To Build and Be Built

JEWISH CULTURE AND CONTEXTS

Published in association with the Center for Advanced Judaic Studies of the University of Pennsylvania

David B. Ruderman, Series Editor

A complete list of books in the series is available from the publisher.

To Build and Be Built

Landscape, Literature, and the Construction of Zionist Identity

ERIC ZAKIM

PENN

University of Pennsylvania Press

Philadelphia

Printed in the United States of America on acid-free paper

10 9 8 7 6 5 4 3 2 1

Published by
University of Pennsylvania Press
Philadelphia, Pennsylvania 19104–4112

Library of Congress Cataloging-in-Publication Data

Zakim, Eric Stephen.
To build and be built : landscape, literature, and the construction of Zionist identity / Eric Zakim.
p. cm. — (Jewish culture and contexts)
Includes bibliographical references and index.
Contents: Belated romanticism — The poetics of malaria — The Hebrew poet as producer — The landscape of a Zionist Orient — The natural history of Tel Aviv — The land bites back.
ISBN-13: 978-0-8122-3903-4 (cloth : alk. paper)
ISBN-10: 0-8122-3903-2
1. Hebrew literature, Modern—History and criticism—20th century. 2. Halutzim in literature. 3. Palestine—In literature. 4. Zionism in literature. 5. Nature in literature. I. Title. II. Series.

PJ5021.Z27 2006
892.4′09006—dc22

2005050361

For Yael

Contents

Introduction
To Build and Be Built

אנו באנו ארצה לבנות ולהבנות בה.

We came to the land to build and be built by/in it.

—A Zionist folk song

This book presents the history of a slogan, "to build and be built," but not simply as a static catalog of its appearances in Zionist culture.[1] Instead, through a critical examination of the slogan's conceptual reformulations over time, this study seeks to understand the complex aesthetic and ideological underpinnings of one of the great revolutionary projects of modern culture, namely, the Zionist transformation of Palestine from an inimical environment into a quintessentially Jewish space. In other words, in looking at Zionist culture, and especially Hebrew writing, during the first four decades of the twentieth century, this study attempts to show how writing and art not merely described and reflected Jewish reconstruction in Palestine, but constituted the very politics that advanced Zionist colonization in the Levant in the first place.

By tying aesthetics to Zionist settlement action, this book aims to present a new and different history of modernism in Hebrew and in Palestine, one that radically inverts a normative understanding of the aesthetics of European modernism which seem to support social disengagement and political disillusionment, a rejection against the political promises of nineteenth-century rationalism and social realism. In the context of Zionism, a different lesson about modernism emerges, where the aesthetics of reaction against realism and against a romantic poetry of object description work to reenliven a vision of nature—that of Palestine—ready and appropriate for Jewish national return.[2]

The project of national renewal and rebuilding required more than a simple physical struggle, and in parallel efforts, the modern Jewish colonization of Palestine sought to exhume Jewish national identity from a dormancy of two millennia while it concomitantly reinvented and "redeemed"—in Zionist terms[3]—the Land of Israel (*Eretz Israel*) from a neglect lasting exactly the same amount of time, that is, since the great dispersion of the Jews in the first century. These two reclamation projects, one psychological and ideological, the other physical and scientific, were viewed within Zionist circles in tandem. The slogan "to build and be built" worked to traverse the distance between these projects and unify the world of national political action and the aesthetics of body and soil. The mutual identification of Jew and land expressed in "to build and be built" thus correlated with repeated efforts throughout the history of pre-state Zionism to theorize each term—the Jew *and* the land—so that the two would fit seamlessly together. As various writers and ideologues during this period would postulate, borrowing from a neat and convenient etymological correspondence in Hebrew, one could not think about man (*adam*) without also thinking about the corresponding term, soil (*adamah*).[4]

However easy it might have been within these parameters to envision man and soil enfolded within the entwined fates of *adam* and *adamah*, the political and aesthetic conceptualization of the terms of that correspondence—the terms of "to build and be built"—was not automatically self-evident. Debates abounded over where and how to begin this project of reclaiming the physical and spiritual nation; over the scope of man's relation to nature and nature's importance to the modern Jew; and even whether Palestine should be the necessary object of Jewish territorial aspiration. In fact, a definitive consensus on Jewish territoriality itself remained elusive throughout much of the early history of Zionism, and interpretations of the slogan's terms passed back and forth—oftentimes in tempestuous argument—from a purely conceptual realm where metaphor and allegory controlled meaning, to a practical footing where the most physical instantiation of work on the soil of Palestine posited significance into the notion of a renewed Jewish identity. While the goal of reinventing modern Jewish identity in a national homeland unified the Zionist movement from almost the beginning, the precise terms of the identification between the "new Jew," as the movement called him,[5] and the envisioned environment of Jewish renewal shifted and were repeatedly refigured as political urgency necessitated.

In this context of shifting meaning and political exigency, the verbal formulation of the slogan marks its inherent inadequacy as a fixed articulation of political aspiration. "To build and be built" ironically and significantly leaves vague the very terms that were to be negotiated and elaborated, namely, *the subject and object of national action.* In the history of the national movement, which began with scant knowledge of Palestine itself and little understanding of how national identity could be constructed around the ideas of place and nature, the invention of the object of Eretz Israel as a hospitable place that could be acquired for the national home necessitated as much the invention of a national citizen who would then inhabit it. Indeed, the very definition of these terms stood at the center of Zionist debate for much of the pre-state period. Within the development of modern Zionist political ideology beginning in the 1880s, and especially after the turn of the twentieth century when Jewish colonial projects in Palestine took on greater meaning as *national* projects of settlement, the elaboration of the slogan constituted the very currents of political and ideological discussion about a new national Jewish identity and an appropriate national landscape.

Those elaborations—the reformulations of the relationship between *adam* and *adamah*, or between Jew and soil—would be repeatedly assigned to literature, which framed political culture's self-understanding through an aesthetic confrontation between this new Jewish subject and the object of nature in Eretz Israel. Partly, the reason behind literature's leading role in the development of these ideas is historical. The origin of a deterritorialized Zionism in eastern Europe during the nineteenth century self-consciously constructed itself on the basis of a culture of writing that worked to invent national expression as it simultaneously formed the national subject.[6] But beyond the historical necessity of writing as national invention,[7] literature offered the type of reflexive discursive opportunity that would accommodate the problems of a deterritorialized nation searching for environmental appropriateness and belonging. In this, it was not merely literature's role to offer the imagined fantasies of national coalescence and unity. Rather, the political problem of expressing the mutual identification of Jew and land for a nation with no ties to nature or to a specific national space became precisely a literary and aesthetic problem of how to bring the contemplation of an imagined nation, Eretz Israel, into a consideration of the land of Israel itself. Thus, the transition from a conceptualized land in the abstract—conceived among diaspora intellectuals and poets in places like Odessa at the beginning of the twentieth century—to something utterly instrumental and familiar—what the land, and especially nature, would become in Tel Aviv by the late 1930s—corresponded to an effort to articulate politically the nature of the modern Jew, transformed from a self-alienated creature to a self-proximate historical agent, one ratified as such by the way in which the fit of the building to the built would itself be constructed.

The Zionist struggle to define an identity within a landscape that reflected the appropriateness of Jewish presence was by nature a modernist enterprise, and not simply because the aesthetic attempts to reach that type of environmental immediacy emerged from late nineteenth-century and early twentieth-century Europe and then traveled to the Middle East. Rather, the entire project itself of de-alienation, of bringing the Jew into a landscape that would reflect the self immediately and immanently (that is, without the mediation of external discursive and political controls) brought this struggle into the realm of various modernist efforts to articulate the self as a willful agent acting in the world. The slogan "to build and be built" thus required an ever more complex aesthetic construction in order to bridge the dialectical tensions inherent within its formulations, and in that demonstrates just how much questions of modernity suffused the entire Zionist project from the beginning.

At bottom, then, this book is a study of how literature attempted to bridge the normative gap between interior contemplation and action in the world surrounding the physical body, a problem for which modernism provided a particularly useful set of aesthetic tools. But unlike in the urban centers of Europe where the aesthetic struggle between idealism and realism in modernism took on particularly decadent and even effete terms, in the Jewish colonies of Palestine, aesthetic debate transcended intellectual and artistic abstraction and engaged a concept of nature that had political consequences. In this, my aim in this book is to show that ideas had very real results in the landscape, and that aesthetics played a constitutive role in the creation of political and environmental history, especially in Jewish Palestine during the decades leading up to the Second World War.

A History Through "Land"

The history of Zionist efforts to elaborate the dialectical relation between Jew and land in no small measure defines the entire history of the movement between 1881 and 1938, entwining throughout this pre-state period a political history of Zionism within a history of intellectual debate over identity and settlement. In fact, by attending to the way the scientific and physical "land issue"—as the British would later describe it—keeps inserting and asserting itself in Zionism, we can understand the extent to which intellectual debate over the relations between identity and place suffuses all Zionist efforts at both political coalescence and actual settlement practice. Thus, when the early nationalist movements of the ovevei Zion and Bilu began to stir in Russia following the 1881 pogroms in Bessarabia, it was Leo Pinsker's pamphlet *Autoemancipation* that embodied both the goals of this first modern wave of immigration to Palestine (what is known in Zionist historiography as the First Aliyah, the first of five waves [*aliyot*] leading up to 1948) and its conceptual and practical limitations, that is, what would lead to its ultimate failure on the ground.

Pinsker's *Autoemancipation* introduced in 1881 a dialectical formulation into the revival of the modern nation by describing the relation between Jew and territory as bound by terms of mutual identification.[8]

But Pinsker's push for "normalcy" and true emancipation for the Jewish nation remains elusively abstract on the question of land and does not posit an essential national bond with Palestine.[9] National territory (Eretz Israel as disembodied place) serves as the ultimate goal of a reflexive plan of action—the *auto*emancipation of the Jew—but identity itself is not defined in specifically spatial terms. The effects of this inability to conceptualize the nation within a particular place had far-reaching implications for the success of settlement. Within the earliest Jewish colonies in Palestine and in the growing forces of cultural Zionism in eastern Europe, which argued for cultural and spiritual cohesion prior to any effort at actual territorial settlement, the coalescence of the nation did not depend on identification with the object of the land. More important than geographic object, Pinsker conceived of a territorialized nation in terms of action and self-transformation. Already in the First Aliyah labor formed an essential ingredient of national rejuvenation if only because of the reflexive meaning that work held for a population bent on transforming itself. But without a parallel sense of a self-contained identity in a specific place, work in Palestine was conceived of outwardly and directed toward capitalist production for export under a system of economic development that mimicked imperial notions of colonial exploitation, focusing on agriculture which looked to markets beyond Palestine.[10] Self-transformation and physical improvement that would produce a healthier nation were not cathected onto the land itself. In this context, viniculture, which encouraged a continued connection to European markets and defined success externally according to sales abroad, became the primary commodity of this early colonial effort, especially in the settlements sponsored by the French branch of the Rothschild family, who underwrote most of the major Jewish colonies in Palestine until the end of the nineteenth century.

By the turn of the century, however, the era of Rothschild domination was coming to a close, hastened both by the inability to develop a sustainable agriculture in the colonies and by the continued insistence on an economic model tied to capital markets. The dichotomy between national transformation and colonial agriculture for export could not sustain itself for long within a capitalist logic. In other words, wine from Palestine never reaped the profits that the Rothschilds had hoped for. In this, the economic woes of the colonies paralleled a continuing ideological debate in Russia over the relationship between nation and place, or, in classic Zionist terms, between diaspora and homeland. Emerging from the confines of the intellectual community of Odessa, Shimon Dubnov and Aḥad Ha'am (Asher Ginzberg),[11] old friends and ideological foes, debated opposing views of territory in the life of the nation, and would come to define the parameters of a Jewish relationship to place and soil. Dubnov's concept of national autonomism supported a continuing diaspora that would nurture Jewish national culture wherever it put down roots within a host nation. On the other hand, Aḥad Ha'am, already one of Zionism's great ideologues, argued against diasporic existence but in an alternate cultural Zionism Aḥad Ha'am still refused to allow for the primacy of territory as *the* defining characteristic of national rebuilding. Cultural and spiritual Zionism, which always saw Palestine as the ultimate goal of national revival, nevertheless maintained the need for deterritorialized national development and psychological autonomy before territorial settlement.

Within the Zionist movement, the hegemony of cultural Zionism was tempered only with the advent of Theodor Herzl to the cause in 1897 and the establishment of a political Zionism that looked exclusively toward territory as a maximalist solution for the nation. In direct opposition to Aḥad Ha'am's notion that a cultural-spiritual center must develop first in the abstract before migrating to the impoverished landscape of Eretz Israel, Herzl fantasized cultural rejuvenation following on the heels of a political mandate in Palestine and the technology-driven environmental improvement of the country. In Herzl's utopian novel *Altneuland*, identity and the natural renaissance of Palestine follow from a political solution to Jewish alienation. National renaissance was indeed tied to an image of land and nature, but the political realm would drive a reinvention of both Jewish identity and the Palestinian landscape.

In these ways, none of the dominant branches within Zionism at the turn of the twentieth century explicitly recognized the dialectical structure of land and identity. However, with the removal of Rothschild family support in the colonies, an independent, practical strain within settlement activity quickly developed under the auspices of the newly formed Jewish National Fund and the Jewish Colonial Trust, which began to envision Jewish presence in Palestine in different terms, ones less centrally controlled and more tied to the very soil of Palestine. Under the mission to purchase land for Jewish settlement, both organizations began to transform ideas of land use and a conception of nature, moving from purely capital-driven incentives as defining land use to national ideological goals of self-renewal. The reasons for this transformation were less ideological than practical. Suddenly bereft of major financial investment and the capital necessary to build an agricultural economy based on export, Jewish land purchasers had to rethink the very reasons for purchasing land, asking basic questions of the major activity of the national movement: Who would occupy purchased tracts of land? How would crops be grown and marketed? What would be the relation between owners and workers on national land?

It was not until the aftermath of the Kishinev pogrom in 1903 that practical settlement received a sufficiently large boost to dominate the Zionist political scene because of a newfound importance placed on building and settlement in Palestine as refuge from the oppressions of Europe. Through the influx of immigrant Jewish workers beginning in 1903 and then especially in the wake of the failed 1905 revolution in Russia came a group of settlers armed with a labor ideology that explicitly disdained profit, individual land ownership, and the use of Arab labor on Jewish soil and thus was ready to reconceptualize the very notion of building as it stood within the national lexicon. Immigration still depended on eastern Europe, but these were the waning days of Aḥad Ha'am's and Odessa's dominance over the cultural future of the nation, even though the lasting triumph of Aḥad Ha'am lay in making culture the ground on which the debates and politics of national revival would always take shape. After Kishinev, Aḥad Ha'am himself quit Odessa, and with him went a sense of cultural Zionism independent of what was happening on the ground in Palestine. After Kishinev, Zionism as a whole worked to recast the individual *within* nature, where the physical world and the identity of the national citizen became mutually dependent.

After 1905 and the end of Herzl's flirtations with Great Britain over an idea to settle Jews in East Africa (the Uganda Plan), all the major entities in the Zionist movement now looked exclusively to Palestine as the site of the future nation. But the legacy of the small band of Second Aliyah immigrants lay in how the Marxist ideologue Ber Borochov and the socialist polemicist Aharon David Gordon developed a concept of a physical Palestine within a dialectic of mutual identification between a reconstructed Jewish subject and the soil. Gordon, whose homespun philosophy of nature and labor would prove to have far more staying power than Borochov's Marxist brand of scientific socialism, arrived in Palestine in 1904 awash in Tolstoyan rapture for the land and the collective idea of a national peasantry of workers tilling national soil. Unlike Aḥad Ha'am's less practical spiritualism, Gordon's romanticism did not obfuscate the materialism of the encounter with the soil, and despite his emphasis on psychological renewal, the entreaty "to build and be built" in his labor philosophy took on a specifically material foundation in work, which came to guide the ethos of the Second Aliyah. Gordon's formulations of individual transformation within the labor of environmental manipulation and improvement emerged as the dominant idea within pre-war concepts of labor working to transform the national landscape.

Until the end of the First World War, any complete hegemony for Gordon's ideas of a labor utopia and Borochov's binational socialist economy were effectively stymied by both the physical limitations of a primitive infrastructure in the country and a continued debate over whether the course of settlement would follow First Aliyah models of intensive farming within a capitalist economy (using Arab workers) or Second Aliyah calls for extensive land use by a collective Jewish proletariat without regard for profit (the idea of *kibush ha-avodah,* the conquest of labor). At stake were not just models of land development but the very place of Jewish labor within a national economy and the relation of Jewish identity to the soil.

By war's end, however, a labor-dominated constructivism held sway throughout Jewish Palestine, and settlement began to take on an exclusively extensive character. The diplomatic achievements of Ḥayim Weizmann, Herzl's successor in the political realm, in securing the Balfour Declaration announcing British sympathy with Jewish national aspirations in Palestine, and the British Mandate itself, which wrested political control from the now moribund Ottomans, paved the way for labor ascendancy both because labor had already developed an extensive institutional infrastructure in the country[12] and because political maximalism of the sort Weizmann was pursuing required extensive agricultural and settlement development on the ground. Thus the political triumph of collective settlement had been determined by its agricultural dependence on extensive farming, which necessitated the acquisition of large tracts of land, and an ideological commitment to an exclusive ethnic culture and economy. In the postwar period—at least until the economic downturn of the mid-1920s—territory was conceived as a political resource, in the sense of what it could yield for national infrastructure, and "to build and be built" assumed a specifically rationalist predication as the movement began to conceive of the land in national governmental terms.

The early 1920s, in fact, marked the height of a reflexive labor ideology that saw action in the land as constitutive of both the self and the nation as a whole. Among the inventions of the post-Bolshevik Third Aliyah entering the country after the war, the Gdud Ha-avodah, the Labor Brigade, emblematized a constructivism that viewed working the land as part of advancing the reflexive reinvention of the working self. In this way, the 1920s mark, too, the greatest efforts to close the gap in a dialectic that held in tension the terms of mutual identification between Jew and land, especially as they were articulated in the work parties of the Gdud. Because of its emphasis on infrastructure improvement (building roads, clearing swamps, establishing settlements), the Gdud saw the collective action of work as a decentralized operation of local labor projects, that is, of physical work as the creation of both the land and the nation through the individual.[13] Against this, the labor leadership of Berl Katznelson and David Ben-Gurion, themselves Second Aliyah immigrants, strove to unify worker and nation within the totalized structure of a political party that would organize labor centrally within a political entity. To this end, in 1919 Katznelson and Ben-Gurion founded Aḥdut Ha-avodah (the United Labor Movement of Palestine). Then in 1920 with the establishment of the Histadrut (the General Confederation of Jewish Labor in Palestine), both political structures meant to solidify a constructivist principle of worker identity on the land within the centralized control of a united labor movement. In this way, Katznelson and Ben-Gurion sought to maintain the essential identification of worker and soil, but placed the control of that dialectic within the structures of an overarching party and labor union.

As the dominant principle of political and social cohesion, constructivism waned by the late 1920s when the internal battles between the Gdud and the Histadrut led to the breakup of the Gdud, an outcome aided by the onset of economic recession in 1925. But at the very heart of the political struggles between the Histadrut and the Gdud lay the question of where to locate an articulation of "to build and be built." Collectivism had taken firm root in the 1920s, especially with the formation of the first *kibbutzim*, large collective farms. But within the labor movement, the role of individual expression and identity in relation to the object of work and the control of the party still remained problematic. While workers began to infiltrate all parts of the country—including a new and growing urban culture—national identity, at least in the official and authorized versions, remained fixed in a contemplation of work on the soil.

By 1929, however, the myopia of the labor movement which ignored external developments in the region—in particular, its refusal to acknowledge Arab displacement as a result of Jewish land accumulation and a cultural effort at self-definition that focused exclusively inward—disintegrated following the Wailing Wall riots in August of that year. While religious access to the holy sites of Jerusalem had been the explicit incitement for violence between Jews and Arabs, investigations by the British cited the displacement of Arabs from lands purchased by Jewish agencies and farmed exclusively with Jewish labor as the primary point of contention in the country. The crisis had been brewing for some years, and itself was only the last in a series of violent outbreaks over Jewish land purchases and Arab dispossession since 1920.

The consequences of the riots on Zionist culture and politics were significant. If before 1929 nativism in the land was never seriously questioned in the Jewish realm because of a naive perception of unfettered access to an ethnically empty space in Palestine (the ideological effect of Israel Zangwill's phrase "a land without a people for a people without a land"),[14] after 1929 nativism emerged as *the* cultural and political question because of a newfound competition in the land, a competition over whose right—Arab or Jewish—claimed greater validity on the soil. In this context, territory became a contested ground, in the sense of what it is at its primordial origin, and the Jew correspondingly came to be presented as "native" and "appropriate" to what the land could hold. As the British demanded that Jewish immigration be capped according to the "absorptive capacity" of the land, the mandate authority reinforced a notion that the landscape and nature's capacity to sustain the population on it would drive settlement. In reaction, Zionist culture reconceived of settlement in terms of ancient nativism, and used the Jew's biblical origin in the land to define the technological goals of extensive agriculture in order to support colonial expansion.

In light of British concern over absorptive capacity in the land, the Jewish Agency did turn toward scientific economic and naturalist arguments supporting extensive settlement and agricultural practices as a way to bolster claims for Jewish presence in the country and the maintenance of immigration rights. Ḥayim Arlosoroff, the young head of the political wing of the Jewish Agency, presented a strong scientific case for the Zionist movement. But this new rationalism would be predicated culturally and scientifically on the ancient origin of the Jews in the country. In the battle over authenticity in the Orient—an Orient of specifically British fantasy (which preferred to see in it a sentimental and quaint agriculture: the timelessness of the Arab *fellah* tilling his native soil using ancient techniques)—Zionist culture reformulated its own relationship to the soil, which was technological and modern but precisely so because it was embedded in historical and mythical authenticity.

The irony of the movement toward authenticity and the search for antiquity was its dependence on a growing urban culture in Jewish Palestine, especially in Tel Aviv, itself a fanciful translation of Herzl's *Altneuland*, "old new land." Tel Aviv had been founded in 1909 as a coastal suburb of Jaffa but had developed as a significant urban center on its own by the 1920s. Arlosoroff himself noticed the growing presence of urban Zionist culture by the end of the 1920s, a result of the Fourth Aliyah, which brought into the country a significant number of bourgeois immigrants from Poland. Arlosoroff had warned about the political effects of ignoring this new urban class and maintaining the political fantasy of a rural society focused on the fields. But the romance of the field would always dominate both art and politics, even if the urban scene came more and more to drive Jewish society. Ultimately, especially after 1932 and the advent of the Fifth Aliyah from Germany—bourgeois refugees from the rising tide of European fascism—urbanism became central to a Jewish concept of nature and dominated the cultural terms of settlement.

The path leading to a final pre-state formulation of nature, land, and national identity was tragically strewn with the dead: the Arab and Jewish victims of violence in 1920, 1921, and 1929, and then Arlosoroff himself, murdered by a right-wing Jewish assassin in 1933 while walking along the beach in Tel Aviv. Violence, in fact, drove much of the Zionist reaction to questions of the land, and the architectural transformation of Tel Aviv in the 1930s reflected a physical and intellectual process of separation, ironically, from the land itself, which was now understood as a violent space subsequent to the encounter with the Arab population. In effect, the withdrawal from nature in the 1930s was made in the name of building nature, buoyed especially after 1936 by the urge to withdraw further into the city in response to the Arab Revolt. In this context, "to build and be built" comes to rest in the pre-state period within the built landscape, that is, it finally describes the metropolis and not the primordial landscape. By 1938, in the midst of the Arab Revolt, the efforts at building an architectural unity in Tel Aviv, one that would encompass and ironically "build" nature within it, resonated only too easily with the development of separate ethnic economies and the withdrawal finally from the field as the site of nature. The city now would present itself as unmediated nature and projected from the metropolis into the field itself, where the architectural model of fortified settlement in the *ḥomah u-migdal* (wall and tower) settlements would mimic urban styles and close off the Zionist farmer from unencumbered access to nature. After 1948, the state would create its own permutations of these histories, but the arrival at a constructed nature—the final inversion of the slogan "to build and be built"—marked the end of a certain formative process and set the parameters for later state development and policy.

The Problems of Zionist History and Hebrew Criticism

In considering the dialectical elaborations of "to build and be built" over time a problem immediately rises for this history. The ways we have come to understand the history of settlement and Zionist identity have been premised upon a separation between Zionist politics and Hebrew culture such that the former is perceived to act independently in the task of nation building, while the latter is perceived to be acted upon as a mechanism that merely reflects the reconstruction of the Jew. Thus, the terms of "to build and be built," originally conceived as reciprocal predicates, have usually been separated in the narration of Zionism. Because of this, the historiography of Zionism, when it takes literature into account at all, has focused principally on the thematic content of literature, without recognizing the crucial ideological dimension of its form. Conversely, literary studies have focused on the conventions of literary form and, when approaching literature's relation to the world beyond writing, have treated imaginary works as adjuncts to the political process without taking cognizance of the way literature in fact constituted the same political project it nominally reflected.[15]

In history's take on Hebrew literature, the act of writing becomes a political and national event, but measured as such exclusively in how it might reinforce through its represented content the assumptions that a positivist study of politics would determine. The poverty of such a historical methodology is evident even in Anita Shapira's otherwise excellent political history *Land and Power: The Zionist Resort to Force 1881–1948.*[16] While outlining the major political and cultural threads of a Zionist outlook toward the use of violence and conflict with the Arab, especially during the 1920s and 1930s, Shapira accepts as important to her historical narrative only those literary texts that explicitly thematize conflict and what she calls a "defensive ethos." But limiting her perspective on culture to a thematic reflection of conflict, Shapira, for instance, cannot account for the relative dearth of references to Arabs in the poetry of the 1920s, explaining their absence within a tautology which claims that missing thematic treatment demonstrates adherence to an ethos that simply would not confront Arab conflict aggressively:

> Perusal of the poetry published [in the 1920s] reveals the extent to which the issue of the Arab in Palestine was suppressed; it also illustrates the predominance of the defensive ethos, with all its concomitant assumptions. In the 1920s, Abraham [sic] Shlonsky's first poems appeared in print. Shlonsky had come with the Third Aliyah and was a member of the Labor Brigade. . . . Arabs rarely appear in his poems and when they do, they play a minor role, as mythological figures or as fixtures in the Palestinian landscape. His thoughts do not concern their presence but, rather, are centered on his private world, his personal experiences. . . . He feels neither hatred nor love for Arabs, almost as though the reality of Arab neighbors did not exist. Yet that can be explained by the personalistic nature of Shlonsky's poetry, which focuses primarily on the realm of private individual experience and does not endeavor to deal with matters of public life.[17]

Shapira's conceptual division between private and public life—borrowed obviously from standard accounts of European modernism—already determines history's consideration of literature, which only takes on meaning as thematic reflection of historical narrative. Thus, Shlonsky's poems are dismissed as private and divorced from public life, relevant only as reflective proof of the ethos Shapira describes, while Yitzhak Lamdan's "Masadah"—indeed an important epic poem of the mid-1920s—better invokes in its content the type of critical political attitude toward the Arab that Shapira is looking for. But nowhere does poetry become constitutive of the history Shapira is describing.

Shapira does allow for the complexity of ideological expression, which may in fact depend quite significantly on aesthetic analysis in order to understand political thought within a discursive framework: "The tendency to speak in two voices, reflecting the presence of an overt, and a subliminal, layer in relating to the Arab question, was integral to the defensive ethos. The relationship between those two layers is a problem that continues to confound the historian, due to the lack of direct documentary evidence."[18] Unfortunately, Shapira's methods occlude any type of investigation that would begin to approach the question she herself raises, and her inquiry cannot proceed beyond an articulation of this problem. Historians such as Shapira tend to resist a critical analysis of politics and prefer to remain insistent on a narrow disciplinary understanding of evidentiary documentation, even when, as Shapira admits, the logic of positivist history itself leads historians to exhume and articulate a particularly discursive question.[19]

Revisionist Israeli history—Israeli new historiography and the like—has been even more resistant than "old" historiography[20] in allowing for discursive analyses of historical phenomena. The methodological conservatism of postzionist Israeli history stems from its structuralist devotion to excavating what it understands as the "truth" of Israeli history.[21] Against that truth stand the obfuscations of national mythology, which is viewed as a simple artifice hiding what really happened in Israel's past. Remarkably, in light of this obsession with truth claims, postzionist history seems completely uninterested in analyzing the mechanisms of this national-cultural artifice. Instead, as Benny Morris keeps repeating, the stage for Israeli new historiography was set by a decidedly positivist event in the progress of academic inquiry, one that clearly places postzionist methods in line with Shapira's own working assumptions about history, namely, the opening up of previously closed state and military archives in the mid-1980s.[22]

Even when historical studies engage discourse analysis, the object of investigation usually centers on the unrevealed intentions of Israeli state actors, in a simplistic application of a Foucaultian understanding of power that completely ignores the subtle influences of Gramscian concepts of cultural hegemony or even the vulgar paradigms of ideology critique. Zeev Sternhell, for instance, unequivocally asserts that the Yishuv's principal concerns regarding settlement always remained focused on ethnic competition and subjugation, in a way that divests even the need for ideology analysis in order to understand the true intentions of Zionist action on the ground in Palestine. In this, Sternhell collapses any division between explicit and implicit expression as Shapira might understand the terms. Instead, Sternhell argues for an even more positivist understanding of historical intention in a method bent on unearthing the truth of political and personal intention within Zionist history. In Sternhell's way of reading intention, history requires no discursive analysis because intention can be easily culled from historical documentation. Thus, Sternhell's analyses read like conspiracy theory where ethnic national competition and suppression were the lightly veiled *conscious* goals of all

Zionist iterations from the very beginning, despite explicit ideological assertions and constructions by Zionism that would have it focus on universal and regional solutions to quite different problems of modernity.[23] As Sternhell demonstrates, postzionist history, for which, to be fair, Sternhell serves as a particularly radical ideological example, has its own difficulties in extending analysis beyond a narrow set of conceptual and methodological assumptions that would subsume all discourse within totalizing historical claims.[24] For postzionism and Israeli new historicism, culture primarily reflects—or, more nefariously, obfuscates—political intention and plays no role in the constitution of that politics.[25]

For the most part, Hebrew literary criticism concurs with history's scission by similarly relegating to Hebrew arts and letters the status of a reflection of historical processes, thus advancing for itself an autonomous vision, that is, one in which Hebrew arts and letters follow their own immanent process of development. In other words, while a poem such as Ḥayim Naḥman Bialik's "In the City of Slaughter" may denotatively respond to the 1903 violence in Kishinev, what remains most significant about the poem is perceived to be its development of a new Hebrew poetic sensibility.[26] Even those works of criticism that do place literature within a significant historical context still only read that history as a closed literary field. In this way, Alan Mintz's nuanced reading of Bialik's "In the City of Slaughter" nicely describes the poem as a response to Kishinev, but only within a study of poetic and literary response to disaster within the textual tradition.[27] In this type of reading, the relation of poetry to national ideology is only reflective, and the major formal advances of Bialik's poem extend merely to the realm of poetics. Politics enters into a consideration of Bialik's poem only insofar as we understand it as a call for the organization of Jewish self-defense in Russia.

Of course, much of this situation emanates from the dominance of formalism in Hebrew criticism, especially in Israel. For instance, Yosef Haefrati's classic and remarkable study of landscape in Hebrew poetry, *Ha-mar'ot veha-lashon* (The Presented World), advances this same paradigm by ceding different conceptions of the Hebrew subject to literary historical causes, thereby permitting landscape to develop autonomously in language.[28] In Haefrati's view, the way landscape appears in Hebrew poetry can only be accounted for as a consequence of the demands of Hebrew poetics itself. Haefrati does flirt with a new sort of historical strategy, one that sees significance in how the encounter with what normatively lies beyond the realm of the imagination—that is, the landscape itself—changes over time in the formal depictions of the real as an imagined space.[29] But Haefrati never, however indirectly, confronts political or historical ideas in his account of landscape forms in Hebrew poetics, that is, beyond the hermetic confines of literature as a separate cultural and discursive field.

This present study begins in a consideration of the consequences of this incapacity of history and criticism—despite their many achievements—to present things in a way that does justice to what the original slogan "to build and be built" actually tried to express. "To build and be built" presents the mutual relation between Jew and land as something other than an identity thesis, where the terms of this reflective formula would present themselves as self-evidently true. Conversely, the two normative forms of Hebrew criticism and Zionist historiography—literary and political—advance precisely an identity thesis that the original formula always found suspect. However, the power of the slogan lies in the way its dialectics must be constantly reinterpreted and newly understood, how the terms of reflection between "to build" and "be built" never achieve a simple stasis wherein meaning can be easily fixed or assigned. Rather, literature and politics themselves must dialectically engage each other within the slogan in order for any history of these people and this place to take on meaning. The slogan thus describes a dynamic process whereby politics and settlement are consistently molded and inflected through an aesthetic understanding of nature and land, an aesthetic understanding dependent on writing and art for its articulation and elaboration. Against this, history in its usual forms falls prey, despite its objections to the contrary, to a process of mythologization that an original Zionism sought to avoid, just as criticism remains trained on a hermeneutical hermeticism that Zionism always sought to dissolve.

New Methodological Horizons

Ironically, one of the most innovative studies to outline the dialectics of Zionist culture and politics emerged from the staunchly formalist Tel Aviv School of Poetics. In *Language in the Time of Revolution*, Benjamin Harshav writes: "In general terms, we may describe a cultural situation as a result of the interaction of two kinds of entities: social, cultural, and ideological *trends* and individual *junctions*. A junction is a cluster of and a selection from intersecting tendencies that constitute an autonomous existential unit, such as a *text* or a *person*. A text, however, is not simply a given intersection of relations, ideas, or poetic principles, but an individualized body of language, marked by partial coherence, and reader-dependent."[30] Here, Harshav begins to outline a discursive reading of how history and criticism might come together. But in general, Harshav, while positing a complex of influences in the "junctions" of cultural production, still reads history as a large structure, as participating broadly in the systems that make up culture and society. Harshav might succeed in bringing political and social ideas into a consideration of language and culture, but the relationship between them is always limited because it remains entirely the product of verbal discourse; politics and culture are not mutually constitutive. Changes over time and the elaboration of political ideas do not, for Harshav, represent challenges to the basic semiotic structure of the cultural realm, which synchronically encompasses history and politics *within* the revolution of expression. Language becomes the focus of his study because of the iterative possibilities opened up in a new ideological medium. In this, both history and literature remain secondary to the totalizing revolution in discourse that determines their particular forms.

Following from Harshav's expansion of the formalist field, postzionist studies of culture offer a certain methodological approach distinct from prior efforts to contain Hebrew literature within studies of poetics. But the difficulty of postzionism in Israel studies as a methodological solution has been its Janus-faced nature, which repeats the division between history and cultural studies. The promise of Israeli new historiography involved the opening up of Zionist history as a field of inquiry, a loosening of nationalist tenets on studies of the past, and a newfound freedom to reach conclusions that may not coexist comfortably with a belief in the ultimate infallibility of Zionist action. But postzionist history and criticism, focused as they both are on archaeology projects of exhuming documentary sources, work to reify the very binary assumptions they seek to undermine. And here criticism has followed closely behind history: the truth claims of the state are simply replaced by the truth claims of a new interpretive strategy where the veracity of various accusations of conscious and unconscious oppression by the Israeli nation can never be resolved. Even those studies of Zionist history and culture that claim sensitivity to a nuanced reading of discourse still blindly and simplistically depend on a facile application of Foucault's understanding of the ubiquitous deployment of state power through discourse and ideology.[31] Ironically, the problem with postzionist criticism lies then in the new infallibility it posits onto Israeli discursive apparatuses, which work with amazing efficiency in dictating mass opinion and maintaining rather narrow controls on the authorized horizons of aesthetic expression.[32]

In the end, neither of the dominant modes of Israeli cultural criticism—ideology critique, which seeks to reveal the unconscious intentions of historical actors, or the excavation of lost voices in the Hebrew wilderness of marginality—offers a methodology that adequately reflects the dialectics of "to build and be built," that is, the interpenetration and interdependence of aesthetics and history. Rather, studies like Hannan Hever's histories of literary and ideological trends[33] and Yael Zerubavel's investigations of the complex mechanisms of public culture in Israel[34] offer the beginnings of a method that looks past the disciplinary confines of literature and history, and starts to show the complex interdependencies of these seemingly separate discursive fields.[35] What marks both Hever's and Zerubavel's work is their refusal to understand cultural production within any sort of narrow disciplinary sphere. Instead, both look beyond the normative boundaries of the field to show how meaning becomes developed and elaborated within both political history and cultural texts.

Immanent Criticism

While cultural studies might point toward a fruitful methodological path of investigation, the transcendental effects of any historical approach must take into account the tendency to reproduce, yet again, the analytical and intellectual divisions spawned by "to build and be built."[36] In other words, any investigation of this history must remain aware of its own collusion in that history and the contribution it is making to the ideas expressed in it. No one stands outside of the historical effort to understand and formulate the meaning of this reflexive dialectical relationship. To the contrary, any analytical conclusions that try to determine meaning for Zionist history and culture must be viewed merely as its latest articulations.

Faced with this critical suspicion, a chronicle of "to build and be built" would have to proceed immanently through such assertions. By a radically immanent procedure, I am referring to a way of conducting criticism that refuses any final reconciliation between critical assertion and the object of knowledge, except as a triumph of reification. In this, my own intervention in the field looks primarily toward formal innovation and transformation within the text as the site of political and social contestation. As national discourse set out to make Palestine into an essentially Jewish place, the struggle to find a critical position between what Theodor Adorno would call subjective immanence (the interiority of self-expression) and objective transcendence (the distance of exterior critique) continuously reasserts itself as the question of Hebrew aesthetics. Adorno saw ideological blindness in both stances and resisted a critical position that proclaimed allegiance to either dialectical thesis. My own methods attempt to follow Adorno's calls for a dialectical stance toward culture, one that shows conflict and struggle instead of the blank, empty promises of an ideological certitude of meaning.

Immanent criticism thus describes a critical position resistant to the claims of historical certitude that rely on analytical distance, and resistant as well to an expressionist faith in the integrity of the human subject to project a unique vision of the world. According to Adorno:

> A successful work, according to immanent criticism, is not one which resolves objective contradictions in a spurious harmony, but one which expresses the idea of harmony negatively by embodying the contradictions, pure and uncompromised, in its innermost structure. . . . [I]mmanent criticism holds in evidence the fact that the mind has always been under a spell. . . . Immanent criticism . . . can neither be vain enough to believe that it can liberate the mind directly by immersing itself in it, nor naive enough to believe that unflinching immersion in the object will inevitably lead to truth. . . . The very opposition between knowledge which penetrates from without and that which bores from within becomes suspect to th[is] dialectical method, which sees in it precisely that reification which the dialectic is obliged to accuse.[37]

Within an immanent criticism, the sections of this book trace the progressive reformulations of "to build and be built" as a series of negotiations with the same problem that the historiography of those efforts begins to reveal. Starting with the reaction to the pogrom at Kishinev in 1903 and ending with the halt in expansion of pre-state Zionist settlement in 1938 (a result of the onset of European fascist aggression), this study examines how literature participated in the political and ideological life of the nation as a constituent element in the progress of ideas. By literature, I mean primarily poetry since it formed the central genre of the nationalist canon. From 1903 until 1938, with the ascendance of a reflexive drive to define Jewish status in the land and the Jew as part of nature, literature worked to describe "to build and be built" within an aesthetic that would recast Jewish life in a new form.

In Chapter 1, "Belated Romanticism," I begin this study by examining early Zionist culture's own reassessment of the relation between Jew and territory as it had been figured initially by Leo Pinsker. This analysis focuses on the way in which, after Kishinev and the ensuing national crisis, the trope of building both the self and national territory started to name Palestine as a necessary component within this dialectical identity. Between 1903 and 1905, within the context of the exhaustion of paternalistic models of colonization advanced in Palestine by the Rothschilds, and the post-Kishinev need for territorial refuge and national "building," Zionist culture looked again to the relation between Jewish identity and territory, arriving at a new predication of that reciprocal relation, one that moves from an abstract idea of place as secondary to a spiritual national renaissance to the concrete building projects of settlement as an answer to the exigencies of external historical urgency. As I argue, Bialik's literary output in the years immediately following Kishinev did not simply respond to historical crisis, but in its form and mode of aesthetic depiction created a new *historical* paradigm insofar as it effected a reformulation of territory and Jewish identity. As such, Bialik both confirms and at the same time points to the inadequacies of subsequent interpretations of the Odessa circle, which have given priority either to the political response of Aḥad Ha'am and his colleagues, or to the literary innovation of Bialik's major poems of these years without adequately examining the necessary relation between them.

The second chapter, "The Poetics of Malaria," analyzes pragmatic responses to settlement and follows the figure of malaria as a trope for the problems faced by the dialectical mirroring of Jew and soil when confronted with an inhospitable landscape unyielding to the romantic projections of the new Second Aliyah immigrants. The invasion of place into the very recesses of the mind of the Jewish settler occurred through the prism of malaria, an ambiguous sign for both a closeness to the land and an enmity based in that encounter. In Jewish Palestine at the beginning of the twentieth century, malaria introduces itself not solely as a problem of the technocrats but no less significantly as the very kernel of the dialectical tension separating Jew and land, around which the relation between farmer and soil would be articulated. In this chapter, I focus principally on the work of Yosef Ḥayim Brenner, who, in his writing between the 1909 essay "For the Hundredth Time (From the Convulsions of One Soul)," published soon after his arrival in Palestine, and the publication of his journal *Ha-adamah* in 1919, develops a new model of Jewish consciousness. In this, Brenner's rejection of the solipsism of romanticism pushes toward the rationalism of naturalist depictions of mutual identification between Jew and land, where the land becomes the object of a mutually hygienic improvement.

Brenner's political and literary writing heralded a labor constructivism by the time of his death in the riots of 1921. But the foundation of "to build and be built" would not remain stable for very long, despite Labor Zionism's political ascendance. At a time when Zionism had not only defined its own understanding of labor, advancing from Borochov to Katznelson, and when Zionism as a whole had advanced from petit bourgeois models of colonization to firmly collectivist ones, these very successes demanded the reassessment of a culture of labor. This is the context in which I situate the early poetry of Avraham Shlonsky and the appearance of a poetic avant-garde in the 1920s. Shlonsky, I suggest in the third chapter, "The Hebrew Poet as Producer," shepherds Zionist thought from the technocratic and political instrumentalism of laborites like Katznelson and Ben-Gurion, for whom labor was implicitly the predication of the relation between Jew and land (insofar as territory would be viewed by them as a natural resource and the Jew as the manager of those resources), and orients it toward a valorization of nature, where territory would not be prized for its productive value but for the way it reflects an organicism within Jewish identity. The Jew of Shlonsky's imagination no longer corresponds with the agent of rationalized farming techniques but rather is a natural man irrationally tied to the soil and the fecund processes of nature. In Shlonsky's work between 1925 and 1929, I trace the progressive refiguration of a dialectical unity between land and Jew as it advances toward a specifically ecstatic and intensely irrational predication whereby the mutual identification of the one by the other depends upon the linguistic act of phatically naming this new political and environmental entity. The self and soil then cannot simply be the materialist outcomes of labor, but the product of a sentimental constructivist act of creation through language and writing, which Shlonsky defines as work in the public sphere.

The efforts of this modernist avant-garde to create a mode of expression that would be productive in itself and untied to previously defined historical discourses proved strangely prophetic of 1929, when Zionists and Palestinian Arabs would be called upon to articulate their prior claims—their nativism—within the country. The masculinist nativism of the modernist avant-garde exemplified by Shlonsky, however, could not offer a significant response to the competitive political realities in the country after 1929. In the wake of the 1929 riots, in response to the various commissions inquiring into the causes of violence, and in the context of the debates between 1929 and 1933 over the absorptive capacity of the land, a different sort of aesthetic outlined a new nativist relation to Palestine. During a period of uncertainty in which even the landscape would no longer be viewed as a reflection of Zionist subjectivity because it was contested, the publication of collections of poetry by women, most notably Esther Raab and Raḥel Bluwstein, signaled an intensified effort to draw upon an alternate way of defining the relation between Jew and territory. At a moment when, in political life, figures like Ḥayim Arlosoroff would find themselves forced to debate Zionism's prerogatives on grounds utterly unfamiliar to them (grounds that pitted a Jewish economy versus a Palestinian Arab one in terms of historical priority and appropriate agricultural land use), these women poets had already begun to advance toward an identification of territory with mythohistorical origin, and of the Jew as the primordial inhabitant of Palestine. Thus, in the fourth chapter, "The Landscape of a Zionist Orient," I examine the poetic efforts of Raab and Bluwstein in particular, focusing on the gendered response to hegemonic poetry and politics and the figure of the primordial woman as a potent political symbol for a new formulation of Jewish presence and identity in the land. In Raab's and Bluwstein's invocations of sensuous belonging to the earth, I suggest one discovers Zionism advancing toward a mythological predication of the relation between Jew and land. In the poetry of Raab and Bluwstein, nature is finally reconciled with origin, and the Jew is reconciled with the East in an Orientalist reconceptualization of the Jew's place in the landscape.

In reading Raab and Bluwstein in this way, I am suggesting an alternative to a dominant way of reading Hebrew women's poetry of the 1920s. I do not deny the oppositional stance of Raab's and Bluwstein's poetics and the way their poetry emerges from within the gaps of male poetry's blindness. However, the gendered differences in writing poetry should not obfuscate the political utility and resonance of a poetry that both explicitly and implicitly coincided with Zionist political and historical aims. This argument is not to say that issues of gender, race, and class were not constitutive elements in a dominant male Zionist poetics. Rather, a writing of opposition—here, to a male-dominated literary canon—does not necessarily translate into a challenge to hegemonic politics. Indeed, in this chapter, I suggest that even minor and marginal writing—in fact, even writing of dissent—might collude with a politics that includes its own suppression.

By 1933 and the deaths of both Arlosoroff and Bluwstein (and the advent of an odd thirty-year silence in Raab), the logic of Zionist Orientalism was already exhausted. Competition of origin in the land was superseded by an ideology of economic separation from the Arab, which reached apotheosis during the Palestinian-Arab national revolt in 1936, thereby rendering territory inaccessible. The national security response to that crisis on the land in the form of fortified settlements, the *ḥomah u-migdal* (wall and tower) constructions, simply echoes and extends a project of architectural transformation of the landscape that began in 1932 in Tel Aviv. In the 1930s, Tel Aviv began to form the center of a new formulation of nature, one predicated on a physical sense of transformation and building. In this context, territory became the built landscape and "building" took on a new, static meaning as a noun. Thus, in Chapter 5, "The Natural History of Tel Aviv," architecture and film lead toward a performance theory of nature, which is then taken up in middecade by the young poet Natan Alterman, whose melding of built and natural landscapes synthesized nature directly into the urban space. The Jew, in this formulation of "to build and be built," becomes the builder and nature becomes, in Georg Lukács's and Adorno's phrase, "second nature," a highly mediated space, where Adorno's conception of "natural history" describes a place engulfed within the dialectical tensions of nature and history, or, as I argue, between artifice and myth.

This study reaches a conclusion by suggesting that Alterman's achievements in synthesizing a vision of nature encompassed by Zionist identity and action led to the conceptual possibility of statist control over nature and the landscape. After 1948, mediation between national identity and territory became a state-sponsored activity. The life of second nature within Israel nourished decidedly governmental goals for the further expansion and conceptualization of territorial settlement, especially in the Negev Desert. In this, the continued existence of a dialectical history of nature and history, of the formulation of "to build and be built," leads to a contemplation of recent events and the ongoing territorial conflicts with the Palestinian Arabs.

A book of this kind, however, with definite historical parameters and interests, can make no direct claim about the current violence in Israel. But the study of a cultural aesthetic that effected both a reflexive search for a new identity in nature and a politics of construction in and of the land certainly adds to an understanding of present antagonisms and the depth of the ideological conceptions that have driven the crisis of this land further into the abyss. This book makes claims about the conflict through culture, not in how literature might have promoted or expressed oppression as a theme, or even in how Hebrew literature might have depicted conflict and the Arab. In fact, this study makes quite the opposite claim, namely, that studying *those* types of thematic content always distracts from the proper view of how Zionist culture came to define a politics of belonging to the land. The slogan "to build and be built," in its reflexivity, finally, refuses to allow anything but a hermetic reading of itself and of action in the name of the nation, and it is within that aesthetic position, which assumes grand political aspiration, that this study might contribute to a lasting understanding of Jewish identity and possession in Palestine.

Chapter 1

Belated Romanticism

News of the Kishinev pogrom that wracked the Jewish community of Bessarabia around Easter of 1903 reached the nearby town of Odessa, then the capital of Hebrew letters and cultural Jewish nationalism, in mythological Zionist fashion, that is, in an extraordinary confluence of the movement's most important historical actors and ideas. According to the memoirs of Shimon Dubnov, the renowned Jewish historian and member of the circle of Odessan Jewish nationalists that included the famous Zionist polemicist Aḥad Ha'am and the poet Ḥayim Naḥman Bialik, the Zionist intelligentsia had gathered on the evening of April 7, 1903 at the Beseda Social Club for a regular meeting of their literary circle, the Committee of Nationalization. The young Vladimir Jabotinsky, who would go on to lead the right-wing Revisionists of the Zionist movement, spoke that evening about Leo Pinsker's *Autoemancipation*, the most famous Jewish text to have emerged in the wake of the previous round of prominent Bessarabian pogroms in 1881 and one of the most important Zionist polemics of the nineteenth century. According to Dubnov, while Jabotinsky spoke news of Kishinev filtered into the hall as refugees from the pogrom began to arrive in Odessa, visceral proof that evening of Jabotinsky's impassioned call for national action coupled to territorial ingathering. Dubnov writes:

> It was the night of April 7, 1903. Because of Russian Easter, the newspapers had not been issued for the previous two days so that we remained without any news from the rest of the world. That night the Jewish audience assembled in the "Beseda" Club, to listen to the talk of a young Zionist, the Odessa "*wunderkind*" V. Jabotinsky. . . . The young agitator had great success with his audience. In a particularly moving manner, he drew on Pinsker's parable of the Jew as a shadow wandering through outer space and developed it further. As for my own impression, this one-sided treatment of our historical problem depressed me: did he not scarcely stop short of inducing fear in our unstable Jewish youth of their own national shadow? . . . During the break, while pacing up and down in the neighboring room, I noticed sudden unrest in the audience: the news spread that fugitives had arrived in Odessa from nearby Kishinev and had reported of a bloody pogrom in progress there.[1]

Even Dubnov, the most outspoken Jewish proponent of a deterritorialized national autonomism, could not escape the implications that Kishinev held for the geographic viability of the Jewish community in Russia.[2] For Dubnov, as for most of Russian Jewry, Kishinev brought on a serious crisis, and he soon left Odessa for the safer climes of Vilna. Indeed, Kishinev sounded the death knell of Odessan nationalist intellectualism in general as all of those he names attending Jabotinsky's talk would presently relocate elsewhere, Jabotinsky back to St. Petersburg; Aḥad Ha'am soon to London; and Bialik to several points in the Pale of Settlement before moving on to Poland and Germany. For the entire community of Russian Jews, Kishinev served as the catalyst for one of the great voluntary Jewish migrations in the modern era, mostly to America,[3] with a small cadre arriving on the shores of Palestine. The geographic impact of Kishinev was thus immediate and far-reaching, throwing into question the territorial certainty of Russia as the "center of gravity,"[4] in Dubnov's terms, for Jewish national revival.

Beyond the geographic transformations portended by the initial news of Kishinev, the moment marks an even more fundamental shift in the way that national identity was now going to be understood in terms of place. With the ground pulled out from under the feet of Russian cultural Zionism, a location for Jewish nationalism became *the* question for the movement, a question that quickly infected political and practical Zionism as well, since none of the major branches within Zionism had yet conceived of place as integral to the political movement as a whole, or landscape as a critical feature in the formation of a modern Jewish cultural identity. After Kishinev, that formulation—the coupling of the nation to a particular national space—became the primary philosophical and political goal of Zionism.

In this, Dubnov's memory of April 7, 1903 begins to outline how thoroughly place, migration, and national action were now to be tied to an examination of national identity and individual consciousness. The loss of Odessa as a cultural national center, one might argue, corresponded less to the physical threat embodied in Kishinev than to a broader, inevitable reorientation of Jewish nationalism away from the deterritorialized cultural terms of both Dubnov and Aḥad Ha'am. Within this context, Jabotinsky's radical territorial solution to the problem of exile and homeland understandably sparks Dubnov's apprehension,[5] as it might in Aḥad Ha'am as well; neither could commit to a territorial solution for modern Jewish identity. But against the dominance of their calls for modern Jewish identity to emerge primarily from a romanticism of self-knowledge and reflexive change, Kishinev disrupted precisely a cultural solution to Jewish national coalescence and pressed for a reconceptualization of place, or rather a reconceptualization of identity as tied to place, which would now be central to the Jewish question in Europe.

This conceptual change had particular implications for Palestine's role within the Zionist movement. Aḥad Ha'am had written repeatedly since 1891 that Palestine could hardly serve as a safe haven for eastern European Jewry given the poor state of the country's infrastructure.[6] In the meantime, however, the crisis over place that Kishinev engendered was compounded by the practical failure of the settlements in Palestine that arose in reaction to 1881. Just as Kishinev pushed the crisis of place within the European Jewish community, Palestine itself required renewed conceptual attention because of the way settlement failure highlighted the problems of plantation colonial models for the movement as a whole. By the turn of the twentieth century, then, as the Rothschild family withdrew support from its financially beleaguered colonies on the ground in Palestine, a new way of approaching settlement had to be worked out, something beyond the monocultural plantations that had sprung up around a doomed vinoculture industry.

With pressure from both sides—European and Palestinian—even cultural Zionism's refusal to conceive of national renewal beyond the abstraction of deterritorialized community could not ignore the fact that the crisis of Kishinev brought the discussion of Zionist identity and the future of settlement in Palestine to a new level of urgency. For those on either side of the practical and spiritual Zionist divide, both factions dominated by the Russians, no theoretical framework existed before Kishinev for envisioning an essential role for Palestine in the life of the nation, this at a time when the more Western political Zionism—the third spoke in the movement's triumvirate—was still toying with territorial solutions outside of the Middle East altogether.

Within the interstice of this gap between political coalescence and territorial viability, the debate over the function of territory in the definition of the deterritorialized nation fissured to the point of broad national crisis. In this context, Kishinev pushed the question of how Palestine might emerge as *the* territorial solution for both the political crisis and the identity crisis in the Jewish national movement. For the cultural and practical factions within Zionism, situated as they were in the east near the epicenter of the pogrom, the impasse of Jewish settlement and personal transformation revolved around the idea of tying identity to a natural environment, that is, to a *national* environment existing beyond an isolated romantic idea of the self. The failures of the first wave of European settlement in Palestine—the reasons Jabotinsky brings Pinsker back into the debate—were tied to the movement's inability to territorialize the nation, to make place not just an inert instrument exterior to the people, but an integral part of national rejuvenation itself. Zionism, in its broadest meaning, had always looked toward the millennial redemption offered by territory and especially the promise of *Eretz* Israel (the *Land* of Israel), but political ideology still needed to connect those millennial impulses to a sense of what nature and place might have to offer the individual Jew. An ideational bridge had to be constructed between the reinvention of modern Jewish individuality and the place of redemption in Palestine.

The solution to this problem could begin only with an aesthetic understanding of the relation of the romantic subject (in the guise of what the movement would call the "new Jew") to the territorial landscape around it. After Kishinev, the task of working out that problem fell most prominently to poetry, in particular the poetry of Ḥayim Naḥman Bialik, who created nothing less than a revolutionary politics within an aesthetic of the self, reinventing the place of individual national identity precisely within a natural environment.

Kishinev and the Struggles for Jewish Autonomy

Dubnov's apprehension in the face of Jabotinsky's territorial polemic begins to show the fault lines in Jewish national thinking between two competing ideas for imagining the structural conflicts in modern Jewish identity, a debate, that is, between temporal and spatial claims on Jewish consciousness. Along the contentious axes of modernity versus tradition and homeland versus diaspora, the tensions of modern Jewish existence vied for conceptual prominence in a movement committed to reinventing and defining Jewish psychology. Pinsker's *Autoemancipation* had been a revolutionary text for the way it combined temporal and spatial axes and attached them to national identity. As a consequence, the pamphlet's practical impact can be measured quite simply in how it fomented both intellectual contemplation and settlement action.

But since 1881, despite the few settlers in Palestine who made up the First Aliyah (the first wave of modern Zionist settlement), autonomism still dominated Jewish national thought, an autonomism that focused on emancipation as a temporal liberation from the bonds of traditional ways of conceiving Jewish identity within Europe.[7] Thus, even though Pinsker and the First Aliyah Zionists of what would be called the Old Yishuv (the nineteenth-century Jewish settlement in Palestine) recognized the transformative value of territory, territory nevertheless remained instrumental to a more profound transformation of the Jewish soul against the strictures of history. The claim for territory's temporal use value had been, after all, Pinsker's strongest argument, leaving the territorial solution as an external tool in the service of a more important interior transformation that would place modern Jewish identity in sync with the major trends of European national thought, trends that indicated progression over time and inevitably arrived at modernity. As Pinsker wrote: "The consciousness of the people is awake. The great ideas of the eighteenth and nineteenth centuries have not passed by our people without leaving a trace. We feel not only as Jews; we feel as men. As men, we, too, wish to live like other men and be a nation like the others. And if we seriously desire that, we must first of all throw off the old yoke of oppression and rise manfully to our full height. We must first of all desire to help ourselves."[8]

Pinsker's call for a self-proclaimed and self-enacted nationalism of modern ideas did articulate a connection between personal and national rejuvenation, on the one hand, and settlement, on the other, but Pinsker did not necessarily situate any future national home in Palestine.[9] Since Pinsker conceived of modernization primarily in terms of old versus new, the actual landscape that would house the modern Jewish nation was unimportant. The principal dialectical vision expressed in *Autoemancipation* remained temporally fixed between the prison of tradition and the promise of modernity.

Until the end of the century, cultural Jewish nationalism steadfastly refused to admit place into a dialectic of personal Jewish identity, remaining bound to a temporal struggle for modern consciousness which was *de*territorial: the "auto" of *auto*emancipation. That, we might conclude, is what bothered Dubnov about Jabotinsky's lecture on April 7, that the metaphor of space necessarily disrupted the immanent call of Jewish nationalism, which Dubnov himself had always supported and given explicit voice to. Just a year before Kishinev, Dubnov had laid out his own dialectical scheme for a Jewish identity caught within the cultural-temporal claims of older Jewish tradition and modern secular European life. Dubnov remained committed to these identity parameters well beyond Kishinev and never fully embraced any of the dominant strands of Zionism, but his work demonstrates at this crucial juncture the terms of the discussion in the air within a broad spectrum of nationalist circles.

In 1902, Dubnov, beginning like Pinsker from a critique of traditional Jewish identity in Europe, proposed a national Jewish education that would avoid both the parochialism of religious textual education and the syncretism (and maximal assimilationism) of the Russian Bundists. The Bundists themselves espoused a certain dialectical reconciliation between Jewish and Russian claims on personal identity, a dialectic that flirted with spatial concepts of orientation inasmuch as for them Jewish national politics remained ever caught between different centers of cultural affiliation. Instead, Dubnov offered a structural resolution dependent on a temporal dialetic, which completely excluded any spatial claims on Jewish identity: "The old school, the *heder* and the *yeshiva*, produces only the Jew; the new school produces the rootless 'man'; the school to come must form the Jew and the man simultaneously."[10] Between old and new, Dubnov's national educational program described a modern *Bildung* emanating from the personal experience of the individual, an educational program, that is, that moved immanently through the individual to the nation. By focusing on the individual's freedom to choose identity, consciousness, as Dubnov described it, clearly and firmly derived from romantic constructions of the self as a hermetic and integral psyche. Indeed, this notion, more than any other, embodied the kernel of temporal descriptions of modern Jewish identity. In this, Dubnov rejected syncretism's dualities of competing cultural affinities, which would pull the Jew out of the hermetic space of romantic consciousness and into a synthetic cultural environment of different claims on identity. More important even, the immanent notion of individual will bypassed a religious essentialism. Dubnov refused to allow Jewishness to define and determine man's soul innately.

Aḥad Ha'am supported Dubnov's educational proposals in 1902 and earlier, before the pogrom disrupted all sense of Russian rootedness for the Odessa group. Even afterward, within Aḥad Ha'am's brand of cultural Zionism, the immanence of personal and national transformation left no room for place as the key to resolving the crisis of Jewish identity. Kishinev did little to break Aḥad Ha'am of this fundamental conviction. In response to the pogrom itself, Aḥad Ha'am steadfastly refused to accept territoriality as either a political or a cultural solution. But because of the obvious territorial implications of Kishinev, Aḥad Ha'am could harness only the most abstract ideas about a deterritorialized people in immediate political reaction to the pogrom, unlike most other responses to Kishinev, which looked specifically to Palestine and emigration as a solution to the dangers of the European diaspora. The intellectual poverty of the temporal reaction to the dialectic of identity—how, that is, this conceptual path had hit a dead end in reacting to Kishinev—comes through clearly in Aḥad Ha'am's answer to the tragedy and what he leaves out of that reaction: specifically, any notion of territory. By focusing on what he saw as the problem of Jewish self-identity, namely a lack of self-reliance which reflected the deficiencies of national culture (as opposed to decrying a violence emanating from outside the nation), Aḥad Ha'am was left to criticize individual Jewish failure through personal inaction. Thus, in direct response to the pogrom, Aḥad Ha'am penned a damning reaction to the violence at Kishinev in an open letter dated April 20 and signed by Dubnov, Yehoshua Ḥana Ravnitsky, Ben-Ami, and Bialik. The letter was addressed to the "Jewish brethren," and in it, Aḥad Ha'am accuses the passivity of a Jewish population that would not seize collective fate:

> What happened at Kishinev was not an isolated incident and we cannot hang all the guilt on the willful malice of a few individuals. The few bad ones who incite and lead the masses against us, they are always the available culprit in these incidents, but they are not the root of the evil, which is our own situation. . . . On

what, Brothers, can we lean, so that this disaster shall not spread again through the country, like twenty years ago, but this time even worse, like we saw at Kishinev? And why therefore must we lose our strength and demean our honor in our request for help and salvation from outside our community after we saw through experience that salvation would not be coming and cannot come from beyond as long as our situation in the country remained as it is. . . . Tears and supplication—these are the only means that we have and since the beginning of the riots—they have not helped us and they have not saved us from this catastrophe that has come upon us. The killings in Kishinev—that is the answer to all our tears and supplication."[11]

Even Aḥad Ha'am's reading of "inside" and "outside" the community held no spatial resonance. National coalescence would remain a completely conceptual and cultural issue, and because of this, Aḥad Ha'am's call for transformation and action would not explicitly point to Palestine. Instead, the message to abandon a reactionary Jewish passivity was couched in terms that echo both Pinsker's and Dubnov's temporal calls for modern national identity: "Brothers! The blood of our brethren in Kishinev is crying out to us: shake off the dust and become men!"[12]

For Aḥad Ha'am the answer to the pogrom lay in individual—and from there national—transformation. To be sure, the specific urgency of the Kishinev crisis did not leave Aḥad Ha'am unaffected, and it did spurn a call for action. But herein lies the dead end of Zionism's deterritorialized cultural logic. Shut off conceptually from the various calls for territorial action in the wake of the pogrom, especially those for a stepped-up pragmatic settlement in Palestine, Aḥad Ha'am's answer to the pogrom is some sort of civil structure within Russia as a solution to what was fast becoming understood as a spatial crisis: "Organization will get us out of this."[13] Organization—coming together in a political movement for self-defense—is an odd position for Aḥad Ha'am, and not only because his nationalist theories always held firm to a belief in romantic immanence as the source for all national action. In purely practical political terms, Aḥad Ha'am had consistently disdained political organization, and the oddity of this call becomes only clearer in light of his scathing criticism of political Zionism's congresses and Herzl's political leadership, against which he had published attacks only the previous year on the occasion of Pinsker's tenth *jahrzeit*.[14] The bureaucratic response in both ways offers placid resolution to Aḥad Ha'am's consistent indictment of traditional belief and passivity.

But lest we simply dismiss Aḥad Ha'am's cultural Zionism as passé by 1903, his critical reaction to the major territorial responses to Kishinev indeed highlights the movement's continued difficulties in conceiving of territory as an essential and integral aspect of Zionism's goal of immanent transformation of the individual. The absence of naming Palestine must have been an obvious exclusion in Aḥad Ha'am's strategies, even without the perspective of historical hindsight. Migration to Palestine was a major and immediate response to Kishinev, ideologically if not actually, and the pogrom promoted broad community support and intellectual sympathy for a territorial solution. We can see the swiftness of the territorial reaction in Aḥad Ha'am's own criticism of how Kishinev became tied to a settlement program whose purpose was to answer the crisis and commemorate the victims of the pogrom. As early as the summer of 1903, just at the time of the Sixth Zionist Congress, Aḥad Ha'am already composed a short essay, "Binyan" (Building), criticizing the building program in Palestine that specifically invoked the victims of Kishinev. In this brilliant little essay mocking territoriality, Aḥad Ha'am manages within the space of only a few pages to criticize a host of political and cultural rivals, especially Micha Yosef Berdichevsky's own comments on "building," as well as Rothschild paternalism and the view that settlement in Palestine could be a legitimate reaction to Kishinev. Most important, the essay clearly demonstrates that Kishinev, within the Odessa circle of Zionist intellectuals, suffused the entire question of settlement and personal autonomy:

> "It is easier to destroy than to build."[15] . . .
>
> In fact it *is* easier to destroy than to build—real building at least, according to a plan devised around true foundations. But simply "to build," to rest stone upon stone, without a deep foundation and without a determined form, and to call this "building"—how easy this is and how difficult to tear down! . . . Here before us is the newest "building," which arose suddenly from nothing, in a single moment . . . on the graves of our sanctified dead in Kishinev.
>
> Rest in peace innocent victims! The fate of those you left behind in the Valley of Tears, don't let it bother your rest! We have already found them redeemers and a good future: "orphans of the community" they will be and to the land of our forefathers they will be sent, to grow and be educated there paid for by the community, and afterward to become "community farmers." —
>
> Orphans of Kishinev—farmers in Eretz Israel! What a beautiful idea!
>
> But we still need to face the question: is it possible really to "make" farmers by educating them in special schools for this purpose?[16] There are experts who say—aided by experience—that educational institutions like these produce what they produce, just not good farmers who will be able to live a farmer's life.[17]

Aḥad Ha'am repeats here the standard divisions between spiritual and practical Zionism, between settlement action, which will produce the new Jew through reification, and settlement as an impediment to a more necessary immanent process of self-transformation. Most important, Aḥad Ha'am reaches these arguments through a debate over language and the meaning of "building" for the identity of the modern Jew.

As much as the political distinctions outlined by Aḥad Ha'am describe very real practical divisions within the organizations of the movement, more significantly, they veil two very different and perhaps even more fundamental aesthetic responses to Jewish consciousness in a modern, national existence. The emphasis on individual autonomy, which derives from Dubnov's insistence on political autonomism but which also describes Aḥad Ha'am's cultural ideology, rejects all but the most romantic notions of the subject, a subject who can, through his own willful spirit, create the world around him as he recreates himself. That is why autonomism refuses territory as a political solution. Autonomy has to be completely immanent, and consciousness thus forms itself intransitively, without reference to the exterior world. Building must be understood as a reflexive metaphor that focuses on building the self; it does not signify action in a world of objects, which will then transform the individual. In Aḥad Ha'am's criticism of settlement, the transformation of "building" from an intransitive, immanently symbolic verb to a transitive, physical act contains the inherent danger of further alienating the individual from the nation since the exigencies of physical settlement place demands on the settler that might transform his external life at the expense of leaving nothing for the more important internal metamorphosis. Hence Aḥad Ha'am's denigrating remarks about "making" farmers, which remains only an external action and part of a wide critique of how Rothschild colonialism in Palestine attempted to educate the new immigrants and externally transform them merely on the outside. Bereft, then, of immanent meaning, "making," a transitive verb, can only be presented and derided within quotation marks as having no inner life.

In general, the threat Aḥad Ha'am perceived and responded to in this essay was located in the symbolic structures of settlement, those that now proposed to guide Zionist action and identity during this new post-Kishinev era. For Aḥad Ha'am territorial action threatened to impose upon Jewish identity a worldview that emanated from beyond the romantic confines of the self. Was not this critique, as well, Dubnov's apprehension and objection to Jabotinsky from April 7, 1903—the rejection not of the perceived threat to Jewish well being, but of the poetics of that threat, the reliance on a spatial metaphor that cast Jewish consciousness within a world where the self could not control its own destiny? Thus, the metaphor of "*outer* space."

In this way, Aḥad Ha'am's new position out of step with the major thrust of practical Zionism demonstrates the important flaws in territoriality as it was being conceived, flaws to which Zionism as a whole was not necessarily blind. Aḥad Ha'am's stature, after all, could not be discounted, certainly not by his followers nor by those moving beyond cultural Zionism's romantic insistence on immanence as the only location for modern Jewish identity. But Kishinev might indeed mark the end of something, perhaps the end even of polemic as the major driving force and dominant literary genre behind conceptualizations of Jewish reactions to national crisis. For the real impact of Kishinev on the Zionist soul would be articulated much more effectively by a poetry that drew the connections among place, nation, and the individual in new ways, trying to work through the competing notions of how Jewish identity might respond to the novel exigencies of a post-Kishinev nationalism.

To understand how far the aesthetic question of temporal versus spatial consciousness infected a representation of the Jewish subject, especially after Kishinev, we might turn again to Jabotinsky, to the introduction to his Russian translation of Bialik's Hebrew poem "Be-ir ha-hareigah" (In the City of Slaughter), which became the most famous political *and* aesthetic reaction to the pogrom. We will return to consider Bialik's poem at some length, but Jabotinsky already puts into relief the terms of the problem that Aḥad Ha'am began to outline and which Bialik attempts to reconcile in that poem. In Jabotinsky's reading, the autonomy of the subject as a romantic, independent consciousness is mitigated and compromised by a national call to arms via the resymbolization of the tradition itself:

Hear O Israel!
Your one and only hope is you yourself
There's nothing worse or more worthy of shame
Than being the object of attack.[18]

Jabotinsky would never deny the power of Jewish will, the need, that is, to act for one's own nation and avoid the passivity of being a victim. But he significantly abandons the temporal dialectic. Spatial goals in the form of political organization drive the poetics of this hackneyed poem introducing Bialik, and the symbols of Jewish tradition—the texts that provide some sort of intertextual meaning to this new cry—maintain symbolic value only by pointing to the forms of modern Jewish consciousness. Placed in a decidedly modern context and significantly introduced and framed by nature, metaphors based on the tradition now appear devoid of the weight of the religious tradition:

Nature beckons with the Spring
Passover beckons, the day of Exodus
Liberation from our chains
They're threatening us once more
As before, in days of yore
Pharaoh's chariots filled
With our enemies' hordes[19]

The threat comes from without, and the tradition enters now simply as a trope in the form of the simile, without any essential power to determine identity. Instead, the tradition is merely an instrument newly endowed by the poet to reflect fear and yearning within the symbols of the nation and of national territory.

The starkness of Jabotinsky's modernism, the way that the self would be understood as the object of multiple cultural and political claims, guides his brand of Zionist politics and disconnects his concept of Jewish identity from a strictly liberal view of self-consciousness and self-reflection. Bialik would not necessarily advocate these views—it is not known whether he authorized the translation—but Jabotinsky shows the terms of the struggle for the self, a struggle that Bialik worked through in order to create a response to the new claims on identity and territory after Kishinev.

Bialik Confronts Kishinev

In the wake of Kishinev, the Odessa group sent Bialik to investigate the site of the pogrom. The choice is not self-evident since for the others—Aḥad Ha'am and Dubnov in particular—journalism and reportage, indeed polemic, constituted a more central place in their writing and thought. But representational veracity might never have been the goal of Bialik's mission, which produced no journalistic report but instead a poetic response, "Be-ir ha-hareigah" (In the City of Slaughter), a poem that clearly ignored some of the actual eyewitness testimony Bialik himself had gathered. But given the popular response to the poem, and the continued critical interest it has engendered, imaginative literature seems at that moment to have held the power to capture and express both the raw horror in the face of violence and the political lessons Zionism sought to extract from the incident. Indeed, on the face of it, "In the City of Slaughter" reads as a poetic elaboration of Aḥad Ha'am's indictment against Jewish passivity in response to immediate danger, a theme that will sustain much Zionist thought and anxiety throughout the decades leading up to statehood.

As a paroxysm of Zionist frustration with traditional Jewish nonresistance, "In the City of Slaughter" certainly expands on Aḥad Ha'am's harangue with great rhetorical power. But the poem does not merely follow ideological dictates. Or rather, by following the response outlined by Aḥad Ha'am the poem inevitably reaches for the same tensions embodied in Aḥad Ha'am's positions and necessarily faces similar dilemmas of where to locate a new Jewish psychology within competing temporal and spatial claims. Bialik himself was clearly aware of the tensions that Aḥad Ha'am's nationalist poetic formulas assigned to the poet, precisely in terms of where the individual stands in relation to the expression of emotion and the nation. In his polemics over "poesy," Aḥad Ha'am had suffused all personal expression within the needs of national renewal, a position that left Bialik the poet with a consciousness of a division within poetry, a division based on Aḥad Ha'am's understanding of national poetry versus personal expression. Time and again, Bialik articulated an understanding that his poetry may not live up to Aḥad Ha'am's nationalist requisites: "[A]lmost half of [my] poems have nothing to do with the nation . . . and among my poems many are of the kind that Aḥad Ha'am describes in *Ha-shiloaḥ* as: 'the out-pouring of the soul and love poetry [which] one finds in abundance in other literatures.'"[20]

"In the City of Slaughter," with its prophetic tone and its ideological confidence in condemning passivity, however, exhibits none of these hesitations. After all, the broad message seems clearly focused on national concerns over suffering and inaction, and the thematic descriptions of the poem direct our attention with unwavering urgency to these issues, mocking the very self-obsession that defines the narcissistic diaspora Jew:

תַּחַת מְדוֹכַת מַצָּה זוֹ וּמֵאֲחוֹרֵי אוֹתָהּ חָבִית,
שָׁכְבוּ בְעָלִים, חֲתָנִים, אַחִים, הֵצִיצוּ מִן-הַחוֹרִים
בְּפַרְפֵּר גְּוִיּוֹת קְדוֹשׁוֹת תַּחַת בְּשַׂר חֲמוֹרִים,

. . . .

שָׁכְבוּ בְּבָשְׁתָּם וַיִּרְאוּ – וְלֹא נָעוּ וְלֹא זָעוּ,
וְאֶת-עֵינֵיהֶם לֹא-נִקֵּרוּ וּמִדַּעְתָּם לֹא-יָצָאוּ –
וְאוּלַי גַּם-אִישׁ לְנַפְשׁוֹ אָז הִתְפַּלֵּל בִּלְבָבוֹ:
רִבּוֹנוֹ שֶׁל-עוֹלָם, עֲשֵׂה נֵס – וְאֵלַי הָרָעָה לֹא-תָבֹא.
וְאֵלֶּה אֲשֶׁר חָיוּ מִטֻּמְאָתָן וְהֵקִיצוּ מִדָּמָן –
וְהִנֵּה שֻׁקְּצוּ כָל-חַיֵּיהֶן וְנִטְמָא אוֹר עוֹלָמָן
שִׁקּוּצֵי עוֹלָם, טֻמְאַת גּוּף וָנֶפֶשׁ, מִבַּחוּץ וּמִבִּפְנִים –
וְהֵגִיחוּ בַעֲלֵיהֶן מֵחוֹרָם וְרָצוּ בֵית-אֱלֹהִים
וּבֵרְכוּ עַל-הַנִּסִּים שֵׁם אֵל יִשְׁעָם וּמִשְׂגַּבָּם;
וְהַכֹּהֲנִים שֶׁבָּהֶם יֵצְאוּ וְיִשְׁאֲלוּ אֶת-רַבָּם:
"רַבִּי! אִשְׁתִּי מַה הִיא? מֻתֶּרֶת אוֹ אֲסוּרָה?" –
וְהַכֹּל יָשׁוּב לְמִנְהָגוֹ, וְהַכֹּל יַחֲזֹר לְשׁוּרָה.

Underneath this bed and behind that cask
Lay husbands, bridegrooms, brothers, peering out from their holes
At the convulsions of the holy corpses underneath the donkey flesh

. . . .

They lay in their shame and saw—and neither moved nor budged,
Their eyes they did not gouge and their minds they never lost—
Perhaps as well each man then prayed within his heart:
O Lord, create a miracle—and let the evil pass me by.
And those that lived through their defilement and awoke from their blood—
To have their lives abominated and the light of their world befouled
Eternal abomination, defilement of body and soul, inside and out—
Their husbands emerged from their holes and ran to the synagogue
And blessed the name of the Lord of their miracles and salvations;
The *kohanim* among them would go out and ask the rabbi:
"Rabbi! My wife what is she? Permitted or forbidden?"—
And everything will be as it was, and everything will return to its place.[21]

The harangue against religious faith, cowardice and passivity—against the femininity of the eastern European Jewish man—while part of an important political message in the poem, also misdirects attention from the central drama depicted. Indeed, even here in this passage, the poem marks its own inadequacy in light of the violence of the pogrom, both formally and thematically. Formally, the poem concentrates on the shards and remainders of violence, thereby reinforcing poetry's inadequacy in portraying the present moment of violence and directing us toward the scene of the harangue's articulation as the principal subject of the poem. Thematically, and tied to the presentness of the expression of the speaker's wrath, the poem ironically announces the exhaustion and impotence of the God who might be the speaker in the poem. Not only does traditional belief and worship come under sharp rebuke, but God himself proclaims his own helplessness:

סִלְחוּ לִי, עֲלוּבֵי עוֹלָם, אֱלֹהֵיכֶם עָנִי כְּמוֹתְכֶם,
עָנִי הוּא בְחַיֵּיכֶם וְקַל-וָחֹמֶר בְּמוֹתְכֶם,
. . . .
. . . יָרַדְתִּי מִנְּכָסַי!

Forgive me, wretched of the world, your god is poor like you,
He is poor in your life and more so in your death
. . . .
. . . I am without possessions![22]

This pseudo-Nietzschean self-indictment first comes in the speaker's attack on passivity cited above where blind belief and faith as a surrogate for action assuage the Jew's guilt. But the attack reflects on the God-figure of the speaker as well, not just in how the lines reject the emptiness of worship but in how those prayers rise to a divine power incapable of effecting change in the face of violence.

The central rhetorical indignation of the poem, then, misdirects us by the very strength of the moral outrage enunciated. Instead, at the core of the drama in this poem lie questions of individual reinvention within the modern world. For beyond the question of political action or inaction, the principal drama of "In the City of Slaughter" describes the unnamed addressee—the nondivine poet-witness who is exhorted to write and aesthetically contemplate the violence in light of God's inability to act:

וְנִצַּבְתָּ כֹּה עַד-בּוֹשׁ וְהִתְיַחַדְתָּ עִם-הַצָּעַר
וּמִלֵּאתָ בּוֹ אֶת-לְבָבְךָ לְכֹל יְמֵי חַיֶּיךָ,
. . . .
וּבְחֵיקְךָ תִּשָּׂאֶנּוּ אֶל-אַרְבַּע רוּחוֹת הַשָּׁמַיִם,
וּבִקַּשְׁתָּ וְלֹא-תִמְצָא לוֹ נִיב שְׂפָתַיִם

You will stand there for long and unite with your sorrow
And you will fill your heart with it for the rest of your days,

. . . .
In your soul you will raise the message to the four winds of the heavens
You will seek but you will not find the proper expression of your lips.

Indeed, the poet's response and personal transformation constitute the principal political message and narrative action in the poem. Bialik's move here is ingeniously modern because of the freedom and responsibility he places on the national action of the individual. If the addressee is thus God's prophet who is exhorted to take in the scene, all within the nationalist context of a strong poetic allusion to God's orders to Abraham to seek Canaan (*lekh lekha*), then, we might say, Bialik actually inverses Genesis's depicted relationship between an omnipotent God issuing commands to an obedient and receptive Abraham. In fact, despite the obvious reference to Abraham in the poem, Bialik seems more interested in a non-national reading of Genesis and makes "In the City of Slaughter," with its emphasis on aesthetic apprehending of the scene—as opposed to the action-orientation of Abraham's movement toward Canaan—a moralistic anti-*akedah*, that is, the unbinding of the prophet Isaac/Abraham, in a reinvention of the prophet as an unbound, independent actor in the world, free to express what he has seen.[23] Still tied to Aḥad Ha'am's concepts of immanence, through self-expression the poet will create national action.

Bialik's personalization of taking in the scene certainly coincides with cultural Zionism's emphasis on immanent reaction, but it concomitantly undermines the simple terms Aḥad Ha'am laid out for response, namely, that action in the face of violence must subsume individual fear and belief within national structures (the "organization" that Aḥad Ha'am called for). As a poem working toward the constitution of the self in the addressee, and not just reacting to a political program, "In the City of Slaughter" must be read ironically against its descriptive power and even beyond the rhetorical strength of its prophetic-divine speaker. Triangulated between these two overwhelming forces in the poem stands the silent addressee, who is cajoled, led, commanded, and impelled to see, all in an effort to create in him some sort of transformation, and through that transformation to constitute a new way for the modern Jewish citizen to look at and understand the physical world. The context for the Jewish soul, then, moves from a textually based dialectic of old and new, between tradition and modernity, passivity and action, and ever so timidly begins to engage questions of how this new Jew might apprehend the landscape and construct national identity in it. Thus, in the poem, turning away from violence and the passive identity of eastern Europe always seems to involve the intrusion of the natural landscape:

וּפָנִיתָ לָלֶכֶת מֵעִם קִבְרוֹת הַמֵּתִים, וְעִכְּבָה
רֶגַע אֶחָד אֶת-עֵינֶיךָ רְפִידַת הַדֶּשֶׁא מִסָּבִיב,
וְהַדֶּשֶׁא רַךְ וְרָטֹב, כַּאֲשֶׁר יִהְיֶה בִּתְחִלַּת הָאָבִיב

Turn and leave the cemetery of the dead,
And for a moment the patch of grass around caught your eyes,
The grass soft and moist, as it is at the beginning of spring[24]

The grass intrudes in a moment of seasonal veracity—the "spring" of Easter and Passover—without any further framing of nature within the overwrought symbols of the tradition or the violence. In general, the dramatic focus on change in the individual's apprehending and understanding certainly derives from the earlier debates within eastern European Jewry over education and the dialectical outlines of a modern Jewish psychology. But they follow as well from specifically poetic concerns which reinforce a reading of "In the City of Slaughter" as treading that fine line between national exhortation and personal transformation, precisely the fault line of Aḥad Ha'am's comments on poesy, which the prophetic exhortation would seem to dismiss. Indeed, in moving beyond the tradition, Bialik places the addressee in a very modern world where the material objects of place become the physical instantiations of a way to reinvent the self while reaching for national coalescence. Granted, all this is being accomplished within the negative provocation of the violent pogrom and within the context of a prophetic-divine speaker who overwhelms and obscures the addressee hovering in the background. But the prophetic harangue has no power if it is not heard, and as it condemns the inaction of the pogrom's passive victims, it gains its power *only* because we understand that there exists a surrogate hearer, an addressee who embeds the hopes of a renewed, powerful national identity. Thus, it is the immediacy in the encounter of the addressee with Kishinev that evinces meaning in the poem, an immediacy of aesthetic response, which is caught up in the relation between the subjectivity of the addressee and the object of the observed aftermath of disaster.

Language then becomes the explicit location of a contestation over meaning, not because the narrative might represent the slaughter, which in fact it does not. Rather, the rhetoric of the poetic language works hard to frame immediacy (for the addressee and *not* for the speaker) and by doing so places us within the consciousness of understanding this place. As a result, an autonomous subject in the form of the addressee emerges from the articulation of the many shards of national disaster left on the place of Kishinev. In fact, the ultimate message of the poem seems to be the conceptual separation it outlines between the independence of the addressee, on the one hand, who transcends the scene both spatially and temporally, taking in the scene and making sense of it, and on the other hand, those victims and passive respondents who are caught within the very throes of history and thus are unable to reflect on their place within a temporal or spatial dialectic, leaving them slaves to history's currents and vicissitudes.

In the specific poetics of the poem, this strategy of immediacy and the focus on the spatial freedom of the addressee emerge through the expression of a romanticism that strives to present the object as a thing in itself, without the mediating use of figuration. Alan Mintz has commented on the exclusive reliance on metonymy throughout the poem, a device of the speaker which pulls the addressee into the scene of destruction. Mintz's powerful reading of the poem stresses how "the indirection of metonymy . . . enables Bialik to eliminate the enemy as a touchstone of antipathy and abomination and to force the reader to transfer those emotions to the interior drama of Jew and Jew, God and His people, the poet-prophet, his sender and addressee."[25] But in this, the effect of the poem and certainly its final political appeal stem less from any represented scene of horror than from the ideological implications of an aesthetic language that would constitute some new sense of Jewish inner life. Thus, drama in the poem emanates from the way the language functions to create meaning for the listener. The "indirection" of metonymy that disdains the objectification of the scene emphasizes how knowledge emerges from the encounter between observer and the physical, spatial fragments of experience. What Mintz calls coercive in the poem—that is, the way Bialik closes the scene off from any non-Jewish perspective, away from any accusation of blame on external perpetrators of the pogrom—is, in truth, a form of aesthetic seduction because it keeps us focused on the figuration of Jewish consciousness and the autonomous experience of the apprehending subject who finally encounters the ineffability of the results of inaction. The interpretive gap from part to whole (the interpretive figuration of metonymy) must be filled through the very act of reading and understanding, which is how the poem maintains its ideological power as national expression.

קוּם לֵךְ לְךָ אֶל עִיר הַהֲרֵגָה וּבָאתָ אֶל-הַחֲצֵרוֹת,
וּבְעֵינֶיךָ תִרְאֶה וּבְיָדְךָ תְמַשֵּׁשׁ עַל-הַגְּדֵרוֹת
וְעַל הָעֵצִים וְעַל הָאֲבָנִים וְעַל-גַּבֵּי טִיחַ הַכְּתָלִים
אֶת-הַדָּם הַקָּרוּשׁ וְאֶת-הַמֹּחַ הַנִּקְשֶׁה שֶׁל-הַחֲלָלִים.

Arise and go [*lekh lekha*] to the city of slaughter and go to its courtyards,
And with your eyes, look, and with your hands, feel at the fences
And at the trees and at the stones and at plaster walls
The coagulated blood and the dried brain of the dead.[26]

The poem opens with an obvious biblical quotation, the exhortation to Abraham to leave Mesopotamia and migrate to Palestine. The reference stresses the individual experience of the national citizen, the *lekh lekha*, a personal address to a man before he enters either the national space or a national community. Even if we must hear the biblical reference as an explicit call to the nation, the chiastic structure of these four lines illuminates the individuality of the aesthetic experience inscribed in the middle two. National concern might frame the stanza—beginning with the biblical allusion and ending at the scene of national catastrophe—but in between, the path toward recognition of national trauma passes through the individuality of sense and interpretation, of the singular viewer encountering the objects of place and making decisions as to their significance. That too is the power of metonymy, which refuses to narrate its own interpretation but rather substitutes the object for the idea, an object that would constitute the idea through the mediating power of the observer.

Mintz astutely couples the rhetorical strategy of the poem to the role of the poet, throwing into question the relation of the poet to a writing about national catastrophe: "Beneath the manifest question of the condition of the people lies the question of the romantic poet, the sources of his authority, the nature of his responsibility to the nation."[27] But the issue of romanticism hardly seems separate from the people, and the drama of taking in the scene cannot be excised from any of the various descriptions the poem offers of violence. In fact, any implied separation between the scene and the apprehending of the scene ignores the very function of romanticism altogether in the poem.

Metonymy then draws the scene of national destruction into the poet: the things, the remains of what had been, stand as fragmentary, material reminders and disembodied parts of what the poet-investigator missed. The remnant signifies the whole, and the metonymic process itself articulates the destructive act of the pogrom: as we construct that passage of part to whole, we are, in effect, reinventing through inversion the violence that forces us into this linguistic trope in the first place. Metonymy thus acts to bridge the tensions between individual and collective participation, an opposition usually accompanying any reading of Bialik as the romantic national poet who disdains that role.[28]

In the tug-of-war between nation and individual, what comes to the fore in the poem is the idea of the individual against the material remnants of the world. Bialik starts to describe this tension for the new Jew by outlining a unified modern self caught within the materialism of the world beyond. In this, a spatial axis finally and significantly replaces a temporal one precisely through the concentration on the metonymic objects of poetic description, which carry no history or mythological force beyond what they in their immediate apprehendability offer to the addressee. Paul de Man describes a similar strain in German romanticism in a critique that has particular application here: "The change [of poetic diction in romanticism] often takes the form of a return to a greater concreteness, a proliferation of natural objects that restores to the language the material substantiality which had been partially lost."[29] De Man's description of a return to the instantiation of the object in language coincides neatly with Bialik's emphasis on metonymy in "In the City of Slaughter."

To be fair, however, Bialik poses a somewhat different question about romantic poetic language, even if there are clear resonances with de Man in the poetics of "In the City of Slaughter." While de Man's criticism of the romantics focuses on the representation of the object, Bialik's goal shifts romanticism's focus onto how the object—the natural world—helps articulate the self. This aesthetic inversion might be due to the belatedness of Hebrew romanticism, which arrived late enough to recognize, with Aḥad Ha'am's aid, that what is truly at stake in the articulation of the nation is the position of the individual observer and not the concreteness of the object being described. In de Man's criticism of Romanticism the poetic encounter with nature ironically veils language's inability (and even disinterest) in truly representing the object. Instead, language—even when it seems to refer to nature itself—only ever refers back to the speaker. In disdaining metaphor, according to de Man, Romanticism nevertheless becomes completely dependent on a broad metaphoric structure where all of nature reflects the person apprehending it. Bialik's rejection of metaphor echoes that type of displacement but it does something significantly different as well, which mitigates romanticism's problem in a very modernist way.

By relying on metonymy, Bialik highlights the inherent falseness of language. In the poem, the shards and fragments of Kishinev literally come belatedly. The addressee has indeed *missed* the action, and metonymy as a replacement of part for whole works to reinforce this temporal lack in our own position in the world. The immediacy of metonymy, then, ironically implies a *lack* of immediacy to the objects described, to the scene of catastrophe, and thus to identity itself. In this way, Bialik's poem begins to tie place to the very problems of temporality. Metonymy ultimately fails to present anything other than the poetic subject's misunderstanding of the world. But it does put in relief how identity must overcome the various temporal and spatial obstacles it confronts. That is de Man's point too, where Romanticism's focus on the object ends in a dialectical paradox: the rejection of metaphor finally relies *only* on metaphor, on the object standing in for a meaning not inherent to it, but one determined by the poet. "At the same time, in accordance with a dialectic that is more paradoxical than may appear at first sight, the structure of the language becomes increasingly metaphorical and the image—be it under the name of symbol or even of myth—comes to be considered as the more prominent dimension of the style."[30] Bialik rehearses this paradox by falling back on metaphor and image at a key juncture at the very end of the poem, which again is a moment when language highlights the drama of the addressee in taking in the meaning of physical destruction. At the end, now, Bialik ties that experience of understanding specifically to a natural environment:

וְעַתָּה מַה-לְּךָ פֹּה, בֶּן-אָדָם, קוּם בְּרַח הַמִּדְבָּרָה
וְנָשָׂאתָ עִמְּךָ שָׁמָּה אֶת-כּוֹס הַיְגוֹנִים,
וְקָרַעְתָּ שָׁם אֶת-נַפְשְׁךָ לַעֲשָׂרָה קְרָעִים
וְאֶת-לְבָבְךָ תִּתֵּן מַאֲכָל לַחֲרוֹן אֵין-אוֹנִים,
וְדִמְעָתְךָ הַגְּדוֹלָה הוֹרֵד שָׁם עַל קָדְקֹד הַסְּלָעִים
וְשַׁאֲגָתְךָ הַמָּרָה שַׁלַּח – וְתֹאבַד בִּסְעָרָה.

And now what's here for you, son of man, rise, flee into the desert
And carry with you there the cup of sorrows,
And tear your soul into ten shreds
And your heart feed it to impotent wrath,
And drop your great tear on the head [*kodkod*] of the rocks
And cast your bitter howl—to be lost in a storm.[31]

The image of Kishinev exists only within the poet's own figuration of the place and the catastrophe that took place there. Metonymy of disaster is set in opposition to the metaphor of contemplation, which now significantly begins to figure nature. At the very least, the invocation of the desert describes an escape for the poet and addressee into a realm untainted by the objective remainders of Kishinev.

A basic dialectical opposition in "In the City of Slaughter" pits the apprehending subject against the immutability of the object of destruction, reminders of a political violence brought about by perceived racial difference. But in locating an aesthetic alienation in that disconnect between (national) subject and object (of place), Bialik points to reconciliation as a coming together of these same forms, if only the proper object can be constructed. Thus, in the poem, language not only creates tension, but highlights how aesthetic expression itself will work to solve the problems of minority for the Jews. These are the same terms as Gilles Deleuze and Félix Guattari's theorization of minority in Kafka,[32] but for Kafka, as they argue, minority demands a constant territorial struggle within the language of oppression. Instead, Zionism worked to essentialize modern Jewish identity within the territorial promise embedded in the dominance of a single, separate language. Language offered escape not just from the temporal bonds of tradition, but from the territorial imprisonment of a struggle with the majority oppressor. Aḥad Ha'am writes about Hebrew as a language of an authentic modern Jewish consciousness, modern because it would be able to will its own identity, once, that is, it coincided with the expression of the nation: "With the Hebrew writers of Eastern Europe and Palestine, for whom Hebrew is still a part of their being . . . the necessity of writing Hebrew springs from their innermost selves. . . . Assimilation, then, is not a danger that the Jewish people must dread for the future. What it has to fear is being split up into *fragments.* The manner in which the Jews work for the perfection of their individuality depends everywhere on the character of that foreign spiritual force which is at work in their surroundings, and which arouses them to what we have called competitive imitation" (emphasis added).[33]

Bialik's "In the City of Slaughter" tries to go beyond Aḥad Ha'am's idea of immanent Hebrew instrumentality and demonstrate the need to reconceive language as a complex medium for encountering a spatial world beyond the self. Metaphor's failure at the end of the poem to do anything but point back at the emotional inner life of the addressee merely outlines the difficulties involved in how language might offer a way to express and constitute the Romantic Hebrew subject beyond the confines of the mind. But those differences point forward, and Bialik's sense that language could begin to construct the bridge between a hermetic self and territorial community addressed a particular post-Kishinev problem and had important resonances throughout the Zionist movement.

The idea of identity as tied to a national landscape infused even the most materialist, antiromantic Zionist interpretations of Jewish history and identity, especially as they began to emerge after the pogrom. Cultural essentialism expressed *by* Hebrew (and not just *in* Hebrew) extended to the ideological extremes of the Zionist movement. Ber Borochov, for instance, Zionism's most ardent scientific Marxist of this early period, echoed these concerns in 1905, even though he might be located far from Bialik in the spectrum of Russian Zionist political thought:

> The system of production of oppressed nationalities is always subject to abnormal conditions. . . . Not only the special interests of every class are affected by this external pressure, but also every individual in the nationality feels it and understands that the source of this pressure is national. . . . Under such circumstances, the mother tongue, for example, assumes greater significance than that of a mere means to preserve the local market. [Within] freedom of language, the oppressed person becomes all the more attached to it. In other words, the national question of an oppressed people is detached from its association with the material conditions of production. The cultural aspects assume an independent significance, and all the members of the nation become interested in national self-determination.[34]

Like Bialik, Borochov pushes language and cultural expression to begin outlining a connection to a national space, here defined in the place of the market, but lying somehow beyond the vicissitudes of a strictly Marxist historical dialectic. Language issues from a fundamental, immanent bond to identity that begins to define individual belonging outside of the mechanisms of production and class. In this, Borochov, in a socialist irony, allows a certain metaphysical function for culture in the forging of the oppressed nation, especially as it would reconceive expression in Hebrew as above the material conditions of production. However, still missing is the precise location of the desert in "In the City of Slaughter," Borochov's place of cultural encounter with the material place of the nation, that is, its market. In the dissolution of Bialik's poem into the disunity of the Jewish soul—"And tear your soul into ten shreds/And your heart feed it to impotent wrath"—Bialik points to the uncompleted project of the poem, which is also Borochov's unsynthesized dialectic. Both reflect national identity within a language tied to place, but cannot as yet locate that identity within a particular landscape.

The Hebrew Sublime

"In the City of Slaughter" initiated a poetic encounter between observer and place that would reach apotheosis in 1905 with "Ha-breikhah" (The Pool), Bialik's major exploration of man's relation to nature. In the passage from "In the City of Slaughter" to "The Pool," the political implications of the aesthetic questions each asks remain similar and build toward a significant aesthetic crisis. However, the connection between the two poems is normally dismissed because of a critical insistence on an oppositional disjuncture between their rhetorical styles and thematic content. Indeed, the move from "In the City of Slaughter" to "The Pool" is always understood as dichotomous, as symptomatic of Bialik's personal oppositional conflict between national and individual expression. In the standard reading of Bialik's aesthetic progress from 1903 to 1905, after fulfilling a national obligation in the wake of Kishinev, in "The Pool" Bialik retreats into the private space of self-expression. Allegory returns to fill the poetic environment, which presents a frail subject caught within the alternating cycles of nature, a far cry from the aggressive prophetic harangue of "In the City of Slaughter." The rhetorical difference between the poems reflects not just a thematic movement from city to forest (the location of "The Pool"), but a political shift as well from an engagement with national history to the mythological retreat into the contemplative self.

However, if we abandon normative readings of poetic opposition that rely on traditional assumptions about form and content, we would then be forced to see "The Pool" as answering significant problems raised in "In the City of Slaughter"—not the national thematic issues of violence and antisemitism but the aesthetic questions of Jewish consciousness and the nation. Thematically, the scene does shift from the violence of Kishinev to the placidity of the forest; from the artifice of the city to the cycles of nature; from the rhetoric of the prophets to a symbolist lyricism. But even on a thematic level, we can link the two in how "The Pool" takes up the call for personal retreat that ends "In the City of Slaughter." In this context, "The Pool" continues to address how language creates difficult barriers to a reflexive articulation of a physical environment, especially the poet's relationship to nature. Language—in this case, Hebrew—expresses an essential national bond, an immanent connection to community, but it still blocks off territory from immanence. Borochov might use language to define an economic community within a territorial space, but the boundaries of that space remain arbitrarily defined, which is why Borochov's use of culture fails to define Palestine except as a multinational space, a solution Zionism was never ready to embrace. What "The Pool" thus succeeds in doing is answer the restrictions of this type of cultural politics by inverting the direction of the encounter with the object in "In the City of Slaughter." If there language flowed from the subject onto the objects that signify place, then in "The Pool" symbolism searches for the inversion, namely, for a language immanent of place which would encompass the subject.

The poem has been read this way, but then only within the broad strokes of personal allegory where the poem's images of the pool and nature represent some hidden meaning for the speaker himself.[35] Bialik complicated the matter. His allegorical pronouncement—"I was like a small little pool of water hidden deep in the woods—a pool that reflects the entire world in silence and in a different hue"[36]—argues strongly for biographical allegory in the poem. But Yosef Haefrati's refusal to take this private utterance as *the* semiotic key to the poem opens up a political reading of the poetics of nature contained within it.[37] For by denying a biographical interpretation of this statement as a definition of how to read allegory, Haefrati, in citing the reference from Bialik, emphasizes the way that allegory itself becomes the poem's thematic content. Thus, instead of a reading that posits a romantic sublime dividing the self and nature, the refusal of biographical determinism pushes for an analysis of the expression of this natural world precisely *as* the immanent statement of the poem's speaker. In this move, representational allegory (the way the critic Dan Miron reads the poem)[38] gives way to a stronger reading of something we might call constitutive allegory, where allegory doubles back on the poem itself and, rather than represent some *thing* as an idea outside the artifice of language, only stands for itself.

In fact, the lines in "The Pool" that open up personal allegory for so many critics—

וּבְשִׁבְתִּי שָׁם עַל-שְׂפַת הַבְּרֵכָה, צוֹפֶה
בְּחִידַת שְׁנֵי עוֹלָמוֹת, עוֹלַם תְּאוֹמִים,
מִבְּלִי לָדַעַת מִי מִשְּׁנֵיהֶם קוֹדֵם

And as I sat there on the edge of the pool, looking
At the riddle of the two worlds, a world of twins,
Without knowing which of them comes first.[39]

might best be understood not as a binary declaration of allegorical correspondence, a mirroring, that is, between nature and the self, but more as describing a romantic problem of linguistic access to the physical world. Here, the speaker announces his apprehensive position caught between the real of nature itself and the lie of nature's representation—a rather Platonic problem. In this, Bialik seems to anticipate de Man's critique of Romanticism's depiction of the object and, with perhaps an inadvertent nod toward modernism, locates the difficulties of identity in the battle to sort out what is real and what is represented, an opposition that troubled Zionist politics quite prominently, as we will see more explicitly in the next chapter.

Instead of allegory, then, should we not see in "The Pool" a more physical encounter with place, where the individual struggles with the artifice of language to get at the kernel of what is real in the world, what Bialik later wrote about in his essay "Gilui ve-khisui ba-lashon" (Revealment and Concealment in Language)?[40] In this context, "The Pool" proposes what we might call a romantic Hebrew repudiation of Plato's cave and a premodern mysticism, instead invoking a sublime meaning for nature, a nature whose unmediated presence becomes the visceral goal of all individual knowledge and desire.[41]

But Bialik's sublime is not completely romantic either because the speaker never truly encounters nature as a thing itself. In "The Pool" Bialik remains ever aware of the power of language to obfuscate, redirect, and otherwise cut off the speaker from the origin of knowledge. We know this from the very opening of the poem, which declares knowledge as both the individual's ultimate goal in the encounter with the forest and an utter impossibility:

אֲנִי יוֹדֵעַ יַעַר, וּבַיַּעַר
אֲנִי יוֹדֵעַ בְּרֵכָה צְנוּעָה אַחַת:
בַּעֲבִי הַחֹרֶשׁ, פְּרוּשָׁה מִן הָעוֹלָם,
בְּצֵל שֶׁל-אַלּוֹן רָם, בְּרוּךְ אוֹר וְלְמוּד סַעַר,
לְבַדָּהּ תַּחֲלֹם לָהּ חֲלוֹם עוֹלָם הָפוּךְ
וְתַדְגֶּה לָהּ בַּחֲשַׁאי אֶת-דְּגֵי זְהָבָהּ –
וְאֵין יוֹדֵעַ מַה-בִּלְבָבָהּ.

I know a forest and in the forest
I know a humble pool:
In the thick of the grove, apart from the world,
In the shade of the great oak, blessed with light and accustomed to storm,
Alone she will dream a dream of an inverted world
And will produce, in secret, her golden fish–
But no one knows what is in her heart.

This struggle to know place might define a particularly Hebrew sublime where the landscape does not offer itself as immediately accessible to the individual, unbound to the strictures of language and artifice. In this, Palestine, or any geographic entity, can never be named because of the way naming itself might be a false designation of the environment, and place must remain an abstract locus for Jewish identity. Specifically, the representation of the land, even in the physical reflection of Palestine itself, cannot substitute as a panacea that would distract from a more fundamental immediacy between the Jew and nature. But then, Bialik readily admits that language is necessary and unavoidable, caught somewhere between Romanticism and modernism. His speaker in "The Pool" is always triangulated within this complex mechanism, more complex, we need to understand, than how Edmund Burke described the sublime beauty of nature, which for him stood as an unmediated object of contemplation. For Bialik, access to nature and place must be constantly negotiated, struggled over, and aesthetically fought for.

Over and against the immediacy of a romantic sublime, "The Pool" in fact outlines a modern struggle to control the symbols that fill nature, and by controlling them the speaker can then get closer to the sublime that nature signifies and might even embody. There is little doubt that this formulation of place has everything to do with Palestine and the post-Kishinev push for Russian Jewish emigration to the Holy Land. Fourteen years earlier Bialik had figured a much different role for nature and even Palestine itself in his poetry. In "El ha-tsipor" (To the Bird), for instance, Palestine presented itself as an unproblematic, accessible object, easily named and represented, just as long as its national meaning remained uncontested and place itself could metaphorically stand for some vague national yearning. In "To the Bird" Palestine as a physical space is allegorically inflected and obliquely represented through the address to the bird, a creature that safely maintains the geographic distance between diaspora and homeland.

After Kishinev, that distance is presented not in geographic terms but in conceptual terms. Access to the forest is thus impossible without first self-consciously knowing its reflections through our own systems of apprehending. In this way, allegory actually is not a rhetorical possibility or even a vague guide to meaning since allegory posits a simple correspondence between signifier and meaning. In "The Pool," every time the poem moves to the interior of nature, to the expected sublime unity of nature qua nature, unmediated by anything other than what it really is, at that very moment ambiguity asserts itself and inverts all expectations for final resolution, always pushing nature further away from human comprehension:

מִבַּיִת לַפָּרֹכֶת שֶׁל הֶעָלִים,
שָׁם יֵשׁ אִי קָטֹן יָרֹק, רָפוּד דֶּשֶׁא,
אִי בּוֹדֵד לוֹ, כְּעֵין עוֹלָם קָטֹן בִּפְנֵי עַצְמוֹ,
. . . .
רִצְפָּתוֹ – זְכוּכִית: בְּרֵכַת מַיִם זַכִּים,
רְאִי כֶסֶף בְּתוֹךְ מִסְגֶּרֶת דֶּשֶׁא רָטֹב,
וּבוֹ עוֹד עוֹלָם קָטֹן, עוֹלָם שֵׁנִי,
וּבְאֶמְצַע כִּפָּה זוֹ וּבְאֶמְצַע אוֹתָהּ בְּרֵכָה,
זוֹ נֶגֶד זוֹ, שְׁתֵּי אַבְנֵי כַדְכֹּד קְבוּעוֹת,
כַּדְכֻּדִים גְּדוֹלִים וּמַבְהִיקִים –
שְׁנֵי שְׁמָשׁוֹת.

From within a curtain of leaves,
There lies a small green island, carpeted with grass.
A solitary island, like a small world unto itself,
. . . .
Its floor—glass: a pool of clear water,
A silver mirror inside a frame of moist grass,
And in it there is another small world, a second world,
And in the center of that dome and in the middle of that pool,
This against that, two keystones are set,
Large and shining crowns—
Two suns.

Once we pull away the veil we still do not get to know the heart of the matter. Rather, the heart of the matter is doubled, once again the real and the reflected. Language, on the one hand, only presents the duality of the real and the represented and remains a barrier to the unitary sublime of a nature that resides in the middle of this place. But on the other, Bialik does not seem overly anxious about needing to traverse this field of images—*leshon ha-mar'ot,* as he describes it—in order to apprehend place and nature. It is in this lack of anxiety that Hebrew literature sheds any strict adherence to romanticism and the ideal of the romantic sublime, and acquiesces to the modern understanding that all objects are mediated and indeed inflected through language. In "The Pool," Bialik, it seems, simply accepts a modernist critique of "second nature," where the world is only a highly contingent place, and language and human understanding mediate all connection to the landscape; thus the dual image of two suns. But unlike Lukács's and later Adorno's criticisms of "second nature" as a bourgeois aesthetic mechanism of political control,[42] akin to ideology critique where the forms of the world do not present the true set of relations underpinning meaning, Bialik instead sees an opportunity in second nature for reintroducing individual consciousness into the world. Rather than caught within an infinite regression of images, as forest and pool endlessly reflect each other, Bialik's speaker in "The Pool" stands as an important and even necessary mediator between image and nature. Nature might present itself through representation, but that fact requires a consciousness whose job it is then to interpret and organize those images:

שְׂפַת אֵלִים חֲרִישִׁית יֵשׁ, לְשׁוֹן חֲשָׁאִים,
לֹא-קוֹל וְלֹא הֲבָרָה לָהּ, אַךְ גַּוְנֵי גְוָנִים;
וּקְסָמִים לָהּ וּתְמוּנוֹת הוֹד וּצְבָא חֶזְיוֹנוֹת,
בְּלָשׁוֹן זוֹ יִתְוַדַּע אֵל לִבְחִירֵי רוּחוֹ,

. . . .
הֲלֹא הִיא לְשׁוֹן הַמַּרְאוֹת, שֶׁמִּתְגַּלָּה
בְּפַס רְקִיעַ תְּכֵלֶת וּבְמֶרְחָבָיו,
בְּזֹךְ עֲבִיבֵי כֶסֶף וּבִשְׁחוֹר גָּלְמֵיהֶם,
בְּרֶטֶט קָמַת פָּז וּבְגֵאוּת אֶרֶז אַדִּיר,

. . . .
בְּלָשׁוֹן זוֹ, לְשׁוֹן הַלְּשׁוֹנוֹת, גַּם הַבְּרֵכָה
לִי חָדָה אֶת-חִידָתָהּ הָעוֹלָמִית.

There is a silent divine language, a secret tongue,
It has no sound and no syllable, only shades of hues;
And it has enchantments and pictures of splendor and a host of visions,
In this tongue God makes himself known to those his spirit chooses,
. . . .
This is the language of images [*leshon ha-mar'ot*], revealing itself
In a strip of azure sky and in its vastness,
In the purity of silver clouds and in the black of their amorphous mass,
In the tremble of the golden wheat, in the crest of a mighty cedar,
. . . .
In this language, language of languages, the pool too
Posed to me her eternal riddle.

This new role of interpreter might then dissolve any last vestige of Romanticism in Hebrew poetry. The language of images and reflections (*leshon ha-mar'ot*) constitutes the serious demise of personal allegory, that is, a reading of nature that would merely reflect representationally on the poet himself. Representation of the world does not participate in the caprice of a sign system (that is, language) tied to a controlling subject whose solipsistic vision and personal desire mold every image. Rather, nature presents its own representation in a language already inherent within *it*, but one that still requires interpretation, intervention, and ultimately understanding. Bialik here advances toward the limits of allegory, but never steps into the allegorical altogether. The subject does not construct itself within any immanent correspondence to symbols, but as a central reader and interpreter of those key symbols. In this, we need to take Bialik seriously at his word and see the problem in the poem as an issue of knowledge and understanding for the speaker and not as an interpretive puzzle for us, where we would allegorize nature as a simplistic reflection of identity.

Through the secret language of nature, which is still language and yet adheres only to physical things, we can finally understand the position of the speaker-poet, not as the reflection of an allegorized nature, but as an interpreter and molder of the very language that he would project. Thus, the "two suns" present a problem of distance between the real and the reflected, but a problem that only man can solve, and only by understanding his place within this world:

וּבְשִׁבְתִּי שָׁם עַל-שְׂפַת הַבְּרֵכָה, צוֹפֶה
בְּחִידַת שְׁנֵי עוֹלָמוֹת, עוֹלַם תְּאוֹמִים,
מִבְּלִי לָדַעַת מִי מִשְּׁנֵיהֶם קוֹדֵם

And as I sat there on the edge of the pool, looking
At the riddle of the two worlds, a world of twins,
Without knowing which of them comes first

Romanticism did not have this problem of duality, nor the question of priority between the real and the represented. What Bialik begins to outline is a question that irked modernist encounters with the world, which will form the basis of a continued Zionist writing of the new Jew's relationship to Palestine. This difference in how a Hebrew sublime might be figured is important because it forms the basis of Zionist intervention in the land of Israel, in contradistinction to the ecstasy of a Romantic sublime, which saw nature as a static object, obtainable only through a transformation of the position of the subject. Bialik rejects stasis in nature and does not tie the function of the subject to the passive apprehending of nature, and in this goes against how Burke originally formulated the power of the sublime: "The passion caused by the great and sublime in *nature*, when those causes operate most powerfully, is Astonishment; and astonishment is that state of the soul, in which all its motions are suspended, with some degree of horror. In this case the mind is so entirely filled with its object, that it cannot entertain any other, nor by consequence reason on that object which employs it."[43] The sublime, then, would suspend aesthetic judgment in the moment when the unmediated object affects the speaker, a position Bialik's "The Pool" clearly refuses.

Romantic poetry itself might not have followed Burke's dictates to the letter, but the basic moment of apprehending nature in a type of aesthetic suspension does translate into a very familiar poetic mode. Thus it is when Goethe encounters the forest:

On every hilltop
Is rest,
In every treetop
You sense
Hardly a breath;
The birds are silent in the forest.
But wait, soon
You too will rest.[44]

Goethe's idealist expression of forest repose works only as an allegorical figuration of the speaker. The expression of the object *as* object signifies the condition of the wanderer, and thus stealthily returns representation to metaphor in a way outlined by de Man. Tranquility *in* the object becomes the repose felt in the speaker.[45]

Within the guise of Romanticism, Bialik does something essentially different by situating the subject outside of these relations. Instead, language becomes available to the speaker only *as* nature. In this way, Bialik attempts to undo a romantic deception. The object becomes both itself and its own representation, just as the pool is both *in* nature and reflective *of* nature. This elision causes that mystical connection in the poem between God's secret language and man as poet, a slippery move that is not completely accounted for in the poem. But the consequences are clear: representation paints the world as itself, which nevertheless comes in a language of poetry created by man, a paradox that begins to address the gap between the real and the represented.

The paradox of this idea is, in fact, quite old. Shakespeare's *The Winter's Tale*, for instance, echoes Bialik's proposition that the reflection in art and poetry creates the intersection between man and nature. As Shakespeare's Polixenes contends, speaking of the relative merits of wild and cultivated flowers:

Yet Nature is made better by no mean
But Nature makes that mean; so, over that art
Which you say adds to Nature, is an art
That Nature makes. You see, sweet maid, we marry
A gentler scion to the wildest stock,
And make conceive a bark of baser kind
By bud of nobler race. This is an art
Which does not mend Nature, change it rather, but
The art itself is Nature[46]

The cultural historian Leo Marx interprets the passage in a way that helps clarify Bialik's own mysticism of the forest's language: "The artificial is but a special, human category of the natural. Man and nature are in essence one. Nature is all."[47] That unity of mind and nature travels through art, whether the art of nature itself or the poetry of man, and in that describes the function of Bialik's *leshon ha-mar'ot.*

The comparison to Shakespeare as well opens a political understanding of *leshon ha-mar'ot,* since in Shakespeare the correspondence between nature and art allows for colonial expansion and the co-optation of new, wild spaces, places outside the origin of those traveling to them, places that can be possessed in art.[48] This same political meaning can be read in Bialik as well, not in any portrayal of imperial expansion or obvious exploitation of nature; even in Shakespeare these political ideas are never self-evident or dogmatically expressed. Rather, once nature and the mind are constitutive of each other, mediating each other through a language emanating from both, the natural space finally opens itself to the visitor, and with that opening up of meaning the ambiguities of knowing and not knowing, which begin Bialik's poem, suddenly and easily disappear. In the end, knowledge and any final notion of objective scientism are replaced by a mystical union:

וּמַטֶּה רֹאשִׁי תַּחַת בִּרְכַּת שָׂבֵי חֹרֶשׁ
מַרְעִיפֵי צֵל וָאוֹר וְשִׁיר וּשְׂרָף כְּאֶחָד –
הָיִיתִי מַרְגִּישׁ בַּעֲלִיל בִּנְבֹעַ חֶרֶשׁ
כְּעֵין שֶׁפַע רַעֲנָן חָדָשׁ אֶל נִשְׁמָתִי

Bowing my head for the blessing of the forest elders
Dripping shadow and light and song and sap as one—
I would feel clearly a silent flow
Of a fresh, new plentitude into my soul[49]

Nature reveals only what one desires it to reveal, but in the guise of only revealing itself. Unity is attained within the depths of the speaker himself who brings together the object and its representation. Nature does not reflect man just as it cannot be an allegory for him either. Rather, nature is fulfilled and completed by man, the two worlds of dialectical separation (the two suns of reflection and the real) becoming complete within the articulation and vision of man, who is thus a conduit for an inherent meaning revealed through the majesty of nature, but reflecting a purely human repertoire of desire. In the final dialectical formulation of "The Pool," nature represents *itself* in the poet's representation of nature. In this, Bialik finally moves to a subject-oriented articulation of place and rewrites the poet-speaker into the objective scene, traversing the divide that had in "In the City of Slaughter" prevented in the end any historical participation by the poet.

From Reflection to Instrument

It might be critically transgressive to posit an environmental ethos in this, Bialik's aesthetic. But the same aesthetic that reveals the unity of man and nature within the reflection of each implies that the desire to transform and express the self would necessarily involve the transformation of nature. Thus, Bialik's speaker cannot be reduced to the *static*, contemplative one of Goethe's poem. Instead Bialik prescribes the active role of changing (that is, *writing*) the object in order to change the self reflexively, finally arriving perhaps for the first time at an active, instrumental expression of place, arriving, that is, at what will become the slogan of just such a dialectical environmental attitude: "to build and be built."

The "belatedness" of romanticism in Hebrew poetry must then lie in its refusal of the sublime.[50] Bialik's speaker in "The Pool" encounters nature not as some transcendent object in whose thrall he is bound, but as the process of the self recognizing itself as reflected nature, that is, as nature's interpreter. In this, Bialik's belated romanticism anticipates and develops a particularly modernist turn. The march into the forest reveals the sublime to be a bad joke played on one's sentimental education, which is always searching for the reflexive truth in the forest. Instead, Bialik's speaker understands that one can never escape from the essential reflections of language, which inflect and mediate our access to and understanding of nature.

Bialik's abstraction—his refusal to commit to place beyond the environmental and natural subject in this poem—attests to his affiliation with Aḥad Ha'am's refusal to sanction a pragmatic settlement program, even after Kishinev and the exodus from Russia. But while politics might have aligned Bialik with Aḥad Ha'am, aesthetics place this poem in particular within the rising tide of Jewish national ideology that becomes the legacy of Aharon David Gordon. Gordon was a pragmatist par excellence, a Second Aliyah newcomer in 1904 who wanted nothing more than to work the land and through work to reclaim his own—and everyone else's—Jewish soul. In this, Gordon and Bialik had little in common, as Bialik's later bourgeois life in Tel Aviv easily attests. But on the aesthetic level, Gordon follows Bialik's heightening of this dialectical relationship between man and nature as *the* essential problem of Zionism and national Jewish identity. Gordon's contribution extends the logic of the dialectic and excludes anything other than the projection of the self on the surface of nature as important for the nation.[51] Gordon obviously went far beyond Bialik, but in his lack of instrumental subtlety we begin to see the extent of Bialik's innovation. Bialik's type of environmental instrumentality remains ever oblique and vague in "The Pool." He never names a place, and in the large rhetorical gestures of both prophecy and symbolism, the linguistic concern of Bialik's Hebrew remains close to the subject, never straying far enough to encounter the object up close.

But the political legacy of a poem like "The Pool" seems clear. It pushed toward an understanding that individual transformation could only be framed by the relation to the object, and that object manifested itself in the form of nature and the land. It mattered little that Palestine bore no actual resemblance to Bialik's forest. As the Second Aliyah enthusiasts who dominated the coming generations of settlement in Palestine would argue, the shape of the land only mirrored the state of health of the people inhabiting it. That idea of mirroring, in instrumental terms of settlement and colonial politics, became the inheritance of "The Pool"; mirroring in nature guided personal transformation as well as national action in the landscape. Bialik's "The Pool" enables these ideas but makes apparent too that the move toward reflection and image was not without its own set of problems, difficulties, and negotiations, which became abundantly clear once the Zionist settler took plow to field in an attempt not just to reclaim the land but to reclaim himself in the vision of reflexive redemption. The land did not easily yield to this vision of reflection. But that became the specific legacy of Gordon's application of these ideas on the land itself, the topic of the following chapter.

Chapter 2

The Poetics of Malaria

The idea of mirroring as the basis of a Jewish relationship to nature, specifically within Eretz Israel, became widespread by the beginning of the twentieth century and went well beyond Ḥayim Naḥman Bialik's concept of *leshon ha-mar'ot* (the language of images/reflections), even though Bialik might have given nature reflection its greatest and most sophisticated elaboration in Hebrew with his poem "Ha-breikhah" (The Pool). During the first decade of the twentieth century, the Zionist movement as a whole produced myriad articulations of a reflexive mirroring of land and people in an attempt to draw some sort of essential connection between Jews and Palestine. One of the most famous and influential came from Israel Zangwill, the British novelist and committed political Zionist, who coined at that time the slogan "a land without a people for a people without a land,"[1] drawing on a normative imperial blindness to the native inhabitant,[2] but coupling the colonial image of empty space to a reflexive rendering of the Jewish people.

Zangwill's phrase resonated strongly within political Zionism because it conceived of settlement in maximalist terms of state interaction (on the level of "the people"), and also because the mirroring of the land in this formulation legitimized and justified Jewish settlement: the land was waiting for Jewish return. In various guises—and mostly as an anonymous folk slogan—Zangwill's phrase has survived for decades as a powerful articulation of mirroring within the national imagination.

But the ideologically dominant ideas of Zionist mirroring emerged from Aharon David Gordon, whose writings on nature and work, and especially those espousing a new psychology for the individual Jew emanating from nature, described a close personal relationship between the new Jewish agricultural worker and Eretz Israel itself: "And when, O Man, you return to nature—on that day your eyes will open, you will gaze straight into the eyes of nature, and in its mirror you will see your own image. You will know that you have returned to yourself."[3] While Gordon's ideas had maximalist implications, his perspective emanated from a cultural Zionist outlook that sought to mirror the Jew in the land in quite personal and individual terms. Gordon remained consistently focused on a broad Jewish renaissance but national considerations always took expression in the guise of individual psychological need and transformation.[4]

Gordon arrived in Palestine in 1904 as part of the Second Aliyah (the second wave of modern Zionist immigration) and became, after some years of toil on the land, the agrarian ideologue of Labor Zionism. Older than most of the other young immigrants and steeped in a Tolstoyan love for nature and the ameliorative effects of working the land, Gordon came to espouse what has been called "religion of work" as the path for Jewish regeneration. "Religion of work" involved a simple equation that relied specifically on the idea of reflection as transformative: by working in and on nature, the new settler would thus be transformed by nature in the improved image of the land. And beyond the benefits agrarian toil accrued on the individual Jew, the process of work was mutually ameliorative; in the end, the worker and nature each reflected the other's condition and the improvements one wrought on the other. For Gordon the land always reflected the condition of those *in* nature.

But nature in Eretz Israel, for Gordon, did not reveal its wonders immediately or self-evidently. Despite Gordon's later guru-like stature in the country, rapture was not his first reaction to Palestine. On initial arrival, Gordon reported back to Russia, explaining his rather vague—but inspired—impression of this place: "Friends! My first letter from Eretz Israel must as usual begin with a depiction of the impression that the land made upon me. But at the moment I can't give myself a clear accounting: there is something strange and complicated going on. I don't know the reason for my current mood: whether the reason is because I left Russia with sad feelings, which still have not passed; or because I cannot forget Russia's nature, which I love. And it is difficult to become accustomed quickly to the nature of a different land."[5] Gordon strives for a self-reflexive account of nature, and in that, the pattern is already set for how he will continue to treat nature and landscape as a reflective entity, like Bialik's pool, but with an instrumental intensity far less subtle. Bialik displaced subject-object conflict in representation by separating the reflected image from the controlling power of the observer in nature. Gordon, however, is incapable of avoiding a vulgar similitude between the condition of the land and the people inhabiting it, no matter the strange feelings that ensue when nature-as-mirror could not produce an image that coincided with his vision for it.

In 1904, if mirroring thus places the Jew as the image of the land, then how does one explain the poverty of previous Jewish settlement? Or at least, in the mutually ameliorative project that must be undertaken to rejuvenate both Jew and nature, where does one start if reflection is the only mechanism for improvement? In simpler terms, if Palestine were to be resplendent and redemptive because of its former ancient glory, then why did it look so terrible? Gordon arrived and, like many before him, faced a land that did not live up to heightened expectations.[6] In the logic of mirroring, the deficiencies of the current state of nature could only be explained as a reflection of the human shortcomings of others. Thus, after proclaiming his ambivalence on sighting the Palestinian shore with its wondrous beauty but the "strange and complicated" feeling it left in him, Gordon's first criticisms are aimed at the local inhabitants, who fail to reflect the marvels of the landscape: "And it seems that the people living here do not understand the nature of Eretz Israel. They are so distant from it! They are so different from it! The glorious nature is enough to amaze, full of dignity—and its occupant, what a polluted, degraded creature, whose life is not a life, everything lacking culture. The wilderness bears witness that the local man does not rise to the level of the Eretz Israeli nature. And furthermore, the farmers have not that healthy and happy complexion."[7] Gordon was not alone in being underwhelmed by his first impression of the land itself. But the disappointment, however neatly it is veiled by an articulation of his love for the Tolstoyan Russian landscape with its sentimentalized view of the Russian peasant, betrays something perhaps deeper than simply revulsion at what Eretz Israel really was. If mirroring guided the vision of nature and reflexive redemption drove the move to Palestine, then the place itself started off quite bereft of those qualities that would guarantee the health and development of the nation.[8]

Gordon's reflections on the polluted inhabitant of Palestine—which, indeed, probably refer to the First Aliyah Ashkenazi immigrants, the native Sephardi Jews, and the early Yemenite Jewish immigrants, as much as to the local Arabs[9]—close his first thoughts on the nature of Eretz Israel where he admits (in opposition to his "polluted" neighbors?) that slowly he "is beginning to adjust his gaze, to become accustomed to the Eretz Israeli nature, and, if it is possible to say it like this, to know the language of nature and nature itself." "The language of nature" might be an odd phrase for a man who would most successfully theorize a direct, unmediated, and personal connection between the Jewish settler and the soil of Palestine. But knowledge of place on Zionist terms always seems to translate into the linguistic ability to express oneself in the language of nature (in the same way that Bialik formed the matter), a language specific to the landscape, which would reflect the inner desires and constitution of the settler. The goal to reflect nature—even a polluted, sick nature, which itself is merely the reflection of the polluted, sick inhabitant—translates into the competition to become part of it and to know its innermost meaning so that the settler might then be able to express and improve it.

Gordon's nature fantasies thus had a specifically physical effect on the land, which was by all accounts in 1904 a difficult and inhospitable terrain. As Gordon and the Second Aliyah reformulated "to build and be built" in light of what they actually encountered on the ground, the slogan would encompass the tension between material and ideal conceptions of Zionist labor. In that, Zionism on the ground produced a vision of the land as necessitating intervention, that is, a vision that paralleled the Jewish settler, who also required fundamental transformation. The reflexive mirroring of nature that Bialik introduced projected into the logic of settlement an illness on the land, a land waiting and needing the involvement of the Jew who would then improve both territory and the self. Blocking the full instantiation of that reflexive image was the land itself, out of which malaria emerged as the principal malaise articulating the extent of resistance and the amount of work to be accomplished. In this context, malaria becomes the driving catalyst for a conception of land improvement that would reflexively cast the Jewish settler in an empathetic relationship to Eretz Israel itself.

The Illness

The contest and struggle for personal Jewish expression in the land of Palestine were articulated in spectacular form four years after Gordon's arrival there when on March 7, 1908, a group of Jewish protesters—mainly itinerant day laborers and members of that corps of young Jewish agricultural workers who had begun trickling into Palestine after 1903—entered the Jewish National Fund (JNF) training farm at Ben Shemen and uprooted several rows of recently planted olive trees. The action formed part of a protest focusing on hiring practices at the farm.[10] Arab workers—both cheaper and more skilled than their Jewish counterparts—had been employed over the previous days to lay out the first olive saplings for the planned Herzl Forest, even though the project had explicitly been meant to enable the employment of Jewish labor on Jewish land. But financial exigencies forcing the JNF's engagement of cheap Arab labor merely acted as a backdrop to the larger national issues at stake in the planting of the trees. The protesters, and the labor movement as a whole, understood the implications of alienation that Arab labor embodied for a nationalist Jewish proletariat. The labor monthly *Ha-po'el ha-tsa'ir*, perhaps the most important Hebrew publication in Palestine at the time, expressed its affront over what had happened at the farm in histrionic and ethnically competitive terms: "Come and see what rights this people has that its labor—and in particular work like this—would be done by others!"[11]

The protest gave expression to what *Ha-po'el ha-tsa'ir* called *kibush ha-avodah* (the conquest of labor),[12] a concept that resonated with various strands within the nascent labor movement and which defined the Zionist movement's idea of the relation between Jewish redemption and territory. The ambiguity of the slogan, which refers to labor as both object and instrument of conquest, begins to outline a reflexive understanding of working the land: the conquest *of* the labor market that will be the conquest *by* the labor movement. At the center, as object of conquest, is the land itself, and the slogan, conquest of labor, quickly transformed within the movement into "conquest of the land" (*kibush ha-adamah*), demonstrating the direct connection between Gordon's concept of work and the attainment of the soil. Both ideas, and in particular the elision between them, begin to reformulate Zionist intervention in the land within the dialectic of "to build and be built," whose reflexive turn itself significantly differentiates the Second Aliyah from prior attempts at Jewish colonization in Palestine.[13]

As a political protest, the demonstration and action at Ben Shemen produced little immediate change in Zionist policy. The relation between alienated labor and the Jewish homeland was to become a point of contention for some years as the various institutions in the Zionist movement struggled to identify what it meant to be a Jewish nation within a Jewish space. More specifically, for the protesters at Ben Shemen, the imperative to work and transform the land was an irreducible element in their vision of Palestine as a Jewish place. As Menachem Ussishkin, the leader of the Russian Zionists, had written in 1905: "Long before the state is established, the territory must actually belong, in an economic and in a political sense, to that people which desires to form a center in it. Its whole life must be dependent upon this people, which must be possessor *de facto*, even though not as yet *de jure*. The people must be bound to the land by eternal ties of heartfelt love and devotion. The earth must be moistened with its blood and sweat."[14]

The protest at Ben Shemen obviously aligned itself with Ussishkin's project,[15] and in so doing it enacted the strange paradox inherent in an ideology of national emancipation through labor which was itself tied to an ideology of nurturing the landscape. After the destructive act of pulling up the olive trees—an action rife with intonations of labor disputes in bourgeois economies of class struggle—the protesters then, apparently with little hesitation or debate, proceeded to replant all the saplings they had just taken out of the ground. The land, the site of worker alienation, would also serve as the stage on which the solution to alienation would be enacted and played out. In this way, nature offered itself in a complex and ambivalent dialectic for the Zionist worker, who was caught between national closeness to nature and class alienation from that very same object of the land. Taken seriously, the performance attests to a larger drama in the crisis of Zionist self-identification between an idealist understanding of the "new Jew" as part of the land and a materialist predicament of a subject alienated from the soil that he would work and which would reflexively define him through labor.[16] But perhaps most important, the replanting showed that even those protesting understood how the problem of alienation was tied not to real consequences in the land but to how the land signifies its relation to those working on it.

The paradox of this problem was not lost on the movement's leadership. Ussishkin himself wrote about settlement in dialectical terms. In *Our Program*, which reads as a Second Aliyah manifesto, he defines "the conquest of labor" as a reconciliation between a purely economic approach to nature (based on the failed settlement experiments of the Ḥovevei Tsiyon during the First Aliyah) and a spiritual Zionism—the deterritorialized, idealized, cultural nationalism of Aḥad Ha'am. Indeed, according to Ussishkin (who seeks to reconcile Second Aliyah ideology with mainstream political Zionism), the sublation within political Zionism of this dialectical split between material and spirit, between Eretz Israel as economic object and Eretz Israel as the physical embodiment of the new Zionist subject, was to be effected precisely in "the conquest of labor."

This transformation of land from the material object of colonization to a conceptual partner in the improvement of the new Jewish citizen began with the economic demise of a First Aliyah program of Rothschild-supported settlement at the turn of the century. After decades of financial subsidies to the struggling Jewish colonies in Palestine, the withdrawal of Rothschild money at the turn of the twentieth century forced the Zionist movement to cast about for alternate models of colonial settlement, and the relative poverty of the movement (coupled with the primitive infrastructure in Palestine) necessitated the move to a system of independent operators and institutions on the ground in the region. But while the transition from centralized European control to local management was initially conceived in purely economic terms, the reformulation of settlement policy and administration quickly devolved into a cultural project of reframing land as the product of Jewish work. The Jewish National Fund, through the leadership of Otto Warburg, effectively became the instrument of this cultural policy.

The JNF had been founded in 1901 primarily as an economic organization for land purchases and agricultural training, to fill the vacuum left as a consequence of Rothschild withdrawal. But quickly the JNF transformed itself and began to connect its scientific economic role to a cultural justification for nation-building. Warburg's Olive Tree Fund campaign, the Ölbaumspende, was instigated in 1905 as the JNF fund-raising effort to finance the Herzl Forest and already began to reconfigure the way nature, and trees in particular, were to be utilized for the propagation of Zionist idealism. From trees as instruments of technological improvement—as the First Aliyah introduction of the eucalyptus had always been represented[17]—trees now fulfilled a cultural role by fundamentally connecting Jews to the soil. And in offering improvement to the land, they also implied the general movement away from disease, which had afflicted the country prior to Zionist arrival, and toward cure—of both the soil and the Jew.

For the JNF and for Warburg, the year 1905 marked the consolidation of cultural notions about Palestine as *the* object of Jewish colonization. At the Seventh Zionist Congress of that year, delegates mourned the death of Herzl while Warburg finally killed the Uganda Plan, which would have explored colonial possibilities in East Africa. At the same time, Warburg also announced the plan for the Herzl Forest as the goal of the Olive Tree Fund campaign, setting in motion the ideas of national collective belonging to the land, and landscape rejuvenation and improvement as the basis of Zionist expressions of possession in Palestine.

Warburg still had to justify land improvement from a utilitarian economic perspective, at least to the Zionist Executive, the executive committee of the Zionist Congress, but the terms of justification quickly elided into a reformulation of the land that figured action on the soil as cultural progress which would make the land healthier and thus more Jewish.[18] In 1904, Warburg had begun framing scientific discussion within the cultural fantasy of ethnic rejuvenation and competition—both for people and for land. In the first issue of *Altneuland*, the Zionist movement's short-lived agronomy journal named after Herzl's novel of the same title (*Old New Land*), Warburg outlined the difficulties of settlement in Palestine: "Against the aspiration to direct Jewish settlement eastward, to Eretz Israel, it is important first of all to make the argument, in addition to the economic and political difficulties that exist, that the land is not fit for settlement, that in response to an absence of a thousand years and because of improper farming, the land has arrived at a state of extreme exhaustion from which there is no reversal."[19] At this point, Warburg recites a litany of physical ills in the land that cascade into a logic of accusation, implying environmental blame on the intervention of unnamed, but obviously Arab, hands: "that the destruction of the forests changed the climate; that the rains flooding in the winter, which were not restrained in their course by the forests, swept away from the slopes of the mountains, parched soil themselves, the thin layer of dust that clung to them, and the valleys and plains became swamps and incubation nests of the worst kind of malaria, since there was no control over the streams of water."[20] In Warburg's rendition, malaria seems to be the logical telos of Jewish absence and the consequent ill effects of poor land stewardship. Much of the physical description of erosion and disease might have been true (if not the fault of the Arab) but the point remains:

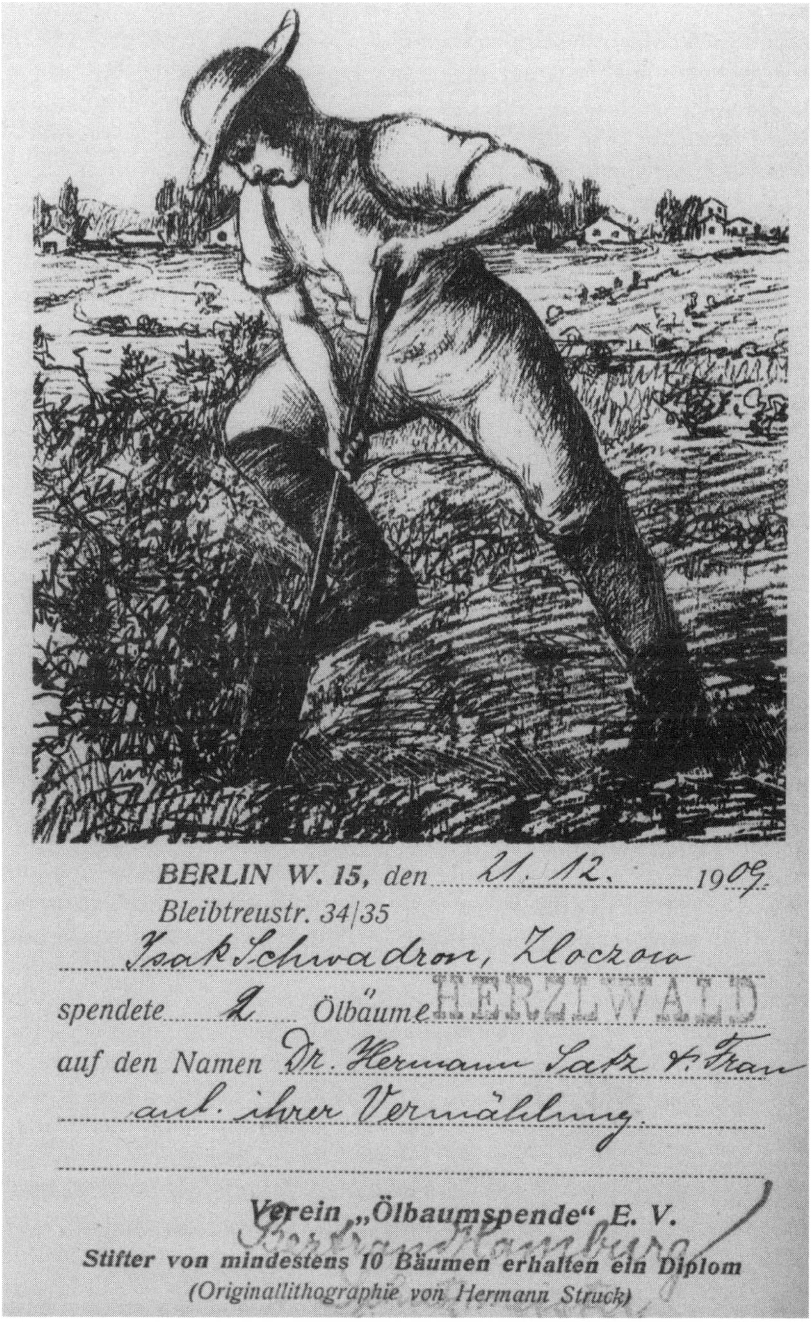

BERLIN W. 15, den 21. 12. 1909.
Bleibtreustr. 34/35

Isak Schwadron, Zloczow

spendete 2 Ölbäume HERZLWALD

auf den Namen Dr. Hermann Satz u. Frau

anl. ihrer Vermählung

Verein „Ölbaumspende" E. V.

Stifter von mindestens 10 Bäumen erhalten ein Diplom

(Originallithographie von Hermann Struck)

Figure 1. A Jewish National Fund (JNF) certificate acknowledging a donation to the Ölbaumspende, 1909.

if he who deforests the land and mistreats it is rendered ineligible to own it, then he who reforests and rejuvenates it is revalidated as the land's legitimate indigene. If along with this accusation came a rhetoric of malaria and torpor until the rightful owner returns, it is because that rhetoric serves to ratify their labor and not just their presence.

As a reaction to these claims for land improvement as the basis of Jewish investment in Palestine, the Ben Shemen protest shows the loss of the symbolic power of older models of colonization that did not figure the return of the Jew as an indigenous, reflective entity in the landscape. In this, trees are implicated, in particular the use of the eucalyptus, the dominant tree of the First Aliyah in fighting malaria and marking the place of the Jew in the land (the "tree of the Jews," according to the local Arab population).[21] The eucalyptus served as a model of individual, market-oriented settlement, and its replacement by the olive tree emphasizes the mimetic value of landscape in the national cause as it is reflected through human labor. Thus, the history of the eucalyptus moves from metaphor—the "Jewish" tree as a stand-in for the colonist, who comes singularly to the new land bearing the tools of modern improvement—to the olive tree forest as discursive reflection: trees and forests, even nature and landscape in general as the means by which national coalescence will be achieved and reified within the population of workers laboring to transform the land within an ancient vision of national redemption.

Warburg, in pushing forward the Olive Tree Fund and forestation projects in general, revealed an awareness that the program portended cultural changes for the Yishuv and the relaxation of a capitalist logic for the planning of future expansion. The success of the JNF campaign lay precisely in the fantasy it offered of self-improvement and self-expression through closeness to the actual earth, and not in any rational economics of capitalist profit.[22] Olives, which would produce a sellable crop only after some years, offered no quick fix to economic problems of productivity in the colonies, a point that the Zionist leadership in Europe was well aware of.[23] When serious objections to the olive's lack of economic sense were raised in the Zionist Executive, Warburg simply reconceptualized the olive forest and instead of economic rationalism, the forest was legitimized by its supposed reflection of a rebuilt lush, shady holy land, an economic refuge for the worker, who would reflexively correct the damage wrought by years of Jewish absence.[24] In this way, the focus on a poetics of the land becomes a mirror of Zionist self-identity and a means to bypass and obfuscate any other intermediary force, namely, the native inhabitant.

The protest at Ben Shemen was thus less about a politics of economic competition than about the dialectical identification of Jew and land, which becomes an aesthetic relation dependent on the performance of action on the soil.[25] Or, by focusing on self-transformation, the Ben Shemen protest obfuscates the larger ethnic struggles of the competition between Jewish and Arab labor. At Ben Shemen, the protest was at once destructive and reconstitutive both of individual expression and the place itself; simultaneously, it expressed the reforestation and reclamation of the neglected land and of the forester. The self-identification model (land and Jew) at Ben Shemen then set the stage for a series of subsequent relations on a larger scale that would only rehearse the constitutive contradictions at Ben Shemen.

The aesthetic questions of self-expression and a subject's relation to the object of the land, which the protest at Ben Shemen opened up, naturally held implications for literary production and for those consciously involved in the production of aesthetic expression. Action on the ground in Palestine reflected far beyond contemporary debates about writing and expression within the Zionist community. Indeed, they recast those debates as aesthetic contestations on the soil of the Jews itself. In particular, the literary conflict between Aḥad Ha'am and Micha Yosef Berdichevsky opened up into a territorial dispute that deployed the holistic figuration of disease that Warburg had already set in motion.

Aḥad Ha'am and Berdichevsky had clashed at the turn of the century over how to express national commitment in Hebrew writing, with the debate falling between premodernist and modernist divisions. In this, Aḥad Ha'am held up the nineteenth-century Hebrew poet Y. L. Gordon as Hebrew's exemplar of committed, deterritorialized national writing: "[M]ost of our poets today do not follow Y. L. Gordon's path of unifying poetry and thought [and relating art to] our lives and great needs. Poesy alone, the outpouring of the soul about the splendor of nature and the pleasure of love and so forth—let our youth seek these things in other national languages to their satisfaction."[26] The internal division Aḥad Ha'am implies for the psyche, between political commitment and aesthetic pleasure, excludes a modernist, twentieth-century sense of internal synthesis. Narration remains a means of expressing *things* within a rational, analytical account of one's interaction with ideas. Aḥad Ha'am does not discount feeling but in the distance of deterritorialized nationalism, the coming together of the nation had to become a willed event, divorced from an interior psychopathology of desire. On the other hand, Berdichevsky offered the entirety of the self toward an inclusive nationalism that would encompass and allegorically reflect national sentiment and desire: "My sorrow is not mine . . . but the sorrow of our entire people, the sorrows of the many people, that becomes my sorrow."[27] Already Berdichevsky uses reflection as a way to move beyond and then collapse onto the self.

At the heart of the matter was the land, not just in a debate over territoriality and deterritorialization for the nation (the political terms of the conflict between Aḥad Ha'am and a younger generation of Berdichevsky's followers who espoused more practical designs on Palestine), but in how to conceive of the encounter with the soil of Palestine. Sickness plays a crucial role in these distinctions and underlies the articulation of the relation between Jew and land. In Aḥad Ha'am, illness ratifies a dispassionate distance from Palestine, from the distortions of the place that still ideally hides the remnants of a lost past and a glorious future.[28] But in his reports on Eretz Israel, Aḥad Ha'am then plays the distanced diagnostician (Y. L. Gordon transposed into a contemplation of soil), and Berdichevsky takes on the inverse and internalizes the despondent malaise of the people (and, by implication, the land). For Berdichevsky, subjective incorporation signifies not only national identification but as well an aesthetic solution to a stricken people.

Berdichevsky's position was most effectively transposed to a consideration of the Palestinian soil through the arrival of Yosef Ḥayim Brenner in 1909, less than a year after the Ben Shemen protest. Before arriving in Palestine in 1909, Brenner had polished his polemicist (and literary) style over four years in Lvov and London.[29] Brenner had always adhered to a cultural Zionism and was most closely associated with Berdichevsky's ideas even though he had ties to Aḥad Ha'am as well, in particular during his two-year stay in London. But that relationship was agonistic, and while in London Brenner had published the journal *Ha-me'orer* (The Awakener) whose commitment to an irrationalism of nationalistic sentiment resonated with a Nietzschean vision of the entire self caught up in the struggle, an idea whose genealogy certainly traces to Berdichevsky.

After arriving in Palestine, Brenner played an important role in the development of a Zionist aesthetic of the land because he effectively translated Berdichevsky's notion of total sentimental commitment to the nation through writing and applied it to the land itself. The reports have it that Brenner arrived in Palestine in a Second Aliyah fervor, ready to devote himself to working the land and redeeming the soil. Whatever made Brenner reconsider physical toil in Eretz Israel as the way for the Zionist writer, he did it quickly and within months of immigrating was writing for *Ha-po'el ha-tsa'ir*, the dominant labor Zionist organ at the time, and working full-time at intellectual endeavors.[30] Brenner's first major essay to confront Palestine, "Be-fa'am ha-me'ah (mi-pirpurei nefesh aḥat)" (For the Hundredth Time [From the Convulsions of One Soul]), was published in July 1909, only five months after he had arrived in Jaffa.[31] The essay, a monologic harangue placed in the mouth of a wizened veteran with years of experience in Palestine, stands out as Brenner's first to confront material realities in the country in the context of literary writing.

Ironically, the general conclusions (and convulsions) Brenner arrives at in this essay concerning the state of settlement in Palestine differ little from Aḥad Ha'am's less impassioned reports of his visits there beginning in 1891.[32] Like Gordon, both Aḥad Ha'am and Brenner disparage the lack of infrastructure and the general primitive conditions throughout the country. Neither seems to posit much hope for the future of settlement on the ground in Palestine. But if content, then, does not signify difference between Brenner and Aḥad Ha'am, then style, or rather the relationship of speaker to form, dictates a very different political attitude toward Palestine as a conjured place. Perhaps the difference comes down to the tourist versus the immigrant, a long overdetermined category in the history of Zionism, where the tourist takes stock and creates inventories of cultural and physical difference, while the new immigrant cathects identity onto the place of Eretz Israel and strives to look through the lens of native authenticity. That difference creates quite varied meanings for similar observations, and it is Brenner who shows that malaria itself (the convulsions?) reflects a fundamental Jewish identity tied to place.

In the persona of the old-timer, Brenner outlines how environmental engagement and transformation—indeed, nature itself as the object of Zionist political aspirations—must be seen *only* as the projection of the Jewish subject into the objective world of Palestine. In this, the dialectics of environmental engagement as they played out at Ben Shemen lead to a literary engagement that begins to write and express place as extension: nature becomes not the allegorical projection of an interior writing, but in contact with, connected to, and revealed through a writing that develops interiority as it moves toward a connection with the landscape. The barrier to a complete incorporation of the land within the body of the settler is malaria itself, the instantiation of the sickness of each and what in the end will tie the Zionist to the land. Thus, the poetics of malaria describe how illness becomes the intermediate bridge between a sick land and a sick people.

From the very first lines, the essay figures an ambiguous and ambivalent relationship to place. Brenner's self-consciousness is that of one who knows what his response to place should be before he feels it. And still, there is something blocking a complete sentimental and discursive identification with the land. The essay begins:

—A person from Israel, a writer from Israel, who all his days, all the days of his toil, from the beginning of his working days, all his life doubted the life force of his people, doubted and worked with all this on his own field, on the field of his literature, worked in the sense of "cast your bread on the waters," and for a long time, because of some reason or reasons—as is said, for example, in the face of hypochondria that "it entered a new phase," or because of some time in Palestine, in the place of the last hope, and saw there everything—it became clear to him—

—Wait . . . in Palestine . . . and he saw there?

—He saw there everything . . .[33]

At once, the work of the nation is given multiple valences and seesaws (indeed, *convulses*) through abstract and material understandings of the signifiers deployed: the work of the nation thus becomes a metaphor for the person, but also an indicator of a need for real contact with a particular place. Brenner opens with "A person from Israel, a writer from Israel," and while this designation signifies spatial belonging—especially as it becomes apparent later on that one of the oppositional motifs of the entire essay will be the *from*-ness of the vitriol versus the geographic and ideological naïveté of the narrator—it also invokes the abstract deterritorialized trope of the disembodied nation: is "Israel" a national or geographic designation? Even if we understand "Israel" as politically metaphoric, the phrase "worked with all this on his own field" brings us back to a realness of description—after all, this is what Brenner had come to Palestine to do—just before the narrative pulls the language once again into metaphor as "field" metamorphoses in the very next phrase to mean something symbolic and perhaps allegorical: "the field of his literature." From the beginning, the discourse of the essay cannot decide where it is, and the disjointed syntax—perhaps itself an allegory for a fragmented land—moves forward not by creating logical syllogisms, but by jerking us suddenly back and forth between counterpoised snippets of semantic and, by implication, political meaning. That fragmentation, too, begins to prefigure the ultimate inability to project any sort of control over the discourse of the land. Instead, fragmentation—a standard trope for the malarial fevers to come—both symbolically represents and emblematically enacts the incompleteness of the bond between the describer and the land being described, and in this begins to instantiate malarial irrationality and disease into the very contemplation of Jewish belonging in the land.

The ambiguity here, this sliding back and forth from physical evocation to disembodied metaphor, from syntax to fragment, from control over language to nonsense, describes both the formal linguistic strategies employed and the thrust of Brenner's message, which laments geography as hindering the realization of a metaphoric idealism, where land and Jew would become one and the expression of both could proceed unhindered. This message becomes abundantly clear at the end of the paragraph when the veteran's rant is interrupted by the narrator's plea for description and observation, something the veteran clearly and emphatically disdains.

Nevertheless, Palestine is named at the end of the very first paragraph and breaks the veteran's spleen, if but for a moment, awakening the first-person narrator, who cleaves onto the very name (and naming)[34] of the place. But the interruption merely reveals the narrator's naive misunderstanding of what is truly important about the landscape, since he shows himself interested only in what is a positivist (and thus distanced) geo-*graphy*, ignoring the more important problem of coming in real contact with the identity of the place. Here the opposition between positivism (the narrator's evocation of "seeing" that yearns for reportage and truth) and subjective identity (the veteran's "seeing" that remains inward and personal) begins to describe the major fault lines of desire over Palestine as a place. Once Palestine is named, it hovers over the vitriol to give it place and fierceness—and perhaps misdirection in the oppositional understandings of veteran and narrator—even though it is human geography that fills the complaint. Place is figured in terms of the human filth and vermin that occupy it and not by the physical features of nature that give it shape.

The divisions between place and mind, between physical space and disembodied nation are therefore already figured in Brenner's first paragraph. For Brenner, Palestine, on the one hand, and the subject, on the other, are actually bridged by the symptoms of disease, either through the inventions of hypochondria or through the real fevers that malaria induces: "And he saw there . . . the best of the 'pioneers' . . . who were brought two-by-two in Russian and Austrian boats to be fodder in the grip of malarial fever and every disease of the place." Malaria in this way bars the mutual identification of Jew and land. But, as barrier, malaria also marks a poetic of convergence in Brenner's thought. Malaria signifies the height of the land's hostility to what human society has wrought upon it and as such is understood by Brenner as its demand for redemption by the Jew.

The specter of Aḥad Ha'am hovers throughout the essay, most obviously later on when Brenner gets to his fierce literary critique of individualism in Hebrew writing, the true reason for the essay. But here at the opening, the struggle for a *real* encounter with the land (malaria versus hypochondria) portends the more explicit attacks on Aḥad Ha'am's distance of reported travelogue. And in the invocation of malaria specifically, the phrase "a person from Israel" chides Aḥad Ha'am, who writes so dispassionately and dryly about Palestine as a place. The ambiguity of the relationship between "person" and "Israel," which could be both physical (from) and nationally symbolic (of) chastises spiritual Zionism's division between territory and people. Nation and nature become inseparable in Brenner; the signifier of the nation designates both.

For Brenner, then, the act of sensing from afar—that is, "seeing"—is something incomplete and naive. Instead, from the perspective of Brenner's pioneer, who has grimly "seen it all," dispassionate vision translates actually into blindness and the naïveté of the narrator since a fragmented inventory of Palestine cannot possibly add up to the totality of experience. The repetition of the phrase "and saw [this] and saw [that]" becomes a blur; there is too much to see, too much to take in. However, despite the criticism of positivist vision and the consequent emphasis on description, Brenner refuses to succumb to its opposite, namely, a purely romantic alternative whereby the land is "taken in" intuitively and then projected solipsistically.[35] Rather, Brenner's "observer"—in repeating the phrase "it has become clear"—modestly sustains a passive construction of his relation to place. Palestine is neither complete projection (seeing what he wants to see) nor objective perception (a thing that would stand self-evidently before one's eyes). In this tenuous position, the character's seeing throws off the romanticism of metaphysical promise in an attempt to create some other way of physically encountering place as a process of self-knowledge.

In the end, Brenner is caught in a dialectic where neither mode of Israel—the metaphysical *am yisra'el* (people of Israel) or the material *eretz yisra'el* (land of Israel)—exists independently of the other. Brenner sums up: "—In short . . . a person from Israel who has looked at all this"—and at that moment finally switches the verb from "saw" (*ra'ah*), with its romantic ties to epiphany, to the more reflexive "looked" (*histakel*). He does this at the moment of turning inward, turning toward the diathetic voice.[36] "Looking" then becomes a reflexive process of self-understanding as opposed to the positivism of Aḥad Ha'am's colonial observations. Brenner writes:

> —In short . . . a person from Israel who has looked at all this and more than this, who has seen *what isn't here,* is able to express, and because of his experiences understands, therefore, that there is no hope and no fix and hope for a fix, because there is no "us," masters of a great history, as it were . . . inheritors of the Bible, settlers of an empty land; because, in truth, there is no Eretz Israel, there is no empty motherland waiting for us these thousands of years. Most of all, there is no Israel, no living Israel, full of strength, full of the strength of simplicity in life, able to create life for itself, able to stand in the face of its enemies, able to create a settlement of living people. Rather, there are wretched, *polluted* little yids [*yidelach*], full of terrible defects, who conduct business with prayers and the receiving of charity and the plunder of charity and torah and . . . In short, there is no Israel and it's impossible that there ever will be . . .—a person like this, a writer like this, who has taken in all this after a decade of looking, of wandering in the wilderness, of storm and desolation—can he live with himself? Can he continue with existence? [emphasis added]

In 1909, with the declaration that neither *am yisra'el* nor *eretz yisra'el* exists, writing does not immediately present itself as the obvious cultural solution to this difficult realization. Indeed, the protagonist-writer can never answer the query repeatedly posed to him by the narrator: "where's the point of difficulty?" that is, what bars a complete identification of *eretz yisra'el* and *am yisra'el.*

However, having dispensed with both the solipsism of an individualized consciousness and its antithesis, the declarative inventories of Aḥad Ha'am who writes the landscape as an objectified idea, the best solution the protagonist (Brenner) can advance in 1909 is a naturalism of sorts. More explicitly, for Brenner, the "people" cannot exist as a preconceived idea which will then be cathected onto place. To him, this is the error of both political Zionism and the spiritual Zionism of Aḥad Ha'am, for whom the nation as a concept supersedes any other subjective content in Hebrew writing. However, if such maximalist ideas of the nation would not suffice to give expression to national identity, then neither would a pragmatic retreat into an individualism of empathy with the land, the sin of Labor Zionism's romantic nationalism.

Instead, Brenner's model for an alternative to this cultural and political impasse presents itself in the writing of Mendele Mokher Sfarim,[37] the famous writer of Yiddish and Hebrew whose texts reconciled first person narration with the world itself, neither Bildungsroman nor documentary, but a natural entwining of a "complex soul" and "the world":

> Mendele. What is he as an individual? What is the principal substance of his soul? What is his basic motivation? . . . —None of these questions touch us so much, because Mendele Mokher Sfarim has not come to tell us—like those of our narrators who have come after him—about himself. Most of his words are indeed in the first person, but that is not because the writer wants to expose his soul before all his friends, but rather he exposes his manner and nothing more. . . . He does not [write] for the purpose of baring his soul. . . . What we, readers of this generation, can see [in Mendele's writing] are the deepening relations of a very complex soul toward the world, the person, and life; but with Mendele even when some vision stirs within him different emotions, even then it isn't amazement, a combination of emotion, but rather a fusion—facing here and here.

Brenner similarly seeks this fusion as a resolution between subjectivity in writing and the objective encounter with place within naturalism.[38] However, the problem as Brenner understands it is that the historical window of opportunity once open to Mendele has since closed. Mendele's mode of writing the "Jewish street," as Brenner consistently and repeatedly describes it, has ended. That type of realism is no longer possible because neither the street nor the writing exists to create the other. Brenner argues that no analogue to the "Jewish shtetl" in Palestine can be written as long as Aḥad Ha'am dictates the ideational content of writing. Brenner actually comes close to naming Aḥad Ha'am, referring to him only as "the great one" in lamenting how "empty words upon words" concerning transcendent and metaphysical belief have supplanted the materialist descriptive poetics exemplified by Mendele's writing some fifty years earlier. However, Brenner is not nostalgic for the realistically portrayed world of the shtetl; his praise for Mendele reaches a climax in a reminder to his readers that when Mendele "penetrates to the very substance of the Jewish street, he has nothing but a cutting judgment [for it]."[39] Realism as such would be impossible in a Palestine whose reality is masked by the discursive gap between Jewish projections and the land itself.

Thus Brenner begins to report the paradox between place as it was successfully integrated into writing during the diaspora, and place as unsuccessfully assimilated on one's own soil. At the same time, in giving voice to the crisis of representation, Brenner shows the power of the negative resolution he is proposing. If the Zionist subject indeed cannot grasp a confirmable engagement with the real (except in the projected forms of solipsism), then the quest to understand what blocks such an encounter would, in Brenner's eyes, constitute the beginning of an authentic writing of place.

For Brenner, therefore, a consideration of aesthetic form finally becomes the tie between a representation of the self and the exterior world. This is why Brenner's first essay concerning Palestine *necessarily* ends in failure, a failure of both speech and writing to place the self in the type of relationship with Palestine to which Brenner's protagonist aspires. In the end, the frustration of this alienated veteran breaks apart normative discourse in its inability to redeem place:

> —So . . . so . . . what I want . . . did you hear . . . this is not the point of difficulty . . . really, all this—understand, it doesn't affect me . . . at all . . . do you understand? . . . words . . . words . . . inertia . . . doesn't affect . . . strange . . . why speak? . . . why write? . . . thus I don't want anything . . . thus all life—please listen: what do I want? . . . isn't it this: I don't want . . . and in spite of this . . . despite my non-desire . . . leaving . . . as if I would want . . . as if . . . the tomb isn't closed—
>
> The eyes and the laugh—they were as wild as before . . .

The wildness, the fragmentation of words and speech, this is the effect of alienated work, of a worker-writer confined to a Jaffa apartment, unwilling to ply in the alienating trades of teaching political or cultural ideas to young immigrants. That wildness of the eyes, reminiscent, as we shall see below, of the discourse of malaria, that infection of place without basis in identity, denotes the inability to close the gap among words, place, and action.

At the same time, this fragmentation of normative language anticipates—indeed introduces—a new normativity in a poetics whose model is the disjointed, feverish spleen of the victim of malaria. To be *of* this place, this poetic would suggest, necessarily meant to be infected by it. Stated differently, the fragmentary nature of the poetics of malaria is the authentic expression of a subject not yet reconciled with the land, but as such gives truth to the lie of prior discursive modes of observation and reconciliation.

The Cure

Finally in 1914 Brenner offered a cure to malaria in his novel *Shkhol ve-khishalon* (Bereavement and Failure).[40] But the cure, in 1914, only points to the problems of a settlement mentality still unliberated from the confines of European thinking. For Ḥefetz, Brenner's protagonist who swoons under the intense sun of Palestine and falls into a malarial stupor while working the fields of a collective farm, the cure consists of a retreat into the shtetl-like confines of Jerusalem and into the bosom of his Yiddish family. Despite the ills of malaria—the way it might designate some gap in the aim to connect identity to place—a cure for malaria is even worse, because it denies the very goal of self-identification with the land. In this, Brenner's *Bereavement and Failure* takes up the social and political-economic impasse that Brenner had described in "For the Hundredth Time." There, with the protagonist's inability to close the gap between the social reality in Palestine and a promise of the land that was unachievable through writing, the protagonist fell into the wildness that suddenly breaks off the text—the necessity of failure, we might describe it in Brenner's literary prescription. Later, in this novel, wildness is transformed into a strange state of psychosis that falls somewhere between malarial fever and nervous breakdown. Ironically, as it had earlier in "For the Hundredth Time," malaria remains the only successful literary trope through which to describe the fusion of the Zionist subject (psychosis) and a natural object (malaria). Indeed, the ambiguity of this stance is inscribed in the protagonist's very name. Brenner's character now has a name, Ḥefetz, but a name that reinforces the anonymous and alienated state of his earlier raconteur since Ḥefetz translates as "thing," "object," "desire"—all undifferentiated and primal ideas but which nevertheless bridge the objective and abstract worlds of the politics of Zionism at the time.

Ḥefetz falls sick of something mysterious, of a psychological malady that *seems* to be malarial fever. We are never quite sure, and Brenner's biting sarcasm seems aimed at a society that retreats into its old shtetl ways in dealing with life (or "nonlife" as Brenner would have it), as opposed to describing and explaining in a naturalistic fashion the hostility of the place. The critic Gershon Shaked is certainly correct when he writes that in this novel "Brenner . . . presented the tragedies of those of the Second Aliyah who did not realize the ideals of the labor movement."[41] But the implication in that statement is of a willful failure, the inability to bring oneself in line with the true path of labor. Brenner can easily be accused of being partisan to the labor cause, but the psychological processes of his characters, especially Ḥefetz and his extended family in *Bereavement and Failure*, speak to a different sort of failure, the failure to gain a rapport with the place of Palestine itself. That is why, upon falling ill with this malarial breakdown, Ḥefetz retreats into the familiar shtetl-like existence of Jerusalem. The failure, which malaria itself might imply from the beginning, is the inability to answer the modernist call to make one's inner life part of the physical surroundings. The "life" that Brenner keeps repeating and that Ḥefetz keeps searching for, ready to abandon his object status in favor of a more active subjectivity, is still fraught with the fears and anxieties of the diaspora, fears and anxieties that work to distance Brenner's characters from where they really are. Certainly, this too was the crux of his complaint in "For the Hundredth Time," namely, the Jewish inability to allow place to become part of the bourgeois, educated settler.

In order to understand just how far Brenner has moved from "For the Hundredth Time" and its portrayal of disease (the "convulsions" that malaria causes in the veteran), to the direction and critique evinced in *Bereavement and Failure,* we might, for a moment, notice how Brenner's story "Atsabim" (Nerves),[42] written a year after "For the Hundredth Time," echoes its themes and form. It is, in fact, a lightly veiled fiction version of that earlier essay. Indeed, what seems of particular importance in the story is the way that malaria in "Nerves," like in the essay, is more a malady of the traveler to Eretz Israel bringing along a mentality unfit for the place than it is a condition of the place itself. In "Nerves," malaria is *brought* to Palestine, echoing the diasporic mentality of all those who come to and then occupy this place.

Against what "Nerves" depicts, *Bereavement and Failure* ends with a certain type of affirmation and critique: the affirmation of a life lived closely to the place (which, at this point, Brenner can only locate within the Arab population) and the critique of a Jewish existence that, despite its location in Palestine, is still based on fear, fear imbued within it from religion, which gets translated into a fear of the environment. As Ḥefetz's uncle Ḥayim, whose name, ironically, means "life," sits on the shore of the Kinneret, the Sea of Galilee, he watches a group of Bedouin plunge into the water:

> The Bedouin spread their flattened hands—and grew distant, and more distant still. "They know how to swim!"—the recliner perked up: he too had once known how to swim. He sat and looked with a kind of envy and self-denial.
>
> But suddenly he was comforted by a funny thought: "In the *mikveh,* ha-ha, even they would not be able to swim, even in the summer"—
>
> He continued to look at the dark, strong swimmers in the distance.[43]

The point of equivalence and competition—swimming between the Kinneret and the ritual bath of the mikveh—actually marks the impasse between this old Orthodox Jew and the authentic natural rapport he believes he is observing in the Arab. The opposition between religion and the reality of the physical realm of Palestine obscures Ḥayim to the truth of the fact that it is the Arab who is truly "living," that fear and the corrupt constructs of the mind are what cause failure in the novel and in the settlement movement in general.

Of course, Brenner's depiction of this opposition might project its own sort of idealism within its Orientalist representation of the Arab in close touch with the soil. In this, he was not alone. Moshe Smilansky, who published in 1911 his popular series of stories *Bnei arav* (The Arab People),[44] worked far more systematically than Brenner at depicting a type of Arab on which to model the "new Jew." Smilansky describes a closeness to the soil, a rapport with the natural realm, and the understanding of how life belongs to the place.

The discourse of Orientalism in both Brenner and Smilansky reflected a frantic search for models of identity in the land and in this are important more for revealing national anxiety than for how they set up political domination in the country. Brenner, for instance, imbues Orientalist qualities in the Arab as an example of Jewish failure, and his depictions of the Arab set off his "yidelach" in an opposition between a relocated diasporism and a type of authentic nativism. But the Arab as model is anything but copyable and remains always a mythological ideal.

Even in Smilansky's *The Arab People*, the depiction of the Arab never veers from the mythological, and the connection to the land does not preclude malaria as an element of that authentic relationship. For example, in the story "Shaitana," Smilansky's protagonist, Ibrahim, migrates from Mesopotamia to the foot of Mount Hermon at the shores of the Hula marsh. The story is a double-edged fantasy: on one side, Ibrahim is a master hunter, come to the country to hunt, and he succeeds precisely because of his knowledge of nature and the ease with which he moves through the physical world. However, on the other side, that world is haunted by the Shaitana, the half-human, half-devil daughter of Satan, who dwells in the darkness of the mud and reeds of the marsh. It is double-edged, too, in its ethnic ambiguity, moving between a strongly biblical discourse (clearly evinced in the very forms of Smilansky's Hebrew) and the narrative depiction of Ibrahim, an Arab believer in Allah. That ambiguity certainly points to a Jewish ambivalence about the Arab as a model of how to live in close rapport with nature in Palestine. The Orientalist sensuousness and physicality in the story lead to both success in the land because of athletic, physical prowess and failure because of the weakness of Ibrahim's mind. Ibrahim succumbs to his feverish love for the Shaitana and throws himself into the Hula swamp to follow her. The irrationality of emotion overcomes Ibrahim, whose dive into the malarial muck of the Hula marsh might be the ultimate victory of the inimical forces of the environment. This Ibrahim describes a physical existence, but he too cannot overcome the emotional fevers with which the Hula envelops him. In the end, the Arab Ibrahim cannot adequately substitute for the Jewish Abraham, despite the obvious etymological similarities of their names.

However much for Brenner and Smilansky the Arab strikes a mythological pose, the model of the Arab offered no solutions for a writing that, in Brenner's terms, sought to straddle the solipsism of an interior monologue infected with diaspora and the distant and mythologizing narration of the newcomer who knows nothing of the place and would write it in order to gain its experience. For this reason, a literary analysis of the Arab, despite Hebrew's obvious participation in an Orientalist idealism, offers little for an account of the development of an aesthetics of Zionist landscape. Before 1914 and the outbreak of war, the suspended and fragmentary poetics of malaria present few solutions to a Jewish environmental impasse.

By the end of the First World War and the beginning of the British Mandate, however, things began to change. The exigencies of history forced a significant realignment of the political conflicts in Palestine and pushed for a rearticulation of the environmental goals of the Zionist movement as a whole. To get at this discursive evolution, the historical transformations that occurred between "For the Hundredth Time," where, we might say, a poetics of malaria is first articulated, and 1919, when it is reversed, deserve some elaboration. The Balfour Declaration of 1917, which expressed British support for the national aspirations of the Jewish people in Palestine, had been a major political victory for Zionism. But the actual results of British sympathy and involvement were not immediately clear. On the ground, the British Mandate initiated a dual economy of Jews and Arabs that set the communities in direct competition for the political favors of the colonial government. Balfour might have initially roused Arab suspicions of British intent toward the Zionists and led to the rioting of the early 1920s over land purchases by Jews in the country. But by 1922, with the official mandatory declaration and the publication of the Churchill White Paper in reaction to the civil disturbances that cost Brenner his life, a dynamic of national competition became institutionalized within the legal structures legitimizing the current governmental setup.

In particular, article 11 of the mandate document, with its admonition for a "land system *appropriate* to the needs of the country" (emphasis added), spurred Zionist constructivism by placing the burden of assimilation and acculturation onto the Jewish population, while it set off a decade-long ideational battle against the intensive agricultural terms of the same article.[45] The sudden need to assert both economic and cultural authenticity did not coincide easily with Jewish agricultural practices, which had already begun to move toward extensive land cultivation. If earlier questions of economic feasibility had initiated debates about the proper thrust of colonial activity, new settlement now took into account purely nationalist considerations. The dual economy and a British Orientalism that idealized Arab presence on the land in a preindustrial romanticism of subsistence farming pushed Zionism to take an oppositional defense of a mechanized and scientific exploitation and improvement of land resources. Later on, after the 1929 riots, as we will see below, these policies developed into a full-fledged defense of technological land improvement because of the need to defend questions of "appropriateness" arising from article 11.

Immediately after the war, however, the origins of these policies can be seen in a Zionist shift toward building as actively changing the landscape and not just taking it into the body. And with this type of landscape and economic constructivism came a concomitant cultural shift on a broad scale that not only worked to place Jewish identity squarely within Palestine but that figured Palestine as both agent and beneficiary of that transformative process. Only by showing how the Jew was tied to the land and how the land was tied to the Jew—both in its history and in its future improvement and development—could the labor movement on a political level and the Zionist settlers on a cultural level justify their own existence in the land and the consequent displacement of the Arab *fellaheen*, landed peasants, who had traditionally worked it and who bore the brunt of the imposition of the economic logic of Western land ownership in Palestine.[46]

It does not seem accidental that these transformations in a cultural program coincide with the final scientific rejection of the eucalyptus as an antimalarial agent in the Zionist landscape. As Brenner had shown, malaria would be the final barrier to attainment of fusion, and it is instrumental here that a maximalist discourse of science finally overcame the allegorical eucalyptus as a particularist symbol for malaria's eradication. This development came about during the war when the Zionist establishment commissioned a series of scientific analyses by American experts on the soil, climate, health conditions, and agricultural potential of Palestine.[47] These reports make clear that while the eucalyptus did indeed consume disproportionate amounts of water and thus worked to dry out swamps and wetlands, it failed to drain the soil completely, leaving small amounts of water where the anopheles mosquito could successfully breed. In fact, it was agriculture itself that bore some of the responsibility for the demise of the ameliorative effects of the eucalyptus. Cited in the report on malaria, the indentations of the hooves of grazing cattle received particular blame. Cattle imprints allowed water to collect in small noncirculating pockets, which provided ideal breeding surfaces to the anopheles mosquito, thus ironically promoting the spread of malaria.

Of greatest significance, however, was neither the conditions around which these reports were produced nor their actual findings. What is so striking, for instance, about Israel Kligler's report on hygiene conditions in the country, "Sanitary Survey of Palestine,"[48] is not the rejection of the eucalyptus per se as effective against malaria, but the fact that these criticisms of the eucalyptus were first known as early as 1902 when John Cropper published his article on the subject, "Geographical Distribution of Anaphilisa and Malaria in Upper Palestine," in the *Journal of Hygiene*.[49] In fact, it was Cropper who first made notice of the hoof imprints and their role in creating breeding grounds for mosquitoes within the eucalyptus forests. Kligler makes special notice of the article but does not seem surprised by its prior existence. And both Kligler and Cropper display equal concern over the extent of trachoma in the country, which Kligler claims to be almost as widespread a problem as malaria.[50]

Admittedly, these are not earth-shattering revelations. Their significance lies in what they say about the culture of Zionism and the way the movement prepared the path to settlement by focusing on particular problems on the ground. The demise of the eucalyptus, then, does not come from a scientific rejection, but rather from a cultural one. During the first decade of the twentieth century, the Zionist establishment focused on the eucalyptus as a metaphoric symbol for environmental progress because of a cultural emphasis on both the settlement of individual farms and a notion of land improvement that would scientifically import ecological knowledge from outside the country. Only with the war's end and the conversion to an effort at settling larger farms and tracts of land in order to produce crops that would maximize employment among the Jewish sector did the Zionist establishment adopt a far more extensive and maximalist method for eradicating malaria.

These cultural and scientific divisions were echoed by debates that preceded the war, namely, debates over two competing economic schemes for the development of Jewish Palestine: one, the further development of colonial plantations dependent on Arab labor and the growing of cash crops for exportation; the other, the expansion of field crops in order to employ Jewish masses, with its attendant implications for collectivization and for the increased role of centralized Zionist organizations such as the JNF and the Jewish Colonial Trust as land-buying agents for national development. As a postwar attitude of maximal settlement reached cultural ascendance, the economic debate simply fizzled. With the rejection of the eucalyptus came a concomitant rejection of an imposed colonial structure, that is, of ameliorative cultural and economic projects that introduced technology through foreign imposition while ignoring the natural features and qualities of the land itself. Not only was the eucalyptus out, but so too the emphasis on small capitalist agricultural concerns. Attention shifted then from the coastal plain and the Hefer Valley to land accumulation in the Jezreel and the establishment of collective farming of field crops dependent solely on Jewish labor. Ditching and oiling—the digging of water channels to drain swamp- and marshland, and then the oiling of the surface of these channels to prevent mosquito breeding—had been a technological option since the late nineteenth century.[51] But as *the* method for land improvement and the eradication of malaria, it only became dominant with a cultural shift in how the Yishuv viewed the landscape.[52]

By the 1920s, science and progress might have finally determined the landscape aesthetic that would dominate Palestine. Ditched and oiled, the waters of the marshes and swamps soon dried up completely, and the Hefer, Jezreel, and Hula valleys came to look like we know them today. But the moment of that transformation, and the way the transformation of the landscape has been conveyed to history came about by the particular cultural negotiations that malaria described. Malaria has a poetics because it does not merely refer to the landscape, that is, a particular way that the natural land looks. Rather, a poetics of malaria describes the development of an aesthetic that depended on the liberation of a certain Zionist political identity of inhabiting this place, one engendered in a writing that moved from the naïveté of individual metaphor to the discursive structural control of constructivism, namely, the totality of an imposed mode of narration. The poetics of malaria determined the writing of the land—the methods of conveyance—and not the referenced land itself.

Thus, the demise of the eucalyptus signals the extinction of the last remnant of First Aliyah models of cohabitation in the land, cohabitation primarily with the Arab population. Not only does the new dual economy of the British Mandate set up ethnic competition but the relation of Jew to nature entailed by this new period of extensive and corporate land development pushed the need for the Jew to become native. While before there was malaria to show belonging in the place through an infected writing, after the war the poetics of malaria point toward a cure that would invert the descent of literature into malarial belonging and see in the "improvement" of the swamp the path toward the eradication of an alienating illness.

Literature sets up these changes by locating writing now directly in the land and not as the anguished reflection of the veteran in the Jaffa apartment or the deterritorialized nationalist of cultural Zionism's prewar ascendance. Right after the war, a slew of new Hebrew literary journals appeared in Europe and Palestine with names like *Eretz* (Land), *Gvulot* (Borders), *Ha-ezraḥ* (The Citizen), and *Ma'abarot* (Transits).[53] The literary culture of Zionism in the late 1910s and early 1920s figured a writing that suddenly accounted for the land while it strove to define the new Jew in the modern world.

Nowhere is this shift in the identification between land and Jew as modeled on malaria more evident than in Brenner's own literary projects of the postwar period. Most prominently, Brenner founded the cultural journal *Ha-adamah* ("the land," in its most physical sense of soil and earth) in 1919, which quickly became the dominant literary publication immediately after the war, especially among those that emphasized land and national citizenship. In this task, *Ha-adamah* received something of an institutional boost in gaining its position. The journal was published by the newly formed labor organization Aḥdut Ha-avodah, the United Labor Movement of Palestine, and served as the movement's platform for the cultural articulation of a new constructivist ethos that saw both the land and the Jew as the products of self-expression.

Conceptually, *Ha-adamah* marks a significant transformation for Brenner, who finally abandons altogether the Nietzschean idealism of *Ha-me'orer* (The Awakener) from twelve years earlier, where creation still adhered to romantic ideals: "—What is this new creation that you are going to create? What is its name?—We don't want to give a name to something that has yet to see the light of day. Thus is the path of creations: at the beginning something takes form in the depths of the heart, secretly, top secretly, and afterward it comes to the masses who call it by its name."[54]

With *Ha-adamah*, gone is any metaphysical idea about national identity. Creation achieves a name in the land itself. In the manifesto, which appeared in Aḥdut Ha-avodah's political journal, *Kuntres*, under Brenner's signature, Zionist identity exists as a negotiation between *karka* (land as soil and physical entity) and *eretz* (land as political concept), or between *ḥakla'ut* (working the land) and *mediniyut* (abstract policy). Instead of an identity determined by imposed concepts of spatial organization (policy) or colonial appropriation (agriculture), a synesthesia occurs between *adam* (man) and *adamah* (land as soil), wherein the two realms collapse on each other. Man and earth are not only tied ideologically. Linguistically and morphologically they emanate from the same thing. According to the journal's manifesto: "The land—meaning not just soil (agriculture) and not just land (policy/politics)—but land as the basis of every side of life, the vision of things as they are, a consciousness of the foundations of reality. By land, we mean the origin of human truth."[55] Not sublime truth, but the truth earlier articulated by Bialik in how nature will lead to human knowledge and personal expression.

The journal rejects—just as Brenner did ten years earlier when he first arrived in the country—a division between the materiality of place (the substance of soil and earth) and the abstracted ideas of nation as policy and politics. Instead, culture, which not only included but focused almost myopically on settlement as the mediation and object of these realms, was to negotiate this opposition within Zionism, an opposition that had once caused the fragmentary alienation of the man working the soil but which now, under the aegis of Aḥdut Ha-avodah and the newfound political and ideological power of the laborites, could be articulated as the central thrust of the movement. Place as fusion of abstraction and materiality, of physical toil and intellectual endeavor, is what would give unity to human consciousness and truth to the actions of the Zionists. As one writer, N. Wagman, declared in the first issue, the time for political rumination and discussion was over: "The center of gravity for all our national movements is the question of settlement—the question of a Jewish culture in the land."[56] Wagman's invocation of a "center of gravity" to define Jewish presence in Palestine chides Shimon Dubnov's defense of diaspora by employing the very term Dubnov made famous and held as the kernel of his beliefs about modern Jewish identity. By mocking the idea, Wagman implicates as well Aḥad Ha'am's notion of a deterritorialized Jewish cultural center for which Palestine, according to the spiritual Zionists, was not ready. In defiance, Wagman turns to the soil and announces that culture in the land—specifically the idea of culture through the improvement *of* the land—will produce the country as it produces Jewish identity in the place.

But while the naming of the land significantly recasts place as the expressive object of natural action, the journal projects further the nativism implied in the terms of natural belonging. With the shift from a romantic idealism that would seek out the metaphysical truth of the nation, this new modernist constructivism casts the land as the product of expression.

To open the inaugural issue of *Ha-adamah*, Brenner and his editors—an impressive group of Hebrew luminaries including Moshe Smilansky and Ya'akov Frishman—chose a fiction story by Alexander Ziskind Rabinovitch, which tells the tale of a tragic love triangle among early pioneers working to settle a collective farm.[57] In the plot of the story, the protagonist, Avraham, silently watches as the woman he secretly loves, Shoshana, is wooed by his best friend, Benjamin. The melodramatic plot, however, seems to have held no particular importance for either the story or its author, who easily and impatiently disposes of the love complications in a few quick, truncated paragraphs. Instead, the ideologically programmatic features of the narrative fill the pages with lengthy and evocative descriptions of pioneering and the land.

Following the journal's title and explicit political aims, the story describes the special relationship Avraham develops to the land. Like his biblical namesake, the pioneer Avraham marks a Zionist trajectory from wandering to settlement, and in the course of becoming acquainted with this land, also becomes one with it: "Within Eretz Israel Avraham doesn't feel at all lonely, even when he is far from human society. All the land is with him, and he is with it, all of it. . . . Even the beasts know Avraham and listen to him."[58] Of course, the land could accept the pioneer because it too was figured as ready for his intervention. Avraham's spiritual journey from an alienated day worker, aimlessly wandering from settlement to settlement, to a Zionist settler putting down roots on a collective Jewish farm, is paralleled by a vision of an alienated land waiting for the pioneers to rejuvenate and reinhabit it. In one of the more polemical statements of a rather transparently ideological piece of fiction, Rabinovitch writes: "The land of the collective farm was acquired by hard labor. The land was almost completely uncultivated because it had been many years since anyone had run a plow over it. The *effendi* who owned the estate lived permanently with his wives in Lebanon and paid no attention to his property."[59]

Avraham's identification with nature, however, does not insure his indigenous belonging to the land and, coupled to that, immunity from malaria. However, malaria, in his case, does not signal an inimical place, nor does it suggest that type of infected belonging Brenner projected in "For the Hundredth Time." Where the representation of malaria has changed is in its location, and while Avraham belongs to nature, what keeps him from belonging to this place and curing the malaria that afflicts him involves a political struggle against the oppressive structures of social organization. Malaria thus moves indoors and this is indeed where we first encounter a delirious Avraham in the very opening of the story, supine in the enclosed space of architecture. We might even conjecture that this is what attracted Brenner to the story, since his own famous literary representation of malaria in *Bereavement and Failure* was coming out at the same time. But what separates the two narratives is not just the five years that Brenner waited between writing *Bereavement and Failure* and publishing it. Over that time, Rabinovitch is finally able to figure a cure for malaria within an identity tied to the construction of the land, an identity that will become part of nature by building it, curing its own illness, and in so doing recreating and reinventing the Jew.

The change in the poetics of malaria between 1909 and 1919, then, indicates the failure of an earlier ambiguity between infection as a signal of the inimical land and infection as a type of penetration of that land into the settler. If before the war, malaria has no cure, if it remains cast in an opposition between infection and alienation (between the veteran of Brenner's "For the Hundredth Time" and an alienated Ḥefetz thrown back into the shtetl of Jerusalem in *Bereavement and Failure*), then after the war, Rabinovitch arrives at a solution to this dialectical prison in the constructivist energies of social organization. Indeed, what Avraham accomplishes on the collective *kvutsah* answers Brenner's literary critique of 1909 which tried to straddle realism and interior monologue. The self-identification with the community that will work the land, improving and changing it, becomes the narrative solution to modes of writing which necessarily had to choose between the solipsism of interior projection and the distance of objective natural description. In a way, Rabinovitch answers the original ambiguity of Brenner's early essay where a "person from/of Israel" had to be differentiated between physical and political meanings. Now in 1919 that distinction collapses and the Jew gains nativist legitimacy by curing a malaria that indicated an essential alienation both from a Palestinian landscape and from true political representation.

To achieve this, Rabinovitch finally posits a natural closeness within the Jew himself, a closeness defined by Jewish action in the land. This is the difference between his Avraham and Smilansky's Ibrahim. Both follow a similar path from wandering to settlement, and both understand the physical place Palestine. But Rabinovitch's Avraham succeeds in achieving a self-understanding and self-control (the contemplativeness and rootedness of agricultural work over the Oblomovian complaints of Brenner's veteran writer) where emotion and an inner life obtain an equilibrium absent in the Arab, let alone Brenner's Orthodox shtetl Jew. Concomitantly, Rabinovitch's move creates a significant political by-product, namely, an important distancing from the Arab, who becomes in the story an interloper into the natural world being built by the Jew. Thus, from the Orientalism of a prewar model of natural savage and idealized inhabitant of Palestine, the Arab becomes a much more nefarious force in the land, who upsets the newly discovered nativist rapport between Jew and place. Indeed, the Arab disrupts rational conceptions of place altogether. As we learn, the only problem faced by the young collectivist Jewish settlement of the story is its neighbors:

> Only the neighbors, the inhabitants of the village next door, were irritating because of their stealing. In this these little Arabs were particularly outstanding. They were agile as devils in the craft of theft. And worse than this, they would drive their cattle onto the planted fields. The workers tried to talk with these pests, to reason with them, and they gave many promises and even suggested they provide guards from among them for very little money.[60]

The Arab is now the devil himself and threatens in how he will trespass on the sense of propriety and proprietary ownership on the land.

But even worse, the Arab remains naively devoted to a money economy, with which he tries to infect the Jewish settlement. Even within the United Labor Movement of Palestine, whose inclusive name belies the exclusion of Arab representation, an anxiety of ownership and acquisition drives the sense of disruption produced by Arab presence. At the labor convention of 1920, the year following the first appearance of *Haadamah,* the United Labor Movement pushed for a strongly ethnic platform that would collapse the distinctions among the four major Jewish labor parties in Palestine. Considerations of working-class solidarity motivated the party but only insofar as they coincided with and protected collective Jewish interests in the country.[61] The economic irrationality of this encounter with the Arab in the story, where the Arab plays an economic game that subverts and undermines any *reasonable* socialist interaction among workers, demonstrates the difference in how each attends to the land: "The young men saw that words were not going to do anything so they gathered up the cattle that had wandered onto the fields of the *kvutsah* and put them in the dairy."[62] Instead of the ambiguity of place and market represented by Arab cattle, Jewish cows have a home.

But what we need to read in the placement of the Arab in the story is how their presence parallels the teleological outcome of the resettlement project as a whole. Avraham begins the story in the throes of malarial fever, a condition coupled to his status as a wandering day laborer within a capitalist market economy. Even though, in this way, he gets to know the country and becomes acquainted with the different branches of work on the farm, the existence is alienating and malaria follows in its course. Then, in the effort to settle down, his first attempt is economically and culturally tentative. He becomes a permanent worker on a privately owned farm. There he insulates himself from some of the vagaries of the labor market, but he still has not reached the rapport with work necessary to the Jewish pioneer who is truly united with the landscape. Again, malaria follows:

> And here malaria, which ambushes especially those who put out but do not take in, gripped Avraham. He made an effort to work even when he was feverish. It's nothing. He'll take the pick in his hand, and strike and strike with it and the chill will pass and the sweating will begin. But the head—what to do with the head? If only it were possible to remove it from his shoulders for a little while so it wouldn't hurt so much, so it wouldn't be a nuisance.
>
> When he stays in bed, then he doesn't get paid, and his debt [to the farm] just keeps growing.[63]

The torment of malaria is both economic and personal, infecting the very forms of literary expression. Free indirect discourse creeps into the paragraph at the moment when Avraham is least able to complete his work. The retreat into the mind denotes neither control nor independence but indeed their very opposites: a surrender to the disease, a surrender to what will disrupt the rapport—how vulnerable the relationship might be on the company farm run within a market system—between Avraham and the land. Work—the striking of the pick—becomes an attempt to set himself free from the exploitative conditions of the farm and the alienating disease that follows this economy. But work alone outside of an egalitarian constructivist system of ownership and land acquisition is doomed to fail.

That movement from feverish delusion to passionate embrace of nature is what we must finally focus on because it is figured as a strange reaffirmation of modernity and progress. In the progressive thematics of the story, Rabinovitch's depiction of malarial fever coincides with an economy fraught by an alienation of labor and the distance from ownership of the land and the means of production. Malaria is not just a physical malady; its poetics mark it as a psychical condition of oppression as well. It is suffered in the closed spaces of both a bourgeois economic architecture and a bourgeois mind-set. Recuperation, then, is ownership in nativist terms, where the environment resonates within the healthy body of Avraham. As Rabinovitch writes, "Within Eretz Israel Avraham doesn't feel at all lonely, even when he is far from human society. All the land is with him, and he is with it, all of it."

The spirituality of this environmental rapport, of Avraham's seeming metaphysical unity with the natural realm, does not disengage from a material notion of progress. But here, progress is inverted. The classic opposition between nature and culture, the mainstay of Western environmental thinking, is thrown on its head and twisted around as malaria—the disease for those who venture into the wildness of untamed colonial spaces of the Orient—signifies a modern civilized problem of economic dispossession. At the same time, malaria frames this existence as ultimately irrational, and progress comes through the victory of reason and the move away from the irrationality of malaria. Reason, that greatest of culture's inventions, figures prominently in the pioneering story, which returns the settler to nature, and also in the love story, where passion acts to support and nurture the new utopian settlement. Lest we miss the point, the story's title, "Sibah doḥah sibah mekarevet" (Opposite Forces), insists on the dialectics of the progress depicted within. The move toward nature is a move toward a human-oriented consciousness, a control of one's mind by the ridding of malaria, and the projection of that control both in the mind and on the land. To make the land one's own, it needs to be transformed, healed, and modified to reflect one's own rational and newly unalienated discourse. In truth, then, Rabinovitch writes: "The land of the *kvutsah* was acquired by hard labor." The final lesson seems to be that progress—the value of labor, a unity with nature, and the rational control of the mind—moves forward despite the violent and irrational death of Avraham's best friend Benjamin at the hands of the Arabs who would disrupt and upset the teleologies of modernity.

Thus, Avraham is only free of malaria once he reaches the *kvutsah*, that is, once he participates in an economy of collective ethnic ownership. Love too follows him to the *kvutsah*, both romantic desire and brotherly comradeship: "When Avraham came to work in the *kvutsah* he became attached to one young worker in particular, Benjamin Hagalili, who knew him already from Yehuda. . . . Shoshana was accepted to work in the kitchen. And Avraham would be seen with her almost everyday. The malaria fevers ceased, and he didn't even suffer anymore from the humiliation of being watched. Only . . ."[64] That "only" is the Arab neighbors, the last obstacle to economic equality, romantic fulfillment, and personal tranquility. Malaria, which marked the last physical barrier to these goals has been lifted with the progress of a reasonable distribution of value (each according to his abilities, as we discover through the course of the reported *kvutsah* discussions) and the acquisition of an economy that places land in proper relation to the desires and needs of the worker.

The irony—and perhaps too the ultimate failure—of the story is the way that reason comes to determine the staid form of the realist narrative. To show the type of nativist rapport that Avraham develops with the land, consciousness must be narrated from the distance of an objectivity that will not allow collapse inward. The narration substantiates Brenner's admonition from 1909 when he refused to admit a writing of solipsism, where writing the physical world becomes mere projection of interior desire and fantasy. But the idealized fusion of subject and object brought together through the writing of the land has instead been replaced by the stultifying restrictions of realist narrative, which even the story struggles with. There, toward the end, as the economy of socialistic equality becomes more and more realized within the *kvutsah*, we lose a sense of Avraham's individual consciousness, to the point where love itself becomes a reasoned and socially determined emotion. When Avraham finally confronts the pregnant Shoshana with his love, pregnant not by him but by the fallen Benjamin, his reasoning is impeccable:

> I don't want the child of my friend to be defamed by bad people . . . I don't want your good name to be destroyed. I want to protect both of you . . . Marry me . . . The child will have my name . . . Afterwards you can leave me, I'll give you a divorce . . . You—woman, you have to do this . . . You understand . . . I have no other intention . . . none . . . Your honor and the honor of my dead friend and his seed require it . . .
>
> * * *
>
> She married him and they were together forever.[65]

At the end, exterior form drives internal behavior in an odd inversion of what the rest of the story seemed to have been about. But then, the reification of identity from the form of narrative and settlement might finally be the poetic of malaria, even though the imposition of form on desire cannot sustain itself. While the ellipses denote the hesitation and ultimate deceit of Avraham's motives for the sake of happiness, love, and a certain logic of settlement, they show also the very breakdown of the discursive control—the *reason* of action and spirit—that would confine and regulate desire. Ernst Bloch wrote about this idea in the 1930s in his debates with Georg Lukács when they argued over these same questions in the context of Expressionism, namely, whether form should be imposed on art and the individual (Lukács in his most soviet articulations of realism)[66] or whether the expression of the self should seek the fissures and cracks in a formal system that would try to confine thought (Bloch in his defense of Expressionism).[67] Through the environmental desires of the story, Rabinovitch tried to straddle both sides, as Brenner did before him in 1909, attempting to understand and articulate how both individual desire and physical form (the land itself) could combine in a discourse that would write Eretz Israel into the very soul of this Jewish worker, this Zionist who was creating the place in his own vision.

Malaria finally outlines its own poetics, then, both in writing and on the ground itself. Form—the poetics of the land—becomes the ground of contestation both for creating Palestine in Jewish nativist terms and for generating a writing that will fuse personal consciousness and reason with a sense of belonging to this place. This is the wound that Adorno writes about in his discussions of nature: the impossibility, that is, of artifice to inscribe nature except through the intermediary filter of aesthetics, despite nature's seduction of offering itself as the transcendent bridge to the sublime immediacy of the mind.[68] The obfuscation of this wound was the greatest triumph of Labor Zionist constructivism, especially as it embraced the realism of scientific rationalism, a disourse that would seem to avoid aesthetics altogether. Realism now narrated the self in a mirrorlike fashion, reflecting the objects of the landscape in the effective conquest of malaria. The dispassionate methods of scientific conquest over the environment might have been decided upon right after the war, but the conceptual conquest of reimagining the land through realistic depiction would be the ultimate outcome of the introduction of science into a mirrored formulation of "to build and be built." And yes, in those final, stuttered hesitations and fragments of Avraham's last speech to Shoshana, right before the literary trope of "happily ever after" decides their fate, one cannot help but hear the distant echoes of all those other fragmented, stuttered malarial speeches.

Realism in the Landscape

With the triumph of realism by the early 1920s, the expansion into the Jezreel Valley was accompanied by both collectivization and central planning. At Nahalal, one of the earliest planned settlements in the Jezreel, the improvement of the land and the preparation for occupation was figured precisely as a mutual identification of the narrating subject with the object of the land. Representation of the Zionist expansion into the valley and the settlement of Nahalal remained constitutive of the very consciousness and identity of those working to transform the landscape. In the engineering drawings of the Nahalal improvements performed by the JNF, landscape emanates from a type of visual poetics that is both dependent on mimesis and sensitive to an interiority of consciousness as the origin of creative desire and agricultural production.

In 1925, after completing the building of Nahalal, the JNF published a bilingual (Hebrew and English) booklet lauding their successes in the valley. *Sanitation Works in the Valley of the Jesreel* [sic] (*Avodot havra'ah be-emek yizra'el*)[69] contains information on drainage, economic uses, and health conditions at the Nahalal and Nuris sites in the valley, and in particular describes the methods used to channel the springs that fed the marshes and swamps in these areas. The work was carried out by a civil engineering firm in Tel Aviv, Yosef Breuer and Shimshon Elek, who produced the drawings and the descriptions of the sites.[70] The primary descriptive text in the booklet declares quite glibly the technical triumph of these works in all its philosophical power. According to a Dr. D. Deutch, who performed a medical examination of the site in 1923 after the drainage improvements were completed, "We might say that man has here conquered nature and even death."[71]

More circumspect are the two maps attached to the booklet: the "before" and "after" representations of the Nahalal site (Figures 2 and 3). In English the maps bear the titles "Nahalal Lands Before/After Amelioration." But the notion of amelioration inadequately renders the Hebrew *havra'ah*, whose translation, we might infer, had already become something of a question since it is used to signify both "amelioration" and "sanitation" on the English side. But *havra'ah* implies a sense of improvement based on health and hygiene, on the one hand, and creation, on the other (the Hebrew root ב.ר.א. [b.r.a.] straddles these lexical fields and alludes significantly to the book of Genesis). In Hebrew, the maps thus represent visually the scientific fantasy of progress and improvement and even creation. Improvement, it seems, does not just imply gradation of quality but the very invention of place.

The translation of *havra'ah* to amelioration fits into a general pattern of colonial thinking from at least the mid-nineteenth century that saw physical improvement and change in concert with questions of hygiene. Within the British Empire—to which Palestine now belonged—from India to the slums of Manchester and Birmingham, the transformation of the landscape came coupled to discourses of progress and hygienic health improvement.[72]

But while the goals of British imperial colonialism certainly affect meaning in the Nahalal drawings, the development of the settlement was never couched as benevolent improvement for the colonized other despite

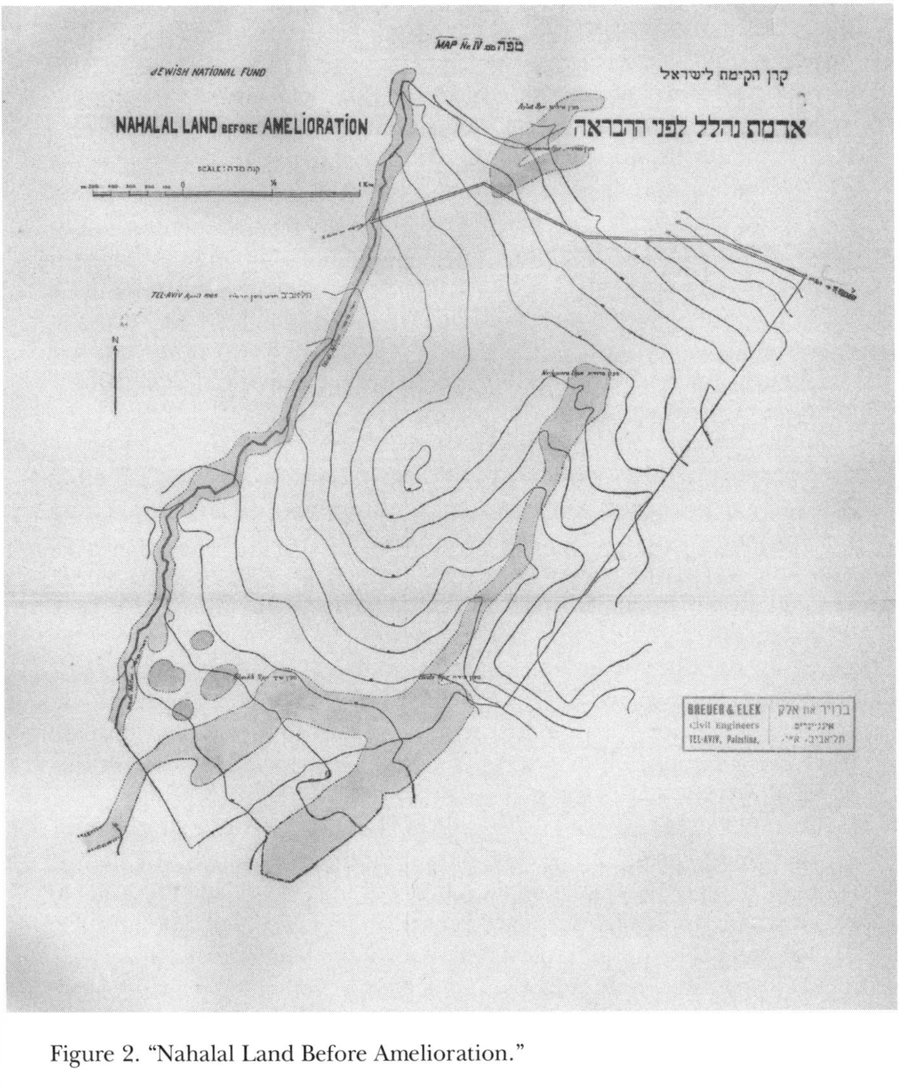

Figure 2. "Nahalal Land Before Amelioration."

the booklet's claims that Arab inhabitants would also benefit from the environmental transformations being effected on the site. Rather, it is the self-reflection—the improvement of oneself—that marks the difference from British colonial paternalism either domestic or foreign. Land improvement by the JNF was fashioned in a spirit of *havra'ah* where the act of changing the land also changed oneself. In this, the imposition of the abstract grid as a visual means of marking change and improvement on the maps signifies much more than just the imposition of human will on the landscape. The grid does not merely organize the site into abstract forms of human organization. Instead, within the logic that the maps here purport, the grid—the imposition of consciousness onto the primitive space—acts to make the land fecund and productive in the first place. The "before" representation (Figure 2) is not merely a topographic description of slope and water drainage. Indeed, it is *only* that, and in a reversal of any intuitive understanding of the grid, the "before" map is the less natural and more artificial of the two. In it, the land is only line and color, completely abstract and as yet unformed. However, in the "after" depiction (Figure 3) and the overlay of the rational grid the landscape comes alive and even becomes more natural. Trees and other flora punctuate the representation as if the grid imposed by the engineer only catalyzed a natural process that then developed on its own. Indeed, the "conquering of land" leads to the more faithful representation of nature, allowing nature, we might say, to become more "natural."[73]

In this context, the translation of *melior* ("better" in Latin, the root of a*melior*ation) to the Hebrew root ב.ר.א. (and its inverse) is rather important and marks a significant linguistic transition from an adjectival Latin understanding of physical place where land is represented as an object with attached attribute, to the nativist Hebrew gerund in a process of *havra'ah* that is dynamic, subject-oriented in its reflexivity, and focused on a process of change that transgresses both sides of the representational divide: the human consciousness that represents and causes improvement, and the land being represented and improved. The grid, that abstract modernist construct,[74] becomes its own opposite, and instead of denoting imposition of exterior form, projects form from within the physical realness of the space.

Nahalal did not originate the use of the grid as a way of organizing and representing the land in Zionist culture. Early JNF certificates acknowledging individual contributions had indeed utilized the grid in an idealized vision of a strangely European-looking landscape (Figure 4). But there the grid is employed to control the land and give it an aesthetically pleasing, ordered look. In contrast, at Nahalal, the grid brings out a natural fecundity and order to the flora which would now thrive within a newly conceived and actualized landscape.

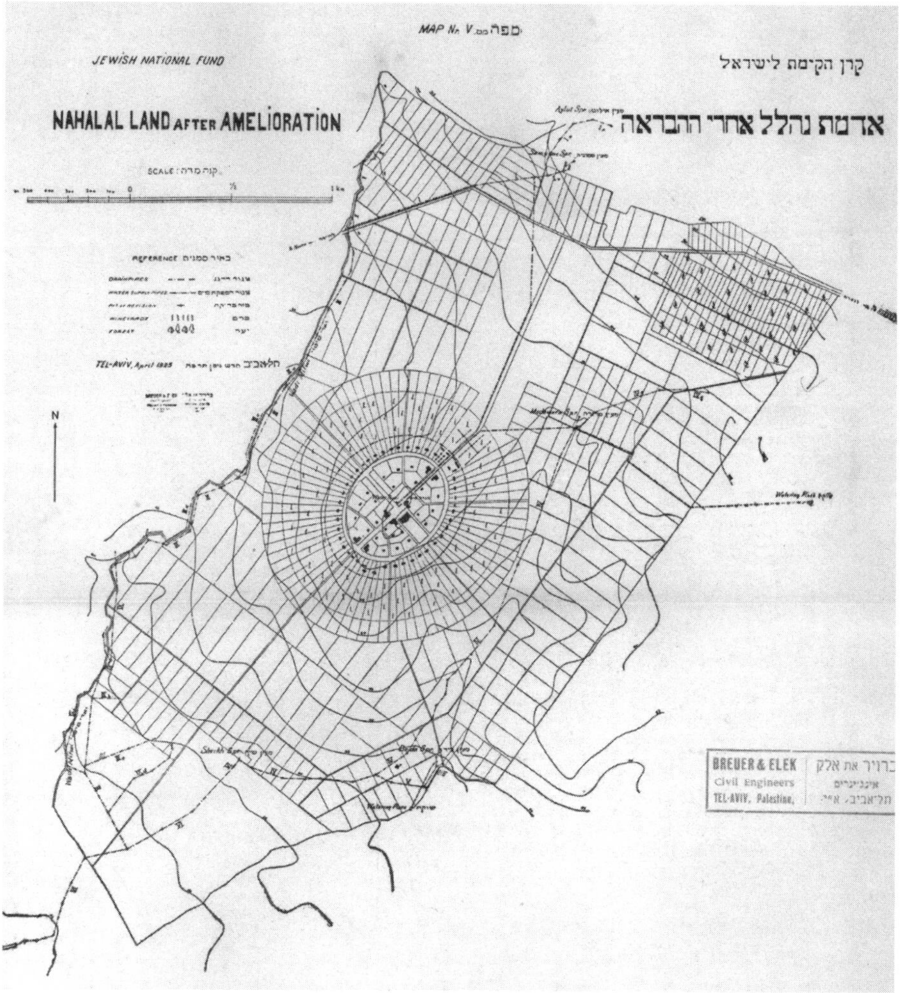

Figure 3. "Nahalal Land After Amelioration."

Nahalal, then, represents the final triumph of a realism that would narrate the self improving the soil reflexively. And it was this contradiction and paradox—a problem, indeed, of prose, which ascended to a centrality in the Zionist Yishuv at only this point—that came under the sharp focus and criticism of a newly developing avant-garde poetics in the mid-1920s. Poets like Avraham Shlonsky, who came to Palestine to work and write, began to see the contradictions in a Zionist constructivism based on a realist aesthetic as the impediment to a truly natural Zionist identity in the land. That, then, becomes the story of the next chapter.

Figure 4. A Rosh Hashanah card whose purchase benefited the Jewish National Fund (JNF), 1910.

Chapter 3

The Hebrew Poet as Producer

The unity of the labor movement in Palestine after the First World War marked the ascendance of a political ideology that would essentially control the Yishuv for some decades to come. From the petty squabbles and ideological tiffs among fractious groups like Po'alei Tsiyon and Ha-po'el Ha-tsa'ir, the laborites emerged united, first as Aḥdut Ha-avodah and then later in the newer, more powerful syndicate, the Histadrut, both of which sought to unify all the Jewish labor organizations in the country. No longer would there be any notion of alienation in a worker's society between those working the land and the structures that would engage the workers in their toil in the fields and in the building of the country. In a constructivism that might best be described as a sort of anticapitalist Fordism, unity within the movement meant the vertical integration of Jewish society,[1] crystallizing the vision expressed years earlier by A. D. Gordon for a workers' society that would unify employer and employee for the sake of a larger transcendent idealism of building the land and fashioning the conditions for the renaissance of the Jewish soul.[2]

Economic and political constructivism held important consequences for culture, and as we've already seen could not develop without deploying a particular aesthetic vision of the land and work. The partnership of the two major journals of Aḥdut Ha-avodah, *Kuntres* and *Ha-adamah*, during the first half of the 1920s speaks to the conscious recognition of the mutual dependence of politics and aesthetics in Jewish Palestine. Together the two journals worked to totalize the party's vision of life in the Yishuv, with literature as a leading element within that project. Brenner's efforts in this direction set the stage for a revolutionary literature that would actively seek to promote Jewish and laborite ascendance in the country.[3]

In art, what labor syndicalism in Palestine meant was a triumph of a *littérature engagée*, that is, the idea of a political culture where aesthetics would synthesize with the larger ideological structures of society and party.[4] But an engaged literature dedicated to the party's political and social aims—what in Hebrew would be called *sifrut meguyeset* (drafted literature)—could not contain all of the aesthetic options in the country.

Like its soviet model, Zionist constructivism would spawn as well a vibrant modernist avant-garde, no less committed to the political goals of a progressive society but which saw the limitations of ideological dictate on a revolutionary aesthetics.[5] Commitment to the cause was never in doubt; the political goals of both "engaged" literature and avant-garde literature remained sharply focused on the notion that art must act for the sake of creating the nation.

But by the mid-1920s, the dominant cultural questions in Palestine would become those that would echo throughout left-wing European literature in the coming decades, especially in reaction to the rise of the threat of the fascist right, namely, how can literature *do* things to engage revolution and not merely reflect conditions within the party? That question reached back to origins in the nineteenth century, but it would especially vex twentieth-century political culture on the left, particularly in Palestine where unity and vertical integration would seem to subsume art under the umbrella of settlement and work.

In this context, the logic of Brenner's naturalism could not last. The inherent tensions of a self-referential naturalism wherein the world operated independently of human intervention and fantasized projection, but only insofar as it would concomitantly reflect the interior of the Jewish pioneer, began to break apart even in Rabinovitch's "Sibah doḥah sibah mekarevet" (Opposite Forces), that first story in Brenner's journal, *Ha-adamah*. When the protagonist Avraham finally gets the chance to voice his inner feelings, they break apart and come out stifled and fragmented. The needs of the community and the needs of the land come together but not in a self-sustaining way. At the end of that story, Avraham's desires might coincide with the good of the community, which is also the good of nature. But the reader cannot help wondering whether something emotionally inauthentic and unautonomous resides in these newfound relationships between individuals in the national space.[6]

That problem of inauthenticity did not bother the new Zionist politics of constructivism, which dominated the Jewish Yishuv after the First World War and which demanded of the settler a personal sacrifice for the nation in order to build the new Zionist citizen. The power of transformation through working on the soil would take care of individual identity. And the notion of settling the land for the sake of both national space and individual revitalization continued to gather strength throughout the decade of the 1920s, especially in the wake of the Bolshevik revolution in Russia, which fed the Yishuv with a new, younger cadre of idealistic workers, members of a Third Aliyah vanguard who had actually witnessed the triumph of collectivism and socialism in eastern Europe. Work projects in the north of Palestine, especially on newly purchased tracts of land in the Jezreel Valley, expanded the scope of settlement and spawned new social and economic formations that directly reflected the constructivist ethos of national rejuvenation on the land as reflective of individual revitalization. In particular, the collectivized forms of the kibbutz and the independent work crews of the Gdud Ha-avodah, the Labor Brigade, laid the institutional foundations for a sustained constructivist approach to working and transforming the land.

However, if in these instances politics followed a type of aesthetic reaction to nature and the need to rebuild the individual, each reflecting the other, then it was only a matter of time before the paradox of Brenner's realism would catch up with political forms and cause a crisis of individual expression. In political terms, the crisis arrived in the mid-1920s when the centralized powers of the nascent labor establishment had assembled enough strength to attempt the exercise of control over the decentralized work units of the Gdud and the kibbutzim. That political struggle between centralized power and decentered work both emanated from issues of expression (the promise of Brenner's constructivist realism) and found its articulation precisely in a debate over writing itself. Specifically, at stake by mid-decade was the value that writing had as individual expression of the constructivist settlement of Jewish Palestine and the reinvention of the Jew within a modern society.

In a way, that debate merely resurrected the older Zionist controversy between Aḥad Ha'am and Micha Yosef Berdichevsky over poesy. But by the 1920s and leading into the 1930s, the terms of that debate grew more real in its consequences for settlement policy in the land and more politically charged in the way it echoed and extended parallel debates in Europe over the relation of aesthetics to politics, in particular, the growing politics of authoritarianism. By 1934 Walter Benjamin would articulate the terms of this debate rather succinctly in his essay "The Author as Producer." There in Europe in the 1930s, Benjamin was responding to the rising tide of fascism, but the question of political engagement for literature suffused the entire question of art for much of modernism. And the perceived consequences for an engaged literature in rousing the proletariat had direct application for the state of politics and literature in Palestine:

> You will remember how Plato deals with poets in his ideal state: he banishes them from it in the public interest. He had a high conception of the power of poetry, but he believed it harmful, superfluous—in a *perfect* community, of course. The question of the poet's right to exist has not often, since then, been posed with the same emphasis; but today it poses itself. Probably it is only seldom posed in this *form*, but it is more or less familiar to you all as the question of the autonomy of the poet, of his freedom to write whatever he pleases. You are not disposed to grant him this autonomy. You believe that the present social situation compels him to decide in whose service he is to place his activity. . . . [The] activity [of an advanced writer] is now decided by what is useful to the proletariat in the

class struggle. . . . [*O*]*n the one hand*, the correct political line is demanded of the poet; *on the other*, it is justifiable to expect his work to have quality.[7]

The opposition between expressive—both political and aesthetic—autonomy and the lack of autonomy defined the debates over writing and settlement politics in Jewish Palestine as well, particularly as they would manifest themselves beginning in the mid-1920s. At issue was not fascist politics and the suppression of free expression within the proletarian masses, the terms of European discussion in the 1930s. Rather, in Jewish Palestine, at stake was the political role of individual expression in Zionist constructivism, that is, how literature could do things to bring about change and mold nature and settlement in the vision of the labor movement while at the same time reflecting on the changing position of the individual subject in the landscape. At stake was the very dialectical inflection—and the very real political control—evinced by the slogan "to build and be built."

Gdud Ha-avodah and the Debates over Hebrew Writing

In late summer of 1925, the fifth anniversary of the establishment of Gdud Ha-avodah (the Labor Brigade) passed without any mention in the pages of *Davar*, the recently founded daily newspaper of the Histadrut (the General Confederation of Jewish Labor in Palestine), which had been founded to augment the older federation of labor, Aḥdut Ha-avodah. The paper's silence was odd, since in 1920s Palestine, labor constructivism—the ideas of building and work as constitutive principles of national identity and labor politics—held a dominant position in the Jewish community. And within the labor movement, the Gdud served an important iconic and physical role in settlement expansion, employing the new influx of young eastern Europeans arriving since the war in national building projects. Steeped in Bolshevik optimism, these pioneers of the Third Aliyah dove straight into hard physical labor throughout the country and fashioned roads out of wilderness, drained swampland, and built settlements, pushing the Jewish Yishuv further into the Jezreel Valley and the Galilee. Ideologically, the Gdud formed itself around the central tenets of constructivism and worked to rebuild the land while concentrating on rebuilding the self through labor and through the radical reinvention of social organization in the newly invented collective farm, the kibbutz, and in various other types of worker cooperatives.

In light of the Gdud's role in the settlement transformations since 1920, *Davar*'s silence definitely forebode a growing political conflict in the movement between the centralizing powers within the labor establishment (notably, the labor leaders David Ben-Gurion and Berl Katznelson) and the decentered principles of local action and organization within the Gdud. Indeed, by 1927 the Gdud would unravel completely, victim both to the worsening economy of Palestine in the mid-1920s and to the political goals of Ben-Gurion and Katznelson, who had always placed greatest political value in a centralized labor organization, first in Aḥdut Ha-avodah and then in the Histadrut.

In practical terms, *Davar*'s oversight (or blatant refusal)[8] in September 1925 to acknowledge the Gdud's fifth anniversary would not pass unnoticed, if only because representation and commemoration were, ironically, already important parts of constructivist action on the ground. And so, the debate over the role of political action and settlement work was sparked by the question of writing itself when a reader of the paper, a certain A. Bar-Adon of Tel Aviv, wrote to complain of the newspaper's neglect of the anniversary: "It is as if the reality of this group did not at all move the minds of our pen-wielding comrades to contemplate this event of great value."[9] Bar-Adon's letter provoked a debate over writing and literature not because of any explicit political accusation concerning the Gdud. Rather, Bar-Adon unveiled the leadership's lightly disguised refusal to accept the decentered controls of discourse and social organization implied by the Gdud's very existence. The letter chides the leadership for allowing the movement's literary mouthpiece, *Davar* itself, to become disconnected from the immediacy of action on the soil: "[The pen-wielders cannot be bothered with] the existence of this organized body within the Histadrut whose shoulders bear the yoke of the great efforts of the workers since the beginning until now." Bar-Adon indicts the growing distance of the party leaders from the constructivist experience by placing his indictment in a critique against writing, and thus attempting to reassert control *by* the worker by controlling the representation *of* the worker.

The ultimate significance of Bar-Adon's critique of *Davar*'s ignoring the anniversary of the Gdud lay in the dialectical separation he outlines between reality (the existence and action of the Gdud) and the contemplation of writing that would look upon and represent that reality in the land (the "pen-wielders" of the newspaper). The dialectic embeds a certain amount of nostalgia already for pioneering, and the turn to nostalgia might, in fact, always accompany the realism of a mimesis where writing is immanently separated from the object being described. In this logic, the contemplating "pen-wielder" of the party mouthpiece becomes part of a hierarchical apparatus that imposes control over the worker's body through the mimetic tool of literature. Instead, Bar-Adon's consistent metaphoric elision (a fundamental principle of constructivist thought) between a social body and the worker's body throughout the brief letter denies a separation between individual experience and the experience of national construction itself. In Bar-Adon's terms, the body is not just the objectified locus of political struggle; rather, it is metaphorically porous, incorporating the paper's insult within both the exterior and interior identities of the worker in Jewish Palestine: "Yes, it hurts not just on the outside, but inside too, in terms of feelings, in terms of every emotion." What Bar-Adon seems to understand is that in the constructivist labor utopia, where the action of the worker builds and constructs a vertically integrated society, the worker's body becomes the site of national responsibility and political will. His indictment, then, speaks to the paradox of mimetic realism where constructivist writing and constructivism itself actually silence the worker, who exists only as a physical body that works and changes the landscape, but has no control over how that work will be valued within a writing that represents it.

Bar-Adon's discursive criticism of the labor movement—that, in truth, a worker's society built from the ground up through the action of work might always already imply the totality of a central authority that sets the terms of national commemoration and discourse—hit a definite nerve and provoked Berl Katznelson himself, who was then general editor of *Davar*, to respond directly to Bar-Adon in a column published adjacent to the letter. Katznelson focuses immediately on the question of who bears responsibility to speak for the movement, parrying Bar-Adon's title "Why the Silence?" which implicitly castigates the labor-union paper, with his own "To Those Silent," thereby totalizing the constructivist experience by deflecting blame from the leadership and passing it onto a rank and file who would not rise up and speak for themselves. Katznelson's logic emanates directly from earlier discourses of nature reflection and the immediacy of acting in and on the land. But it might then expose the dialectical contradiction of Katznelson's and Ben-Gurion's repeated attempts to centralize labor organization in the country while consistently claiming that the significance of labor lies intrinsically in its very action, that is, in the immediacy of the encounter between worker and soil.

In order to sidestep this contradiction of central discursive control over decentered political action, Katznelson's argument focused on the value of professional writing to the labor movement, dividing it between documentary reportage and a writing that has itself as a goal. Katznelson thus resurrects Aḥad Ha'am's old arguments against "poesy" but reconciles them with his deceased friend Brenner's defense of personal expression by arguing that the workers in the fields must be the source of literary production. True writing must still connect to the source of personal immediacy but only as a reproduction of the action that drives a labor society. Literary writing, then, falls outside of immediacy, becoming instead reportage and representation of that experience:

> The greatest value and weight in the literature of labor in the country are those narratives and clear visions that come not from the "pen-wielders" but rather from those participating in these things. Not by strength of literary talent has our journalism grown to this point, but by the purity of the words that come from the inside. The moment that the transmission of matters of labor and life to the readers becomes the purview of those knowing how to write, then labor literature will stop being what it has been until now. It will become a literature of research and reason and learning. Perhaps too it will raise itself up and take on great importance in the eyes of "foreigners who don't understand." But it will lose its importance for us. And woe be to us if the events of our lives and our deeds will be told and discussed only within the narrow confines [*eshnabim*, lit. small windows] of this paper.[10]

Within the complete social integration of constructivism—"On the division of our camp into two: [between] plain comrades, who have the right to be silent, and 'pen-wielding' comrades whose duty is 'to contemplate events'—I cannot allow. . . . [Professional writing] cannot appease us and uncover the life force of our works"[11]—writing takes on a contradictory and self-negating purpose: it must seek the "purity" of true expression, a conduit from the workers in the fields, but only as an intermediary force that would not displace the self-revealing truth of work itself or the very forms of settlement that give truth to writing in the first place.

Earlier that year in February, David Ben-Gurion had issued a similar call for a totalizing politics, borrowing from the terms of discourse and writing to describe a constructivism that would meld subject and object through the action of labor, but explicitly within a transcendent political structure that could provide the framework for worker expression. Writing nostalgically of the foundation of Aḥdut Ha-avodah, Ben-Gurion states, "In Petaḥ Tikvah [where Aḥdut Ha-avodah was founded] the movement demanded the creation of a single vessel that would include both the subject of the movement and its predicate: a general framework inclusive and undivided in content."[12] In the call for unity, Ben-Gurion ironically expresses the dialectical form of the movement, that is, how the discursive collapse of a subject-object opposition defines the totality of constructivist experience, exactly Katznelson's political message to Bar-Adon. The worker might be the origin of expression, but Katznelson reveals in *Davar*, just as Ben-Gurion does here, how discursive control cannot be allowed to stray too far from the centrality of the party itself. Action becomes the starting point for any expression of the political subject, and action—the building of the country, which in 1925 looked to the collectivized settlement of the Jezreel and the Galilee—was ever more part of a structure of central planning.[13] For both Katznelson and Ben-Gurion, history is embedded in the dialectical process of subject-object resolution, with the remainder, a writing of what they saw as immanent subjective experience, always extraneous—the *musaf* (supplement), as Katznelson would call it—to the expressive structures of history itself.

For the young avant-garde poet Avraham Shlonsky, who had himself spent time since his arrival in Palestine in 1921 laboring in the construction projects in the Jezreel Valley and who was equally committed to a labor ideology, Katznelson's response concerning "professional writing" could only be disingenuous. In a response to Katznelson published in *Davar* that October, Shlonsky too took up the issue of immediacy in the writing of the labor movement, but posited responsibility for literature on the shoulders of those, like himself, for whom writing was more than an avocation. For him, the issue was less the professionalism of writing itself than the independence and political importance that writing was to hold within the life and institutions of the Jewish Yishuv. By focusing criticism on Katznelson's decision to separate the literature section of *Davar* from the main body of the paper and call it a *musaf*, specifically the "Sabbath and Holiday Supplement" (Musaf le-shabatot ule-mo'adim), Shlonsky poked sardonic fun at the separation implied for literature, namely, that literature and writing had become elitist activities in the eyes of the party leadership and divorced from the "work" (or "action") of the party:

> A man [*adam*] who places his writing table on the holy soil [*adamah*], he does not need to give up on "literature" [*literatura*] from anywhere . . .
>
> And here is the literary supplement of "*Davar*": a special section that until now was inside the paper and now will be separated from it for some reason. I know why; everyone knows. The editors certainly know—but to say it simply and forthrightly is forbidden. It's as if "Supplement for Sabbath and Holidays" is more proletarian and less "intelligent" than Literary Supplement or simply: Literature Section.
>
> What is this shame?
>
> God almighty! What is this shame.[14]

In the very language of his response, Shlonsky mocks Katznelson's xenophobia (just as he makes tangential reference to Aḥad Ha'am's formulation of the poesy debates): the closing of labor society around a totalized vision; the fear of a Jewish writing that will have foreigners as its audience. He does this by referring to literature as *literatura*, a clearly foreign word to displace the Hebrew *sifrut* (literature). Here, and throughout the essay, Shlonsky's point remains focused on the intrinsic and mutual relationship between man (*adam*) and soil (*adamah*) which he maintains within the synesthetic closeness of their Hebrew roots. Writing, for Shlonsky, does not displace this closeness, but becomes constitutive of the relationship in the first place. The writer claims his position on the soil—not separated from it as a type of excess (a *musaf*) or disconnected from it by virtue of his "literariness." But right there on the land itself. In this,

Shlonsky attacks the disingenuousness of the entire idea behind the newspaper *Davar*, where the "word" (*davar*) that stands for the labor movement would disdain writing itself. That is why "*Davar*" is surrounded by quotation marks, highlighting thereby not only the newspaper's name but the denotative meaning of the word that stands for the word.

Shlonsky leaves unsaid what he "knows," but he had already alluded to it earlier: the shame of the elitist cachet that "literature" brings with it to the laborite establishment. Shlonsky mocks the euphemisms that have taken the place of "literature" in the official vocabulary of the movement: "professional pen-wielders," "written things." And he laments the way literature has been excluded from the political system: "This isn't accidental. It's not coincidental at all—it's systematic. It's the principle. It's almost a type of new 'ism.'"[15] Yet Shlonsky falls short of calling for the dismantling of a labor structure or even a Marxist paradigm for the place of writing. His is not an attack exterior to constructivism. Indeed, within the folds of ideology, Shlonsky sees the place of writing as central, "within the paper," or, in a reading that complicates his previous rejection of "isms," within the *ma'arekhet*, which in the narrow context of the essay refers to the newspaper itself (*ma'arekhet* as "editorial board"), but which resonates more broadly (*ma'arekhet* as "system") with the entire structure of society.

The critic and literary historian Hannan Hever explains the ideological resistance between Katznelson and Shlonsky as historical and generational, pointing to a division between the two that derives from competing artistic affiliation and allegiances stemming from their respective experiences in Russia and with Russian literature.[16] Katznelson, like Brenner, immigrated to Palestine after first being inculcated within a nineteenth-century tradition of realism and dissent in prose. Dostoyevsky and Chernyshevsky echo throughout their polemical and imaginative prose, especially in Brenner who is the true agonistic figure for Shlonsky. Shlonsky names him as the progenitor of the separation of literature from the intelligentsia in Palestine by citing *Ha-adamah* and Brenner's propensity to privilege writing from the fields.[17] Shlonsky does not attack the realism of the journal, but rather the effects of a literature that emanates only from a *committed* writing. In arguing for writing untied to party dictate, Shlonsky rejects the mimesis of *Ha-adamah*, which would only represent the external processes of physical renewal in the country. Against this mode of writing, Shlonsky self-consciously molds a poetry based on the Russian futurism of Mayakovsky and a writing that rejected a sense of literature as supplemental to the fundamental expression of the individual within a collectivist political system.[18]

By defending literary professionalism and rejecting mimetic prose Shlonsky has naturally fallen prey to claims of elitism, as Hever suggests.

But we need to differentiate Shlonsky's valuation of writing from a bourgeois modernism that acted to separate literary endeavor from the banalities of everyday life. Shlonsky might argue against Katznelson's celebration of a literature that comes directly from the fields, but in criticizing a labor attitude toward literature as supplement he still does not argue for art as an end in itself. Professionalism might be necessary, but only because writing becomes as instrumental within the political redefinition of a proletarian Jewish society as any working of the soil. Indeed, Shlonsky allows for no separation between the two. Unification of writing and landscape motivates a Shlonskyan modernism. As Shlonsky writes, in a moment of dialectical seriousness: "We cannot agree with this division between higher and lower, between Sabbath and workday . . . and why should a report on a strike or a tractor, which are secular matters and part of a person's daily existence, not be called literature—and a poem or a critical essay and everything that comes from it—this is literature? . . . why is it possible to create classes in the midst of ending the 'class war'?"[19]

Shlonsky's view of art articulated a new modernist reformulation of Zionist identity in the land. Now, writing itself would not merely reflect this new identity. Instead, it would self-consciously constitute the Jew in the soil through expression itself. In this, Shlonsky's poetics required an even greater struggle against the Hebrew textual tradition than prior generations in order to rid historical meaning from a modern poetry. His poetic mantra—"freedom of the word"—oscillated between metaphors of political and religious independence through writing. In general, Shlonsky's modernist manifesto, guided by both a Russian futurist desire for free linguistic invention and a Zionist politics of identification between place and text, required as well the reformulation of Jewish discourse within the weight of the tradition: "free love among words, without the canopy and marriage vows of the holy text."[20] The move away from a textuality subsumed within an intellectual religious tradition saw as an alternate model for expressive concentration the physical encounter with the land, and not the interior abstraction of "freedom" as espoused by European modernism. The circumstances of Hebrew textuality—the overwhelming strength of the Bible, the Mishnah, and the Talmud, which echoed down through the literature—might have been a unique phenomenon, but in that uniqueness, it marked the split for Shlonsky from a Russian whose textuality was less determined by the hegemony of its cotexts. Thus, in Hebrew, form could not offer itself as an unmediated retreat from literature as a supplement to political activity. By locating modernist writing within the place of national return, Hebrew had to look both backward and forward: back to a prebiblical origin of an unmediated literary expression and forward to a technology of environmental manipulation that would show the presence of a productive consciousness.

In political terms, the independence Shlonsky demanded of writing translated into attacks on what he called a "drafted" literature (*sifrut meguyeset*), which represented a new Hebrew consciousness, but one bound by party dictate. Throughout the latter part of the 1920s, and especially after being fired from *Davar* for obvious ideological conflicts with management, Shlonsky continued his assault on the objectivist aesthetics of the party, primarily in the pages of the independent daily *Ha-aretz*, where he wrote a self-consciously titled column, "From the Side." In October 1928, the entire structure of settlement culture as encapsulated in the trope of the "new Hebrew," an idea and slogan that had risen to popular prominence in the constructivist labor campaign, came under his attack: "Blast the trumpets! Sing out with a great voice! The new Hebrew, here he comes!"[21] The attack on the new Hebrew included oblique references to the quasi-militarism of Gdud Ha-avodah itself: "One, two! One, two!—Forward march, new Hebrew! [. . .]—'Battalions' [*gdudim*], 'companies,' 'officers' etc." Shlonsky mocked the regimented structure of a labor ideology focused on the forms of settlement, an ideology that ignored what Shlonsky had earlier described as the need for Hebrew expression free of such imposed structures: "They will pass, they will stream by in single file: One, two! One, two! And hollow hearts and diligent pens will become hoarse greeting them: the new Hebrew, here he comes!"

The concept of the new Hebrew does not necessarily conflict with Shlonsky's push toward the reinvention of language and, along with that, the invention of a new Jewish consciousness. But for Shlonsky that transformation came precisely from the "freedom of the word," a revolution that reinscribed expression not within the "arrays" of newfound systems of ideological compliance but within a free articulation of the individual Jewish settler, free, that is, of the historical and ideological layers of both a totalizing history and a totalizing politics.

Shlonsky's cultural and political criticisms would parallel a poetic struggle to free both personal expression and the representation of the land from the mediation of political organization. That triangulation of individual, land, and party—which Brenner had advocated, which Rabinovitch had given direct expression to, and which Katznelson and Ben-Gurion strove to institutionalize—in Shlonsky's view obscured the immanent relationship between the creativity of the self and its connection to the soil. In his journalistic attacks against a "drafted" literature, Shlonsky aimed to liberate expression from the party and thus liberate expression from an objective prison of bland and uncreative (that is, unreflexive) reportage and mimesis.

Shlonsky's struggle ensued in poetry as well as in polemic, although in poetry the aesthetic difficulty of maintaining such a radical political position became all too evident. The prescriptive politics of Shlonsky's view of writing did not easily and effortlessly translate into an aesthetics of immediate rapport between poet and the object of expression, the land itself. Instead, we can trace through Shlonsky's poetry of the mid-1920s a deeply complex aesthetic confrontation with politics, where the "freeing" of the word—Shlonsky's mantra since 1923—becomes not a static description of a mode of writing, but something part of a difficult dialectical process of negotiating that old divide between subject and object, that is, between the settler working the land and the land itself, all the while mediated through writing. While Katznelson certainly saw that connection as mediated and indeed facilitated by the political party—and specifically within the party's journalistic organ, *Davar*—Shlonsky demanded a purer immediacy in the encounter with Palestine, one that would be completely constitutive of both the settler and the land. In this way, poetry for him became the site of the fundamental work of the entire political movement.

"Here Is My Land"

What Shlonsky had in mind for a poetry of new Jewish identity tied to the land begins with raw form, which is then defined and inflected through the artistic vision of the speaker himself. "Here is my land, a wild body," Shlonsky writes at the commencement of the cycle of poems "Gilboa" from the mid-1920s, a cycle whose references to settlement work and the Jezreel specifically invoke images of both Jew and soil. Already in this first line, Shlonsky constitutes place in the utterance of the poet. "Here is my land" Shlonsky proclaims, opening "Gilboa" with an exclamation of possession. He continues with "a wild body," a phrase that goes further and identifies the land with the physical image of the new Jew, land metaphorized as body in a dialectical understanding between speaker and the object of possession. The wildness—the inverse of all that was left behind in history, left behind in civilized Europe—is Shlonsky's consistent trope for the land ("wild" and "long-haired," he will still write of it in 1947, more than two decades later),[22] and while provoking the opposition between tame and untamed—a category that also went by other names, good/bad, healthy/malarial—the wild land resonates too with sexual energy: the body of the land, wild, feminine, and needing to be tamed.

But if "wild" thus names some primal, free state of being, a way to connect to the land within the type of discursive freedom the poet would seek, it also marks the beginning of the aesthetic struggle to constitute that body as the land. Possession, we might say, is not enough, especially with the realization that ownership requires a negotiation through the legal texts of the tradition. Shlonsky's speaker might then call the land his own and begin to metaphorize land as body, but that figuration also outlines the extent of the distance—both political and literary—embodied in that sort of trope. Possession thus is merely Shlonsky's starting point, the beginning of a more important effort to transform a legal trope into a constitutive immediacy between body and land where instead of any sense of object ownership (and the implications this type of ownership would have for a parallel alienation from place), metaphor might work itself into synesthesia where the one (body or land) necessarily implies and indeed *produces* the other. In that way, the aesthetic struggle is over making literature *act* in the land.

In pursuit of that goal, the title of this initial poem in "Gilboa," "Hineh" (Here Is), already disavows description in favor of presenting some sort of artistic consciousness. The title directs attention toward the voice of the poet rather than any mimetic object or representation of the land. But then—as perhaps a way to highlight how even poetics will not suffice in presenting the land as it is, or as it must be, that is, as the product of Jewish consciousness—the first two stanzas outline the legal terms and textual questions that need resolution before immediacy in the soil can be attained:

הִנֵּה אַרְצִי גְּוִיַּת-פֶּרֶא.
עוֹר כִּקְלָף לָהּ, קְלָף לַתּוֹרָה.
וּבְחֶרֶט-עַד מְחֻקֶּה דְבַר אֱלֹהֶיהָ
עַל הַקְּלָף.

מִי הַפֶּרֶא אֲשֶׁר יוּכַל קְרֹא הַמְּגִלָּה
שֶׁלַּבְּרֵאשִׁית?
וּמִי יִזְכֶּה לַעֲטֹף טַלִּית פֹּה
וְלַעֲלוֹת לַתּוֹרָה?

Here is my land, a wild body.
Skin of parchment she has, the parchment of the Torah.
And with an eternal pen the word of her god is marked
On the parchment.

Who is the wild one who can read the scroll
That belongs to Genesis?
And who will be able to wrap a *talit* here
And rise to the Torah?[23]

The possession of language and discourse—of writing on the parchment of the land, of reading the scroll that is the wild body—forms an integral part of the entire settlement project. The battle to sever the past (of the text, of the diaspora) from a modern consciousness is laid out right here at the beginning. These are problematic lines and confusing in how they seem to run counter to the prescriptive poetics Shlonsky himself outlined in the pages of *Hedim* in 1923 where he speaks of the "freedom of the word." The repeated references to the religious tradition mitigate such a modernist surrender to immediacy. But in that, this first poem in a book about settlement in the Jezreel clues us into the difficult process ahead, the difficulty both of actually settling the land and of creating that necessary aesthetic figuration of it in the face of a tradition—especially a *Hebrew* tradition—that would a priori load the language's signifiers with an entire history. The struggle, then, for freedom takes on its own dialectical character of freeing the very idea from its own prehistory.

In this, it is not so much that these metaphors of *talit* and Torah (which will expand later to include *tfilin* and the early morning prayer, *shaḥarit*) define the land, as that these figures and the poet's struggle with them are indispensable to a *process* of defining the land as both essentially Jewish and essentially modern. And one poem will certainly not suffice to answer these questions. The involvement of soil and nature in reading and writing—of who will decipher and act on the land—begins the course of a poetic structure that runs throughout "Gilboa," encompassing the volume's best-known cycle, "Amal" (Labor), and reaching a climax in the parallel cycle of poems, "Adamah" (Soil). Genesis ("Who is the wild one who can read the scroll / That belongs to Genesis?"),[24] as both idea and text, is the disputed ground in this literature: who will finally prevail in uttering and thus creating this land? Who will own the right and primacy to create the land through a performative discursive act? In the long arc of both of these cycles of poems, Shlonsky's goal becomes clear: to reverse natural syntax and transform the land from object, and work from represented action, and make them into the product of the very utterance of the speaker himself, where writing *becomes* the work of making the land.

This first poem, "Hineh," already moves in that direction by destabilizing the land as object, first through metaphor and then by defining it through action:

סִרְקוּ סָרוֹק, הַחַמְשִׁינִים, הַקָּרַחַת בְּגָלִילִי,
אָנוּ נַדְשִׁיא מָחָר דֶּשֶׁא,
יָהּ-חַי-לִי-לִי
עֲמַלִי.

Comb, desert winds, my bald Galilee
We will plant a lawn tomorrow
Ya-ḥai-li-li
My labor.[25]

This final stanza in the introductory poem begins the transformation that the poems of "Labor" and "Soil" will enact by breaking down both text and meaning in poetic form. Here, as the lines contract, they lead into a simplistic rhyme scheme and the phatic reflective utterance of the final word: *amali* (my labor). Action now defines the speaker, as opposed to the metaphorical associations of the previous stanzas that equated various objects with the position of the subject: camels, milk, ivory. Central to this entire process of disintegration of discourse is the futurist fragmentation of language into phonemes. Words themselves lose their significance and contract into mere sonic games within the lines of the poem: *sirku sarok, nadshi maḥar deshe.* Historically, Hebrew has always favored alliteration and Shlonsky's *sirku sarok* follows and competes with a tradition tracing as far back as Genesis's *lekh lekha.* Here, however, the tonal playfulness of the words and the breakdown of meaning have a specific purpose and point directly to the creative power of the speaker. Just before the invocation of action in *amali,* the sound fragments and their repetitions culminate in the near-nonsense word *ya-ḥai-li-li,* an inversion of *hallelujah,* which directs our attention specifically to the speaker and not at God.[26] The strategy of Genesis is sustained; the idea here is competition over the process of creation and production on the level of both world and word. But the land's author becomes the poet himself, the one who can create the language that will speak this place, *ya-ḥai-li-li.*

All the language games accomplish that same goal, both by mixing body and land ("comb . . . my bald Galilee") and by the way neologism reiterates the speaker-poet's primacy. Phonetic wordplay reflects the speaker precisely because of its nonsense, which lifts the word out of the transparent syntax of a signifying rhetoric. Rather, action in the land (which is the same as action in the text) reflects the speaker's presence there, and the poet's ability to express himself drives this poem and indeed sets the ground for the next cycle, "Labor" (Amal), itself a lengthy exposition and elaboration of this final word, *amali,* and the significance that action and intention in the land (and in the poem) will have for defining the identity of the poetic speaker.

"Labor"

The movement from linguistic figuration ("here is my land") to the textual substantiation of action ("my labor") begins to bring speaker and land close, but both entities, land and speaker, are still contained within the words that represent them, nouns specifically whose *thing*-ness in Hebrew is reflected through the body: the *shem-etsem* of the noun. Thus "Labor" as poetic cycle and "my labor" as a collapsing of action and thing only constitute an intermediate move: the new poetic figures that Shlonsky uses do reformulate the relation between subject and object, but Shlonsky already indicates their limitations to move past a traditional discursive relationship of static objects. Land and man regain their reciprocal relation to one another, but only as instances of the abstraction named in the "body" of the noun object, namely, "my labor." Metaphors of land—a "wild body," a combed-over Galilee—do work to bring Jew and Palestine together, but it happens only within the physical world of objects. This transformation is certainly significant in and of itself, especially since Shlonsky articulates and elaborates that connection at length, striving to move beyond the simple reflection of nature and the body:

הוֹ זֵעָה!
הוֹ אֶגְלֵי בְּרָכָה הַיּוֹרְדִים מִמִּצְחִי הַגָּבֹהַּ
כַּטַּל מִשָּׁמַיִם טְהוֹרִים.

הִנֵּה בְּשָׂרִי צַח וְשָׂעִיר,
וְהַשֵּׂעָר דֶּשֶׁא שָׁחוֹר.
הוֹ זֵעָה, זֵעָה מְלוּחָה,
הַטְלִילִי נָא אֶת בְּשָׂרִי כִּשְׂדֵה שַׁחֲרִית סָמָר.
הַלְלוּיָהּ!

O sweat!
O blessed drops descending from my high forehead
Like dew from a pure heaven.

Here is my fresh and hairy flesh,
And my hair is a black lawn.
O sweat, salty sweat,
Please bedew my flesh like a bristly field at dawn.
Hallelujah![27]

The drops of sweat that are like dew—a romantic figuration of metaphoric relations between objects—are transformed into an action of bedewing the body. The relationship of object to object is, then, a transformative act: the noun "dew" becomes the verb "to bedew," denying any syntactic separation between the body and nature. Objects are not *like* other objects. Instead, they begin to act upon and define each other. Thus, the metaphor of the body presumes nothing, not even the existence of the body, which emanates and only finds expression in nature. In fact, the metaphor redoubles on itself and each side significantly inflects and defines the other. This is Shlonsky's modernist triumph where no figure is static. For him, nature labors upon (and thus builds) the body, just as the body labors upon (and thus builds) the land. Labor, as the pivot between both entities, renders the one in terms of the other, but only by subordinating both to a newly transcendental principle, labor itself. In this way, work (and action) carves out a space for the reinversion and reintroduction of the phatic exclamation "Hallelujah," which returns in its original form, inscribed now within this new field of transcendent meaning.

The poem cycle "Labor" is thus aptly titled, not because the poem describes labor as an idea. Rather, as action, labor enables language to take on meaning as it connects subject and object. The mutual identification of Jew and land erects the universal equivalence of labor, just as laboring on the soil constitutes this relationship. In this way, any identification with Palestine must come about through action in nature. However, Shlonsky's process does not end here. While transformation of the environment creates subjectivity, it does so only as the object of that abstraction, defined by it and relegated to the actions it prescribes. Already we can see the breakdown of the logic of labor—even as it is being articulated—and why Shlonsky will not end things here in this cycle. The "I" that is also "labor" ("*Ani—he-amal,*" Shlonsky proclaims at the very end of this poem, trying to phatically instantiate this new entity) shows the poet, like an actor playing Hamlet or King Lear,[28] only realizing a character in the performance of labor. The question then becomes how to reemphasize the "I" of the speaker, how to reconstitute a subject out of this abstract equivalence of acting upon land and body.

The process of reconstituting the subject as a creative entity in the environment (and not just as an actor subordinate to the master-script of labor) begins with the apostrophe of the vocal address ("O sweat!"), the exclamation that announces the disembodied voice. In the voice we hear the attempt to transcend the rhetorical confines of the body-land equivalence in the object. In this poem, those steps are still tentative, but the apostrophe already hints at a metatextual solution to a textual problem. The "Here is" and the "O!"—particles in a poetic discourse, standing almost outside of grammar—point back toward the speaker's voice, heightening and announcing its presence. The apostrophic "O!" opens up a metapoetic space, just as the body blurs any strict grammatical function as object or subject and becomes the very action at the heart of this relationship. In the poem "Labor," just as Shlonsky defines work as a prism blending the first-person subject and the land, he significantly moves as well toward pure apostrophe:

רִתְמוּ הַמִּדְבָּרִיּוֹת!
וּכְמוֹשְׁכוֹת מַתְּחוּ כְּבִישִׁים!
אֲנִי יוֹשֵׁב עַל הַדּוּכָן!
אֲנִי – הֶעָמָל!

Harness the wilderness!
And like reins stretch roads!
I am sitting on the dais!
I—labor![29]

What moves from apostrophe to the product of labor ("O sweat!"), to an address to the object of action ("Harness the wilderness!"), ends in an attempt to equate action with the subject: "I—labor!" The subject has collapsed into action and intention where the transformation of the environment is meant to create subjectivity and not merely reflect subjective action. I—labor is a single entity unencumbered by a discourse of equivalence or metaphor; it pronounces the collapse of subject and predicate (as Ben-Gurion had proposed) and the displacement of bodily objects (sweat, hair, and the like). Finally free of any mediation through objects, I—labor sits on the dais, producer of action and creator of environmental transformation.

The end of this third poem in the cycle on labor would thus seem to reach apotheosis in this articulation of a new entity—the I—labor that collapses distinctions between the poetic "I" and the abstraction of labor itself. And if we skip the often anthologized fourth poem of the cycle and move directly to Shlonsky's next major cycle, "Soil," we could easily see how he continues to work out this large aesthetic-political narrative that moves from object through action to arrive at a redefinition of a new Zionist subject for both the land and the Jew. But how then to read the fourth poem, the most famous of Shlonsky's entire large cycle "Gilboa"?

The problem of the fourth poem is not just that it seems to repudiate all the work that had pushed Shlonsky's aesthetics toward the unification of subject and action. Indeed, it does that. But by reintroducing the tradition through the metaphors of *talit* and *tfilin*, the fourth poem would seem to bring us back to the very beginning of this poetic struggle as if nothing had happened in the interim. Syntactic regularity creeps back in, apostrophe is purged past the opening line, and now tradition itself, through metaphors drawn from religious symbols, lends meaning to the poetic language.

הַלְבִּישִׁינִי, אִמָּא כְּשֵׁרָה, כְּתֹנֶת-פַּסִּים לְתִפְאֶרֶת
וְעִם שַׁחֲרִית הוֹבִילִינִי אֱלֵי עָמָל.

עוֹטְפָה אַרְצִי אוֹר כַּטַּלִּית.

Dress me, pure mother, in a striped tunic of splendor
And with dawn bring me to my work.

Wrap my land in light like a talit.[30]

The poem invokes an entirely different and radically conservative type of meaning, even if the tradition is recontextualized within the settler milieu where *tfilin* signifies the work crews of the Gdud. The images of the poem certainly deploy traditional symbols within a radical Labor

Zionist setting, but the poetics here do not successfully challenge the type of representational malaise that Shlonsky seemed to have been working against. On the other hand, in a consciousness raised and elevated by the previous poems in the cycle, can't we now gaze on the empty signifiers of the tradition, the symbols and metaphors and intertextual allusions that pronounce a sentimentality completely void of any significance? Within the context of the larger structure in this book of poems, shouldn't we better read the language of the poem as explaining that the tradition can now itself be finally purged, its symbols recast within the requirements of a labor that would transform the land? Or rather, does the conservatism of this poem admit that the work of discursive challenge and transformation is not over, that the project of this cycle cannot rest on the concept of work as a static signifier?

וּבָעֶרֶב בֵּין הַשְּׁמָשׁוֹת יָשׁוּב אַבָּא מִסִּבְלוֹתָיו
וְכִתְפִלָּה יִלְחַשׁ נַחַת:
הֲבֵן יַקִּיר לִי אַבְרָהָם,
עוֹר וְגִידִים וַעֲצָמוֹת.
הַלְלוּיָהּ.

And in the evening father will return from his toils
And like a prayer he will whisper contented:
My dear son Avraham,
Skin and veins and bones.
Hallelujah.

As a serious moment in Shlonsky's large politico-aesthetic narrative of subject transformation, labor as idea cannot really change the textual tradition that lends meaning to the work in the fields. Thus, the finale of this intermediate cycle of poems fails to rise above the textuality of its own abstractions, and that is certainly the point. Language might be reinterpreted to infuse new meanings into old tired signifiers now dependent on settlement itself for significance. But lost in that is the speaker, who remains the actor in the drama, now not acting out the script of a metapoetic voice, but inscribed within the drama of the intertexts themselves, subordinate to the demands of meaning and the tradition, and in the end, only skin and bones after the work he performs.

The poet, Leah Goldberg, one of a later poetic triumvirate with Shlonsky and Natan Alterman, and herself a professor of literature at the Hebrew University of Jerusalem, outlined a convincing reading of this poem, but a reading that inadvertently highlights the poem's inability to challenge the tradition that it would oppose.[31] For Goldberg, poetic symbols are freely associated, the cultural context of the poem no wider than the textual religious tradition it evokes. In that, Goldberg's analysis is a strange reading, taking the poem out of the context of the cycle by analyzing it first among the four, divorcing it from the crisis of subjectivity toward which the cycle builds.[32]

What Goldberg misses—and what makes this last poem point straight toward the next cycle, "Soil"—is how Shlonsky's attempt to write a synesthesia between the "I" and nature could not end with the static entity I—labor because of how subjectivity would then always be subordinate to the abstracted action of the predicate. The title "Labor" and the equivalence of I—labor certainly begin to destabilize the object relations of body-nature, but only by replacing them with this new abstraction. The fourth poem, which reintroduces the questions of "Hineh" into the foreground of the poetic narration, marks both an interim triumph and failure. In the context of the entire cycle we can certainly read the intertextual allusions as divested of their usual power to signify. *Tfilin* and *talit* less project meaning than gain it from this new entity of labor. Within a certain sarcasm and irony, which go unaccounted for in Goldberg's reading,[33] the newly paved roads that are straps of *tfilin* and the romanticism of the light of the Middle East wrapping the land like a *talit* go to show the distance traveled from these figures and their power to define meaning within the Jewish tradition.

On the other hand, the "I" which had so forcefully and strenuously proclaimed itself free through the apostrophe that announced "here is"—"here is" the land *and* the "I"—is finally subsumed formally within a Hebrew of an antiquated morphology. Action completely subsumes the subject as perhaps only Hebrew can make happen textually: the two verbs that define the opening and closing stanzas of this final poem—"dress me" and "bring me"[34]—graphically and morphologically encompass the speaker, who retreats textually within the very body of the verbs. Unlike their English translations, the Hebrew verbs, *halbishini* and *hovilini*, embody the "I" within the word that would represent action. The cycle, then, might arrive at some new formulation of the "I" and the land, whose relations are now blurred and significantly indistinct. But the new Jewish subject has yet to gain its full independent articulation as producer of the land through writing.

The Natural Voice of the Poet

In the wake of the failed exclamatory strategy ("I—labor!") to lay claim to subjectivity, Shlonsky moves to the poem cycle "Soil" by articulating a subjectivism premised upon consciousness and not labor. This notion is a striking performance of the paradox already encountered in malaria where the subject emerges from a reconciliation of an idealist consciousness and the very materiality of the soil. "Soil" articulates the materiality of both by, in effect, reinventing language itself. If I—labor could only approximate some new entity and imperfectly render its articulation in language, then language itself now becomes the object of change and manipulation with an intensity far greater than Shlonsky's earlier experiments at neologism. In what seems a direct response to the fourth poem of "Labor" and the problem of subjectivity embodied by *halbishini* and *hovilini*, in the opening stanza of "Soil" verbs and their morphologies tell a new tale of a modernist consciousness tied to the earth and free of any discursive bonds.

כָּל הַלַּיְלָה נָדְדָה שְׁנַת הָרוּחַ
וַיְיַלֵּל.
חֲלוֹמוֹת רָעִים בִּעֲתוּהוּ:
כִּי יָדַע
אֲשֶׁר אָנֹכִי עֵר.

אָנֹכִי עֵר
כִּבְקֶדֶם אֱלֹהִים עַל פְּנֵי הַמָּיִם:
בְּרֵאשִׁית!
וְצַר לִי,
צַר לִי עַל כָּל כּוֹכָב וְכָל מַזָּל:
רַק חִפּוּשִׁיּוֹת קְטַנּוֹת הֵן,
הָרוֹמְשׂוֹת בְּתוֹךְ דָּמִי,
הַלְלוּיָהּ.

All night the wind lay awake
And howled.
Bad dreams frightened him:
Because he knew
That I am conscious.

I am conscious
Like from before God on the surface of the water:
In the beginning!
And I am sorry
I am sorry for every star and every constellation.
They are like little beetles,
That course within my blood,
Hallelujah.[35]

Human consciousness competes with God in a contest over ontological primacy played out on the level of the word. These stanzas represent finally the ultimate struggle for the "freedom of the word," that is, a way to wrest poetry and creativity from the confines of external meaning and return it to the inheritors of the land. When God enters explicitly in the second stanza, the speaker is already a presence, not just in the way that "wind" (which means also "spirit" and "God" himself) stands in opposition to the consciousness of the speaker, but in the very language of the stanza, which sets the stage for competition. Indeed, language pits man directly against God. The enjambed second line produces an aspectual form of the verb, a decidedly biblical form that reflects on God as the "howler" and begins a deflation of metaphysical meaning in the poetic language. The morphology of the predicate in the third line, which, like *halbishini* and *hovilini*, archaically embeds both verb and object in a single word, stands in sharp contrast to the naked—modernist, ornamentless—verb of the fourth. Competition still exists within the representation of action, that is, in the poetic form of the verb, but it now implies a consciousness existing prior to and behind action, not subsumed within it.

From the word, competition with the Divine envelopes the power of expression itself. In the second stanza, the speaker declares that what ties his body to nature materially is no longer what binds them together significantly. Instead, the consciousness that makes God shudder not only antedates the Bible and the textual tradition but serves as the central focus of the animated world. In this celebration of self, the speaker declares: "I who am raised by the songs in the book of Psalms, / Who is called: the world."[36] Psalms acts in concert with Genesis to show that beyond the competition over the possession of the utterance, the "freedom of the word" resides in the consciousness that controls the poem. Psalms, we should remember, are composed texts of the Bible and present an author other than God. In this, the authority of creation, namely, the creation of the word that also instantiates the world (the very question from "Hineh": "who is wild enough to read the parchment?") keeps returning in the stanza through the exploration of an independent subjective voice. Indeed, an answer to the original question of reading and writing presents itself in a consciousness antecedent to Genesis, a voice whose utterance is not only creative but which in fact defines the world. Consciousness competes with God, and now nature reflects that consciousness, both as its creation and its creator. Thus the world of Shlonsky's speaker is antediluvian and perhaps even pre-linguistic in how the speaker prefigures any social construction, any transcendent social organization. The speaker exists *before* Genesis, before "in the beginning" (*bereshit*).

This notion of individual consciousness as identified with fundamental social and natural structures definitely constitutes the recuperative side of the modernist project, what Trotsky called at roughly the same time a recognition of the coincidence of the self with history, although here environment and nature would substitute for history.[37] As a modernist, Trotsky needed to avoid the determinism of a romantic dialectic by melding that dialectic with a Bolshevik consciousness. This did not deny the mechanisms of history but placed them at the disposal of those who could identify with them. This is the same type of dialectical consciousness that Shlonsky attempts to perform in poetry as he moves away from the romanticism of Bialik and also away from the modernism of

European urban alienation in the Hebrew poetry of poets like Avraham Ben-Yitzhak and David Fogel.[38] Shlonsky avoids both by rejecting the distance of Bialik's relationship to nature, on the one hand, and Fogel's dispersed subjectivity, on the other. Instead, Shlonsky focuses completely on a self-articulated subject; the repeated incantations of *anokhi* (I) drone in our ears as a physical substantiation of the speaker in nature. Around this "I" then stands an expressively free nature, ready to be formed and created, in contrast to the civilized and designed gardens of the bourgeoisie. The raw creative potential of wildness is defined by ridiculing external bourgeois form, which opposes the true expressive freedom of nature:

וְאַתֶּן, בֻּבּוֹת-פְּרָחִים,
מַה כְּעַרְתֶּן בַּעֲרוּגוֹת גַּנֵּי-בִּיתָן וַעֲצִיצִים וְאַרְמוֹנוֹת!
אִתְּכֶן יִשְׁאַג לִבִּי מֵחַלּוֹנוֹת-הָרַאֲוָה:
עַל אֲדָמָה.
עַל מִדְבָּר.

And you, flower puppets,
How ugly you are in rows of house flowers!
With you my heart will roar from the display windows:
On soil.
On desert.[39]

In contrast, within "Soil," Shlonsky frames the entirety of the represented universe within the unity of *anokhi* (I) and *adamah* (soil/earth), the first and last poems of the cycle. In between, from primordial physicality and enlightened consciousness—*ani er* (I am conscious)—the speaker begins to figure nature, and in so doing comes to discover himself. But if this then implies a decadence in the poetry—a move toward a solipsism that retreats into an allegory of man as universe—the poem remains sensitive to precisely this issue as well. Thus, what emanates from this poem is neither allegory nor mimesis; neither man nor nature is quite independent but rather, as primitive prearticulate entities, they become whole through poetic discourse itself. Before the materiality of the body comes to define the speaker, both nature and speaker are transforming into a primordial state, evolving into a *de*volved condition of wildness:

הַצְמִיחִינִי אֶת צִפָּרְנֵי-פֶּרֶא-פֶּרֶא,
וְעָרֵל בְּשָׂרִי מֵרְגָבַיִךְ וּמִדִּשְׁנֵךְ,
כְּחָרוּל עֶרֶל-שְׂאַר וּפֶרֶא-קוֹצִים.

Grow my nails wild-wild,
And would my flesh become uncircumcised from your dirt and your dung,
Like a bramble of unpruned growth and wild-thorned.

The meaning of the word *aral* slides between uncircumcised and unpruned to characterize both man and nature as inseparable and striving for the same state of wild symbiotic existence. The precircumcised/prepruned body radiates creative power because it has yet to be touched by culture. The rejection of stars and constellations in the poem works the same way because they are bound within the discursive limits of a preset arrangement.[40] Instead, authentic articulation derives from a closeness to nature where human expression is caught up within the creation of nature itself:

אֲדָמָה!
הִנֵּה שָׂרִיתִי עִם אֱלֹהִים
וְעִם אֲנָשִׁים,
וָאֱהִי אָדָם.
אֲנִי – הַבָּשָׂר.
וְאַתְּ – אֲדָמָה.
וּמִי כָּמוֹנוּ יוֹדְעֵי-לֶדֶת!

Soil!
Here I have struggled with God
And with people [*anashim*]
And I became a man [*adam*].
I—the flesh.
And you—soil [*adamah*].
And who is like us knowers-of-birth![41]

Birth—the very moment of creation and production—becomes the sought-after immediacy where man and nature are bound in a similar fate. The complementary sexual imagery is unmistakable in how flesh and soil form a complete dialectic, coming together through the knowledge of synthesis. Shlonsky's move is regressive and antibourgeois by pushing man from social organization under God's dominion (*anashim*) in order to rediscover an entity (*adam*) that will be identifiable with soil (*adamah*). By rediscovering these primordial states—*adam* and *adamah*/flesh and soil—the dialectic moves to synthesis in the very knowledge of production, creativity, and birth, where the poet, and poetry, becomes the instantiation of that unity.

"דָּבָר – אָמְרוּ – הִנֵּה הָאָדָם!"
הֲיֵּדְעוּ יָדוֹעַ שַׁאֲגַת בְּרֵאשִׁית:
– שֶׁמֶשׁ!
– מַיִם!
– אֲדָמָה!
וְהֱיוֹת כָּל מִלָּה
כַּאֲבָנִים אֲשֶׁר יִרְמֶה צַיַּד-מַמּוּתָה פֶּרֶא
וְגִדְיֵי אוֹמֵר לָכֶם:
"הָאָדָם הוּא לֶדֶת."

"Speak"—they said—"here is man!"
Who knows the knowledge of roaring Genesis:
—Sun!
—Water!
—Soil!
And the being of every word
Is like stones cast by the hunter of the wild mammoth
And my goat-kid says to you:
"Man is birth [also: becoming]."[42]

In the poem, textuality itself must be freed of any preexisting discursive forms. But the need to create a productive discourse goes further. It is the power of the voice—and really nothing else—that finally makes man a producer, recreating Genesis not just through the apostrophic speech act that names and in so doing, as Walter Benjamin points out, creates the definition that would then organize and discipline knowledge.[43] Shlonsky's voice, in fact, does much more, performing a natural alchemy: the phatic exclamations of sun, soil, and water constitute a recipe of fecundity and production, an agricultural speech act that turns voice into the maker of the natural realm. This, then, points beyond allegory and language as a stand-in for a conceptualized nature. Rather, the alchemy of these speech acts is the alchemy that transforms voice *into* nature, in an immediacy that follows the cycle of poems, from "I" to "Soil," flowing through the life cycle of the four seasons as well. The poetic journey mimics both the natural course of seasons—here in the binary oppositions of heat and rain, death and rejuvenation that are specific to the Middle East—and the revitalization of man, or specifically the Jew, who now lives in touch with the soil.

The poet's voice finally connects subject and nature, bypassing the discursive limitations of grammar and objectified rhetoric. This is a funny gig for a poet, who denies the very forms of poetry and transgresses written discourse to avoid the essence of what the poet is ostensibly trying to achieve: an articulation of meaning. The same thing was true of the Russians like Mayakovsky who scoffed at standard syntax and vocabulary in order to focus on individual consciousness. But in the national program that was Shlonsky's—this was, after all, a cycle of poetry entitled "Gilboa," pointing straight to the Jezreel and the pioneering activities of the emerging nation—the breaking of rules and the development of a maximalist poetics could only reflect straight back at the speaker not as an individual but as a national entity who returns to a specific place. Shlonsky, in approaching solipsism, does not advance consciousness quite so much as he advances the voice of the phatic utterance, which cannot be dissociated from or appropriated by an abstraction like labor. Instead, in "Soil," Genesis serves as the model for an alchemy that conjoins voice with nature and soil, suggesting that the more the medium's conventions are abandoned—syntax and the like—the stronger the mutual predication of man and nature, those "knowers-of-birth" (*yod'ei-ledet*).

Thus, for Shlonsky, the expressive dimension of language creates the world. In poetry's acoustic properties, the voice of the poet becomes constitutive of the natural realm of the country. Sun, soil, water do not describe or represent place. Rather, they *become* that place, rising above the limitations of a textual order that would only allow naming (of objects and places) as the essential character of texts. This strategy is not merely a modernist melding of form and content—the newness of syntax and vocabulary allegorically relating a mimetic content of the rejuvenated landscape—but the bypassing of the form-content nexus altogether.

The Limits of Music

The idea of voice as a metatextual element, that is, the notion that expression (and performance) has its own significance independent of content and form, has been a vital idea in music for several years, certainly since the publication of Carolyn Abbate's work on opera: "In an effort to go beyond words and syntax, voice in music . . . can be understood in larger senses as the power of sonority, as a presence or resonating intelligence."[44] But while the antimimesis of music pushes Abbate to search for a narration that will issue ontologically from the surface of musical discourse and especially from the moment of musical performance, Shlonsky's phatic voice vies with a medium that would signify meanings outside of what the poet might intend. The natural voice of the poet thus flows from the text, from the sonorities that would issue only from the poet and define the poem as an articulation of nature and man's place within the specific reality of Palestine. This is a strong and new idea for a Zionist articulation of nature, and the triumph of Shlonsky's expression of the closeness between man and nature is only tempered by the instrumentality he projects onto nature. After all, his project is a nationalist one of transformation and control. The land might reflect and mutually constitute the creative will of the poet-settler, but only insofar as both would then be changed, improved, and re-formed.

וְהָאֲדָמָה – פְּסַנְתֵּר-אֲדִּירִים:
מְנַעַנְעָיו – אֶלֶף, אֶלֶף.
מִזְמוֹרָיו – רְבָבָה, רְבָבָה.
אַךְ בְּפָרְטִי עָלֶיהָ בְּאֶצְבְּעוֹת רַגְלֵי הַיְחֵפָה,
וְחָבְרוּ הַמִּזְמוֹרִים יָחַד:
אֲנֹכִי.

And the soil—a great piano:
Its keys—thousand, thousand.

Its melodies—tens of thousands.
But in my wandering upon her with the toes of my feet,
And bound together in melodies:
I[45]

In the piano that is to be played, the earth that must be walked over, Shlonsky cannot erase completely the instrumental function of nature for man, the way that nature, both in its physical presence and in its allegorical discursive form, projects onto man the ability of articulation. In this, the ugliness of the arranged bourgeois flowers are only ugly because they participate in a discourse that does not coincide with the speaker, one that is not instrumental to his notions of fecundity and immediacy. Music, with its apparent lack of representation and its seeming freedom from social discourse, represents a Schopenhauerian source to immediate transcendence.[46] But the inability to see music's discursive functions and artifice reveals the very limits of music as a successful national allegory. The figure of performing music upon the soil only reinforces a subjectivity that would mold and transform the environment in the name of closeness to it. Instrumentality discloses just how much Shlonsky's strategy for subjectivity cannot veil its reliance on a set of assumptions at odds with what the poems are trying to perform.

Throughout all of these poems, the speaker works to strengthen his own materiality and physical presence by drawing an ever smaller separation between himself and nature. In the phatic announcement of the self, which builds to a new type of spiritual ecstasy, knowledge is replaced by a coincidence of feeling and creative energy. But materiality does not involve the complete loss of subjective control and, in the end, this material closeness to nature also breeds self-knowledge and enlightenment, as the cycle ends with an expression of the definite centrality of the speaker:

וָאָבִין:
אָנֹכִי הַנַּעֲלֶה בְּמִזְמוֹרֵי סֵפֶר-הַתְּהִלִּים
שֶׁקֹּרָא לוֹ: תֵּבֵל.
וּבְשָׂרִי – הֵיכַל אֱלֹהִים
עִם כָּל הַבְּהֵמָה אֲשֶׁר תִּגְּעֶה פֹּה אֶל נֹכַח הַשָּׁמָיִם.

I understood:
I the exalted by the melodies of the book of Psalms
Who am called: world.
And my flesh—a theater of God
With every beast that touched the presence of heaven.[47]

This final move reintroduces a rationalist consciousness and then attempts to reconcile a philosophical break between the subjective ecstasy of the "I" in nature and the objective materialism of an external reality in the land.

This synthesis between material primordial being and enlightened modern subject ultimately centers singularly on the consciousness and body of the speaker. *Adamah* and *adam* might be parallel producers within the world but one cannot be both material object and projecting subject, all the while maintaining a unity with nature. Rather than sink into the lost rapport of Bialik's romantic separation from and desire for the natural environment, Shlonsky's speaker, in the end, asserts the modernist position of projector, where *adamah* becomes the tool for the expressive powers and desires of a centralized "I." Nature is still controlled, organized, and discursively figured, even if the ideology of redemption has fantasized an environmental unity between man and soil.

The lessons of subjective consciousness for a politics of natural inclusion in Palestine were not lost on a younger generation of ideologues rising in the Labor Zionist ranks during the late 1920s. Ḥayim Arlosoroff, generally considered the most brilliant of this generation, echoes Shlonsky's appeal to a consciousness that would appropriate the natural essence of the country as the solution to the debates within the labor movement leading up to the final unification of parties in the early 1930s. Writing of working-class consciousness in Zionist society, Arlosoroff posits its strong presence in Palestine, arguing that it must become commensurate to the conditions of the place:

> Marx, in his book *The Eighteenth Brumaire*, points to the fact that the peasants, who composed the majority of the population in France in the period of Napoleon III's war, were a crystallized class from the objective economic point of view, but lacked any consciousness of this. They composed a class in itself, but not for itself. It is the opposite with us. The workers of the Land of Israel became a class in its own eyes before they developed into a class in itself. This abyss between reality and consciousness would have been impossible if our ideology had developed solely in the conditions of the reality of the Land of Israel.[48]

Arlosoroff not only inverts the dialectic of class and consciousness, but significantly mediates it through environment, both by asserting an appropriate consciousness based on the natural attributes of place (agrarian economics in Palestine) and by claiming that a Jewish proletarian consciousness had to precede the encounter with the land.

The abyss that Arlosoroff writes about between "reality" and "consciousness" is what Shlonsky strove to traverse in order to create a subjectivity appropriate to the place, and one that would, in the end, constitute that place. Shlonsky's failure lay in his faith that that voice was primary, that reality was a static condition, not contingent on the very dialectics he sought to bridge. Shlonsky failed finally to understand the true dialectical character of the relationship he was describing, where the reality of the place—nature in Palestine—did not stand still against the subjective claims of this new class of Jewish workers. For Shlonsky, that meant ignoring anything other than the projection of the masculine Jewish subject: women, Arabs, the environment as an uncontingent space.[49]

Ironically, Shlonsky the political provocateur and poetic rebel came to articulate precisely the politics he would disdain. Not only would Shlonsky the poet come to represent a normative Labor Zionism during the 1930s and 1940s, but that very normativity, we might claim, emanated from the blindness of a poetics that hid instrumentality in the environment behind an ideological expression of freely associating with nature.

However, before this type of poetic of a mutually constitutive nature and Jew could gain complete hegemony throughout the Zionist political spectrum in the mid-1930s—ushered in more by the aesthetic triumphs of Shlonsky's immediate successor, Natan Alterman, than by Shlonsky himself—those left out of this aesthetic, namely, Arabs and an uncontingent notion of the environment, came together in a violent spasm in 1929. The Wailing Wall riots of that August and the aesthetic reconfiguration of nature that they entailed significantly deflected Zionist politics and led to an alternate poetic model of nature, as we will see in the next chapter.

Chapter 4

The Landscape of a Zionist Orient

Avraham Shlonsky's strategy of poetically announcing Jewish identity in nature through the phatic declaration of the new Zionist citizen could not survive the upheaval of the Wailing Wall riots of August 1929. After all, Shlonsky's ideas of what constituted a new Jewish "I" (*anokhi*) relied upon an image of the land as primordially unformed, politically unencumbered, and free to be phatically possessed. The riots of 1929, of all their impact on Palestine and the future of Jewish settlement, were a definitive reminder that this constructivist image of an empty landscape coupled to a politically unmediated Jewish subject did not coincide with any real situation on the ground.

The lesson did not go unheeded. After August of that year, Zionist politics and aesthetics would never again take for granted a natural landscape that easily yielded to the free imaginings of the Zionist subject. Rather, the riots introduced competition over land resources, and the successive British investigations into the violence forced the Zionist leadership in Palestine and abroad to develop with a certain level of detachment a defense of settlement that scientifically analyzed and scrutinized place as a dispassionate object. If constructivist poetics represented some sort of subjective response to the land, where the "I" and the land would each be formed by self-expression, then the riots ushered in an era of objectivist defenses of the Jews' very presence in Palestine. Nature and the land would now be the object of direct Jewish action upon it, an object of reflection, to be sure, but yet an object that would reflect Zionist belonging only in how the Jew might act upon it.

Zionist politics were no less affected by the riots than were aesthetics. But politics found a renewed vigor in its reaction to violence, in contradistinction to the crisis that ensued for aesthetics. As a political entity, the Yishuv was particularly proud of how Jewish militias banded together to repel Arab attacks throughout most of the country. Competition over land—indeed, the idea that the land itself might have competing ideational claims made over it—was brought to the fore by the riots and might have trampled upon the very underpinnings of Shlonsky's poetics. But the riots also catalyzed a fascinating turn in Zionist political discourse, which emerged from 1929 focused on collective citizenship and away from any sense of individual spiritual responsibility for the nation. The 1929 riots rescued Zionist politics from the discursive dead end of constructivism.

The poetic response to 1929 was no less radical even if the loss of a prior concentration on interiority required more time for literature to find its bearings. For some, in fact, the new politics offered little for a poetic encounter with the land. Cut off from an unfettered and unmediated image of nature, Shlonsky cast about for new models of poetic discourse. Turning his back on Palestine altogether, Shlonsky entered into a poetics of symbolic abstractions that would be politically safe: the *tohuvavohu* (the pre-Genesis enigma) of an undefined, amorphous, chaotic national space.[1] In this, Shlonsky was not alone, and Zionist art, it seems, abandoned landscape too, taking up visual abstraction in order to represent national desire.[2]

Not all art fled from the encounter with nature, even if Zionist aesthetics after 1929 seemed to lag behind politics and certainly did not give voice to the elated reaction to Zionist civil defense during the riots. However, in locating an aesthetic that did respond to this new political reality, rather than a canonical literary response that would have rewritten the land in the image of postriot politics, we must look instead to the women poets of the 1920s and their struggles to construct an oppositional poetics to the avant-garde of Shlonsky's *moderna* group, an alternative that by 1929 coincided neatly with a politics now focused on the land as an object, that is, as a place preexisting the Jews' return to it. As a marginal aesthetic on the edges of the Zionist literary system, a feminine poetics always imagined the land in opposition to the subjective assertions of the masculine modernist avant-garde, even as it shared the idea of a reflected nature. After 1929, the reflected image of the land as object coincided with a counterpoetics of a subjectivity for the Zionist woman.

Until this chapter, this study has focused on men who wrote as political-historical actors in the development of the institutional structures of Zionism. By turning to the margins of the literary system, the arguments that bind poetic discourse to political ideology become decidedly more associative and less actively ideological in the way that poetry might constitute the politics it reflects. Yet, despite the move away from the canonical center of literary production, the writing of nature on the feminine edge of Hebrew poetry was never meant to challenge a political commitment to settlement. Indeed, political allegiance to Zionist goals transcended poetic association in Palestine. And so we are left to ponder: what relationship existed between a counterpoetics and the hegemonic politics of the Yishuv? How did a woman's writing against a dominant masculine avant-garde nevertheless articulate a cogent political position within the country? If before 1929 the position of a feminine poetics was tenuous in relation to the obvious masculinist predilections of constructivist thought, then after the riots we might discern how that same counterpoetics began to coincide with a new objectivist way of looking at Palestine.

In this regard, within the complex reactions to 1929 one of the historical occurrences worthy of notice is the sudden appearance of publications by women poets in 1930, especially since women's poetry in the 1930s remained consistently focused on landscape. [3] To be sure, throughout the 1920s women poets like Esther Raab and Raḥel Bluwstein, two of the most popular and important, were able to publish their work in literary journals alongside poems by Shlonsky and other *moderna* poets.[4] Nevertheless, 1930 marks some sort of threshold for feminine Hebrew poetics, just as it did for a masculine poetics. However, does the appearance of volumes of poetry in 1930 signal a discursive legitimacy that goes beyond the gender politics of a segregated literary market? Do politics supersede purely literary struggles for poetic dominance? After all, despite the marginalization and critical debunking of women's poetry during the course of Hebrew modernism, all of the most prominent women poets were nevertheless avowed Zionists. Somehow, we must place their work as well in the poetic narration of the nation and not beyond it. In the very least, the success of Bluwstein and Raab, despite their marginalization, would require a critical look at how their poetics might have suddenly coincided with some sort of larger discursive need within the Jewish Yishuv. Indeed, 1929 seems to mark an important heightening of a basic aspect of feminine poetics in the writings of Bluwstein and Raab. By following the historical progression of their work from its oppositional stance in the 1920s through its intensification after 1929, we can begin to see how a marginal poetics began to coincide with and perhaps even help constitute a dominant political position in this history.[5]

The Shifting Discourse of Tel Ḥai

The changes in how the Yishuv approached the conceptual challenges of settlement after August 1929 are conveniently encapsulated in the developing commemorative discourse surrounding the earlier massacre of Jewish settlers at Tel Ḥai in the north of the country in 1920. From the immediate aftermath of the incident at Tel Ḥai conscious attempts were made to create a public memory of the martyrs killed in the massacre. The commemoration of Tel Ḥai had, in fact, always been connected personally to the public persona of Berl Katznelson, and his deployment of the massacre as a political trope in his writings both before and after the riots of 1929 serves as an informative litmus for how far 1929 pushed the Zionist establishment into transforming its attitudes toward the land.

In March of 1929, on the ninth anniversary of the battle at Tel Ḥai and the death of its famed defender Yosef Trumpeldor, Katznelson commemorated the tragedy—as he had done every year since 1920—with a brief address devoted to the martyrs of the northern settlement, eight of whom had fallen at the hands of Arab marauders. Back in 1920, Katznelson had published in the pages of *Kuntres* a famous memorial poem, a secular *yizkor* prayer, that quickly entered the canon of national texts and solidified Tel Ḥai's position in the Zionist pantheon.[6] In March 1929, long after Tel Ḥai had already come to reflect the settlement values of a wide spectrum of views within the Zionist Yishuv because of the way commemoration had always focused on individual sacrifice and personal political participation,[7] Katznelson once again turned his attention to the personal plight of the Tel Ḥai martyrs, valorizing sacrifice for the benefit of both national and ideological principle: "The small group of people that stood during their lives at the northern guard, there—alone and abandoned, tattered and worn out, hungry and cold—they earned the right in Hebrew history to be crowned after their deaths, with splendor and glory, as heroes of the nation."[8] The settler mythology Katznelson invokes here is a common one and traces its genealogy back at least as far as the turn of the century and the modernism of the Second Aliyah. The heroism of these martyrs is located in their internal struggle, the loneliness of their confrontation with the difficulties of defending the land and transforming it into a habitable Jewish domain.

The focus on the internal struggles of the settlers as individuals working and dying on behalf of the people leaves little room for even the mention of an external enemy, let alone the demonization of the Arabs who attacked the settlement. In this, Katznelson's brilliance as a populist ideologue, like Aḥad Ha'am's after Kishinev,[9] lay in his ability to turn the bite of national commemoration back on the structures of the movement itself and the inaction of the Jewish collective, rallying the troops whom he depicts as unresponsive to the needs of the individuals manning the front lines of settlement, the true heroes of the struggle. Tel Ḥai thus came to symbolize "a double battle [in which] the heroes of Tel Ḥai stood and fell: not just in the battle against robbers and plunderers from outside, who came to destroy the natural beauty of peace and work, but also a battle against the apathy, weakness, the alienation and fear from within, within the Yishuv itself and among its leaders."[10] Just as in his response to Bar-Adon four years earlier in the pages of *Davar*, Katznelson makes settlement the constructivist solution to this double struggle. For him, Tel Ḥai serves as a national symbol because its members, in their personal struggle to settle the land and reinvent themselves, combined political belief with devotion to settlement, "the vital mixture of love of the people and the land, with the principles of the work ethic and socialist correctness."[11]

Five months later, *after* the riots, the political significance of landscape and working the land—even the emphasis on individual transformation and the characterization of the Arab—had changed dramatically, a consequence of the violent confrontation which seemed to wake Zionist culture from its fixed gaze inward. Indeed, August of 1929 marks the end of a Zionist modernism in politics and aesthetics that was based on the fundamental principles of internal individual transformation.[12] The Wailing Wall riots of that August were sparked ostensibly by questions of religious access to and control over the holy sites in Jerusalem. But as violence quickly spread beyond Jerusalem, the country became engulfed in a paroxysm of broad Arab frustration at Zionist encroachments on Arab lands and the consequent displacement of peasant agricultural workers, the *fellaheen*. Violence over land had occurred before, most notably in 1920 and 1921. But the conflagration of August 1929 had a more profound and long-lasting effect, perhaps because of the British response, which looked for a more comprehensive accounting of this violence and required both the Jewish and Arab leadership to defend their communities' positions on the land. In the early 1930s, with British political limitations placed on both land purchases and Jewish immigration, the landscape became a contentious space, and the Jew in it had to conform therefore to a British vision of what it meant to belong to the landscape.

In the immediate aftermath of the August rioting, the necessity for this type of radical reorientation and repositioning was obviously felt within the Jewish political leadership. At that point, Katznelson revisited the symbol of Tel Ḥai, but now the same image as before the violence, described in the same language, came to represent a political landscape far removed from the individual constructivist ideals of his commemorative address only five months earlier. Indeed, after August, Tel Ḥai came to symbolize for Katznelson the movement as a whole, and he drew direct comparisons between the violence of 1920 and 1929, defining national progress since Tel Ḥai as the coalescence of the pioneering ethos into a unified culture: "In the earlier riots, the defender saw himself alone and abandoned by the Yishuv, and the Yishuv as a body saw itself alone and abandoned by the entire people. This feeling of loneliness . . . has disappeared this time. Perhaps this is the first time that we have not felt alone, that the people is with us, that the people of Israel has responded. Truly responded. It did not hear our cries in the days of Tel Ḥai. . . . This time it heard and answered."[13] Katznelson is certainly referring to the improved national infrastructure in the country, especially the organized Jewish defenses throughout Palestine during the August violence.[14] But these facts have also discursive implications, and the repeated phrase, "alone and abandoned," has been transformed from the mark of individual devotion and commitment (of what must be done *in spite* of individual isolation) to become the attribute of those lacking a collective structure of political, social, and cultural identity. In the aftermath of August 1929, individuality and personal resolve melt before the collective singularity of a settled people.

Within this newfound national unity, Katznelson goes even further, presenting Arab violence as nothing more than a catalyst to that collective identity, as evinced by the project of settlement itself: "The attack of 1921 gave us the building of the Jezreel Valley, mighty Tel Aviv, the urban neighborhoods. The attack of 1929 will bring us sevenfold: settled valleys, consolidated workers' neighborhoods, united and fortified settlements [and] the expansion of the domestic market for Hebrew products. . . . Shacks were burned, concrete will be built. Corrals were robbed—we'll erect cattle sheds. . . . That's our only answer, that's our only revenge. We have no other desire for revenge except for this: the scheme of our enemies will be thwarted, and Eretz Israel will be built."[15] The phrase *admat yisra'el* (the soil of Israel), which had dominated Katznelson's *yizkor* prayer of 1920 where it only designated the geographic entity of Jewish Palestine and marked an ethnic principle of labor, has now been transformed into a political signifier, *eretz yisra'el*, which Katznelson never used in 1920. Land as redeemed by labor is no longer the cause of inner renewal for the Jew, but rather reflects a Jewish subject who emerges *in competition* with an enemy over the same land. The objects of possession, built in ethnic competition and contention, mark the extent of national identity and belonging in Palestine.

Katznelson's adoption of abstraction—from *admat yisra'el* to *eretz yisra'el*—was emblematic of a general attitude in the Yishuv, which withdrew from all representational considerations of Palestine after 1929 and moved from the close embrace of nature and soil to a formal abstraction that disdained figurative representation. Israeli art criticism has pointed out how stylistic transformation characterized a certain response to violence and a withdrawal further into the recesses of a modernist, creative consciousness.[16]

But the new objectivist politics that became necessary after August to defend Jewish settlement practice and agricultural methods in front of successive British commissions of inquiry fostered as well a concomitant self-representation in literature and politics that embraced the land fervently as an object of depiction and possession, reflecting, we might say, not Katznelson's abstract politics but a litany of real objects on the ground. For both types of response, after August, a modernist preoccupation with the subjective voice in the land gives way to the representation of something *not* within the Jew, where the landscape as either abstract idea or material object becomes a more distant and separated entity. Building and improving the land continued to reflect a Jewish subject but one defined within a basic conflict and competition between Jew and Arab, where building was the product of that competitive identity and not constitutive of an identity that could ignore the political environment beyond the Jewish settlement. The Jew now had to conform to a land that was objectively discrete, possessing its own unique set of physical characteristics, which might or might not coincide neatly with Jewish desires in the country.

The Poetics of Absorptive Capacity

Katznelson's shift from subjective possession of the land to the building of competitive objects reflects the new way Zionist discourse envisioned settlement as the material instantiation of national desire. In this, Katznelson's reaction to the riots simply portends the findings of the Shaw Commission of Inquiry itself, sent by the British Parliament to investigate the actions, causes, and complaints that led to and emerged from the August disturbances. The commission articulated a basic incompatibility between the self-articulation of Jews and Arabs, on the one hand, and the available territory on the other, thus bifurcating national aspiration and settlement policy. In other words, since the Balfour Declaration, the governing authorities had been faced with the realities of intense economic and social competition over limited space, a condition exacerbated by contradictory promises to both national camps. But in 1929, settlement, euphemized in colonial jargon as "the land issue," loomed large over the commission's deliberations and came to define the central questions concerning ethnic tension in the country.

To alleviate the ponderousness of maximalist national assertions by either side, the commission sought to abrogate any transcendent claims of either Arab or Jewish nationalism by defining land according to the immanent characteristics of the land itself, in an inverse move to Katznelson, who looked at the land through a logic that progressed from national abstraction to physical materiality. Thus, the structure of future land development in Palestine would follow from the essential character of the place—that is, land as signifier with inherent meaning—in what was spoken of as the "absorptive capacity" of the land, namely, what the physical, scientifically defined resources of the land would allow. Even this dispassionate understanding of physical resources and natural geography was fundamentally discursive. After all, someone, namely the British, had to determine the meaning inherent in the signifier.[17] The commission's scientific formulation of absorptive capacity as an inalienable quality stemming from the essence of the soil, however, laid out a seemingly incontrovertible method for calculating the appropriateness of settlement, a process that had profound consequences for a Zionist self-understanding of its connection to Palestine. In its conclusions, the commission inverted Zionist constructivism's formulation of an immanent connection between body and soil, and instead, within the terms of absorptive capacity, which elevated physical place as primary over any abstract claims of national politics, the connection between nature and the Jewish "I" was crudely recast in a vulgar equation of economic sufficiency, thus dividing, in Zionist terms, body and spirit as they had been conceived as unified in the land.

Within the scientific logic of absorptive capacity, Jewish immigration came under intense scrutiny, and the limits on immigration effected physical, as well as conceptual, separation between Jew and Eretz Israel. Immigration controls had been in place before, most notably in response to the mass violence of 1920 and 1921. But now, the commission linked immigration to land directly, giving support for restrictions of immigrants based upon what the land could scientifically handle. Plainly, science was inflected by cultural attitude since population controls depended solely on agricultural capacities. Absorptive capacity assumed a Palestine that was to remain agrarian but only within the scientific horizons of British Orientalism.[18] In this, all three sides party to the commission's investigation acceded to the assumption that the basis of the Palestinian economy (and its cultural foundation) lay within a strictly agricultural understanding of land use and development, an assumption that both reflected and dictated much of Zionism's self-understanding of action in the landscape and the economy.[19] According to the conclusions of the commission's report, which came out in March of 1930, exactly a year after Katznelson's remarks about the inner strength of the settlers at Tel Ḥai, "Palestine cannot support a larger agricultural population than it at present carries unless methods of farming undergo radical change. With more intensive cultivation, should this prove to be possible, room might be found for a number of newcomers in certain districts."[20] These conclusions—and their attendant conceptual assumptions—reversed a tacit understanding between Britain and the Zionists (an understanding that the Arabs seem never to have participated in) concerning the relation between land and people.[21] In effect, the new politics after August 1929 would give priority to land as physical object and determinant over the fate of these populations.[22]

The extent of Zionism's understanding of its own national movement as foreign to the colonial terms set down by the British government can be heard in the transcripts, where the last gasps of Zionist political modernism were articulated by the Jewish leadership arguing for land policy based on individual control and free will. Against the claims of displaced Arab agricultural workers (displaced by Zionist land purchases throughout the 1920s), the Zionists argued for a liberalism of individual choice, claiming that an uncontrolled and unlimited land market merely allowed for individual opportunity among those participating in the free-market exchange of property. In land purchases, so the argument went, Jews paid fair (if not inflated) market prices in transactions freely entered into by the Arab seller. Because of this, the Jewish leadership had little concern for collective material effect, namely, the permanent displacement of the peasant *fellaheen*. Indeed, land prices had risen sharply over the previous two decades as Zionist agents began looking to purchase large tracts of land. But the general assumptions of the argument reflect, more importantly, the extent of Jewish thinking about the relationship between land and individual action in the soil. [23]

Perhaps because of Zionism's inability to conceive of land outside of the immanent self-identification of land and Jew a concerted refutation of the Shaw Commission report emerged only after some time and by a new political voice untied to the constructivist generation of Katznelson and Ben-Gurion. The time lag and the conceptual catch-up required to shift thinking and understand the new colonial reality of absorptive capacity might explain, too, why the Shaw Commission report garnered greatest Zionist scrutiny, even though subsequent British policy declarations (in particular, the recommendations of the Passfield White Paper of 1930) had a larger impact on immigration and land transfer rights.[24] In fact, the parade of subsequent British officials and their pronouncements—the Passfield White Paper of 1930; the MacDonald letter of 1931 that mollified, in Zionist terms, much of the damaging tones of the Shaw Commission report and the Passfield White Paper; and then, John Hope-Simpson's investigations of 1930 into Arab displacement and Jewish land transfers—put policy into effect and implemented the conclusions of a view of land that was transcendent over any ethnic claims for national identity. In this, the Shaw Commission had laid down the discursive foundations for all reassessments of land use, and for this reason, when Ḥayim Arlosoroff, the young head of the political division of the Jewish Agency, finally wrote a rebuttal to the commission report in 1931, well after the publication of the Passfield White Paper, the MacDonald letter, and John Hope-Simpson's arrival in the country, he focused on the original text and the implications it held for Zionist policies of land use and thus Zionism's understanding of nature.[25]

Arlosoroff directed much of his argument about the "land question" to the issue of intensive cultivation, a vexing problem because it was authorized by the language of article 11 of the Mandate Authority itself, which specifically designated "appropriate" settlement on lands that were intensively cultivated.[26] The British reversion to a stricter interpretation of article 11 fostered a grander sense of a nostalgic Orientalism for how the Palestinian landscape should look, which presented quite a problem for Zionist settlement. Within the Jewish Yishuv, extensive cultivation had been the dominant agricultural practice of settlement since the end of the First World War. Extensive cultivation both expanded the physical domain of Jewish settlement in Palestine and also contributed to the separation of ethnic labor markets because Jewish workers could be exclusively employed on extensively cultivated farms; higher skilled Arab labor was not necessary. Extensive landholding thus enabled the constructivist ethos of the 1920s, whose cultural and conceptual formulations were supported by a scientific discourse espousing the environmental, as well as the social, need for extensive cultivation as the basis of Jewish settlement. The Zionist agronomist Arthur Ruppin, for instance, had already published in 1925 a detailed social and scientific critique of the intensive cultivation of small farms (twenty dunams or so) as an alternative for Jewish farm production.[27] An insistence by the British on intensive planting meant the very breakdown of the Jewish settlement economy and culture.

As opposed to Ruppin's earlier refutation of intensive farming, which was based squarely in the discourse of agronomy, Arlosoroff focused his argument on the imperial implications of intensive agriculture, as he saw them, which would bring back to the country a colonialism of interdependence among the two colonized peoples. This was, in fact, the explicit aim of British policy, especially as it had been devised in the Shaw Commission report where the future of ethnic cooperation in the mandate depended on a sentimental vision of an Orientalist history predating the war (and British political involvement in Palestine). According to the British version of that prehistory, peaceful coexistence reigned between Jewish settlements and Arab villages in an Orientalist fantasy of premodern intensive agrarian codependence. Arlosoroff's criticism of the commission report thus centers on the social and colonial implications of the British institutionalization of this Orientalist history. "How much excitement," Arlosoroff writes, "the report invests in an account of the cooperation between Jewish and Arab settlement before the war."[28] Arlosoroff then makes his next critical move by complicating the colonial status of the ethnic and political triangle in Palestine, attacking British romanticism as a hidden source of worker exploitation: "What is being called here cooperation is nothing but a system of exploitation, exploitation of the many by the few, in whose place the Jews had established in the period after the war a settlement program on the basis of independent labor. It seems that the commission still does not understand that the exploitation of the indigenous people by a minority of European immigrants is today an illegitimate system for social and political reasons, according to scientists engaged in land settlement."[29] The comment is somewhat odd because it seems a self-indictment of Jewish action in the country before 1914. But then, as an argument for separate ethnic economies as a means for breaking the yoke of colonial control, Arlosoroff resurrects Ber Borochov's ideas about the economic development of emerging national ethnicities. Arlosoroff thus concentrates his critique on the economic effects such a romantic colonialism would have on Arab culture, let alone Jewish culture. In this, Arlosoroff's analysis of British colonial sentimentality mocks the consequences it would imply for agricultural progress in the region, drawing attention to how the arrest of cultivation within traditional holdings and farming methods could only scientifically support primitive Arab crops such as watermelons and what he calls *hilfa*, probably referring to *Eragrostis*, a genus of grasses. Arlosoroff fundamentally argues that British defense of Arab land rights within a sentimental Orientalism only leads to the further oppression of the Arab.

The importance of the analysis, however, might lie less in the way Arlosoroff attacks sentimental British paternalism as a form of Orientalism (a desire by the governing authority to suspend history within an ideal state of colonial dependence) than the way he himself acquiesces to that discourse as well. It is not so much that Arlosoroff argues for an Orientalist colonial benevolence toward the indigenous Arab. Rather, by relying on the scientism of economics and a rationalism of agrarian exploitation in order to argue for an ethnic settlement policy of modernist progress and national independence, Arlosoroff abandons a modernist constructivism and argues instead for the very same objectification of nature that initially roused Zionist anger toward the British commissions. Indeed, Arlosoroff absorbed well the new conceptual realities of post-1929 political competition and understood that the basic foundation of settlement and a defensible conception of soil had evolved into a perspective on nature as an object to be used and exploited. His doctorate in economics must have prepared him for this conceptual shift as Arlosoroff himself represented a new mode of Zionist thinking. He was a new type of Zionist ideologue, whose education derived not from the field but from rational analyses of land resources. Because of this Arlosoroff could understand the British and how absorptive capacity as the determination for Jewish national identity forced onto Zionist thought a reconceptualization of the land itself as the primary object of focus and contemplation. Both economics and culture now issued primarily from the object of the land, a static, contested site of competition around which the ethnic body must contort itself. In this context, Arlosoroff understood well the new discursive function and limitations of colonial politics, namely, how the romantic assumptions of British imperialism would determine the objective analysis of environment and nature. Arlosoroff tied the Jew to the land by showing how identity emerged from an essential connection to the soil, that is, how Jewish agriculture was essentially connected to the land in an objectivist manner. From Arlosoroff's point of view, the new politics of absorptive capacity had to be made to conform to deeper Jewish interests and aspirations. But that task required some sort of aesthetic intervention—a vision of an objectivist belonging in the land—beyond what Arlosoroff himself had already accomplished in his political critique of a British colonial understanding of land and ethnic identity.

The Oppositional Subject in Feminine Poetics

The post-1929 shift of ethnic politics in Palestine neatly coincided with a feminine poetics that had already developed in the country during the 1920s. In opposition to the phatic assertions of Shlonsky's masculine relationship to the land, poets like Raḥel Bluwstein and Esther Raab asserted a view of nature as an object that produces, reifies, and forms the Zionist subject, thereby creating an identity most suited to the place. If masculinist poetics—as in Shlonsky, Brenner, or even Katznelson—developed a dialectical reconciliation between subject and object that would create the individual through the very expression of a natural Palestine, then a feminine poetics sought the earth itself, the realness of the soil and the antiquity of a connection between Jew and land, in this way later reinforcing the new politics of Arlosoroff's search for appropriate forms of settlement in the land. The connection here between politics and poetry is not simply associative, even if a feminine poetics never gained ideological dominance in the Yishuv. And women Hebrew poets never entered public life the way that Bialik, Brenner, and Shlonsky did. But the intensification of a feminine poetics of the land after 1930, especially by deploying a discourse of Orientalism, pushes toward a reading that situates the poetry historically and not merely as poetic opposition on the political margin. Because of this, any analysis of a post-1929 aesthetic of an objectified landscape needs to reencounter an earlier opposition to the hegemony of masculine writing.

The poetic I am calling post-1929 emerged out of an intra-Zionist opposition to masculine forms of writing in the 1920s.[30] This was always a poetry ensconced within pioneering ideology, but one that emphasized the earth itself as the primary force determining individual identity in relation to nature. Raḥel Bluwstein's simple lyric "Here on the Face of the Earth" seems in this way to speak directly against a masculinist, avant-garde poetics of expression:

כָּאן עַל פְּנֵי אֲדָמָה – לֹא בֶּעָבִים, מֵעָל –
עַל פְּנֵי אֲדָמָה הַקְּרוֹבָה, הָאֵם

לְהֵעָצֵב בְּעָצְבָּהּ וְלָגִיל בְּגִילָהּ הַדַּל
הַיּוֹדֵעַ כֹּל כָּךְ לְנַחֵם.

לֹא עַרְפִלֵּי מָחָר – הַיּוֹם הַמּוּמָשׁ בַּיָּד,
הַיּוֹם הַמּוּצָק, הַחַם, הָאֵיתָן
לִרְווֹת אֶת הַיּוֹם הַזֶּה, הַקָּצָר, הָאֶחָד,
עַל פְּנֵי אַדְמָתֵנוּ כָּאן.

בְּטֶרֶם אָתָא הַלַּיִל – בּוֹאוּ, בּוֹאוּ הַכֹּל!
מַאֲמָץ מְאֻחָד, עַקְשָׁנִי וָעֵר
שֶׁל אֶלֶף זְרוֹעוֹת. הַאֻמְנָם יִבָּצֵר לָגֹל
אֶת הָאֶבֶן מִפִּי הַבְּאֵר?

Here on the face of the earth—not in clouds above—
On the face of the near earth, the mother;
To be saddened in her sadness and rejoice in her humble joy
Which knows so well how to give comfort.

Not a foggy tomorrow—the concrete today in hand,
The solid, hot, strong day
To drink one's fill of this short, singular day,
Here on the face of our earth.

Before the arrival of night—come, come all!
A united effort, stubborn and alert
Of a thousand arms. Is it really impossible to roll
The boulder from the mouth of the well?[31]

The poem dates from 1926 and has been often anthologized as typical of a certain settlement ethos. Written in Tel Aviv, ironically far from the earth it sentimentalizes and long before the political realities of the early 1930s, the poem's critical tone focuses on the Yishuv itself in a political statement emphasizing an alternate collective endeavor to the phatic poetics of Shlonsky's avant-garde.[32] The first line already announces a metapoetic critique even as it embraces the physical earth and soil. This is a poetry of place, but place as something that can be felt and touched, not the ideational transcendence of art that hovers above, unconnected to nature's soil. To emphasize that point, the earth takes on anthropomorphic features—"on the *face* of the earth"—bringing the body closer to the soil. Zionism's avant-garde—as Brenner's naturalism before—also cathected body onto the land, but here that relation becomes the primary contact for the settler and issues from the land itself. The aesthetic is now all about form, about nature as a real entity, and not about ideas *about* form and nature. Because of that, the poem drapes itself in conventional form as a way of proclaiming the poem's transparency and simplicity.[33] Rhyming couplets and neat stanzas of metrical symmetry resonate throughout the poem with a consistent prosody.

From form, then, the speaker follows, not just in how she will present poetry, but herself as well, formed in body and mind through the passive constructions of verbs that place agency in this land: "to be saddened in her sadness and rejoice in her humble joy." The land takes on the role of mother, of progenitor of both thought and feeling. In the alliteration of this line—*lehe'atsev be-otsbah ve-lagil be-gilah*—Bluwstein uses physical sonic echoes to define the individual within the object of the land. Action, then, is subordinate to description; verbs play a secondary role to the noun objects of "sadness" and "joy," whose represented emotions and form give significance to the line. Meaning in the sentence does not emerge from the changes that might be wrought within the verb. Instead, the action of the verb merely reflects the situation and condition of the earth itself.

The rest of the poem further emphasizes the objects of earth and day by stressing the characteristics possessed by nature. The concreteness of the day takes on meaning through attributes that emphasize its *thing*-ness: solid, hot, strong, short, singular. Even the discovery of the well and the collective action of the pioneers to improve the land only emanate from the earth mother herself. The well reveals not the work of man. Rather, it is discovered, a hidden treasure of nature herself, giving physical instantiation and resonance to the metaphor of "drinking one's fill" from nature. Even the call to the community—"come, come all!"—maintains an instrumentality always secondary to nature, where humanity ("a thousand arms") is composed merely of the various parts that fill this space. Again, adjectives—united, stubborn, alert—create the description and emphasize human intervention as anonymous and selfless; the lines focus more on the soil than on any Zionist consciousness that might self-reflexively form nature. Instead, parts signify the whole in a reversion to metonymy, which distances the poem from the obsessions of both the avant-garde *moderna* and a politically drafted literature of constructivism (*sifrut meguyeset*). This short, simple poem poses a strong, even ingenious, feminine challenge to a masculinist poetics of control and centralized discourse, centralized through both party apparatus and poetic voice.

The challenge of this aesthetic to a constructivist subjectivism is nowhere so explicit as in Bluwstein's "Ani" (I), a direct response, we might understand, to Shlonsky's own "Anokhi" (I) from the same year. While Shlonsky (and the Hebrew avant-garde generally) reconciles a dialectical separation between man and nature through the collapse of discourse and the heightening of the speaker's interiority, Bluwstein's "I" performs a dialectical resolution that depends on objective representations of the exterior. Like Shlonsky, Bluwstein's "I" negotiates a world dominated by nature, the constant in any Zionist response to Palestine, but a nature defined by phenomenological experience:

כָּזֹאת אָנֹכִי: שְׁקֵטָה
כְּמֵימֵי אֲגַם,
אוֹהֶבֶת שַׁלְוַת חֻלִּין, עֵינֵי תִינוֹקוֹת
וְשִׁירָיו שֶׁל פְרַנְסִיס זַ'ם.

בְּשֶׁכְּבָר הַיָּמִים עָטְתָה נַפְשִׁי אַרְגָּמָן.
וְעַל רָאשֵׁי הֶהָרִים
לְאֶחָד הָיִיתִי עִם הָרוּחוֹת הַגְּדוֹלוֹת,
עִם צְרִיחַת נְשָׁרִים.

בְּשֶׁכְּבָר הַיָּמִים . . . זֶה הָיָה בְּשֶׁכְּבָר הַיָּמִים.
הָעִתִּים מִשְׁתַּנּוֹת
וְעַכְשָׁו –
הִנֵּה אָנֹכִי כָּזֹאת.

I'm like this: quiet
Like the waters of a lake,
Loving the tranquility of the everyday, eyes of babes
And the poems of Francis Jammes.

Long ago I wrapped my soul in purple.
And on the heads of mountains
As one I was with the great winds,
With the shrieks of eagles.

Long ago . . . that was long ago.
Times change
And now—
Here I am like this.[34]

The best way to hear Bluwstein's poetic account of her "I" surrounded by the objects of nature might run through Amy Lowell's praise for Francis Jammes, the French poet Bluwstein names here.[35] In celebrating Jammes's writing, Lowell attacks the very foundations of a modernism based on "interiority" as an older, passé poetic and equates "modern" with a mode of writing she calls "exteriority": "Somehow, that fashion [of interiority] worked itself out, and 'exteriority,' as I call the characteristic modern touch, came in. By this extremely awkward word, 'exteriority,' I mean an interest in the world apart from oneself, a contemplation of nature unencumbered by the 'pathetic fallacy.'"[36] The description echoes much of the power in this poem as well (indeed, Bluwstein might in fact have been far more successful than either Jammes or Lowell in expressing these ideas). Right from the opening line, the speaker recedes among the objects of nature that will intimately describe her, a litany of *things* whose significance then produces meaning for the "I."

But if this poem means to define a subject position by, in essence, denying it, by placing the *ani* ("I") of the title within an object world where action derives only from the indistinct states of feeling that objects create when they come into contact with each other, there exists too a self-referential textuality in both the poetics and thematic content of the poem. In this, language itself becomes part of the world of Palestinian objects. In the first line—"I'm like *this*"—the emphatic statement mirrors the self (and perhaps too responds to the phatic assertions of Shlonsky's "Hinei," a poem Bluwstein would easily have been familiar with) but refuses the very primacy of language to create meaning for the speaker. In the unspecified deictic utterance "this," nature is freed of the subject's linguistic pronouncement and instead the "I" is suspended until it can be defined within the surrounding world of nature. The dialectical divide between Jew as subject and nature as object is bridged by denigrating language and especially poetry, leaving them powerless to produce anything beyond themselves. Thus, the dispersion of the subject among the objects of the world suffuses the reference to Jammes. The object of equivalence in the poem in this case is itself a poem, an intertextual assertion that leads into nostalgic sentimentality not only because it picks up thematically from Jammes's own hackneyed sentimentalism, but because the textual reference always already connotes the mediation of *another* consciousness. In this way, Bluwstein consistently makes clear the artifice of her own poem, the way that poetry can only refer obliquely to a prior experience taking place beyond the text—which by implication is originally and authentically located in the landscape.

The consciousness of textuality in the poem begins to account for the audibly nostalgic sigh in the final stanza and the reference to days past. There is a hint here of that antimodern discourse of immediacy within nature, of a sublime once known in the past but now lost, a nostalgic sentiment common to pastoral. Time figures in both these poems by Bluwstein to describe immediacy within nature, an immediacy of the moment, but that connects through nature to an authentic past. The circularity in "Ani," which begins and ends ostensibly in an endlessly recurring moment of rapport between present and past, begins to blur any chronological distinctiveness. This sense of history in place where the past infuses the moment of the poem pushes toward a notion of authentic experience in the landscape, one where the natural landscape creates connection between the individual and the nation.

These poetic claims for authenticity in the landscape, especially as it might reflect the nation through individual experience in the land, are even stronger in the poems of Esther Raab, who highlighted the entire issue of authenticity by consistently referring to herself as the "first native poet in Palestine."[37] In the poems themselves, Raab's lyricism surrounds and defines her speaker within the attributes of nature, here a nature of even greater descriptive objectivity than in Bluwstein's work. While Raab's invocations of brambles and thorns are usually taken as unmediated signs of her environmental appropriateness and sensitivity, we might look instead at the figuration of the imported eucalyptus to see how carefully she writes nativism into nature. The authenticity of Raab's natural depictions is so successful that even the eucalyptus, which could not stand the test of indigenousness in a different poetics, thrives in her poetry. More important than the tree's botanical appropriateness, Raab's poetic figuration creates the depiction of a truly natural place, with the physical eucalyptus at its center, which then creates the subject. The explicit references to the eucalyptus in Raab's first collection, *Kimshonim,* occur in two untitled love poems, which each stake a position for the speaker's feminine independence. From one of these:

לְעֵינֶיךָ הָאוֹרוֹת, הַמְלֵאוֹת,
מַה טּוֹב חֲיוֹת;
לְאוֹרָן כָּל אֵבֶר מָתוּחַ
כְּאֶקָלִיפְּטוּס אַחַר סַעַר אָתָּה:
עָיֵף, אֵיתָן וְנָע עוֹד בָּרוּחַ –
רֹאשִׁי יַגִּיעַ עַד חָזֶךָ,
וְעֵינֶיךָ מִמַּעַל
חֲמִימוּת עָלַי תִּרְעַפְנָה.

For your bright, full eyes
How good it is to live;
In their light every limb flexes
Like a eucalyptus after the storm you:
Tired, strong, still swaying in the wind—
My head will reach your chest,
And your eyes from above
Will dote on me warmly.[38]

Raab's speaker entwines her lover in the natural world of the eucalyptus, which represents the male lover as protector and comforter. But while initially introduced as a simile, the eucalyptus takes on a role far greater than a mere discursive instrument. The love poem, in fact, seems much more about the relationship to nature than to any human lover, not only because of the dominance of the eucalyptus simile, but because of the elaboration of the simile through the metaphors of physical attribute—"tired, strong, swaying"—which begin with personal description but then move easily and effortlessly back into the natural realm. The effect of the line inverts the usual direction of metaphor, and now human attribute works to make the tree more alive, more the primary participant in the relationship. We understand that idea in how the poem relies on physical description to define both the lovers and what connects them. The delay of the specific referent of the metaphor, "you," postponed to the end of the line, initially blurs the discursive instrumentality of the tree and enhances both its physical presence and its signifying ability to encompass both lovers. Thus, emotion emanates from the materiality of the natural scene where the inaccessibility of the male's interiority sends us looking to nature to fill the gaps left in the description.

Dressing the lover in nature's garb and vice versa was something of a normative trope in Hebrew literature and especially Orientalist Zionist art.[39] But in Raab's use of the figure, nature lacks any of the sexual instrumentality usually employed by the trope. In this, Raab's poetics work against a phatic poetry and anticipate Shlonsky's final return to nature in 1947 after his extended hiatus through abstract symbolism. Only then could Shlonsky return to the soil in "Harei at" (You Are Hereby) where nature appears as lover in an extended metaphor of woman and land, both objects of a male sexual national desire. Against Shlonsky's strategy, Raab in this poem about the eucalyptus might be accomplishing the very opposite of instrumentality in nature by employing the metaphor of the land within the love poem in order to claim nature as a feminine domain of identity.

Of course, one could read the poem ironically as well and then the gender divide between female lover and male eucalyptus creates another type of opposition between authenticity in the guise of the woman and foreignness projected onto the land through the imported Australian tree. But then, the specific ambiguity of the third and fourth lines—"In their light every limb flexes / Like a eucalyptus after the storm you"—which begin, it seems, by referring to the speaker herself before pointing to the masculine "you" at the very end, implicates the female lover in the eucalyptus simile as well.

In either reading, the figurative language of nature points back at the speaker, for whom the land serves as a rich ideational field that gives meaning to expression. Raab's vocabulary issues from the entire physical realm surrounding her, the eucalyptus as well as the thorns and brambles, with which she is usually associated. The objects of the landscape reflect on an identity that will in turn form and reify this place. "The landscape of dreams for desert wanderers," Raab wrote in a 1924 poem while she was living in Egypt, a line that punctuates a description of the East:

כַּעֲנָקֵי פְּרָחִים
עֲלֵי גִּבְעוֹלִים דַּקִּים,
צָפוֹת מִמַּעַל הַצַּמָּרוֹת
כָּרֵי-דֶּשֶׁא, צִיּוּרֵי-הֲזָיָה
תּוֹךְ הָאוֹרוֹת אוֹבְדִים –
נוֹף הַחֲלוֹם לְתוֹעֵי-מִדְבָּר.

Like necklaces of flowers
Atop thin stems
The treetops float above

Grassy meadows, fantasy paintings
Lost within the light—
The landscape of dreams for desert wanderers.[40]

The landscape cannot escape the projection of the speaker even as it defines the subject. Here especially, the vision of the speaker falls on the physical attributes of place, finding in nature itself the material for its dreams. But the syntax of the poem collapses into the vision of the wanderer; the sentence disintegrates into fragments that culminate as a particular image of the fantasized world of the observer. The place is vivid and the descriptions of the land remain sharp, evoking real experience. For Raab, natural description always falls back onto a subject defined by physical place, and not the opposite.

A focus on natural authenticity connects Raab and Bluwstein and functions to differentiate their search for an expression of feminine Zionist identity from the normative masculine poetics of the 1920s. The way that the physical attributes of an authentic landscape describe and even define a feminine speaker builds a poetics where meaning derives from the correspondence their work makes to what could scientifically be claimed for nature. But Raab's elegant and effective deployment of the imported eucalyptus certainly points out as well the gap between representation and science and shows how both sides are inflected by the ideological positions they stake. Both Raab and Bluwstein successfully created a poetry of description that framed authenticity of Jewish identity by fundamentally connecting that identity to a vision of an actual landscape, a vision shared by a wide spectrum of Zionist pioneers in Palestine.

Movement to the West, Movement to the East

The cultural aftermath of the 1929 riots has usually been measured by the riots' effect on the normative institutions of artistic production. The comprehensive rejection of oriental visual themes in Zionist art, for instance, or the abstract symbolism of avant-garde Hebrew poetry.[41] To be sure, the disappointment articulated by Zionist politics in finding itself within a hostile competition with the Palestinian reflected a certain turning away from Orientalist models of the Jew's return to the East. But the wholesale rejection of the Orient as a legitimate aesthetic cannot account for the types of political justifications Arlosoroff made against the colonialist sentimentality of the British. The politics of absorptive capacity required a type of cultural response that would not completely turn its back on the object of the land as its primary focus. Authenticity in the landscape—what Arlosoroff was forced to argue from August 1929 onward—could not easily coexist, we might say, with a complete aesthetic rejection of a representational depiction of physical connection to a specific place.

Indeed, it did not. But to see this, we need to account for parallel movement in both Zionist politics and poetics. Just as Arlosoroff himself moved to the East in casting Jewish settlement as "appropriate" to the physical attributes of Palestine in a kind of counter-Orientalism, one more scientifically authentic and culturally truer than how British sentimentality saw the East, a concomitant Zionist politics began to look myopically westward across the sea in an effort to further isolate the Jewish economy and society from interaction and dependence on its Arab neighbor. Throughout the 1930s, much of Zionist politics focused away from the land in order to recast identity as bound to the current situation.[42]

In poetry, this bifurcation of Zionist politics received expression in an intensified divergence of masculine and feminine poetics. A feminine response to the political issues post-1929 points to writing as a primary means for expressing new political sensibilities. This seems particularly true since the singularity of the feminine literary response is marked by the complete avoidance and absence of any masculine engagement with the politics of appropriate and indigenous occupation of Palestine. While politics now directly confronted the question of Arab presence in the land—something Zionist culture had refused to take on in the previous decade[43]—Hebrew culture turned away from Palestine and especially from any representational consideration of the indigene.

Shlonsky himself perhaps best exemplifies this trend. Others have remarked about the transformation in Shlonsky's poetics after the events of 1929,[44] but while the poetic implications of Shlonsky's more intense abstract symbolism have garnered attention, the reflective nature of symbolist politics remains less clear. However, what can easily be noted is how Shlonsky turns his attention away from the land after 1929 and effectively abandons all poetic reflection of Palestine until well into the 1940s.[45] Even here, Shlonsky's removal from the land into the abstraction of symbolism might itself ironically depend on a reengagement with Orientalism as a mode of discourse that writes Palestine as an objective other. Despite, or perhaps because of, Shlonsky's turn to abstraction, after 1929 Palestine emerges in his poetry within an objective consideration of the land. Gone is the synesthetic ability to express both Zionist identity and creativity in the landscape. Instead, from the early 1930s, Shlonsky heads out to sea in poems like "Yas'ur" (Albatross),[46] which announces the poet's departure from the local scene:

וְאַחֲרָיו אַחֵר [גּוּפוֹ – חֶדְוָה שֶׁל עֶשֶׁת,
וְעַל פָּנָיו – שִׁכְרוֹן יַמִּים וְטַלְטֵלַת צִיָּם]
וְסָח לִי:

"אִמָּא-מָא, לֹא תִשָּׂאֵנִי הַיַּבֶּשֶׁת,
נִכְסוֹף נִכְסַפְתִּי אֶל הַיָּם".

. . . .

זָכַרְתִּי צְרוֹר יָמִים – בָּעֵמֶק, בַּגִּלְבֹּעַ:
הָרִים רָבְצוּ לִשְׁתּוֹת מִנַּחַל עֵין-חֲרֹד.
בִּצְרִיף הָעֵץ, כִּבְתוֹךְ מִקְדַּשׁ אֱלֹהַּ,
אָמְרוּ תְּהִלִּים רַגְלַיִם שִׁכּוֹרוֹת.

שָׂדוֹת עֻלְּפוּ מִכָּרְסְמֵי חַמְסִינִים,
הִתְפַּלְּלוּ עַל טַל בִּשְׂפַת הָאֲבָנִים.
מֵאֹהֶל עַד כּוֹכָב בְּזֶמֶר-הַכְּנִיסִינִי
הִמְרִיאוּ כִּסּוּפִים כֹּה מוּבָנִים.

הָרִים מְצֻלָּקִים זָקְפוּ אֶת הַדַּבֶּשֶׁת
וְהִתְגָּרְדוּ בְּחַדּוּדֵי-כוֹכָב.
"הָהּ אִמָּ-מָא, לֹא תִשָּׂאֵנִי הַיַּבֶּשֶׁת".
וְהִתְרוֹצֵץ כְּפֶלִי בֵּין אֶחָיו.

הָיָה זֶה לְפָנִים. כְּמוֹ אֶשֶׁד עֲבָרַנִי.
יָמִים כַּיַּעַר. וּבַיַּעַר - אֵשׁ!
עַכְשָׁו הוּא עַל יָדִי. אֵלִי, הַהִכִּירַנִי?
הֵן מָה-שֶּׁהוּא נִכְמַר בִּי וְקָרָא לוֹ: גֵּשׁ!

וְהוּא נִגַּשׁ – פָּרוּעַ וְגָבֹהַּ:
יַסְעוּר פָּדוּי אֶל אֵיתָנָיו חָזַר!
שָׁאַלְתִּי: "טוֹב?" אַךְ הוּא עָמַד בְּלִי נוֹעַ:
אֲסוּף כְּנָפַיִם וּמוּזָר.

And then another one approached [his body—blissful steel,
And on his face—sea drunkenness and undulations of their fleet]
And said to me:
"sweet Mother, the land will not carry me,
I long, I long for the sea."

. . . .

I remembered many days—in the Valley, the Gilboa:
Mountains kneeled to lap at Ein Ḥarod Creek.
In the wooden hut, as in a godly temple,
Those drunken feet sang psalms.

Fields faint, consumed by hot, dry wind,
They prayed for dew in the language of stones.
From tent to star, with nostalgic songs
Simple yearnings were sent airborne.

Scarred mountains with their humps erect
Scratched against the jagged stars.

"Oh, sweet Mother, the land will not carry me."
He rushed about, a secret being amongst his brothers.

That was then . . . like a waterfall passing through me . . .
Days like a forest. And in the forest—fire!
Now he is near. My God, does he know me?[47]
Then something stirred within me and called to him: approach!

And he approached—wild and tall:
An albatross released, enlivened!
I asked: "Well?" but he stood motionless:
Wings tucked in and unfamiliar.[48]

The poem can be read through the lens of postriot Zionist disappointment: now, in the 1930s, the promise of nature has faded, and rather than the ideology of fecund potential and renewal, ideas imbued in all the earlier poems of "Gilboa" that reflected action in the Jezreel, the land here appears as a denotatively described object—the Gilboa only a memory of the past. The metaphors remain vivid—"scarred mountains . . . jagged stars"—but now only as descriptive attributes. Hung onto the objects of the noun, they sound almost hackneyed in their dependence on a sentimental visual poetics that works only to distance nature from the speaker. Unlike those of five years earlier, this poem is *about* nature, and while it might not explicitly articulate alienation from the land, the speaker is constantly deferred and postponed. The first stanza delivers the weariness of the settler in the ventriloquized "I" of this seabird, "sweet Mother, the land will not carry me," which resonates (almost as direct quotation) with the Shaw Commission report: "Palestine cannot support a larger agricultural population than it at present carries." The land that "will not carry" embodies the disappointment of sundering expression of the land from the creation of the land itself, just as the poem alludes to Bialik's forest, but now it is invaded and violated, the individual reverie and closeness to the Divine all in shambles as the forest is cut off from the settler, ablaze; knowledge of identity is suddenly requestioned.

The thematic allegory of the weary settler turning back to Europe, however, seems less important as a political strategy in the poem than the transformation of its poetics. The poems of *Avnei bohu* (Stones of Chaos), the volume that includes "Albatross," appear, on the one hand, to be Shlonsky's least abstract, the most removed from the free-flowing world of figuration that will follow in the mid-1930s. Indeed, this is Shlonsky's most denotative encounter with place as physical object, a type of sentimental poetics he refused in the 1920s. But now, in a leave-taking from these places, he names the Jezreel, the Gilboa, Ein Ḥarod in an outburst of nostalgia, a figure that not only objectifies the landscape but separates the encounter with nature from the speaker. How far these poetics have come from the prelinguistic inventions of earlier, from the Genesis-like promise that language held to invent both man (*adam*) and soil (*adamah*). It is the rhetoric now that is so alienating: the dislocation of nature and its expression from the subject, which so markedly contrasts the primal phatic utterances of the mid-1920s. Instead, the albatross acts as an aesthetic doppelgänger, reinforcing the artifice of the poetic discourse and distancing the speaker from himself in a return to the figuration of alienation. As referent to Coleridge's poem "The Rime of the Ancient Mariner," the bird-cum-settler transforms into the wedding guest, tired and weary after being kept from his real, natural environment. Added to that is Shlonsky's speaker as a mirror of nonterritorial, abstract desire and yearning—the yearning to quit this land that in no way feels a part of him anymore.

If Zionism's masculine poetics thus looked to the west after 1929, to the civilizing mission of settlement and to the Zionists' own arrival as the harbingers of a new natural and cultural identity, then a feminine poetics—if indeed we can talk in such generalized terms—looked further east to the anterior as the progenitor of an identity both for the land and for the Hebrew. Something of this sensibility is captured in Raab's consistent claims to have been the first Hebrew poet born in Eretz Israel. The language of the "authentic" propels Raab's poetry, like Bluwstein's, into a radically new formulation of the mutual identification of land and Jew, where identity emerges from the soil itself. And after 1929, these trends only intensify. The title of Raab's first book of poems, *Kimshonim* (Thorns), published in 1930, highlights the objectivist, antiromantic stance in her poetics, and in that begins to outline the book's resonance with the political discursive transformations in Zionist thought after the violence of 1929. Although most of the poems in this volume predate the riots, the authenticity of a landscape of thorns anticipates a new way of addressing the nature of Palestine.[49] And if we look specifically at writing emerging after the riots, the convergence of a certain poetics and politics seems even clearer.

The Primordial Jewish Indigene

While Bluwstein's poems from the 1920s, "Here on the Face of the Earth" and "I," might constitute a potent challenge to how masculine aesthetics posited in nature only instrumental value, they corresponded easily to a Zionist politics wherein nature itself becomes the reifying object of action among two competing minor communities. Identity defined by its relations to the object of the landscape asserts itself in an Orientalism of authenticity, the Arab competing for appropriateness with a natural Jewish indigene. Thus, after 1929, the writing of land as object still necessitated a dialectical negotiation between a new identity for the Jew in the land and the alienated object of nature. But the reconciliation of that dialectic shifted for Bluwstein and Raab. While authenticity had never previously been expressed in Orientalism's terms, that is, as the closeness of the Jew to a particular history of Palestine and the competition with Arab culture, after 1929 that identity is expressed almost exclusively as such.

Among her final poems, Bluwstein turns consciously to an Orientalist theme, and the "Ivriyah" (Hebrewess) becomes the model for the authentic encounter with the land.

אֲנִי מַבֶּטֶת בָּהּ נִפְעֶמֶת,
נִדְמֶה: הִנֵּה זֶה אַךְ
בְּחֵן קְדוּמִים, בִּשְׁחוֹר וְלַהַט
עָלְתָה מִן הַתַּנַ"ךְ.

וְגֶשֶׁר פָּז נִתְלֶה מִמֶּנָּה
אֶל אֶרֶץ הָעִבְרִים.
וְזִכְרוֹנוֹת יְמֵי הַחֶסֶד
בַּנֶּפֶשׁ מִתַּמְּרִים.

בְּנוֹף נֵכָר הָלוֹךְ וָנוֹעַ
(דְּרָכִים בּוֹ מִי יְסַפֵּר?)
אֲנִי הֵמַרְתִּי שְׁחוֹר וְלַהַט
בִּתְכֵלֶת וּבְנְהוֹר.

אַךְ אִם מָעַלְתִּי – לֹא לָנֶצַח,
כִּחַשְׁתִּי – לֹא עַד תֹּם.
וְשַׁבְתִּי שׁוּב כְּשׁוּב הַהֵלֶךְ
אֶל כְּפַר מוֹלַדְתּוֹ.

כֹּה אֶעֱמֹד פֹּה לְפָנַיִךְ
נִפְעֶמֶת, אֲחוֹתִי,
בְּחֵן קְדוּמִים, בִּשְׁחוֹר וְלַהַט
אָזִין עֵינֵי תְּכֶלְתִּי

I look at her in awe,
It seems: she has just
With grace of yore, in black and burning
Emerged from the Bible.

And a golden bridge is hung from her
To the land of the Hebrews.
And memories of days of grace
Arise in the soul.

In a strange landscape walking, moving
(who can count its paths?)
I exchanged black and burning
For blue and bright light.

But if I betrayed—not forever,
I lied—not all the way.
And I returned like a wanderer
Returning to the village of his birth.

Thus I will stand here before you
In awe, my sister,
With grace of yore, in black and burning
I will nourish my eyes of blue.[50]

In 1926, the connection between present and past remained vague for Bluwstein, named but not specified as to its significance for present Jewish identity in the land. Now, any ambiguity is gone. The poem thematizes return and historic connection, but not in the transformations and labors characteristic of a masculine poetics of improvement. Rather, the speaker is embraced by and through the landscape. Adjectives dominate a poetics where the predicate is de-emphasized, displaced from its normative syntactic position in the sentence, and thus its teleological stress on the grammatical subject. Instead, attributes now completely guide rhetorical thrust. And form—of the poem, of the land—defines the feeling of home in a Zionist return "to the land of the Hebrews."

In this way, description evokes the realness of place, which is echoed in the text by the steady, fixed stasis of the adjective, the form perhaps least inflected or affected by grammatical position in Hebrew. In Bluwstein's poem what changes is the person behind the descriptive gaze, who develops a feminine identity reflexive of the authentic history of the physical description. If earlier in "Ani" (I), Bluwstein's speaker nostalgically outlines a lost connection with a present land—"Long ago . . . that was long ago"—then this poem from after 1930 presents that connection with the past as something recuperated and sustaining for an identity in the here and now. Through the feminization of the land, the ancient, primordial place confirms the speaker's own sense of identification with the homeland and her own identity. As before, attributes describe both the speaker and the Eastern Hebrewess, Eastern in her blackness and her "burning" against the blue brightness that the speaker acquired in her wanderings throughout the diaspora. The land does not necessarily figure here as thematic *object* of description and representation. Rather, in the poetics of attribution, the land *gains* objectivity and authenticity by its ancient and Eastern attributes, through its equivalence with this woman of the Bible: "And a golden bridge is hung from her / To the land of the Hebrews."

The intensification of Bluwstein's temporal dialectic naturally excludes the Arab, whose presence is traversed and significantly displaced by the "golden bridge" represented by the *ivriyah* who connects Zionist identity directly to the authenticity of antiquity. Any lingering doubts in the earlier poems about the very possibility of creating identity in the land and connecting to the past have simply vanished. Distance between the speaker and the nature of the "land of the Hebrews" has given way to the intervention of historical authenticity, namely, the *ivriyah* herself, who announces a deep, essential connection to a primordial oriental origin.

In a similar way, Raab also thematized the Orient after 1930 in order to point in the direction of an authentic identity in the land.[51] In this, Raab likewise employed the opposition of modernity and prehistory to create a sense of a pre-Arab appropriateness in nature. However, the *way* Raab goes about this transformation bears striking differences to Bluwstein. First, Raab represents Arabs directly and places her critique in an Orientalist description of authenticity and inadequacy. And second, she does so in prose, which highlights the objective truth of what she is describing. Like Bluwstein's writing, in the story "Ribat-shoshanim" (Rose Jam) from 1933, Raab inscribes authenticity in an Eastern feminine subject. Curiously, that subject is not explicitly Jewish. Clementine, the adolescent protagonist in the story is denuded of any essential ethnic markers. We are not meant to read any denotated identity in her; her cultural place is not specifically named. Rather, through her complex stance within an oriental world of competing claims on her identity, her identification with the East emerges and points us toward a politics of natural belonging that would compete with Arab political claims in the Middle East.

Set in Egypt, the story articulates a brief sensual moment within the life of an adolescent girl on the cusp of sexual awakening. Sensuousness characterizes the entire story, and the liminality of adolescence reinforces the idea that individual identity forms as a negotiation with the physical world that surrounds the body. Sexuality then is the product of a world of sensation where the rose jam of the title activates a host of other stimuli through taste, smell, touch, and sight. Individual action and control are subordinated to a verdant world of sense images, which are objects that take on life only in an interplay of their physical attributes.

At the beginning of the story, Raab's anonymous and transparent narrator scans the physical scene: "The wild pigeons are cooing in the dense pepper trees. The sun rises and gilds the flat roofs; palms cut the sky with their trunk-pillars. The gardens in front of the houses give out the remains of the night-scent before the day prevails."[52] The sentences remain simple, plainly describing the landscape. Prose allows for that simplicity, shedding artifice and figuration in order to allow objects—human and natural—to meld together: "The desert sky, transparent and wide without end, hovers, rises quickly, and opposite, long white streets stretch with their edges ending in the horizon." Nature begins with inanimate things, but then encompasses the human traffic of the village: "The black-skirted *leben* sellers are already pouring their anguished ornate soprano into the dewy morning. Immediately after them the fishermen rise from the Nile, their wet baskets on their heads; with a short, abrupt cry, they announce their arrival into the four corners of the town . . ." The ellipsis that trails off saves the paragraph from becoming a litany of anthropological observation of an exotic Eastern other who melds into the countryside, united with the natural ebb and flow of the landscape. The ellipsis, at least, returns us to the text, and even while the story remains outside and never penetrates the consciousness of its protagonist, Clementine—that's *not* the point, after all—it does pull us toward her, letting us know that these impressions are hers, even if they are never conscious. The surrounding context of the physical world impresses on her and forms her identity.

The girl, too, blends into the place and appears only as an object among other objects. Clementine's name nicely plays with the entire idea of individual identity formed within the land. She is not just a citrus fruit ready to be plucked in ripeness, the obvious metaphor of the name, which then allows her to circulate through the space as a sexual creature, the object of desire in an Orientalism that places people in close sensuous relation to the nature realm. Beyond that, Clementine is a particular type of fruit, a natural hybrid that emerged only at the beginning of the twentieth century from an encounter *in* nature, produced and defined by the soil in which it takes root. In her name, Clementine signals the melding of natural and human, and like the sensuous pleasure of the rose jam being cooked in large vats of pungent syrup, the human realm fuses with the physical: "The jam in the cauldron emitted a warm intoxicating smell, the smell of roses. The people here would call it 'the perfume of women.'" Individuals become their descriptions, as in the introduction of "Mohammed, the youngest of the servants, a long-waisted Berber whose arms and legs are like thin iron bars, and his skull as narrow and polished as dark copper." He undresses—"[he] took off his outer garment . . . [and] removed his waistcoat also, remaining in his white tunic"—just at the moment when the jam stimulates the senses.

But lest we conceive of the story completely within an Orientalism of exterior depiction, of a discourse that describes and depicts a primal sensual existence, cathecting onto the Eastern other the fantasies of imagined Western desire, Clementine negotiates a far more complex and undialectical world. Black and white oppositions of race and gender do begin to define sexual desire. But the sensuousness of nature in this particular place is not embedded in a parallel contrast between East and West. That battle is definitely here, left to be played out in a male realm. But then femininity, at least in the overlooked adolescent Clementine who still falls for the most part outside of the male gaze, becomes free to explore an independent sensuousness:

> At that moment the strange and awful thing happened: Clementine ordered glass jars be brought up from the cellar and filled with the new jam; while at the entrance of the moldy and dark cellar, suddenly Mohammed appeared nearby as if rising from the earth [*adamah*]; with one movement of the arm he grabbed her chest, pressed her small breasts with his iron fingers and then up and down along her body: like a black, crazed insect, his hand buzzed over the dress that was now white in the darkness of the cellar; the smell of roses they were steeped in escaped from them and she stood as if petrified and couldn't move a limb, so self-evident and awful was what happened that moment; the very event petrified her.

The adolescent Clementine begins to awake to the commodity that her body has become, but continues to play with it as a childish game of innocent touching. That moment of sexual epiphany—of the dark authenticity of Berber African sensuousness, of bodies intersecting in the darkness of the cellar as if just emerging from the depths of the earth, each entwined within the physical objects of this world—contrasts the real exploitations in male society, which is described as an Arab world of oppressive and abusive marriages and artificial social convention. In that realm of civilized society, what happens in the privacy of the bedroom (the privations and oppression of women) stands in contradistinction to the desire of the cellar and the awe-full (*nora*)[53] experience of natural objects touching. Clementine's Arab betrothed, Naguib, stands absent and removed both from her naturalness and from a society of sensual honesty. Instead, he repeats the worst and most typical deprivations of Arab society, which appear distant and detached from honest sensuality. Indeed, Naguib is anything but authentic; he is the Arab trying to pass as white, consumed by colonial anxiety. In his attempts to transcend his native origin—through costume, the Parisian mistress he brings to Egypt, and the like—he reveals and indeed highlights all too well his failure to transcend the colonial anxiety that drives him: "there was no difference between him and Mister James, who lives in the compound."

The contrast then is not between Naguib the Arab and Mister James, the authentic white person, but between Naguib and the real Oriental, the Berber Mohammed, who is more authentic, more of this place, and more natural. The comparison is clear and the bifurcation cuts through both attribute (his bodily presence) and character, that is, in how these differences are intellectually understood and emotionally felt by Clementine. Raab writes: "Clementine knew all of this," meaning all of the violence and oppressions of marriage and the world of her Arab sisters, who are prey to the deprivations of their colonially anxious and inauthentic Arab husbands. On the other hand, completing the sentence about Clementine's knowledge, but separated by the divide of intellectual and immediate experience, stands the not-quite-so-Arab Mohammed: "and here was the black slave, like an ancient Egyptian god from the museum in Cairo." Mohammed's touch was real, even if he is, ironically, repressed in this oriental society, but only because oriental society in its modern garb is anything but authentic to the East. In contrast, authenticity lies in a primordial, pre-Arab Egyptian identity.

Clementine's adolescence, her marginal existence to the adult world at a time when she is first able to see it as such, defines both the tragedy of the oppressions she will experience and the vast potential of her unspoiled identity, unspoiled because it has yet to be initiated into the inauthentic artifice of adult Arab culture. In a text of clear ethnic division, Clementine stands undefined, an identity not yet tethered to anything other than sense perception and the physical space, not yet named or defined within the corruption of Arab society.

Despite Clementine's unfixed ethnic identity and the story's setting in Egypt, the story is still about a competitive ethnic fantasy, about an Orientalism free of the Arab, who now stands strangely for the West. The Berber shuffles the standard East-West opposition and, like the Jew, with whom he has been seen to have a special relationship,[54] disrupts a clear sense of where he belongs politically and culturally. But the Berber, more authentic than the Arab, closer to the earth and the physical attributes of his own description, does not simply stand in for the East within a new Orientalist fantasy that would then truly describe this place. Rather, he triangulates the encounter within the Orient and shows how Clementine's identity will be formed among various competing entities. In this, it seems banal to point out Clementine's citrus affiliation with what was the persistent sign of Zionist agricultural settlement, capitalist drive, and identification in the West, that is, the export of the Palestinian Jewish field, particularly in the form of the Jaffa orange. But if we posit a complicated ethnic configuration in the story, where Clementine stands somehow outside the East-West opposition of an imperial fantasy, then we can see a purer, more natural feminine identity emerging from her close encounter with the physical, ancient objects of this place, at least those unfettered to constructs of ethnicity. Could we not then read in this story an expression of Jewish identity in the East as an alternate site of relations to the soil?

The move from poetry to prose in Raab's career hardly seems innocent, even if the evocative language of the story resonates with the figural texture of a poetic environment. Still, the writing of prose, dislocated from the centrality of a strong voice, works to dissipate identity further into the described world. The artifice of representation retreats into the metaphoric descriptions of physical objects. And in that sense, Raab moves toward Arlosoroff's rhetoric, not with any sort of enhanced scientism (although could we not read the removal to Egypt as the distancing through objectivity that Arlosoroff tries to maintain in the political rhetoric of his economic argument?). Rather, Raab further separates the land from the apostrophic address of the written utterance. The land no longer issues from the word itself, not just in how Shlonsky defined the land, but in how poetry cannot rid itself from its self-generation, its own artifice. Instead, the land now simply is there, and artifice hides behind a prose style that never identifies its own point of view, thereby assuming—as did Arlosoroff—the land as a given thing.

Orientalism, we might argue, generally demands prose over poetry as it extends discourse to encompass the other, even when, as here in Palestine after 1929, the other might be the environment of the east and not the easterner. Poetry worked, for Raab and Bluwstein, to challenge the dominance of a male poetics where the poet's view figured the land from nothing and defined a politics of environmental invention and natural identity, casting aside those deemed marginal. After 1929, however, with a new politics of colonial competition and the ascendance of an object-oriented discourse, prose as poetic idea becomes the obvious telos, the fate of a literary politics that would compete in and for the land.

The End of Objectivism

By the mid-1930s, however, this minor ascendance of a feminine aesthetic was finished. In 1931, Bluwstein was dead, felled by tuberculosis, a disease, ironically, of enclosed spaces and constricted urban environments. In 1933, Arlosoroff was assassinated as he strolled along the beach in Tel Aviv; he, too, we could say, a victim of the discourse he so passionately embraced, a discourse of Eastern politics and environmental affiliation. By 1934, as well, Esther Raab fell silent and published nothing more until the appearance of her next book of poems in the 1960s, a hiatus of three decades.

There were others—the poet Yocheved Bat-Miriam, to whom Bluwstein had dedicated "Ivriyah" (Hebrewess); and the artist Anna Ticho, whose sparse, antiromantic landscapes echoed Raab's nature descriptions—but no one matched the iconographic status of Bluwstein's sentimental portraits of pioneering and the land, or Raab's self-promotion as an authentic poet of the land, the first Hebrew poet, as she persistently reminded the public, who had been born in Eretz Israel. That sense of authenticity still persists, and even though contemporary critical assessment at the time marginalized Raab's position within the centrally accepted canon, we cannot overlook her coincidence and collusion with a discursive political project that belied an ideological affinity with a larger hegemonic outlook for Palestine.[55]

Most important, with the death of Arlosoroff, perhaps the greatest Arabist of Zionism's leaders, a political outlook focused on the East died as well. By the mid-1930s Zionism's political and cultural energies were committed to Katznelson's image of a post-1929 future for the Yishuv: building an aesthetic and physical infrastructure that would be based on ethnic separation, with a concomitant rejection and erasure of the Arab from Jewish horizons in the country. The consequence of this strategy was tragically predictable. By the mid-1930s, the ethnic struggles of two colonized peoples contending for economic and political dominance erupted into one final paroxysm of colonial violence, the last, that is, before statehood rearranged competition into other discursive arenas. The Arab Revolt that began in 1936 and lasted three years demonstrated how powerful the Jewish market had become, how, that is, separation had successfully cordoned off Jewish society and identity from its surroundings. Thus the Arab Revolt marked the final collapse of a Hebrew modernism that looked to the land "as it was," a modernism that sought to build a new Jewish identity through the encounter with nature. If the violence of 1929 killed a constructivist poetics that would utter the land in the utterance of the self—a subject-oriented writing of the land that reflexively wrote the self at the same time—then its opposite—the object identity of a feminine poetics—died of its own impossible logic, dead long before the Arab Revolt ever began.

The final chapter, then, of this saga of modernism in the land involves the abandonment of nature itself, in the name of nature, to build nature as an unmediated and unmarked space of infinite potential and economic opportunity. The story then moves back to the most artificial and reviled space of Zionist settlement: the city. But in Tel Aviv, away from the ethnically confusing land and the failures to control the discourses that would write the landscape as an essentially Jewish space, Zionist writing turned, ironically, to its European urban origins, this time to construct and colonize nature within the political safety of a built environment.

Chapter 5

The Natural History of Tel Aviv

By the early 1930s, Ḥayim Arlosoroff was able to recognize a rapidly developing urban segment within the Jewish population of Palestine.[1] The observation had several critical implications. Not only was the Yishuv quickly becoming dominated by urban economics, but urban culture marked an ever greater proportion of Jewish experience in the country. In particular, the rising Jewish metropolis of Tel Aviv, the erstwhile garden suburb of Jaffa founded in 1909, came to symbolize this urban growth away from the field. As the Jewish economy expanded into increasingly industrial modes of production—factories that produced marketable goods; a hydroelectric power plant at Naharayim;[2] a Jewish port in Ashdod,[3] south of Tel Aviv—the Jewish population clustered in urban centers, farther and farther from the fields that had defined Zionism's fundamental identity.

Yet, despite Zionism's traditional antipathy toward the city, and despite the labor establishment's wariness of the potential political hostility of a bourgeois urban populace,[4] Tel Aviv was never conceived outside of the discursive space of settlement, cut off from the agrarian values of the farm. Indeed, urban experience would never replace the cultural importance of nature, even after urbanism and industrialism had come to dominate the development of the Zionist economy. This is not to say that the city had no impact on the culture and politics of the country. In the wake of Arab violence and the newly defined contestation over the land, the city in fact became something of a cultural haven for the Yishuv and opened up a new space for the expression of the mutual identification of land and Jew. If "to build and be built" had always been predicated on a concept of nature that somehow encapsulated a certain Jewish anxiety over the distance that might exist between the Jew and nature, then ironically the retreat from nature in the 1930s ostensibly articulated a much closer and secure relationship between settlement and nature as if that anxious gap no longer existed. Nature was now framed aesthetically and ideologically within a reimagined built environment. In the city, architecture and the industrial building projects of the decade would define the essential performance of Jewish building in the land.

The constructions of an industrialized society thus embraced and formed the natural landscape within a unified vision of what constituted both the city and what traditionally lay beyond it, namely, the field. In this new idea of nature, artifice, especially in the form of urban experience, underwent a process of being reconceptualized as part of nature, as something in itself natural. Building, in fact, became a performance of what nature in Palestine must be.

During the 1930s, within this process of redefining nature, literature actually lost its leading role to other arts, newer arts for which the new technologies of the decade invented innovative ways of perceiving the landscape. As Tel Aviv began to explode culturally and physically in the early 1930s, literature remained caught in an anachronistic opposition, caught, that is, in a dialectic of static subject-object representation, trapped between abstract interiority and objective exteriority. On the other hand, the aesthetics of modernist architecture, cabaret, and talking pictures—all performance arts—seized the expressive vacuum literature had left and developed a new dialectical articulation of "to build and be built," one that attempted to synthesize artifice and nature in the very act of building the country. In the end, that elaboration engulfed poetry as well, specifically the poetry of Natan Alterman, who would come to be its greatest proponent, but only after a notion of performance in the land had developed in order to replace the moribund poetics of the previous generation. Indeed, if we look to standard poetic genealogies of the Hebrew literary canon of the 1930s, we would find a troublesome lacuna in the articulation of a nature aesthetics, a gap between Shlonsky and Alterman's poetry of the mid-1930s. Even then, Alterman emerges not as what we might expect from a nature poet, but ironically as a city poet, indeed a poet of Tel Aviv. But it was there in the city where nature could be encountered, a nature, that is, reconceived and reimagined within the buildings of Zionist identity and the Jewish nation.

Tel Aviv Between Bauhaus and the Kibbutz

In 1932, the young former kibbutznik Arieh Sharon returned to Palestine after studying architecture at the Bauhaus. Now armed with an aesthetic arsenal of modernist building techniques and ideas, Sharon had nothing but disdain for the ethnic eclecticism of the chaotic Tel Aviv street:

> [W]hen I came back from the Bauhaus after six years of absence, I walked through Tel Aviv, and I was very depressed by its architecture. After Berlin, which, in the late twenties, was the liveliest city in the world, making its unique contribution to literature, the arts, theater and architecture, Tel Aviv was a shock. I walked along the main street, Allenby Road, and found it was a commercial center of a provincial Mediterranean town. Around it, two and three-story houses

with little mediocre shops lined the streets. There were generally small apartments on the two upper floors, a mixture of street elevations, decorated with various different balconies and alcoves in the poor style of Eastern Europe.[5]

Sharon offers scant praise for the "few, somewhat charming, oriental facades designed by the pioneering architects of the early twenties." Overall, he shudders at the lack of a clear, unified visage in the city. The "restless, heterogeneous building facades" reveal far too much their ethnic character: "Mediterranean," "oriental," and "Eastern European." For a young man "dreaming of contributing to the architectural development of a new country," the lack of (ethnic) unity in the urban design of Tel Aviv was quite discouraging.

By 1938, however, Sharon and handful of other like-minded architects had completely succeeded in transforming the Jewish city. Despite the broad architectural eclecticism that characterized Tel Aviv throughout the 1920s, International Style architecture and urban planning quickly came to dominate the Tel Aviv scene. Within a mere six years of Sharon's return, and due much to his concerted efforts,[6] the city would be transformed into an urban space of outstanding uniformity of architectural design, especially in its newer northern quarters. Indeed, what we think of as the typical Tel Aviv street (Figure 5)—boxy three- and four-story apartment buildings raised up on pilotis; apartments facing the street through large balconies—emanates from the architectural vision of the 1930s and this modernist explosion of building. With few formal modifications, the basic elements of European modernism were adapted for the strong, hot climate of the eastern Mediterranean: the flat roof; the cubic geometry of the building's structure; the ribbon windows, which were redesigned as ribbon balconies; Le Corbusier's pilotis, which became a de rigueur design element, allowing for free air flow around the entire structure and the penetration of the garden into the building itself.[7]

As might be expected, the meteoric rise of German modernism to stylistic hegemony in Jewish Palestine has elicited several critical explanations. Most claim to concentrate on formal analysis, but they usually devolve into a combination of rationalist pragmatism (climatic exigency) and nationalist spiritualism (positing stylistic unity alternately on the 1930s wave of bourgeois German immigrants with their imported aesthetic predilections or on sudden national coalescence).[8] Common to all of these arguments—no matter the historical and critical inconsistencies among them—is their reliance on a rather limited oppositional assumption, well known in Israeli and other colonial studies, that depends on the proposition that stylistic appropriation in the colonial space indicates either universalist aesthetic affiliation or unique atavistic allegiances.

Recently, this opposition has been effectively challenged for modernist architecture in Palestine by Daniel Bertrand Monk, who argues for a resonance between the terms of aesthetic analysis and a political attitude defined by specific ethnic assumptions.[9] In his analysis of the interdependencies of transfer (of style/people/knowledge) and autonomy (of community/art/expression), Monk dismisses any sense of conceptual opposition between these terms and demonstrates the dangerous political obfuscation that occurs when transfer and autonomy come to represent the entire spectrum of critical alternatives.

We can hear the power of Monk's argument, and his critique of a political silence that ensues within responses to architecture, when we read, for instance, Gilbert Herbert's description of German aesthetic dominance in Jewish Palestine: "There were many reasons for this unexpected flowering of modern architecture on the remote shores of the eastern Mediterranean. Its austere, cubic geometry was *somehow* completely congruous with the climate, the landscape, and the indigenous forms of the vernacular architecture of the region" (emphasis added).[10] What Herbert refuses to analyze—and what seems to lie at the crux of a critical interrogation of the deployment of specific art forms—is how to understand the "somehow," which displaces and postpones questions about the political significance of architecture. Doesn't the "somehow" stand in for the ethnic marker, the inflection through Jewish colonialism, whose influence on making things seem natural or "indigenous" is

Figure 5. A Tel Aviv street in the 1930s.

precisely the thing we need to investigate? Ita Heinze-Greenberg's rather inarticulate paroxysm of explanation for the Bauhaus in Tel Aviv—"Because: it was appropriate"[11]—does little to make the matter any clearer. Appropriate to what? And how are we to understand the odd use of the term "appropriate," which resonates with the violent history of competition in this land?[12]

By the time Sharon wanders through Tel Aviv on his return from Germany, the city certainly embodied all of these ethnic questions. Despite attempts to maintain the original vision of a small, aesthetically and commercially (and ethnically) controlled satellite Jewish community on the outskirts of northern Jaffa, Tel Aviv had metamorphosed into a mixed urban center. Even then, in the 1930s, the city continued to debate its urban identity. Since Tel Aviv's foundation in 1909, two comprehensive master plans had been devised, the most significant by the Scottish academic Patrick Geddes in 1925. Even though Tel Aviv had expanded well beyond its origins by the 1920s, Geddes still looked to the English garden suburb as the foundation for the city, maintaining and even emphasizing many of the original conceptions for the suburban space: the single-family house; large lot sizes; and green space within and between blocks. Ironically, Sharon's disgust with the city, despite being aimed at the commercialism of Allenby Road, which neither the founders nor Geddes had anticipated, finds its clearest articulation in an attack on the garden concept of Geddes's plan for the city: "The town obviously suffers to this day," Sharon wrote, "from its first misconception as an urban garden city."[13]

Despite this disdain for the conceptual origins of Tel Aviv as a garden city, Sharon's solution is not to counter garden with city. Rather, his criticisms seem primarily focused on the city aspect of the garden city, which explains his mistake in even talking about the original conception for Tel Aviv as a garden *city*.[14] Ironically, both he and the other Bauhauslers returning from Europe to work in Palestine benefited greatly from the aesthetic parameters Geddes set up for the urban environment. Indeed, in 1932 the Geddes plan was still very much alive as a debated issue in Tel Aviv and continued to be bandied about various city departments until it was officially adopted in 1938, well into the most intense years of Tel Aviv's urban transformation. In a formal sense, some dissonance might exist between Sharon's modernist predilections, on the one hand, and the garden suburb concept, on the other. However, formal dissonance only distracts us from seeing a clear ideological agreement in how all these design concepts integrate nature within the city space. As the urbanization of Tel Aviv progressed, the idea of remaking the city as closely associated with nature clearly reflected the ideological and personal experiences of these architects, who were, in general, less bourgeois

German immigrants of the Fifth Aliyah importing their European cultural sensibility than returnees from sojourns abroad, pioneers who were inflecting the values of the field through the urban training they received in Europe.[15]

In this, too, Sharon was typical and his own personal history emblematically reflects a growing intensification in the Zionist orientation toward melding technology, design, and nature.[16] Sharon never lost his original agrarian interests and returns time and again to the kibbutz, both as the primary locus and impetus for Israeli urban design and as intellectual and ideological origin. His migration from kibbutz to Germany and then back to Tel Aviv tells a fascinating story of developing Zionist attitudes and intellectual transformations, from rustic ruralism to an urbanism informed by European modernism. But we cannot ignore, as Sharon himself never does, the intense influence of the rural experience on the making of Tel Aviv and Zionist urban aesthetics in general.

Sharon's text never strays far from its fundamental natural telos, that is, the need to synthesize what the architect learned in Germany with the fundamental agrarian values he originally absorbed in Palestine. Indeed, his narrative of wandering through Tel Aviv in 1932 becomes a sort of modernist nature parable. In his peregrinations beyond Allenby Road, the architect encounters a young woman he had last met in Germany, and it is she who takes him to see a house built in the modernist style on the city's northern edge. In a series of happenstance encounters reminiscent of early Kafka, that house, in turn, is inhabited by old friends of Sharon from his kibbutz days. In this way, the narrative describes a triangulation of experience: from urban wanderer to German savior who shows the way back to an indigenous, nature-based modernism. It is not so much the importation of urban elements into Palestine that marks a trajectory of the dissolution of the divide between city and country so famously outlined by Raymond Williams,[17] but precisely the opposite: the fantasy of nature overcoming the urban. This type of vision had real consequences, and not just in a metropolis like Tel Aviv. At Nahalal, for instance, which meant to express a rational Zionist control over the land in order for nature to blossom, theories about the new, modern garden city consciously informed design.[18]

The comparison to Nahalal is not capricious; in at least one important way, that is, the rejection of commerce, the natural space of Nahalal echoes Tel Aviv. Tel Aviv originated as free of commerce, and, as an indication of the way urban space might corrupt nature, the presence of commerce continues as a problem for the Zionist city. In fact, in what truly reveals the Tel Aviv architectural revolution as modernist, and fortifies as well its connections to the original vision for the garden suburb, Sharon's narrative reacts initially not to the forms of the buildings themselves, but to the very presence of commerce on the street: "I walked along the main street, Allenby Road, and found it was the commercial center of a provincial Mediterranean town." Sharon's disappointment in the commercial street is integral to a redemptive design tale that moves away from the city as an eclectic menagerie of representational systems and toward the collective articulation of the group and the return to nature. For, when Sharon arrives at the modernist house on the edge of the city, the most significant changes occur not in the exterior forms of the architectural object, but in interior personal perspective, now refracted through the cultural activities of a modernist avant-garde: "Informal gatherings of the Tel Aviv cultural leaders . . . took place there. . . . On the mornings after these sessions . . . the Tel Aviv landscape came to look different and more hopeful . . . the play of light and shade over the white elevations of the apartment buildings changed my mood."[19] The city emerges as an optimistic space but only if one can see it through the prism of a collective understanding of the national environment.

Sharon's urban critique is thus not completely Bauhaus-influenced and certainly evolves from traditional Zionist reservations about the city, reflecting broadly on many of the sentiments behind Herzl's own critical urban vision articulated in his 1902 novel *Altneuland*, from which Tel Aviv derives its name. There, Herzl fulfills the anti-urban fantasies of his protagonist, Friedrich, by whisking him off to the tropical utopia of the rich, older Kingscourt's South Pacific island.[20] In this, Herzl merely enacts a critique of the ills of urbanism generally associated with a range of contemporary social commentaries on the European city, none more famous (or infamous) than those of his close associate in the political Zionist movement, Max Nordau.[21]

But the cultural critique of urbanity's ills was not limited to Zionism. Indeed, Georg Simmel's 1903 essay "The Metropolis and Mental Life," for instance, reads almost as a primer for the type of criticisms both Herzl and Sharon hurl at the city: "The deepest problems of modern life flow from the attempt of the individual to maintain the independence and individuality of his existence against the sovereign powers of society, against the weight of the historical heritage and the external culture and technique of life. This antagonism represents the most modern form of the conflict which primitive man must carry on with nature for his own bodily existence."[22] Simmel's concern, the "mental life" of the individual and the relations between urban modernity and the natural proclivities of the individual within community, marks a new modernist attitude toward urban critique, and in this he shares with Herzl the idea that it is precisely the subject that must emerge from the struggle with the totalizing forces of the metropolis: "The development of modern culture is characterized by the predominance of what one can call the objective spirit over the subjective; that is, in language as well as in law, in the technique of production as well as in art, in science as well as in the objects of domestic environment, there is embodied a sort of spirit, the daily growth of which is followed only imperfectly and with an even greater lag by the intellectual development of the individual."[23]

Herzl would agree, and for this reason sent Friedrich on his way to develop an inner life, of which he was bereft at the beginning of the novel, sitting alone in his alienating urban hovel, contemplating suicide. Like Herzl's utopia—and Sharon's fantasies for the Tel Aviv street—Simmel ignores the physical structure of the city itself and anchors his critique in the representational systems of urban life, which would displace true relationships among people. In large part, money becomes the ultimately nefarious signifier that would stand in for true relations, a critique Herzl also responded to, banishing money from his utopian vision of a technologically advanced Jewish Palestine.

What differentiates Herzl's Friedrich from Sharon's ideas about Jewish urbanity in Palestine are the possibilities opened up during the thirty-year gap dividing them. Friedrich could only reflect on and take in the changes Herzl envisioned, a passive observer of this newly built utopia, built, that is, offstage from the narrated action of the novel. We never do see the hard work of building. Sharon, however, begins to enact the place in a newfound individual confidence of projecting a design vision onto the landscape. Thus, what Sharon's fleeing the commercial life of the urban center rejects is a place for the individual alienated from the basic structures of mental existence. Sharon turns toward self-reliance, toward individual control over urban signs, and away from the external commercial discourses of Allenby Road that assign arbitrary values to objects. Over against the interchange of the urban space, Sharon knows that his reflexive vision will converge with the community and connect to the nation. Erich Mendelsohn, who was brought to Palestine by Salmon Schocken to design several buildings there, expresses this same millennial vision for the architect at the beginning of his text *Palestine and the World of Tomorrow*: "It seems to be no matter of mere chance but rather *natural*, that it is the architect—accustomed to the conception of a building as the sum total of all the requirements of his time—who should be among the first to realize the change in the structure of the world because he feels the structural element to be his own personal prerogative" (emphasis added).[24] Structure, in Mendelsohn's sense, does more than bridge form and content, where the physical building articulates a deep architectonic awareness. Beyond that, structure also designates a fundamental, essential sympathy between the vision of the builder and the natural—that is, unarbitrary—structures of society.

The Performance of Nature

In Mendelsohn's "personal prerogative," building as the reinvention of society emanates from the architect's vision, the product of a willed construction in the land that will build society anew. For Jewish society in Palestine, that correspondence between builder and environment translated into the articulation of Tel Aviv *within* the natural landscape. After all, that was the thrust of Sharon's critique of the garden city: not that it obfuscated the true urban nature of Tel Aviv, but that it accomplished precisely the opposite, namely, the separation of the city from the land surrounding it. As the 1930s progressed, the interpenetration of builder and built environment—where nature elides into the concrete world of construction—became an explicitly articulated element of Zionist settlement.

Performance, then, and not literary articulation comes to define Jewish space in the 1930s. The difference is subtle, but performance takes on meaning from public enactment, the "personal prerogative" of the architect expressed in public building. Articulation, at least as Zionism had usually understood it, had been a private matter: intransitive, reflective of nature, drawing on nature's fecundity, but creating no substantial object. Performance, on the other hand, produces the object through public intercourse. Because of this, the stage might, next to the architect, embody the paradigmatic locus of 1930s Zionist expression. And indeed, in the 1930s, the stage flourished in Tel Aviv, and from it emerged a new type of pioneering performance, the cabaret song.

"Mi yivneh" (Who Will Build), for instance, made famous by the Yemenite singer-dancer Bracha Tsfira, another returnee in 1932 from the sophisticated salons and stages of Berlin, defines nature by the building of the city. In "Mi yivneh" Tel Aviv's new place as the principal object of Zionist performance is made clear. Drawing on the old pioneering ethic of building, the song transforms nature as contemplative object into the transitive product of public construction:

מִי יִבְנֶה, יִבְנֶה בַּיִת בְּתֵל-אָבִיב?
אֲנַחְנוּ הַחֲלוּצִים
נִבְנֶה אֶת תֵּל-אָבִיב.
הָבוּ חֹמֶר וּלְבֵנִים
וְנִבְנֶה אֶת תֵּל-אָבִיב!

מִי יִזְרַע, יִזְרַע שָׂדֶה בְּתֵל-חַי?
אֲנַחְנוּ הַחֲלוּצִים
נִזְרַע אֶת תֵּל-חַי.
הָבוּ לָנוּ זֵרְעוֹנִים
וְנִזְרַע אֶת תֵּל-חַי!

מִי יִשְׁתֹּל, יִשְׁתֹּל פַּרְדֵּס בִּרְחוֹבוֹת?
אֲנַחְנוּ הַחֲלוּצִים
נִשְׁתֹּל אֶת רְחוֹבוֹת.
הָבוּ לָנוּ שְׁתִילִים
וְנִשְׁתֹּל אֶת רְחוֹבוֹת!

מִי יִטַּע, יִטַּע כֶּרֶם בְּרִאשׁוֹן?
אֲנַחְנוּ הַחֲלוּצִים
נִטַּע אֶת רִאשׁוֹן.
הָבוּ לָנוּ גְּפָנִים
וְנִטַּע אֶת רִאשׁוֹן!

Who will build, build a house in Tel Aviv?
We the pioneers
Will build Tel Aviv.
Bring material and bricks
And we will build Tel Aviv!

Who will sow, sow a field at Tel Ḥai?
We the pioneers
Will sow Tel Ḥai.
Bring us seeds
And we will sow Tel Ḥai!

Who will plant, plant an orchard in Reḥovot?
We the pioneers
Will plant Reḥovot.
Bring us saplings
And we will plant Reḥovot!

Who will plant, plant a vineyard in Rishon?
We the pioneers
Will plant Rishon.
Bring us vines
And we will plant Rishon![25]

The song creates a new place for the city Tel Aviv, inventing a new way to articulate and, indeed, *perform* settlement. Thematically, building is now infused with purely material industrial meaning: "bricks" and "houses" parallel the agrarian fields. In fact, the signs of bourgeois urban life themselves initiate a litany of Zionist tropes of nature and settlement: from bricks, we get trees, plants, vineyards, and the like. Nature receives impetus and gives its bounty only at the initiative of urban building. And beyond the thematic presentation of the city within an agrarian fantasy, the incorporation of the built environment into a vision of nature dictates a new type of syntax in the very sentence of the lyric, reflecting as well a new conceptualization for building on the land. The hesitation of the first line in each stanza—"Who will build, build a house in Tel Aviv?"—

repeats the predicate which then concludes in a direct object, performing through grammar the cultural transformation of an intransitive idea, taking the reflexive notion of working in order to form the self and giving it a decidedly material object. The stammer—the last gasp, we might say, of consciously understanding the implications of this new performative aesthetic—pushes aside reflection and forms the object in the land, beginning, in what seems a *natural* progression, from the urban environment. Laboring in the land, in this song, does not merely create the worker reflexively; it also produces something external to the self, namely, the land.

In each stanza, as the song moves through a list of canonical settlements, not only do the *means* of action receive concrete material expression in an object—bricks, seeds, saplings, vines—but these material objects are now the instruments in the creation of larger conceptual spaces in the country—from a house in Tel Aviv to the city itself, from the fields of Tel Ḥai to Tel Ḥai itself, and so on. Access to nature now passes through a double filter: through the named settlement that stands in for and completes nature; and through the material objects that will allow the Zionist to build there in the first place. In both instances of building, that is, as both verb *and* noun, nature is completely instrumental to larger conceptual ends.

Much of this transformation was no doubt due to the technological novelties of the decade in industry, building construction, and entertainment. Alongside the stage, even as a product of the stage, talking pictures flourished in Palestine both as an entertainment form[26] and as a medium for promoting Zionist settlement throughout the world. Indeed, promotional sound films replaced scripted slide shows read at local meetings of diaspora Zionist groups as a way of disseminating a feel for the country.[27] The difference was radical; from the mid-1930s on, animated labor and action on the land could be represented with an authentic sound track of nature and of building alongside it. Logistically, film did away with the detailed instructions to the local Zionist narrator on how to present the slides and inflect the script. Thematically, film allowed the abandonment of static visual representation and emphasized the rejuvenation of nature in Palestine as an active process being performed by Jews. Thus, as opposed to the passive tours of the slide shows, film supported a notion of a built environment that followed the architectural projects of the young International Style architects and thematized architecture and building on the screen. Juda Leman's *Land of Promise*,[28] the highly publicized and widely distributed propaganda film produced by Keren Ha-yesod in 1935, frames nature within a telos that ends in Tel Aviv and gives meaning to the process of Jewish redemption in Palestine within a dialectic that synthesizes building and nature.

Among images of agricultural improvement and expansion, in truth, the scenes of construction in Tel Aviv narratively sum up Jewish efforts in the country and give expression and meaning to an advancing control over nature that would effectively *enact* nature as something natural. Within the film's narrative language, urban building frames meaning for the battalions of agricultural workers marching to the fields, in a choreography utterly derived from the ordered, modernist cityscape.

Most iconographically striking in this respect is the film's poster, which carefully outlines the connections and associations to be understood from the new architecture and the idea of performance in the land (Figure 6). The visual lexicon in the poster is familiar: the peasant couple in the center with field implements slung over their shoulders proudly announces the work on the land, a desert landscape lying quietly in the background, made fertile only in the foreground at the feet of the two workers. Promise is embodied in the agricultural implements, which will transform and make the land yield its crop.

Off to the right, however, stands another product of human technology: a modernist structure, with a caravan of riderless camels passing in front. The image of the Bauhaus structure and the camels (minus their Arab handler) comes directly from the movie but the poster erases any human presence in the camel train, as if we are to understand the signifier of the camel as carrying inherent meaning.[29] However, what was being erased in any image of the camel as a signifier must have been clear, even for the myopically focused Yishuv. By 1935 the configuration of modernist architecture and Middle Eastern ethnicity could not have been so innocent, especially in the context of Nazi propaganda that had depicted the degeneracy of Bauhaus design in 1933 with a touched-up photomontage of the Weissenhofsiedlung in Stuttgart as an Arab village. There too camels mark the space as authentically Middle Eastern, but clearly of Arab descent (Figure 7).[30]

While the Nazis tied architecture to degeneracy and Orientalism, the Zionists consciously move away from ethnicity to couple building to the land itself. Gone is any hint of human habitation—especially Arab—except for the ruddy European peasants of the foreground, marked in their modernity, and thus ironically their distance from any true indigenous pedigree, by their short pants, still today the clear mark of the colonial outsider. But that didn't matter. Instead of an Arab village, where the camel contextualizes the purported evils of modern architecture, modernism in the Zionist representation works to contextualize and romanticize the camel in an inversion of the Nazi image. The place in the land, the poster seems to say, must be built, artificially constructed to sprout both wheat (the product of extensive farming) and society as a product of human action.[31] Modernist building did not reflect an ethnicity inherent

Figure 6. Poster for Juda Leman's *The Land of Promise*, 1935. The first line "Spre o viață nouă," in Rumanian, reads: "Toward a new life"; the second line, in Hungarian, "Az igéret földje," reads "The Promised Land." (Steven Spielberg Jewish Film Archive)

in the land, but in a modernist way, building invented new ethnic possibilities for the land on which the architecture stood. The workers of the land, with tools in hand, stand before their creations in a dialectical relationship, at home both with the natural image of the camel and with the artifice of the modernist structure. Together, both elements generate meaning in the landscape.

The isolation of the modernist building and the lack of any urban context should not be ignored, for it seems to resonate with more than just an allegorical abstraction of conjured features within the landscape. The separation of the structure certainly echoes a Zionist notion of creating *ex nihilo* on the land, as in Sharon's journey to the very edge of Tel Aviv in order to encounter a redemptive modernism. But it also signifies a monumentality and fecundity for modernist buildings that might indeed have been unique for Palestine at the time. Instead of taking the poster solely as a lexicon of Zionist desire in the land, the rural space reclaimed as a modernist landscape, within the context of the building projects in Tel Aviv in the mid-1930s, the poster expresses perhaps denotatively the iconic significance of a building program emerging of great monumental value. The photographs of the original construction of Dizengoff Circle, designed by Genia Averbach and begun in 1935 (Figure 8), clearly show the disproportionate size of the plaza against the scale of

Figure 7. Nazi photomontage of the Stuttgart Weissenhofsiedlung as an Arab village, 1933.

the rest of the city. The *Land of Promise* poster might indeed reflect a real everyday sight in the city and mark a confluence between fantasized landscape and actual building.

In a strikingly similar way, the poster for Baruch Agadati's promotional film *Das ist das Land* (Figure 9),[32] also from 1935, takes the same visual language of desert, camels, modernist architecture, and a couple of workers and blows them up into a modern fantasy of man's vision in the environment. Thematically, here too the land is void of Arabs. The camels move in a caravan on their own, marking that we are in the Middle East, but one newly constructed and imagined—the product of a transcendent consciousness. The empty footsteps leading into the background signify more the trace of the worker suspended above the scene than any Arab who might actually have trod this ground. Hovering above that ground is the fantasy of building, which means construction—of rational structures, of neat rectilinear proportions, of a melding of man and modernist building.

The connection between building as object and human figure marks the strongest difference from the image in *The Land of Promise*, which

Figure 8. Aerial view of Dizengoff Circle, Tel Aviv, 1939. (Zoltan Kluger; Central Zionist Archives)

Figure 9. Poster for Baruch Agadati's *Das ist das Land*, 1935. (Steven Spielberg Jewish Film Archive)

maintains at least a modicum of realistic portrayal. Instead, in the *Das ist das Land* image, abstraction takes over to convey a similar sort of belonging in the land, again, one significantly figured through construction. But now the dialectical relationship between these elements is more clearly outlined. The human figures hover over the landscape and collapse into the building structure itself: the arms of the woman, the sleeve of the man mimicking and even synesthetically becoming rectilinear outlines parallel to the skyscrapers that similarly float in this ideational space above the soil. While earlier we might have thought of a dialectical reconciliation in the fantasy of man and land coming together in a bridging between human desire and the realities of nature, now that projection is figured within a narrower syllogism of moving from the human subject to the built environment as the product of artifice. The land remains exterior to the central figures in this image: an outcome, a remainder of the essential relationship between actor and construction within the space. Nature, then, becomes the final product of that equation, the promise of the subtitle, *The Wonder of Modern Palestine*, which places Palestine as the invention of psychological wonder.

For the Zionist movement in general, with its anxieties to compete as native in Palestine, the inability of representation to close the gap between a phenomenology of place and the abstraction of subjective consciousness pushes even greater alienation into the text between the worker in action on the land and the landscape itself. As I am trying to argue here, a solution to that problem—*one* solution—certainly was the abandonment of textual resolution in favor of a performative enactment of nativism. For instance, any grammatical difficulties in "Mi yivneh" are significantly ameliorated by the performance itself, by Bracha Tsfira as a Yemenite dancer-singer who lends authenticity to the manipulation of the countryside. Similarly, the title *Das ist das Land* functions itself as a performative utterance, whose pointing to the land ties its vision to a speaker who will enact it. Film performs what the static visual image of the poster or the slide show can only vaguely promise.

Building then becomes native, transformation is deemed authentic because the subject performing the articulation of this action already embodies both the land and the identity of native belonging. The sojourn through Berlin—for Tsfira as it was for Sharon—acts to legitimize the self-reflexive Orientalist gaze that authenticates the subject as appropriate to the landscape. After success in Europe, Tsfira can be successful in Palestine because Berlin—with the likes of Einstein himself granting the imprimatur of authenticity[33]—accepts the oriental image as proper and the performance of the fantasized indigene as authentic. The by-product of that journey, especially for Sharon, might have been the acquisition of a new aesthetic vocabulary (Tsfira, too, ostensibly went to Germany to "learn" her craft of singing the eastern songs she made famous in the Jewish salons there),[34] but the ideological success and impact of the turn back to Europe was the authentication of a nativism tied to the performative utterances of an always already nativized Jew, of the subject *as* object.

Natural History

The outcome of this process is not just building as "appropriate" to this place by its nature, a nature carefully controlled, formed, and discursively defined—but a performative language and dramaturgy denuded of its historical and aesthetic contexts. Thus, Bracha Tsfira stands on the Tel Aviv stage in Yemenite garb singing Zionist pioneering songs constructed of the simplest European diatonic harmonies. For this reason too the Bauhaus building stands alone in the desertscape, the product of a Zionist fantasy of belonging to the land, of living a new native life there risen *ex nihilo* from the landscape. This is a new language based on action and intention, a set of neologisms meant to perform what language alone could not accomplish. Always implied in that new articulation of place and nativism is the idea of an immutable association between what is historically contingent—the Bauhaus structure in the desert, the Yemenite singing Zionist ditties on the Tel Aviv stage—and the natural essence of the place—the camels that define the Easternness of the desert. This relationship between the contingencies of history and the spirit of national will, on the one hand, and the universality of unchanging natural structures, on the other, defines the forms of Zionist representation in the 1930s and ties the city to the natural landscape.

Theodor Adorno had already articulated a critique of this type of modernist practice in 1932 when he addressed the currents of recent philosophical trends. Because of this, his essay on natural history can certainly be read in the context of Zionism and sheds light on how the movement attempted to derive universal (natural) principles from the resistance of phenomena to submit to strict empirical schemes: "[P]recisely where an element fails to dissolve into determinations of thought and cannot be made transparent, but rather retains its pure thereness, precisely at this point the resistance of the phenomenon is transformed into a universal concept and their resistance as such is endowed with ontological value."[35] In the context of Zionism, we can invert the critique into a willed ideological maneuver and understand perhaps a conscious resistance to the contingencies of nature, namely, a resistance to the dialectical interconnections between those aspects of the landscape deemed immutable and the products of human articulation. In this, the dialectics of natural history open a point of departure for understanding a

Zionist ideological refusal to acknowledge how the dramaturgical performance of nature tautologically fulfills the fantasies of political prophecy for a land made better by Jewish presence. Adorno's dialectical thinking would then offer a serious challenge to Zionist modes of representation because it upsets the very basis of Jewish presence in nature: "The division of the world into nature and spirit or nature and history, a tradition set by subjectivist idealism, must be overcome and its place must be taken by a formulation that achieves in itself the concrete unity of nature and history."[36]

Within this context, we can speak of the natural history of Tel Aviv because of the way discourse about the city articulated a resistance to the type of dialectic relationship Adorno describes between artifice and being. The envisioned city derives from the landscape and disavows any border between building (spirit/history) and natural landscape (fields/soil). The design appropriations of Tel Aviv modernism—ribbon balconies, flat roofs, pilotis—each acted to emphasize and heighten the sense of interpenetration between the built and natural realms. Even beyond purely formal considerations of design, Tel Aviv, through the unity of its building program, attempted to construct a conceptual bridge precisely between history and nature. In the Zionist search for native identification with Palestine, the built environment becomes the enactment of a subjectivity that unifies the "possible and the real" in a denial of both the contingency of that move and the stasis it creates for a language that would describe this place. In this sense, Bracha Tsfira's performance of nativism could only work as an imported poetic, appropriated from outside, legitimized beyond Palestine, and then brought back and cathected onto the nature of this "old-new" place in order to make it more appropriately and intrinsically Jewish.

The Return of Poetry

Economic development and expansion certainly played a hand in filling Tel Aviv's theaters during the 1930s, as did the influx of bourgeois German immigrants after 1933. But the success of performance as a poetic goes far beyond the stage, and if the 1920s were marked by the constructivist privacy of the individual utterance, then the explosion of performance in the 1930s signals an important aesthetic and ideological shift in how action and nature would interact in the creation of the nation. By mid-decade, nature poetry would return to outline this shift, but now as a public act, taking on significance as a performance, thematized that way within the new technology of film.

In *The Land of Promise*, action is not just represented by the intersections of landscape aesthetics and human labor—as in the lines of agricultural workers marching off to improve the land, flanked and paralleled by neatly planted rows of cypress trees, the ubiquitous symbol of Zionist and later Israeli heroism.[37] In the film, too, performance plays a more active thematic role and reintroduces poetry into the discourse of how the land will be improved.

Several songs were composed for the movie, the music by Daniel Sambursky, a recent immigrant in 1935, with words by Natan Alterman, a young poet who was beginning to make his mark on the literary scene. The music for the songs "Shir ha-emek" (Song of the Valley),[38] "Shir ha-kvish" (Song of the Road),[39] and "Shir boker" (Morning Song; also known as "Be-harim kvar ha-shemesh melahetet" [In the Mountains the Sun Is Already Ablaze])[40] rehearse standard European Jewish sonorities of D and E minor and add little to the scenes they accompany. However, the represented social context for the songs as work songs and marches that imitate and accompany the armies of workers heading off toward the fields and the construction sites, reinforces the collective role of music and lyric in society. The apotheosis of this idea in the film occurs when Sambursky himself sits at the piano in the dining room of Kibbutz Givat Brenner, teaching "Song of the Valley" to a group of pioneers. In the middle of the song, the visual stream breaks off and underneath the continuing sound track of the song we see images of pioneers singing the song as they labor throughout the workplaces of the kibbutz.

As poetic texts, "Morning Song" is in fact the most interesting because it reintroduces personal allegory into a Zionist discourse of the land. To be sure, Alterman's poetic achievement owes a great deal to the inherited legacy from Shlonsky, but here symbolist technique yields a new relationship to both nation and land. The poem begins with several standard tropes: the blazing light, the sparkling dew, a declaration of love for the motherland expressed through the munificent aura of the landscape.

בֶּהָרִים כְּבָר הַשֶּׁמֶשׁ מְלַהֶטֶת
וּבָעֵמֶק עוֹד נוֹצֵץ הַטַּל,
אָנוּ אוֹהֲבִים אוֹתָךְ, מוֹלֶדֶת,
בְּשִׂמְחָה, בְּשִׁיר וּבְעָמָל.

In the mountains the sun is already ablaze
And in the valley the dew still sparkles,
We love you, motherland,
With joy, with song, and with work.

The apostrophic address in the song figures nature within a definite community of speakers and performs an intimacy magnified by the plurality of the "we." The apostrophe, however, does not merely invoke the rhetorical trope of nature. Love might open up the connection between speaker(s) and land, but the infusion of the people happens through the adverbial modification of action: "With joy, with song, and with work." Poetry and labor parallel each other, each serving to set up the conditions of national definition in the land. This poem is not simply an ode to the beauty of the land, or a mere litany of places that define the boundaries of place and love. Rather, the simple declaration of love sets up a series of transitive statements, transforming love as an abstract idea into the concrete expression of change and modification. In a way, Alterman takes the performative aspects of Shlonsky's 1920s poetry and adds to it a transitive object, putting phatic individualism into a social national space:

מִמּוֹרְדוֹת הַלְּבָנוֹן עַד יָם הַמֶּלַח
נַעֲבֹר אוֹתָךְ בְּמַחֲרֵשׁוֹת,
אָנוּ עוֹד נִטַּע לָךְ וְנִבְנֶה לָךְ,
אָנוּ נְיַפֶּה אוֹתָךְ מְאֹד.

From the slopes of Lebanon to the Dead Sea
We will cover you with plows,
We will plant you and build you,
We will make you very beautiful.

Love for the pioneer is anything but unconditional, and nature, which started off as a figurative trope, begins to resonate with actual agrarian policy. To achieve that, Alterman, in an ingenious move, slips metaphor in through the back door and inverts the usual way allegory lends meaning to nature thereby giving greater naturalism to the entire concept of building or artifice. The song begins with a series of linguistic figures that evoke naturalism, and only after the establishment of an allegory to encompass the land as lover does the poem reach toward a more realistic representation of nature and labor. Reality thus gains substance from the very figurations of the imagination, and actions like planting and building take on meaning from the allegorical power of the line "we love you." Love justifies improvement based on the promise to beautify that which the lover, in the pluralized form of the nation, touches. The artifice of this sort of action becomes clear in the third stanza when the speaker declares:

נַלְבִּישֵׁךְ שַׂלְמַת בֶּטוֹן וָמֶלֶט
וְנִפְרֹשׂ לָךְ מַרְבַדֵּי גַּנִּים,
עַל אַדְמַת שְׂדוֹתַיִךְ הַנִּגְאֶלֶת
הַדָּגָן יַרְנִין פַּעֲמוֹנִים.

We will dress you in a gown of concrete and cement
And we will lay out for you carpets of gardens,
On the soil of your redeemed fields
The grain will make bells shout with joy.

That first line—"We will dress you in a gown of concrete and cement" —flies in the face of the Zionist poetic tradition, consciously inverting how both Bialik and Shlonsky had viewed the relationship to nature, and indeed how figuration in nature was meant to comfort and envelop man. For Bialik and Shlonsky nature enveloped man and the call for protection—*hakhnisini, halbishini*—always reflected a passive stance in the face of nature's power.[41] Alterman, on the other hand, purposefully introduces an urban element into the natural, agricultural scene, wrapping Palestine within a construction project that reflects the subject in how he would reconfigure the place. Alterman still avoids an oppositional position to nature, an antagonistic encounter between city and country, by making improvement of nature the telos of the built environment. The garden carpet does not mediate artifice in building but itself parallels the industrial fervor of concrete by improving the land.

The dialectics of this simple poem seem forthright: to meld nature and history into a simple project of performative intervention. And here, intervention receives not only a physical instantiation in urban building materials, but a particularly militaristic and aggressively millennial articulation. But the idea of melding action (history) and place (nature) also outlines its own critique, especially in how the song evinces an original problematic in Zionist settlement, namely, the presentation as reconciled of a dialectical division between action in the land and the land itself. Here, the deflation of the allegorical moment by the introduction of the banality of concrete and cement certainly de-idealizes allegory. But the effect raises the quotidian value of work—both of improvement and of defense—to fortify the power of a fantasized landscape.

הַמִּדְבָּר–אָנוּ דֶּרֶךְ בּוֹ נַחְצֹבָה,
הַבִּצּוֹת–אֲנַחְנוּ נְיַבֵּשָׁן.
מַה נִּתֵּן לָךְ עוֹד לְהוֹד וָשֹׂבַע,
מַה עוֹד לֹא נָתַנּוּ–וְנִתֵּן?

בֶּהָרִים, בֶּהָרִים זָרַח אוֹרֵנוּ,
אָנוּ נַעְפִּילָה אֶל הָהָר!
הָאֶתְמוֹל נִשְׁאַר מֵאֲחוֹרֵינוּ,
אַךְ רַבָּה הַדֶּרֶךְ לַמָּחָר.

The desert—through it we will chisel away,
The swamps—we will dry out.
What more should we give you for glory and pleasure,
What more have we not given—and we shall give?

In the mountains, in the mountains our light shines,
We will climb the mountain!
We've left yesterday behind us,
But long is the path to tomorrow.

Ultimately, any meaning for the poem's discourse, be it the morning dew or the cement of the factory, derives from the powerful poetics of the built—and here, performed—environment. "Concrete and cement" frame and perhaps create what is most natural in this version of nature, reminders of Adorno's critical observation that "what is expressed in the allegorical sphere is nothing but an historical relationship. . . . Nature itself is transitory. Thus it includes the element of history."[42] Only from concrete and cement, as we read or hear the song linearly, emerge the redeemed spaces of desert and swamp. The sudden deflation and introduction of the banal give meaning to a nature already denuded of anything but the transience of a rhetorical trope.

Alterman reveals the ideological fervent of his poetics in the final stanza of the lyric, whose ultimate couplet recapitulates the ending of the first stanza, except for one important interjection:

אִם קָשָׁה הִיא הַדֶּרֶךְ וּבוֹגֶדֶת,
אִם גַּם לֹא אֶחָד יִפֹּל חָלָל –
עַד עוֹלָם נֹאהַב אוֹתָךְ, מוֹלֶדֶת,
אָנוּ לָךְ בִּקְרָב וּבֶעָמָל!

If harsh and treacherous is the path,
If even more than one soul falls—
Forever we will love you, motherland,
We to you in battle and in labor!

"Battle," which substitutes for the more open and individually marked actions and emotions of "joy" and "song," finally reveals the meaning of the march rhythm in the melody and demonstrates the hidden contestation in this place, for which labor will work to create what "we [are] to you." Left unsaid and only implied (an impossibility in English, but normatively ambiguous in Hebrew) is the predicate that bridges the first-person speaker and the second-person addressee. But the predicate precisely does not matter and in this its absence demonstrates just how far Alterman has removed himself from Shlonsky. The specific modifications and definitions of action—the adverbial interjections of the individual and *not* the verb—create the specific character of the object that would reflect the subject. The verb matters little. The Zionist subject fuses to the land through the quality and character of his individualized performance of action on the soil.

The dialectic in Alterman's poetry between nature and the city has been commented upon. Dan Miron, perhaps Alterman's most significant reader, draws on the central stanza of "Morning Song" to place the poet in a literary-political dialectic that saw a sharp opposition between urban and agrarian development.[43] For Miron, Alterman's poetry brought together and articulated an oppositional stance that had been codified in Tel Aviv literature during the 1920s and took a stance as either pro- or anti-city:

> Alterman needed therefore the entire opposition in anti-Tel Aviv poetry and tried to break it down. He tried even to break apart the accepted opposition of nature-city of cement and concrete. In the famous lines of the popular song "Morning Song" . . . which in fact does not relate directly to the topic of Tel Aviv, he asserts: "We will dress you in a gown of concrete and cement / And we will lay out for you carpets of gardens." The parallelism teaches that there is no opposition between gardens and cement, just as there is no opposition between the soil of the city covered in concrete and the "redeemed soil of your fields." About which the grain will make the bells rejoice throughout the poem.[44]

"Morning Song" draws urban and rural elements together and begins to mend the ruptures within a Zionist ideology that expressed great antipathy for the city. But even though Miron writes of reconciliation of a city-nature opposition, he nevertheless maintains that division himself in this criticism by seeing a parallelism between concrete and garden as distinct from nature. Both are indeed the same thing, especially in ecological terms where garden and cement each intervenes and modifies the landscape, in opposition to a concept of nature as unmediated and unmodified. But even in a more forgiving understanding of the garden as part of nature, a breakdown of the opposition between concrete and garden would lead us to see that concrete inhabits not a realm separate from nature but nature itself. If the opposition between concrete and garden is false, then so is the dialectical divide of a criticism that supports it.

Within Miron's dialectical reading, Alterman's poetry still cannot account for the untamed spaces of wilderness, which must be controlled and redeemed. If thematically Alterman is able to go beyond the depictions of desert by Shlonsky and posit a natural city that would incorporate and then "dress" the desert, poetically, his position still depends on a single series of structuralist oppositions, as Miron himself points out: "Alterman absorbed all the tensions and oppositions of Tel Aviv poetry from the 1920s and beginning of the 1930s, and certainly absorbed well these tensions and oppositions as they became apparent in Shlonsky's poems, which were at that time his immediate basis for all of Hebrew poetry."[45] That assessment might be accurate, but it places poetry within a structure that always remains hermetic. The concrete-garden opposition turns out to be a false dialectic not because both sides issue from a built environment designed by human hands, thus to the exclusion of nature, but because that dialectic, and the myriad structural oppositions that present themselves as efficacious alternate readings (nature-culture and old-new), obfuscate how the poetics acts to reify and create the dialectic in the first place. Alterman pushes nature back into a poetics of metaphor and allegory that can only offer artifice as a resolution to the tensions of a natural-historical divide. The sun is ablaze and the dew sparkles only because of how these figures reflect on the transformations man has wrought, that is, on how nature has been redeemed and made more natural.

The Built Environment

At the heart of the discursive transformation Alterman directs toward the city lies the issue of metaphor and the possibilities it holds for poetic innovation. Certainly, in Alterman's Tel Aviv poems from the 1930s, especially the more serious ones from *Kokhavim ba-ḥutz* (Stars Outside),[46] metaphor separates Alterman from a Shlonskyan poetics of the 1920s. This difference reflects too a particular political stance, an attitude toward the social function of poetry and discourse. Shlonsky ignores the city and with it any social system. For him, rapport with nature comes through the boundless potential of the primal utterance untied to any interpretive community; or at least, it issues from the ideological fiction of a chaotic prelinguistic state. That is why neologism abounds in his language. Creation in the land comes within a discourse that is itself creative, the projection of the interior self through expression.

Alterman's language, on the other hand, is filtered through the city, through a community that will define it and give it meaning, and thus, too, give meaning to the world that language encompasses.

His poem "Yom ha-shuk" (Market Day) conveys these grand ideas through something as simple as the homophonic play of *ir* (city) and *or* (light), two leitmotifs that bind the urban environment to the majesty of the natural realm. But all the while throughout the poem, we are cognizant as well of the performative nature of *poetry* as represented consciousness that performs an alchemy and eventually combines these oppositional phenomena. Apostrophe appears here as well, this time in a speaker addressing not nature but the city itself, and in so doing inflects the bustle of social activity through the figuration and physical representation of nature.

The large architectonic development in the poem is contained in a simple scheme that unites *ir* and *or* and gives meaning to a dialectical understanding of the title, "Market Day," whose terms stand in for the very separation between city and nature that the poem intends to transcend. Thus the title "Market Day" already announces the dialectical scheme of the poetic narrative. Immediately it is sundered into its smaller building blocks, "day" and "market," before being rejoined within a newfound, fundamental interplay of city and nature, a life-affirming and life-giving amalgam. At the end is a teleology of building. The city embodies both the majesty of nature and the subjectivity of the interlocutor whose poetic constructions enact this dialectical synthesis.

אוֹר שׁוֹעֵט! רְאֵם הָאוֹר הַמַּקְרִין בַּזָּהָב!
אוֹר שׁוֹעֵט! בְּהָמוֹן, בִּנְהִימָה וּמַמְלֶכֶת!
. . . .
וּמִלְמַעְלָה – אֶל שִׂיא הֹר-הָהָר הַכָּחֹל,
מַעְפִּיל עוֹד הַשֶּׁמֶשׁ, אַכְזָר וְזָהִיר.
מְסֻנְוֶרֶת,
בַּיּוֹם הַסּוֹבֵב כְּמָחוֹל,
בַּמַּבּוּל הַנִּפְלָא,
עוֹמֶדֶת הָעִיר!

Trampling light! Great light shining golden!
Trampling light! Numerous, roaring, and regal!
. . . .
And from above—toward the summit of the blue heights,
The sun pours forth, fierce and brilliant.
Dazzled,
By the day that turns as in a dance,
In the wonderful torrent,
Stands the city![47]

Assonance—not just in the *ir-or* elision but also in the rhyming scheme—helps pull the city into the natural description of the day. But the typographic placement of the stanza on the page tells the full story. The convention of rhyming couplets cannot contain the rhetorical thrust of the stanza that introduces the city, as if the textual line were unable to contain the significance of each word's meaning within the structure of the artifice. Of course, breaking out of the artifice only serves to highlight artifice itself, making us, the readers, aware of the construction of the discourse and the artificiality of its prosody. Against that tension, the typography emerges as more natural and more authentic, connecting light to the city and setting up the leitmotif structure that builds from "day," denuded of its social function in "market day," continuing through "city," and arriving at the end in the dialectical construction of *ir/or* (now abstract stand-ins for city-market, on the one hand, and light-day, on the other). These elements synthesize into the final exclamation, the last word and ideological telos of the entire poem: "united!" The concept of "united!" then synthesizes in a political utterance the physical spaces of nature and the city.

כִּי חוֹמוֹת מִן הַדֶּרֶךְ תִּפְנֶינָה הַצִּדָּה
וְחַיֵּינוּ גָּאוּ לְלֹא גְבוּל וּמִדָּה.
אֶת עֵינֵי הָאָדָם וְיוֹמוֹ כְּבָר הִצִּיתָה
אֵשׁ לְבָנָה,
יְחִידָה!

Because you will clear aside the barricades from the path
We live proud without limit or measure.
You have already instigated the days and eyes of man
A white fire,
United![48]

The city acts as conduit and instigator of man's search for the natural realm, where the market becomes a place of intersection for human activity and the world of nature. Clearly, this is not Simmel's marketplace of money, where interchange is dictated by a signifying system that displaces real relationships through representational constructions, always substituting the signs of money for exactly what it represents. In Alterman's market, like the ideological origins of Tel Aviv itself, money is conspicuously absent, and in its place the market allows for moments of true rapport between man and nature. In denial of its own bourgeois etymology, the city is thus a place of real intercourse where city and nature interpenetrate, not necessarily in social interaction but something both oddly public and private: an individual rapport between the self and all that surrounds it, meaning both commerce and the beauty of nature. As Alterman writes, the city allows for boundlessness; it throws down the barriers of representational limit and allows man's eyes to be formed, that is, to take in the hues of light that illuminate external, social space, external, that is, to the completely hermetic confines of a modernist self. And there, within the boundless possibilities of the market, nature begins to shine:

אֵצֵא אֶל הַשּׁוּק הַמַּפְשִׁיל שַׁרְווּלַיִם,
אֵלֵךְ מִתְנוֹדֵד בֵּין צְבָעָיו הַדּוֹלְקִים
סְחַרְחַר מִיֵּינוֹ, מֵרֹאשׁוֹ בַּשָּׁמַיִם,
מֵאֵשׁ הַקְּלָלוֹת שֶׁל מוֹכְרוֹת הַדָּגִים!

זוֹ הָעִיר! מֶה חָזָק מִקַּלּוּת הַדַּעַת?
מִי, לוּ פַּעַם, לִבּוֹ לֹא יִשָּׂא לָהּ כְּשֶׂה?
בְּשָׁלְחָהּ בָּנוּ רֵיחַ תַּפּוּחַ וּדְלַעַת,
מַה נַּעֲשֶׂה לָהּ, מַה נַּעֲשֶׂה?

I will go out to the market that rolls up its sleeves,
And I will walk among its lighted colors
Becoming dizzy from its wine, from its head in the sky,
From the fiery cries of the fishmongers!

That's the city! What is stronger than levity?
Who, even once, hasn't had his heart lifted up like a lamb?
From the fragrant wafts of apple and pumpkin,
What will we do for her, what will we do?[49]

Indeed, the city is actually alive—"Alive! Alive! Roars spill forth!"—and takes on properties of the body. The image of the city as body returns over and over again, defining the organicism of social construction, which will subvert the moneyed alienation that Simmel describes in an artificial urban space. The figuration of the body inflects the constructs of the pioneer himself through the natural realm. The body creates resemblance between city and speaker, as if only within the social construct can we really absorb and know the day. The city thus opens the individual to the light and majesty of nature.

But missing from Alterman's depiction of the urban market is any awareness that the erasure of money merely obfuscates the creation of an alternate representational system. The boundless symbolism of Alterman's city works hard to frame figuration into meaningful units. But those poetics refuse to admit what Simmel understood about the city, namely, that the necessity to create representational systems of interchange obscures any outlet toward nature, toward a realm that would lie beyond the enclosure of social relations: "[I]n the life of a city, struggle with nature for the means of life is transformed into a conflict with human beings and the gain which is fought for is granted, not by nature, but by man."[50] From here, Simmel would arrive again at money. Simmel's point about money is that it is inevitable, and the escape from its debilitating effects lies only in a modernist retreat inward: "That we follow the laws of our inner nature—and this is what freedom is—becomes perceptible and convincing to us and to others only when the expressions of this nature distinguish themselves from others."[51] The city could not deny its own representational character; real relations between people were in fact contained within discourse, the discourse of a money economy; it was unavoidable. Thus, the inner life becomes the antidote to the objective quality of urban experience, and while we might then criticize Simmel's idealization of "inner nature," we can see in his modernist dependence and belief in interiority a rejection of the imposition of objective layers of representation and a critique of a naive belief in constructing discourse outside of urbanity's character.

Alterman takes the opposite turn wherein the city projects the fantasy of a utopian totality in Palestine, one more pure, more real, and more natural than the commercial relationships in the European city. Where Alterman would seek the phenomenology of experience in city-nature, Simmel would counter that all cities will create their own systems of representation and thus a true inner life can only be maintained through the fiercest interchange of people.[52] Instead of interchange—that is, instead of cultural negotiation within the marketplace of the city—Alterman's market constructs itself as an alternate, truer totality. The city finally becomes the extent of everything; boundless, yes, but in the way that any sense of the world—of nature, of society—can be knowable only through the constructs of the city, through a city that encompasses and defines—indeed, *builds*—what we need to know.

Ḥomah u-migdal

In the large scheme of the path of Hebrew landscape poetics and politics, Alterman represents an arrival of sorts. If we can talk about a path of development for Zionist discourse of the land, then the incorporation of nature and landscape into the artifice of the built environment finally allows for the complete formation of a new Jewish identity within Palestine, complete because nature and place would issue in real terms only from the intervention of the Jewish pioneer. The dialectic that saw within representations of politics, literature, and the self the need to reconcile a modernist alienation in the land (the historical separation of the Jew from the nation's homeland) was finally overcome by the synthesis of culture and nature within the powerful poetics Alterman was able to build. Natural history in Tel Aviv, then, announces an ideological success just as it points to a critical position in understanding how poetry and Zionism came together to define how building and being built would work discursively in the country.

Of course, by 1948, one could claim, the need to resolve these dialectics had become moot once the land lost its abstract ideational quality and became a set of legal borders, part of a state structure of political control. If nature poetry and discourse about the land prior to 1948 worked to reconcile and smooth out the complex system of competing ideological claims made by the Zionists in Palestine, then after 1948 those types of cultural anxieties and political struggles came out into the open. The power of how looking at the land and writing the land had been formulated—and where it had arrived by the late 1930s—dictated the possibilities for much that both the state cultural apparatus and the reactions against it would write and describe throughout the coming decades.

The natural history of Tel Aviv, then, is a culmination of a discursive process that begins as far back as Kishinev, a process that melded political need and aesthetic interest, and worked to make history intervene into the natural landscape in the name of nature. This was not only an aesthetic and intellectual journey; we cannot speak only of the abstraction of ideas. The physical culmination of this ethos came during the Arab Revolt of the late 1930s, an era that in Zionist historiography is referred to as the period of *ḥomah u-migdal* (wall and tower).[53] In the face of Arab attacks on Jewish settlements throughout the Yishuv, Zionist defense took on a decidedly architectural icon (Figure 10). As reaction to Arab attack, the Yishuv extended Katznelson's prophetic 1929 calls for retribution through construction,[54] which now developed a specific design motif, transforming the verb "to build" into the static and material force of the object, "building." In disputed areas of the country, overnight settlements would be erected inward, away from and closed off to nature: a watchtower surrounded by a fortified corral. The dynamic process of dialectical tension and struggle for individual meaning and identity had become by the late 1930s a fixed notion of the object bounded by a meaning imposed on it through design. The wall and tower that defined settlement inscribed notions of building and national identity onto the very landscape itself, in an aesthetic that was consciously and explicitly inflected through political aspiration. The reaction to external political competition coupled itself to a definition of the land, both of which were expressed in building itself. By the end of the pre-state Yishuv, which effectively came to its final formulation in Alterman's poetry and the cessation of major settlement activity in 1938 with the rise of tension in Europe, the slogan "to build and be built" became but an empty political cliché and came to rest within the lexical ambiguity of "building," whose meaning as noun-object (the physical instantiation of a fixed identity reified in the landscape) overcame any dynamic process of dialectical tension and individual reflection.

Figure 10. A *ḥomah u-migdal* settlement in 1937. (Central Zionist Archives)

Conclusion

The Land Bites Back

By the 1940s, the constructedness of the Zionist landscape was already gathering critical reactions from a population not completely immune to the way nature had become framed within the built environment. The growing metropolis of Tel Aviv, especially, provoked a nostalgia for an origin of the city that denied its urban character and instead embraced the natural surroundings that had encompassed the first steps in the construction of a Jewish landscape. In 1942, no less than the great Hebrew poet Shaul Tcherniḥovsky, whose nature poems described an environment generally free of ethnic affiliation and determinations, complained about the demise of an older moment in the history of Tel Aviv when man, house, and tree stood as singular peers in an interdependent formula that had built the foundations of the country:

> There is another Tel Aviv, whose borders are narrow, and which grows smaller by the day. Our Tel Aviv is a major city. She is thirty-something . . . [but] there still remain some corners of Tel Aviv of ten, fifteen, twenty, and maybe even thirty years ago. . . . There are small corners and modest houses whose gardens are larger than their buildings. Sometimes you stand in front of huge (old?) trees beautiful in their natural beauty, which have not been cut or pruned. Each designed house has its terrible style, but each unstylized house has its own originality. It is impossible not to love such a house. . . . Back then, every tree that was planted was a source of pride. [Owners] didn't consult with a gardener, but rather with the entire family. They didn't introduce a stranger's opinion into the private garden, but only what they liked. Together with the tree they were saddened during droughts, and rejoiced in its shade when it grew.[1]

Tcherniḥovsky's description of an older Tel Aviv embraces that natural origin of the country when man and nature stood together. "To build and be built" may not reside, in Tcherniḥovsky's complaint, within the Bauhaus construction of a modern environment—he was, after all, from a generation for whom nature was attained through work—but the construction of a Jewish landscape in Palestine, for Tcherniḥovsky, is nevertheless mediated through the built environment—through the house—which ties together the fates of both tree and human owner. Even within the critique, the mutual identification of man and nature makes itself felt through a newly erected nostalgia for the purity of pioneering.

Tchernihovsky's natural organicism of wild, untamed growth—or at least growth that tied man to nature without the artificial interventions of the outside expert (the gardener)–also raises a more critical issue for aesthetics. Even though Tchernihovsky's concerns here can be seen within a settlement logic encompassed by "to build and be built," his own poetry, like his 1942 criticisms, stood outside of a strict instrumental reflection of Zionist politics. In the generation of forty years earlier he and Bialik had forged something new within the language. However, by the 1940s, a poetics of organicism would appear, we might say, could only appear, in a complaint, thereby signaling not the margins of expression but the extent to which a national discourse of a "second nature" had worked to embrace Zionist thinking.

We can understand Shmuel Yosef Agnon's great novel satirizing Zionist settlement in similar terms. In 1945, on the eve of Israeli statehood, Agnon, by then one of Hebrew's most celebrated and idiosyncratic writers, opened *Tmol shilshom* (Only Yesterday), his satirical novel about Zionist settlement in Palestine, with a critique of both the same nostalgia Tchernihovsky represents and, more deeply, the entire settlement ethos itself. The first line begins: "Like the rest of the brethren of the Second Aliyah, people of our salvation, Yitzhak Kummer left his country and his homeland and his city and immigrated to Eretz Israel to build it from its ruins and to be built by it."[2] The sentiment was familiar, the terms of action already well a part of Zionist culture: uprooting and reinventing oneself through work in the ancient land of the nation. But the critical message runs even deeper. Alongside the supple interplay of Talmudic and biblical quotation—the intertextual fabric of multiple texts from the tradition, what usually marks Agnon's particular prose style—here Agnon entwines Yitzhak Kummer's fate within that instrumental slogan of the settlement period: "to build and be built."[3] In 1945, the slogan resonated strongly throughout the Zionist movement, and the question raised by Agnon's text relates not only to the realities of the pioneering experience. Rather, the intertextual nexus announces, in farcical irreverence, the slogan's emptiness, its identity as cliché. By entering the pastiche of Agnon's prose, writing itself already demonstrates the descent into nostalgia for the pioneering slogan and the values that vacuously follow from it. The idea of mutual identification was innocent and beautiful in its simplicity, and Agnon focuses on that idea to hone his critique: no matter how hard Kummer and his friends try, no matter how self-evident the ridiculousness of the environmental challenge itself, what they are incapable of achieving is precisely the personal transformation they so crave. Throughout Agnon's *Only Yesterday*,[4] Yitzhak Kummer tests himself within this place, and traverses the enduring symbols of Zionist success—draining swamps, making the desert bloom—which embrace the slogan in all its strength and make improvement of nature the test of Zionist self-worth.

It was that anxiety of reflexive self-worth that pushed an ever expanding technological intervention in the land. For the Zionist, the invention of nature would, ironically, suppress nature in order to create something more natural. Back in 1920, when the swamps were being drained in the Jezreel Valley, nature was ironically both the goal and competition of the entire enterprise. As Dr. D. Deutch wrote in his hygiene report about the improvements at Nahalal, "We might say that man has here conquered nature and even death."[5] The work of changing this place, of bringing it back to that glory of former times was a daunting task. The synesthetic dialectic of "to build and be built"—of seeing the fate of the land and the people tied together, of linking the invention of the "new Jew" to the rejuvenation of this devastated landscape—required an aesthetic that would motivate and mobilize political forces as well as a fundamental individual yearning for identity in the land. Thus, throughout the history of Zionism, the aesthetic of environmental identification had to be invented and refined. Only after some time would a Zionist subject emerge from this alienating place and meld into the landscape, to become one with the land, as the great Zionist naturalist Aharon David Gordon, put it.[6] The Zionist and the land did not just stand side by side, but instead became entangled together in an aesthetic that could not differentiate between them. Place itself becomes the phantasmagoria of the individual envisioning it and not merely the material outcome of a realist aesthetic process. Agnon had something to say about this too, alluding to the idea of melding with nature when Kummer emerges for the first time from his Jaffa hotel, ready to meet the day and conquer the land: "He hadn't managed even one step when both legs sank into the sand."[7] The land, it seems, was not going to cooperate easily with the utopian plans of these early ideologues; or, at least, melding with the land too had its ridiculousness.

Sinking into the sand—we are reminded as Yitzhak Kummer struts toward the open field, ready to throw himself into this national environmental enterprise, that ideology always ignores nature itself. The landscape to emerge reveals itself as the projected fantasy of the subject, as the mirror, according to Gordon, in which "you will see your own image." Zionism was a perfect foil for this type of thinking: already a return in an abstract longing for home, the physical instantiation of return required first an idea of a land to be the object of that return. Of course, implied in return, as Gordon pointed out, was the Jewish separation from nature after centuries of urban alienation.[8] Nature might be the cure, but getting to nature was a difficult and drawn out process. As the failures of the early settlements made clear, arrival in the land did not assure a oneness with it.

But where Agnon's critique truly surpasses Tcherniḥovsky—beyond the humor of the farce—is in an understanding of how discourse itself (and not mere desire or fantasy) mediates this relationship between man and nature. Kummer's demise toward the end of the novel comes from a misapprehension of the power of the word and the text to create the natural environment, of how language is not just a play of signifiers in the hands of the Zionist pioneer. Kummer, in perhaps the most famous incident of the book, paints the words "mad dog" on the back of Balak the dog, and sets the dog free in the streets of Jerusalem. The panic that ensues is precisely Kummer's intent, but what he cannot anticipate is the way that nature will be reified by the words on Balak's back. Unbeknownst to Kummer, Balak indeed contracts rabies; nature becomes what the signifier signifies, and the manipulation of man returns to bite as Kummer approaches and falls victim to an infectious bite by the rabid Balak, tricked by his own discursive utterance to believe in a nature independent of his very intrusion into it.

In this way, the power of the text and of aesthetics goes beyond a hermetic cultural realm of abstraction and leisure and infects the very nature of the world the Zionists lived in and created. In the name of constructing the place, conquering the land, and restoring it to its former glory, Zionism built a landscape of its own image—and in that sense fulfilled the promise of the slogan "to build and be built"—but one that, half a century later, finds itself under attack for the environmental damage it wrought.[9] The lessons of pollution in Israel—of the environmental toxins that attacked the Australian athletes at the opening of the 1997 Maccabiah Games in Tel Aviv after falling into the Yarkon River; of the lawsuits by former army soldiers stricken by cancer after training extensively in the Kishon River; by the public health complaints issuing from the industrial plants north of Haifa; by current efforts to undo the greatest mark of early Zionist pride on the land and return the wetlands to their original state—pollution might indeed mark the triumph of Alterman's poetics and the discursive success of Zionism's conception of nature. The ironies of Tel Aviv's natural history, where nature becomes precisely the built environment in a hegemonic instantiation of "second nature," led not just to complaints and satire by Tcherniḥovsky and Agnon. More effective and instrumental to the future history of the country were the appropriations of this lesson by those in power, like David Ben-Gurion, who quickly saw the ideational strength of conceptualizing a particular type of nature for the newly established state. Thus, the future history of Israel in the 1950s was marked by the cultural and agricultural reformulation of the Negev Desert as a site of Jewish settlement and the

Zionist conquest of nature. Ben-Gurion understood the discursive need to enlist culture for state purposes, especially those that would expand into new hostile landscapes.[10]

Just a few years after statehood and the triumphant ascendance of Jewish nationalism, David Ben-Gurion, then prime minister and forever "the old man" who would emblematize the state, answered Israel's first census by proclaiming his personal roots clearly within the soil of Palestine, now Israel: in response to the census query about personal occupation, Ben-Gurion replied that he was a farmer.[11] It had been a good forty years since Ben-Gurion had wandered, like Yitzhak Kummer, with the other immigrants of the Second Aliyah, begging day jobs as transient farmworkers, finally agitating for workers' collectives. Even that gig had been fleeting, a brief interlude between childhood in Russia and the political work for which he was to be known. But like all sorts of national leaders, especially those from the emerging socialist and postcolonial nations of postwar underclass ascendance, Ben-Gurion claimed his role as farmer, as worker on the land—within a modernism of immanent action, where the body of the ruler no longer metaphorically signified the nation; instead, it was the role of transformation in the landscape that defined the qualifications of a leader.

On the pop charts of the early 1950s, "Horah mamterah" (Sprinkler Horah), buoyed by the military culture it came out of but ultimately embraced as a pop culture phenomenon on its own, resounds with the same environmental confidence that prompted Ben-Gurion to claim his place among the nation's farmers. Culture was certainly an artifice of the state, agitprop of a socialist realism—the *horah* a folk manufacture devoid, as was all folk culture, of any authentic folk. But the popular embrace was genuine. "Turn, turn sprinkler," goes the chorus:

סֹבִּי, סֹבִּי, מַמְטֵרָה,
לְפַזֵּר פְּנִינֵי אוֹרָה,
סֹבִּי וְהַתִּיזִי מַיִם!
עֵץ יָרִיעַ בַּשְּׂדֵרָה,
אֲדָמָה תִּתֵּן פִּרְיָהּ
בְּאֵין גֶּשֶׁם מִשָּׁמַיִם,
גֶּשֶׁם מִשָּׁמַיִם.

Spread your pearls of light,
Turn and sprinkle water!
A tree will cheer in the avenue,
The ground will give forth its fruit
Without water from the heavens,
Water from the heavens.[12]

The quasi-repetition of the last two lines might encapsulate the arrogance of the whole movement and articulate the competition with nature that then substitutes for nature itself, replaced in the repetition by the mechanism of human industry and invention. If no water arrives from the heavens, the song declares, we will create it, and in that tricky repetition of the popular lyric, the repeated line instead undermines and replaces what came before. Without water from the heavens, we will sprinkle with water from irrigation pipes—

רַן קִלּוּחַ בַּצִּנּוֹר,
צִנּוֹרוֹת–עוֹרְקֵי הַנֶּגֶב,
זֶה דַּרְכּוֹ שֶׁל הַמִּזְמוֹר–
מִן הַבֶּרֶז אֶל הָרֶגֶב
יַעֲלוּ מֵימֵי–תְּהוֹם.

The flow sings in the pipes.
Pipes—arteries of the Negev,
That's the way of its song–
From the valve to the dirt-clod
Torrents of water will pass.[13]

Caught within this network of images, culture melds with both body and land: each is renewed and given life only through the mechanistic intervention of man, mechanistic and yet tied inextricably to its own sense of what is natural in the landscape, an idea whose lead came now from the state. For the Zionist, that was the goal: the invention of nature that would reproduce nature in order to surpass it with a fantasized vision of what is truly natural.

The instrumentality of the landscape in the hands of national ideologues continues with little hesitation as the political contestation over the land becomes consistently articulated as a contestation over nature itself. "Our first answer to these murderers and animals is that the government and people of Israel will stay here, build here, live here. . . . We will remember [these victims] with every home we build, every road we pave, every family we raise." Thus spoke Benjamin Netanyahu as prime minister in 1996, and the echoes of the sentiment resonate throughout both Israeli and Palestinian discourse. The contest over land has always been a contest over landscape, and a contest over aesthetics, not in a competition for the instrumental control of art, but in the self-fashioning of art itself and the form that cultural expression takes. "To build and be built" thus describes more than just a political slogan and more than just a pioneering ethos. Rather, the dialectic inscribed within it can only arrive at a construction of a Jewish subject in the land that hungrily strives to control the landscape in order to construct itself. That, in the end, might be the legacy of early Zionism and an explanation of how Palestine did indeed become a Jewish space.

Notes

Introduction

1. The entirety of the lyric consists of the one line in the epigraph, and its exact origin is not known (the song is listed in Israeli encyclopedias as a "folk song"). On the use of folk lyrics in Zionist culture and their dominance in forming cultural attitudes and assumptions, see Ziva Ben-Porat's "Zionist Reads Palestinian: Interpretation and Dialogue in the Light of Cultural Differences and Political Conflicts," in *Arcadia*, Band 31, ed. H. Rüdiger (Berlin: Walter de Gruyter, 1996) Heft 1/2, 231–44. Ben-Porat's essay outlines the general problem of translating the preposition in this lyric, which can be either positional (. . . *in* it) or instrumental (. . . *by* it). The difference implied by the different actions of these translations reveals the difficulty of the slogan as an articulation of ideological certitude.

2. For the idea presented in this paragraph, see Carl Schorske, *Fin-de-Siècle Vienna* (New York: Vintage, 1981); Gregory Jusdanis, *Belated Modernity and Aesthetic Culture: Inventing National Literature* (Minneapolis: University of Minnesota Press, 1991); M. Bradbury and J. W. McFarlane, *Modernism: 1890–1930* (New York: Penguin, 1978); and Neil Larsen, *Modernism and Hegemony* (Minneapolis: University of Minnesota Press, 1990).

3. On the topic of "redemption of the soil" (*ge'ulat ha-karka*), see Ruth Kark, ed., *Ge'ulat ha-karka be-eretz-yisra'el* (Redemption of the soil in Eretz Israel) (Jerusalem: Yad Yitsḥak Ben-Tsvi, 1990). See in particular Shmuel Almog's essay, "Hage'ulah ba-retorikah ha-tsiyonit" (Redemption in Zionist rhetoric), 13–32.

4. Gideon Ofrat highlights this connection in his study of pioneering drama in the Yishuv: *Adamah, adam, dam: Mitos he-ḥaluts u-fulḥan ha-adamah be-maḥazot ha-hityashvut* (Earth, man, blood: The myth of the pioneer and the ritual of earth in Eretz Israel settlement drama) (Tel Aviv: Tscherikover, 1980).

5. I am aware of the gendered terms of this reference. Historically, the argument was usually cast in masculine terms, and I will use them here consistently, especially since there is a point where a feminine challenge makes itself felt. Much work has been done on these subjects and is worth review; see, for instance, Naomi Seidman, *A Marriage Made in Heaven: The Sexual Politics of Hebrew and Yiddish* (Berkeley: University of California Press, 1995); and Michael Gluzman, *The Politics of Canonicity: Lines of Resistance in Modernist Hebrew Poetry* (Stanford, Calif.: Stanford University Press, 2003). In Gluzman, see especially his chapter "The Invisible Revolution: Rereading Women's Poetry," 100–140.

6. The idea is common in much writing about Zionist culture and especially about modern Hebrew writing. See Amos Oz, *Israeli Literature: A Case of Reality Reflecting Fiction* (Colorado Springs: Colorado College, 1985); and Lev Hakak's assertion: "From the beginning of Modern Hebrew literature until the 1930s, the authors who wrote in Hebrew did so by their own choice, for idealistic reasons," *Modern Hebrew Literature Made into Films* (Lanham, Md.: University Press of America, 2001), 1.

7. Hebrew certainly acted as one of the key factors in national coalescence and a justification for the imagined community. In this, the language and the literature served functions described by both Benedict Anderson in *Imagined Communities* (London: Verso, 1983) and Homi Bhabha in *Nation and Narration* (London: Routledge, 1990). The particular history of Hebrew national culture would challenge many of Anderson's and Bhabha's specific claims for nationalism, but their general theoretical frameworks apply to the case of Zionism.

8. This relation between Jew and land remains highly instrumental as territory functions either as refuge or as a productive base for Jewish national activity. However, Pinsker does begin the process of tying emancipation not just to territory but to a psychological vision of a revivified Jewish nation: "The civil and political emancipation of the Jews is not sufficient to raise them in the estimation of the peoples. The proper and the only remedy would be the creation of a Jewish nationality, of a people living on its own soil, the auto-emancipation of the Jews; their emancipation as a nation among nations by the acquisition of a home of their own." "Auto-Emancipation," in *The Zionist Idea*, ed. Arthur Hertzberg (Garden City, N.Y.: Doubleday, 1959), 198.

9. Pinsker makes explicit his disdain for the reinvention of the ancient biblical home in Palestine: "[W]e must, above all, not dream of restoring ancient Judaea. We must not attach ourselves to the place where our political life was once violently interrupted and destroyed. . . . Perhaps the Holy Land will again be ours. If so, all the better, but *first of all*, we must determine . . . what country is accessible to us." Hertzberg, 194.

10. The exception to the colonial goals of the First Aliyah was Bilu, which already embodied the reflexive cultural aspirations of the Second Aliyah and beyond. See Shlomit Laskov, *Ha-biluyim* (Tel Aviv: Ha-sifriyah Ha-tsiyonit, 1981).

11. For a concise outline of Dubnov's and Aḥad Ha'am's intellectual thought, see David H. Weinberg, *Between Tradition and Modernity: Haim Zhitlowski, Simon Dubnow, Ahad Ha-am, and the Shaping of Modern Jewish Identity* (New York: Holmes and Meier, 1996). Of course, on Aḥad Ha'am, the standard has quickly become Steven J. Zipperstein, *Elusive Prophet: Ahad Ha'am and the Origins of Zionism* (Berkeley: University of California Press, 1993). On the subject of the tension between diaspora and homeland in modern Jewish thought and ideology, see David Biale, *Power and Powerlessness in Jewish History* (New York: Schocken Books, 1986).

12. The wartime situation of the Zionist Yishuv in Palestine, and particularly the state of development within Labor Zionist institutions during these years, has been the topic of some important studies. See, for instance, Nathan Efrati, *Mimashber le-tikvah: Ha-yishuv ha-yehudi be-eretz-yisra'el be-milḥemet ha-olam ha-rishonah* (From crisis to hope: The Jewish community in Eretz Israel during the First World War) (Jerusalem: Yad Yitsḥak Ben-Tsvi, 1991); Mordechai Eliav, ed., *Bematsor uve-matsok: Eretz-yisra'el be-milḥemet ha-olam ha-rishonah* (Siege and distress: Eretz Israel during the First World War) (Jerusalem: Yad Yitsḥak Ben-Tsvi, 1991).

13. The early chapters of Hillel Dan's memoirs of working in Solel Boneh, *Bederekh lo slulah: Hagadat solel boneh* (On the unpaved path: The story of Solel

Boneh) (Jerusalem and Tel Aviv: Schocken, 1963), capture both the conditions of work in northern Palestine right after the war and also the political complicities of this work.

14. The theme of the empty land was captured in the popular slogan: *eretz lelo am le-am lelo eretz* (a land without a people for a people without a land). Baruch Kimmerling attributes the slogan to Israel Zangwill, and quotes it as: "a people without a land returning to a land without a people," *Zionism and Territory* (Berkeley: Institute of International Studies, University of California, 1983), 9.

15. The question of representations of Arabs in Hebrew literature and Israeli culture is an exemplary subgenre of Hebrew criticism because it focuses almost exclusively on content analysis. For instance, despite the political poignancy of both Menakhem Perry's and Gilead Morahg's important essays on the subject (respectively), "The Israeli-Palestinian Conflict as a Metaphor in Recent Israeli Fiction," *Poetics Today* 7, no. 4 (1986): 603–19; and "New Images of Arabs in Israeli Fiction," *Prooftexts* 6, no. 2 (1986): 147–62), neither delves into aesthetic questions when analyzing the way Arab characters have been depicted in literature. Both essays certainly break new and important political ground, but they remain limited to commenting on literature as a separate discrete field of activity. Neither can make claims for literature other than as a reflection of some realm (called history or politics) that exists beyond literature.

16. Anita Shapira, *Ḥerev ha-yonah: Ha-tsiyonut veha-koaḥ, 1881–1948* (Tel Aviv: Am Oved, 1992); the book was translated as *Land and Power: The Zionist Resort to Force, 1881–1948* (New York: Oxford University Press, 1992).

17. Shapira, *Ḥerev ha-yonah*, 195; *Land and Power*, 139.

18. Shapira, *Ḥerev ha-yonah*, 483; *Land and Power*, 357.

19. Sociology might point toward a disciplinary alternative to history's deficiencies, and indeed, Israeli sociology has been a progressive force in pushing Israel studies forward into new areas of inquiry. But while sociology has introduced semiotics and discourse studies into Israel studies, these generally have remained focused on sign systems as merely reflective of social and political developments that progress independent of the semiotics that would reflect them. A good example of this trend is Oz Almog's interesting article on Israeli hairstyles: "From *Blorit* to Ponytail: Israeli Culture Reflected in Popular Hairstyles," *Israel Studies* 8, no. 2 (2003): 82–117. In Almog's study, hair does nothing more than act as an empty signifier, taking on meaning as it would be assigned by society.

20. "Old" history was a phrase Benny Morris used to differentiate the "new historiography"; see Benny Morris, "The New Historiography: Israel Confronts Its Past," *Tikkun* 3, no. 6 (1988): 19–23, 99–102. Morris later rescinded the oppositional structure of that original article, allowing for much less division between old and new; see the introduction to his collection of essays *Tikun ta'ut: Yehudim ve-aravim be-eretz-yisra'el, 1936–1956* (Jews and Arabs in Palestine/Israel) (Tel Aviv: Am Oved, 2000), 13–14.

21. Ilan Pappé's first book, *Britain and the Arab-Israeli Conflict, 1948–51* (New York: St. Martin's Press, 1988), focused on the British in order to avoid the necessary distortions of Zionist and Arab accounts of this history. But Pappé never seems too interested in British distortions arising from particularly British cultural and political assumptions in acting within the region.

22. Morris, "The New Historiography," 19–23, 99–102.

23. Zeev Sternhell, *The Founding Myths of Israel: Nationalism, Socialism, and the Making of the Jewish State* (Princeton, N.J.: Princeton University Press, 1998).

24. Postzionist history has been the subject of several studies over the past

decade, for instance: Gulie Ne'eman-Arad, ed., *Israeli Historiography Revisited*, special issue, *History and Memory* 7, no. 1 (1994); Laurence Silberstein, *The Postzionism Debates: Knowledge and Power in Israeli Culture* (New York: Routledge, 1999); and Anita Shapira and Derek J. Penslar, eds., *Israeli Historical Revisionism: From Left to Right* (Portland, Ore.: Frank Cass, 2003). Of these, only Silberstein treats history as part of a larger cultural context.

25. The issues of conscious and unconscious action lie at the core of much of Israeli debates over revisionist history. Aharon Megged's response to Israeli new historiography, "One-Way Trip on the Highway to Self-Destruction," in *Zionism: The Sequel*, ed. Carol Diament (New York: Hadassah Books, 1998), 318–25 (originally published in the *Jerusalem Post* [June 17, 1994] and based on a series of articles published that year in *Ha-aretz*), defends the intentions of the original settlers, who, he argues, came to Palestine with utopian and altruistic political motives. Against a statement of intention, Israeli revisionist history has little in the way of an answer. The same argument, but poised as an attack on the motives of the Second Aliyah, forms the basis of Sternhell's entire history, as it does for Gershon Shafir in *Land, Labor and the Origins of the Israeli-Palestinian Conflict, 1882–1914* (Berkeley: University of California Press, 1996). Shafir's argument differs from Sternhell significantly in that he applies sociological structures of analysis to draw parallels between imperial colonialism and Zionist colonialism. But Shafir can only work through a positivist understanding of colonialism, which is quite the opposite of discursive analyses. Shafir applies a list of necessary and sufficient conditions in order to define and compare colonialisms. In doing so, he arrives at a colonial description of Palestine that seems far removed from the actual history and particular discursive forms that Zionist colonialism took. Again, the methodological failures of the study—despite its fascinating conclusions—involve the inability to take into account the specific discourses of Zionist ideology and debate. Conversely, discursive analysis and confrontation constitute the strength of Yoram Hazony's polemical attack on Israeli left-wing intellectualism in *The Jewish State: The Struggle for Israel's Soul* (New York: Basic Books, 2000). Hazony understands something fundamental which new Israeli historiography and most postzionist scholarship refuse to confront, namely, that the internal political struggle within Israel for dominance in viewing national identity and in dealing with the Arab conflict is situated within a cultural and discursive contest. For Hazony, the major political struggle is over the control in the public realm of national interpretation of meaning.

26. The politics of Kishinev and the Zionist movement always remain in the background as a vague filter onto the poem itself. Thus, when Dan Miron, who is sensitive to the political atmosphere and goals of Bialik's prophetic poems, refers to "In the City of Slaughter" when discussing the prophetic genre in modern Hebrew poetry, he writes: "[I]n the years 1904, 1905, and 1906, faced with the crisis in the Zionist movement because of the Uganda controversy and Hertzl's [*sic*] untimely death, and in the wake of the abortive Russian Revolution of 1905, with its backlash of widespread pogroms, Bialik wrote more prophetic poems, each grander, more somber in tone, and more desperate in outlook." *H. N. Bialik and the Prophetic Mode in Modern Hebrew Poetry* (Syracuse: Syracuse University Press, 2000), 5–6. But that is the extent of the way that political or historical development might impose itself on the poem, according to Miron. Miron does cite the conflict over the prophetic mode as indicative of internal Zionist debates over poesy and national expression, but by focusing almost exclusively on the generic and poetic requirements of prophetic verse, Miron does little to situate Hebrew poetry within a context larger than Hebrew poetry itself.

27. Alan L. Mintz, *Hurban: Responses to Catastrophe in Hebrew Literature* (New York: Columbia University Press, 1984).

28. Yosef Haefrati, *Ha-mar'ot veha-lashon: Le-toldot ha-te'ur ba-shirah ha-ivrit ha-ḥadashah* (The presented world: Evolution of the poetic language of nature description in Hebrew poetry) (Tel Aviv: Porter Institute, 1976).

29. In an article published soon after his death, "Tmurot be-shirat ha-teva ke-degem shel ma'avar mi-tkufah le-tkufah ba-historiyah shel ha-sifrut" (Changes in nature poetry as a model of transition from period to period in literary history), *Ha-sifrut* 17 (September 1974): 50–54, Haefrati makes an even stronger historical argument by connecting change in nature poetry to differing reflections of interiority of the poetic speaker. The emphasis still remains focused on literary history, but here formalism allows for the intrusion of an extraliterary consideration, at least an element exterior to a self-defined poetic discourse.

30. Benjamin Harshav, *Language in the Time of Revolution* (Berkeley: University of California Press, 1993), 54.

31. A particularly telling example of such a narrow understanding of ideology, one that leads to the critical reification of the state as wielding ubiquitous discursive power, is Gabriel Piterberg's "Postcards from Palestine," *New Left Review* 17 (September/October 2002): 150–57, where he criticizes Daniel Bertrand Monk's book, *An Aesthetic Occupation: The Immediacy of Architecture and the Palestine Conflict* (Durham, N.C.: Duke University Press, 2002). What bothers Piterberg is Monk's unwillingness to assign clear blame in the conflict and to show absolute political and historical hegemony in the Zionists from the beginnings of the twentieth century. Such a conclusion might indeed emerge from Monk's study of political discourse surrounding the architectural monuments in Jerusalem from the nineteenth century until the 1930s, but Monk clearly is uninterested in allowing a totalized history to determine criticism, and what emerges is a discursive analysis of the conflict wherein both Arab and Jewish collusion in maintaining the violence comes under scrutiny.

32. Straddling the line between Zionist and postzionist modes of criticism and history is quite a difficult task, mostly because of the tendency in Hebrew literary studies to see national discourse as inclusive and apolitical, marginalizing no one. Hannan Hever, in his essay on Anton Shammas's novel *Arabesques*, "Hebrew in an Israeli Arab Hand," in *The Nature and Context of Minority Discourse*, ed. Abdul JanMohamed and David Lloyd (New York: Oxford University Press, 1990), makes this point in analyzing Amos Oz's response to Shammas's novel. Dan Miron, on the other hand, demands an inclusiveness for Hebrew literature which ignores the complications of history and ideology. In his attack on what he calls "the Berkeley School" (a group I am associated with) for its work on the modernist poet David Fogel, Miron sees politics as the determining factor in the criticism. Miron's critique certainly has application in many cases of postzionist criticism, but as I argue below, the application of such a critique must implicate all criticism, and certainly encompasses Miron's work as well. The problem of politics in criticism is when it would refuse its own presence and not reveal itself as a critical matter, something the Berkeley group was careful to outline and explicate. See Dan Miron, "Ahavah ha-tluyah be-davar: Toldot hitkablutah shel shirat David Fogel" (Conditional love: The critical reception of David Fogel's poetry), in *Aderet le-Binyamin* (An overcoat for Benjamin), vol. 1, ed. Ziva Ben-Porat (Tel Aviv: Porter Institute and Ha-kibbutz Ha-meuḥad, 1999), 29–98.

33. See, in particular, Hannan Hever, *Paitanim u-viryonim: Tsmiḥat ha-shir ha-politi ha-ivri be-eretz-yisra'el* (Poets and zealots: The rise of political poetry in Eretz Israel) (Jerusalem: Mosad Bialik, 1994); and *Bi-shvi ha-utopiyah: Masah al*

meshiḥiyut ve-politikah ba-shirah ha-ivrit be-eretz-yisra'el bein shtei milḥamot ha-olam (Captives of utopia: An essay on messianism and politics in Hebrew poetry in Eretz Israel between the two world wars) (Beersheva: Ben-Gurion University Press, 1995). Hever's first book in English, *Producing the Modern Hebrew Canon: Nation Building and Minority Discourse* (New York: New York University Press, 2002), also follows the political career of Hebrew, and here takes a large perspective on the entire twentieth century. Most recently, Hever has turned to analyze the poetry and politics of Uri Zvi Greenberg in *Moledet ha-mavet yafah: Estetikah ve-politikah be-shirat Uri Zvi Greenberg* (Tel Aviv: Am Oved, 2004).

34. Yael Zerubavel, *Recovered Roots: Collective Memory and the Making of Israeli National Tradition* (Chicago: University of Chicago Press, 1995).

35. One more work deserving citation is Tamar Berger's *Dionysus ba-senter* (Dionysus at Dizengof Centre) (Tel Aviv: Ha-kibbutz Ha-meuḥad and Siman Kriah, 1998), which constructs a multilayered and complex history of a central space in Israel.

36. The limits of recent Israeli history to transcend the conflict were nicely analyzed in a series of articles on the death of postzionism, which appeared in the Israeli newspaper *Ha-aretz*: Dalia Shehori, "Perhaps Postzionism Is Dead, Perhaps It's in a Deep Freeze" (Hebrew) (April 20, 2004); "There's Even a Postzionist Bookshelf" (Hebrew) (April 28, 2004); and "Postzionism Has Entered the Phase of Mutual Mud-Slinging" (Hebrew) (May 3, 20004). What these articles point out is that postzionism has been singularly unable to rise above the effects that politics have had since the beginning of the Al-Aksa Intifada in 2000. As a critical approach to understanding the production of knowledge, postzionism is bereft of any serious intellectual underpinnings that would allow it to analyze its own position within the new realities of the conflict.

37. Theodor Adorno, *Prisms* (Cambridge, Mass.: MIT Press, 1981), 32–33.

Chapter 1

1. Simon Dubnow, *Mein Leben* (Berlin: Jüdische Buchvereinigung, 1937), 135–36; my translation. The account of April 7 of Dubnov's daughter, Sophie Dubnov-Erlich, adds further drama where the German translation of the original Russian memoir leaves things less adorned: "Dubnov listened to [Jabotinsky's] fiery tirade . . . with a heavy heart. He was thinking, was it really necessary to instill in the wavering Jewish intelligentsia terror in the face of their own national shadow? In the intermission he was pacing along about the foyer when distraught voices and bitter weeping suddenly attracted his attention. Refugees from Kishinev who had escaped the massacre had brought word of the horrors they had just survived," *The Life and Work of S. M. Dubnov: Diaspora Nationalism and Jewish History*, trans. Judith Vowles (Bloomington: Indiana University Press, 1991), 122. According to Jabotinsky's memoirs, which claim he only met Bialik *after* Kishinev, there is reason to doubt the entire incident; cf. Michael Stanislawski, *Zionism and the Fin-de-Siècle: Cosmopolitanism and Nationalism from Nordau to Jabotinsky* (Berkeley: University of California Press, 2001), 160; and Alice S. Nakhimovsky, *Russian-Jewish Literature and Identity: Jabotinsky, Babel, Grossman, Galich, Roziner, Markish* (Baltimore: Johns Hopkins University Press, 1992), 45–46.

2. In the immediate aftermath of the pogrom, Dubnov softened his stance on Zionism and Jewish involvement in the socialist movements of Russia. In the face of catastrophe, communal participation overrode all other concerns and thus allowed for support of Zionism, however fleeting that support might have proven

to be. See Shimon Dubnov, *Mikhtavim al ha-yahadut ha-yeshanah veha-ḥadashah* (Tel Aviv: Dvir, 1937). Weinberg, in *Between Tradition and Modernity*, 163ff., discusses Dubnov's reactions to the pogroms and their effect on his intellectual work.

3. America as destination was the goal of Dubnov's own appeal following Kishinev, as he stated in an essay published in Voskov after the pogrom. Dubnov-Erlich, 123; Dubnow, *Mein Leben*, 39.

4. Dubnov developed the term "center of gravity" in his study *Jewish History: An Essay in the Philosophy of History* (Freeport, N.Y.: Books for Libraries Press, 1972). The notion of a "center of gravity" describes the shift from Jewish associations built around political organization to survival in the diaspora predicated on social and spiritual community. This fundamental transformation in Jewish history, according to Dubnov, allowed for the survival of the people and explained why cultural matters unrelated to territory were paramount to the nation. The Zionists would later mock the idea. See, for example, N. Wagman's article, "Nekudat-ha-koved" (The center of gravity), *Ha-adamah*, no. 1 (July 1, 1919): 56ff. The importance of this journal as a platform for a consolidated expression of territorial writing is discussed in Chapter 2 below.

5. On the relation between nation and land, Dubnov, *Jewish History*, 20–21, wrote: "The nation is the kernel and the land is but the shell; the shell may be broken but the kernel remains intact, and if the seed is a healthy one the nation will always be able to preserve its autonomy against the heteronomy of the alien surroundings." Dubnov's terms significantly echo how Bialik would describe meaning in language in his 1915 essay "Gilui ve-khisui be-lashon" (Revealment and concealment in language), *Divrei sifrut* (Writings on literature) (Tel Aviv: Dvir, 1965), 19–24. The difference in how they each deploy the imagery of seed and kernel is quite telling. Dubnov adheres to a Hegelian notion of history dictated by the development of the nation. In contrast, Bialik's description of language searches out immanent meaning in individual words.

6. Aḥad Ha'am traveled to Palestine several times beginning in 1891, each time reporting on his visits and criticizing the state of the settlements and the possibilities for transforming Palestine into the cultural center that he envisioned for it. See "Emet me-eretz yisra'el" (Truth from Eretz Israel), in *Kol kitvei Aḥad Ha'am* (The complete writings of Aḥad Ha'am) (Jerusalem: Dvir, 1946), 23–30. For discussions of the importance of the essay, see Zipperstein, *Elusive Prophet*, and Alan Dowty, "Much Ado About Little: Aḥad Ha'am's 'Truth from Eretz Yisrael,' Zionism, and the Arabs," *Israel Studies* 5, no. 2 (2000): 154–81. For a discussion of these reports in comparison to Yosef Ḥayim Brenner's view of Palestine, see Chapter 2 below.

7. Dubnov and Aḥad Ha'am differed in their views of autonomy in a significant way. Autonomism mostly describes Dubnov's concept of deterritorialized Jewish nationalism, which Aḥad Ha'am severely dismissed at least twice in print: "Shalosh madregot" (Three steps), in *Kol kitvei Aḥad Ha'am*, 152; and "Shlilat ha-galut" (The negation of the diaspora), in *Kol kitvei Aḥad Ha'am*, 399. However, while Aḥad Ha'am attached autonomy only to individual redemption—the creation of the new modern Jew—and always argued for the impossibility of Jewish national survival in the diaspora, in practical terms, with Palestine still inhospitable to Jewish settlement on a broad cultural level, Aḥad Ha'am's Jewish autonomy of the individual did not look so different from Dubnov's national autonomism. Any difference can be gleaned from Aḥad Ha'am's criticism of Dubnov in "Shalosh madregot," which attacks Dubnov's more Hegelian beliefs in large historical principles. The difference between them lies in how they view

the overarching metaphysical structures of history. Weinberg, *Between Tradition and Modernity*, 205, also describes the disagreement over autonomism but only in terms of questions of national viability as a minority within host nations.

8. Quoted in Hertzberg, *The Zionist Idea*, 194–95. Hertzberg publishes the text of the pamphlet in its entirety.

9. The selection of land for Pinsker only had to meet certain instrumental criteria: "This land must be uniform and continuous in extent. . . . This piece of land might form a small territory of North America, or a sovereign pashalik in Asiatic Turkey" (Hertzberg, 197). Pinsker never connected individual transformation to land directly; the temporal and spatial axes remain quite separate in *Autoemancipation*. This is why the land decision relies completely on a politics of governmental relations: "Of course, the establishment of a Jewish refuge cannot come about without the support of the governments" (Hertzberg, 197).

10. Dubnow, *Mein Leben*, 118. See also "Ha-limudim ha-ivriyim" (Hebrew studies), in Aḥad Ha'am, Shimon Dubnov, and Judah Leib Benjamin Katzenelson, *Ha-lashon veha-ḥinukh* (Language and education) (Krakow: Hotsa'at lishkat ha-merkaz shel "Ivriyah" Bran, 1906), 20–28. Dubnov delivered the lecture printed in this volume in May 1902.

11. Aḥad Ha'am, *Kol kitvei Aḥad Ha'am*, 501–2. Unless otherwise noted, all translations from the Hebrew are my own.

12. Ibid., 502. The obvious masculinist tone of the letter can not be dismissed purely as generic practice. Gender and the issues raised in this letter about Jewish passivity go hand in hand, as they did for Pinsker in 1881. In the 1890s, the matter received specific scientific expression from Max Nordau in his formulation of Zionism as "Jews with muscles," which derived from his more general diagnosis of a European cultural malaise in *Degeneration*. From Nordau, Herzl formulated his own fantasy about masculine refiguration in *Altneuland*. For more nuanced readings of gender and the need to transform the Jewish body within the development of Zionism, Hebrew literature, and the Israeli state, see Naomi Seidman, *A Marriage Made in Heaven*; Meira Weiss, *The Chosen Body: The Politics of the Body in Israeli Society* (Stanford, Calif.: Stanford University Press, 2002); Michael Gluzman, *The Politics of Canonicity* and "Ha-kmihah le-heterosexualiyut: Tsiyonut u-miniyut be-*Altneuland*" (Longing for heterosexuality: Zionism and sexuality in Herzl's *Altneuland*), *Teoriyah u-vikoret* 11 (1997): 145–62; and Jacob Press, "Same-Sex Unions in Modern Europe: *Daniel Deronda, Altneuland*, and the Homoerotics of Jewish Nationalism," in *Novel Gazing: Queer Readings in Fiction*, ed. Eve Kosofsky Sedgwick (Durham, N.C.: Duke University Press, 1997), 299–329.

13. Aḥad Ha'am, *Kol kitvei Aḥad Ha'am*, 503.

14. Aḥad Ha'am, "Ha-torah veha-avodah" (Ideal and work), in *Kol kitvei Aḥad Ha'am*, 164–73.

15. The reference is obviously to Micha Yosef Berdichevsky's article "Stirah u-vinyan" (Destruction and building), which came out that same year. Aḥad Ha'am and Berdichevsky already had a history of conflict concerning the role of "poesy" in the writing of the nation (see Gluzman, *The Politics of Canonicity*, 21–26), and by 1903 the issues began to center on how to interpret the word "building"—whether in a physical or allegorical sense. Otherwise, Berdichevsky seems in agreement with much of Aḥad Ha'am's and Dubnov's programs for identity: "The enlightened, who stand in the middle [between secular affiliation and Jewish parochialism], possess two faces: half Western—in their lives and their thoughts; and half Jewish—in the synagogue. The life force continuously dissipates and the

nation moves toward ruin." Berdichevsky takes Dubnov's ideas a step beyond purely intellectual considerations and ascribes physical action to the need for a new identity. His new Jew is less the product of institutionalized education than of the process that melds internal transformation and belief with exterior action: "We find that this revival must be both internal and external at the same time . . . we need to stop being Jews by virtue of an abstract Judaism and to be independent Jews, as a living and existing people. The usual 'I believe' has already ceased to be enough for us. . . . We have a great responsibility. Everything is in our hands! We are the last Jews or we are the beginnings of a new nation . . . " The last ellipsis is part of the original text, the future left off mid-gasp in all its awesome potential. Both quotations from Micha Yosef Berdichevsky [Ben-Gurion], *Kitvei Micha Yosef Ben-Gurion [Berdichevsky]: Ma'amarim* (The writings of Micha Yosef Ben-Gurion [Berdichevsky]: Articles) (Tel Aviv: Dvir, 1948), 30.

16. The reference to agricultural schools is assuredly a pointed dig at the failures of the institutions developed under Rothschild patronage in Palestine to train Jewish settlers as farmers. The promise of agricultural enlightenment—the promise of change through education—did not meet with great success; see Derek Penslar, *Zionism and Technocracy: The Engineering of Jewish Settlement in Palestine, 1870–1918* (Bloomington: Indiana University Press, 1991).

17. Aḥad Ha'am, "Binyan" (Building), in *Kol kitvei Aḥad Ha'am*, 334–35.

18. The entire text of the poem is found in English translation in Stanislawski, *Zionism and the Fin-de-Siècle*, 188–89.

19. Ibid.

20. Bialik to Y. H. Ravnitsky, March 17, 1897, *Igrot* (Letters) (Tel Aviv: Dvir, 1938), 1:93–94. For an excellent discussion of this history and Bialik's position vis-à-vis Aḥad Ha'am, see Gluzman, *The Politics of Canonicity*, 19–21.

21. The Hebrew is found in Ḥayim Naḥman Bialik, *Kol shirei Ḥayim Naḥman Bialik* (The complete poetry of Ḥayim Naḥman Bialik) (Tel Aviv, Dvir, 1970), 352–53.

22. *Kol shirei Ḥayim Naḥman Bialik*, 356.

23. In contradistinction, that is, to the biblical Avraham, who casts his eyes downward, lifting them in Genesis 22:4 to see the landscape only when God explicitly commands and directs his vision.

24. *Kol shirei Ḥayim Naḥman Bialik*, 356.

25. Mintz, *Hurban*, 142.

26. *Kol shirei Ḥayim Naḥman Bialik*, 350.

27. Mintz, *Hurban*, 143.

28. According to Israel Efros, the American Hebrew poet and critic, "[T]he tragedy and humiliation [of Kishinev] caused a crisis in the poet's heart, a burning sense of duality, a clash between his individual and national personalities, between the internal and external claims," from his introduction to *Selected Poems of Hayyim Nahman Bialik* (New York: Bloch, 1965), xxvii. Or Leon Yudkin: "Much confusion has reigned with regard to the twin voices of Bialik—the public and the private. . . . [W]e are aware of a great deal of tension within the poetry itself, which not only refuses its label, but asserts the very opposite tendency," in "The Quintessence of H. N. Bialik's Poetry and Its Seminal Influences," in his *Escape into Siege: A Survey of Israeli Literature Today* (New York: Routledge and Kegan Paul, 1974), 21. Or Aliza Klausner-Bar: "In our opinion, one must make a complete distinction between Bialik's personal poetry and his public poetry . . . his national poetry. . . . The national interest became a part of his life to which he

dedicated a large part of his poetry. However, in parallel to his national poetry emerged his personal poems, poems of childhood, poems of nature, poems of love, and poems of struggle between love and tradition and between man and God, and this poetry endured even after his national poetry ran its course," in "Al hashpa'ato shel Aḥad Ha'am al Ḥayim Naḥman Bialik" (On Aḥad Ha'am's influence on Ḥayim Naḥman Bialik), in *Meassef 10*: *Mukdash li-ytsirat Ḥayim Naḥman Bialik*, ed. Hillel Barzel (Ramat Gan: Agudat Ha-sofrim and Masadah, 1975), 316. See also Reuven Tsur, *Yesodot romantiyim ve-anti-romantiyim be-shirei Bialik, Tcherniḥhovsky, Shlonsky, ve-Amiḥai* (Romantic and anti-romantic elements in poems by Bialik, Tcherniḥovsky, Shlonsky, and Amichai) (Tel Aviv: Papyrus, 1985), 7–9.

29. Paul de Man, *The Rhetoric of Romanticism* (New York: Columbia University Press, 1984), 2.

30. Ibid.

31. *Kol shirei Ḥayim Naḥman Bialik*, 360.

32. Gilles Deleuze and Félix Guattari, *Kafka: Toward a Minor Literature* (Minneapolis: University of Minnesota Press, 1986).

33. Aḥad Ha'am, "Ḥikui ve-hitbolelut" (Imitation and assimilation), in *Kol kitvei Aḥad Ha'am*, 89.

34. Ber Borochov, "The National Question and the Class Struggle," in *Class Struggle and the Jewish Nation*, ed. Mitchell Cohen (New Brunswick, N.J.: Transaction Books, 1984), 72–73.

35. See Fischel Lachover, "Ha-breikhah ha-roga'at" (The tranquil pool), in *Shirat Bialik* (Jerusalem: Mosad Bialik, 1953); Baruch Kurzweil, *Bialik ve-Tcherniḥovsky: Meḥkarim be-shiratam* (Bialik and Tcherniḥovsky: Research on their poetry) (Tel Aviv: Schocken, 1968); and Arieh Strauss, *Be-darkei ha-sifrut* (On the path of literature) (Jerusalem: Mosad Bialik, 1959).

36. Ḥ. N. Bialik, *Igrot Ḥayim Naḥman Bialik* (Letters), vol. 1 (Tel Aviv: Dvir, 1937), 162.

37. Haefrati, *Ha-mar'ot veha-lashon*, 109.

38. Dan Miron, *Ḥadashot me-eizor ha-kotev: Iyunim ba-shirah ha-ivrit ha-ḥadashah* (News from the polar zone: Essays on Hebrew poetry) (Tel Aviv: Zmorah Bitan, 1993), 463–67.

39. Bialik, *Kol shirei Ḥayim Naḥman Bialik*, 361–69.

40. The essay is dated October 3, 1915.

41. Shimon Sandbank goes even further and, while repudiating a strict allegorical reading of the "pool," sees in it a competing consciousness in the world of the poem—not an object but a parallel sentient force: "It's clear that the relationship of consciousness to the pool is still not enough to change the pool into a conscious being, and within that into a metaphor for human consciousness. But the consciousness [in the poem] does not just relate to the pool from the beginning, but rather to the consciousness of the pool. Because even though the poet knows a forest and knows a pool, he does not know 'what is in her heart,' he does not know what the pool is thinking. Already from the beginning, of the poem, therefore, the pool appears as a thinking being." *Shtei brekhot ba-ya'ar* (Two pools in the forest) (Tel Aviv: Tel Aviv University, 1976), 33.

42. Lukács discusses the concept of second nature in *The Theory of the Novel: A Historico-Philosphical Essay on the Forms of Great Epic Literature* (Cambridge, Mass.: MIT Press, 1971), 63–65. For Adorno, see his "The Idea of Natural History," *Telos* 60 (1984): 111–24. For a more detailed discussion of these ideas and their role in a Zionist articulation of the land, see Chapter 5 below.

43. Edmund Burke, *A Philosophical Enquiry into the Origin of the Ideas of the Sublime and Beautiful* (Oxford: Oxford University Press, 1990), 53.

44. Über allen Gipfeln
Ist Ruh',
In allen Wipfeln
Spürest du
Kaum einen Hauch;
Die Vögelein schweigen im Walde.
Warte nur, balde
Ruhest du auch.

45. The innocent belief in the ontology of the object which then presents itself to the poet became the point of derision for modernism, in its view of romanticism generally and in its parodies of this poem in particular. See for instance Bertolt Brecht's "Liturgie vom Hauch," in *Die Hauspostille–Manual of Piety* (New York: Grove, 1966), 40–49; and in Hebrew, David Fogel's "Be-leilot ha-stav" (In the nights of autumn), in *Lifnei ha-sha'ar he-afel* (Before the dark gate) (Vienna: Ma'ar, 1923).

46. William Shakespeare, "The Winter's Tale," act 4, scene 4, in *The Works of William Shakespeare* (New York: Oxford University Press, 1938), 1120.

47. Leo Marx, *The Machine in the Garden: Technology and the Pastoral Idea in America* (New York: Oxford University Press, 1964), 67.

48. Shakespeare's ideas of nature as expressed by Polixenes are further elaborated and given specifically colonial application in *The Tempest,* which is the point of departure for Marx's discussion. Since 1964 when Marx wrote *The Machine in the Garden,* the political analyses of these issues in Shakespeare have come under increased scrutiny. See, for instance, Ania Loomba and Martin Orkin, eds., *Postcolonial Shakespeares* (London: Routledege, 1998); and Ania Loomba, *Shakespeare, Race, and Colonialism* (Oxford: Oxford University Press, 2002).

49. Bialik, "Ha-breikhah," 367. Cf. Walter Pater's *Marius the Epicurean,* where knowledge and the world "flow" from the objects surrounding the body, which are then known immanently. As the critic Harold Bloom describes Pater's subjective materialism: "The self . . . knows that it is joined to no immortal soul, yet now believes also that its own integrity can be at one with the forces outside it". Harold Bloom, *Figures of Capable Imagination* (New York: Seabury, 1976), 27.

50. Adorno's critique of subject-object relations might also get at the point of Hebrew romanticism's belatedness. Adorno's early essay "On Subject and Object" points to what the romantics set into motion and in a materialist way reacts against the independence of the subject. In the context of the Zionist movement and Hebrew's move toward a modern romanticism, Adorno's critique of abstract continental philosophy resonates with concrete political and environmental consequences: "The separation of subject and object is both real and semblance . . . the separation is manifested in their being mutually mediated, object by subject, and even more and differently, subject by object. As soon as it is fixed without mediation, the separation becomes ideology, its normal form. Mind then arrogates to itself the status of being absolutely independent—which it is not: mind's claim to independence announces its claim to domination. Once radically separated from the object, subject reduces the object to itself; subject swallows object, forgetting how much it is object itself. The image of a temporal or extratemporal original state of blissful identity between subject and object is romantic, however: at times a wishful projection, today just a lie." Theodor Adorno, "On Subject and Object," in *Critical Models* (New York: Columbia University Press, 1998), 246. In Bialik's poems, Adorno's subject-who-is-also-object remains little more than an aesthetic exercise; Bialik's speaker treads that dialectic blithely between reflection and separate image: the forest and pool both a projection of

the controlling subjective voice and independent ontologies that are always already beyond reach, the "knowing" of the opening a cruel and ironic inversion of what might actually be happening throughout the epiphanic narrative of the poem.

51. This idea of instrumentality in Gordon is not how he is usually read and understood. Rather, his legacy has been irrationalist and metaphysical in the history of Zionism. As Eliezer Schweid writes about Gordon's concept of man in nature: "Man is a continuity of nature. In fact, he puts himself opposite nature as its master and exploiter, but that is both his crime and his punishment—the source of all his flaws and sorrows. Man has no other remedy than to return to nature, whose watchword would be: life within it and from it." *Ha-yaḥid: Olamo shel A. D. Gordon* (The Individual: The world of A. D. Gordon) (Tel Aviv: Am Oved, 1970), 98.

Chapter 2

1. As noted above, Baruch Kimmerling quotes Zangwill as writing, "a people without a land returning to a land without a people," *Zionism and Territory*, 9. Kimmerling dates a certain demise to the notion of an empty land to before the onset of the Second Aliyah. But that opinion relies too heavily on a positivist scientific and observable understanding of "emptiness," and indeed, Kimmerling makes his case dependent on documents concerning land purchases and thus fails to take into account cultural discourses. "Frontierty" (Kimmerling's term for a sense of openness and possibility in settler communities) may never have been very high in Palestine but there is little evidence to differentiate between First Aliyah and Second Aliyah experiences in terms of how much open land was available to Jewish immigrants. Besides, the myth of the empty land was alive well into the 1930s as a cultural trope: see Eliezer Smolly's *Anshei be-reshit* (People of Genesis) (1931; Tel Aviv: Am Oved, 1982); and Yael Zerubavel's analysis of Smolly in "The Forest as National Icon: Literature, Politics, and the Archaeology of Memory" *Israel Studies* 1, no. 1 (1996): 60–99.

2. Anne McClintock discusses this idea in terms of British imperial attitudes in *Imperial Leather* (New York: Routledge, 1995).

3. Aharon David Gordon, "Writings for the Future" (1910), quoted in Hertzberg, *The Zionist Idea.* Mirroring forms the basis for much of Gordon's nationalist philosophy of nature. See, for instance, *Ha-adam veha-teva* (Man and nature), in *Kitvei A. D. Gordon* (The writings of A. D. Gordon) (Tel Aviv: Ha-sifriyah Ha-tsiyonit, 1955), 2:43, where Gordon uses the metaphor of the mirror to indicate the ubiquity of nature in man's existence. Gordon's closest articulation to Zangwill's slogan came in a letter from 1912 concerning worker idealism in the country and urging employers to understand and be sympathetic to the idealism that drove the Jewish proletariat to immigrate to Palestine: "What have we come to do in Eretz Israel? To redeem the land (in either its widest or narrowest meaning—for us there is no difference) and to bring the people to life. But these are not two separate tasks, but rather two sides of the same thing. There is no redeeming the land without the renaissance of the people [*tḥiyat ha-am*] and there is no renaissance of the people without the redemption of the land [*ge'ulat ha-aretz*]," May 31, 1912, in *Mikhtavim u-reshimot* (Letters and short articles), in *Kitvei A. D. Gordon,* 3:51. Unless otherwise noted, all translations are my own.

4. In Gordon's notion of the land, the particularism of the individual still played a reflective role: "In my dream—here I have come to the land. And the

land is empty and desolate and in the hands of foreigners. . . . And far from me and strange to me is my beloved land. And also I am far and foreign to it. The one connection that binds my soul to her . . . is that my soul is also desolate like her and given over to foreigners who have devastated and degraded it." "Heḥalom u-fitrono" (The dream and its solution) (1909), in *Ha-umah veha-avodah* (The nation and work), *Kitvei A. D. Gordon,* 1:86.

5. Aharon David Gordon, "Mikhtav me-eretz yisra'el" (Letter from Eretz Israel), 1904, in *Kitvei A. D. Gordon,* 1:77.

6. I am referring here not just to the written impressions of Aḥad Ha'am and Yosef Ḥayim Brenner, which will be discussed below. Beyond their influential work, an entire genre of sentimental reminiscences developed in Hebrew which looked back to the origins of pioneering and lamented the sorry state of infrastructure and the poverty of the land. See, for instance, the two-volume collection of reminiscences *Zikhronot eretz-yisra'el* (Eretz Israel memories) (Jerusalem: Hahistadrut, 1947). Commemorations of First Aliyah and Second Aliyah pioneering had already been published before and during the war: Shmuel Dayan, *Ḥatsi yovel shanim shel Degania* (Twenty-five years of Degania) (Tel Aviv: Stybel, 1937); Eliezer Smolly, *Ḥayei rishonim* (Lives of the first settlers) (Tel Aviv: Am Oved, 1942).

7. Gordon, "Mikhtav me-eretz yisra'el," *Kitvei A. D. Gordon,* 1:78.

8. This notion, in fact, would drive Gordon's writings until his death and contributed significantly to his concept of the individual, which he defined always as distant from fulfillment. On the topic of the individual in Gordon, see Schweid, *Ha-yaḥid.*

9. Gordon saw the Arab primarily as an economic competitor with the Jewish worker. For Gordon's early views from 1910 on Arab worker competition in the economy of Palestine, see Yosef Gorny, "Ha-ideologiyah shel 'kibush ha-avodah'" (The ideology of *kibush ha-avodah*), *Keshet* 10, no. 2 (1968): 68.

10. Shafir, in *Land, Labor and the Origins of the Israeli-Palestinian Conflict,* makes a convincing case that, in essence, the origin of collectivity in Jewish Palestine can be analyzed as a reaction to the threat of Arab labor competition (cf. 165ff). In that sense, all labor unrest in the colonies and on the training farms can be seen as protests against Arab competition. This idea would certainly coincide with Ber Borochov's defense of labor competition even within a Marxist analysis of proletarian struggle. See his essay from 1905, "The National Question and the Class Struggle," in *Class Struggle and the Jewish Nation.*

11. "Kronikah," *Ha-po'el ha-tsa'ir,* February-March 1908, p. 23. More details about the protest can be found in Zvi Shilony, *Ideology and Settlement: The Jewish National Fund, 1897–1914* (Jerusalem: Magnes Press, 1998), 126–28; Yehuda Slutzky, *Mavo le-toldot tnu'at ha-avodah ha-yisra'elit* (Introduction to the history of the Israeli labor movement) (Tel Aviv: Am Oved, 1973), 197; Derek Penslar, *Zionism and Technocracy,* 98. Details about the protest are sketchy in each of these accounts and not well documented in any.

12. Yosef Gorny offers a fascinating analysis of the development of the concept *kibush ha-avodah* during these years (roughly 1907 until 1912). His focus on the principal differences between Ha-po'el Ha-tsa'ir and Po'alei Tsiyon are particularly instructive since the various labor movements indeed perceived developments on the ground and in theory with much difference and rancor ("Ha-ideologiya shel 'kibush ha-avodah'").

13. On this, see Hannan Hever, "The Origins of Eretz Israeli Poetry," in Sheila Jelen and Eliana Adler, eds., *Jewish Literature and History* (College Park: University of Maryland, forthcoming).

14. Menachem Ussishkin, *Our Program,* trans. D. S. Blondheim (New York: Publications of the Federation of American Zionists, 1905), 1–2. Shafir, *Land, Labor and the Origins of the Israeli-Palestinian Conflict,* 42–43, reads "Our Program" in very policy-oriented terms and considers the practical impact of the manifesto on capitalist ideas of land purchasing and the ownership of land.

15. Especially on land owned and operated by the JNF. Ussishkin, *Our Program,* 25–26. Ussishkin was certainly no socialist and was still quite committed to settlement on the basis of the Old Settlement, the small individual capitalist colonies of the First Aliyah. However, on lands owned by the National Fund, Ussishkin does make an early call for cooperative settlement: "Upon the largest portion of the lands of the National Fund, however, co-operative colonies must be established, in accordance with Oppenheimer's project" (25). Franz Oppenheimer's cooperative settlement plan had been championed by Herzl, and his influence had been instrumental in the writing of *Altneuland.* The cooperative plan outlined a phased worker ownership of settlements that would be founded and supervised by technocratic experts; see Penslar, *Zionism and Technocracy,* 55–59.

16. Some years later, David Ben-Gurion, recalling the achievements of the Second Aliyah years, attributed success to the "independence of thought" of the group, the lack of a priori ideological convictions to determine a particular course for the Yishuv. Beit Berl Archives, file 23/55, meeting of the Mapai Central Committee, February 20, 1955; quoted in Sternhell, *The Founding Myths of Israel,* 75.

17. Aharon Ever-Hadani, *Ḥaderah (1951–1891): Shishim shnot koroteha* (Tel Aviv: Hotsa'at masadah ve-"ḥevrat meyasdei ḥaderah," 1951), 96. Herzl talks about the eucalyptus as well in instrumental economic terms in *Altneuland.* Theodor Herzl, *Old New Land* (New York: Bloch, 1960).

18. From a flyer soliciting funds for the Ölbaumspende: "The product of this forest will enable us to educate the children of our people in our land in a Jewish spirit and to develop Jewish culture upon a genial soil so that it shall blossom anew. The Olive Tree Fund enables us to acquire a safer and higher profit out of our landed property in Palestine, although we are cultivating the Olive Tree at less expense, at a quicker rate, upon poorer soil, with inferior labour and with less risk, than is possible in the case of the methods of agricultural colonisation which are usual and necessary elsewhere" (CZA KKL1/472).

19. Otto Warburg, "Eretz yisra'el ke-eizor le-hityashvut" (Eretz Israel as an area for settlement), in *Sefer Warburg,* ed. Ya'akov Thon (Herzliyah: Masadah, 1948), 156. This is a translation of Warburg's essay "Palästina als Kolonisationsgebiet," *Altneuland* 1 (January 1904): 3–13.

20. Warburg, *Sefer Warburg,* 156.

21. Early JNF propaganda films from the 1900s proudly reported this fact; see *Frühling in Palästina,* a silent film, which in one title states: "Die Araber neunen ihn den Juden-Baum" (Steven Spielberg Jewish Film Archive VTDA 276 2a & 2b). Also see S. Raskin, "Die Baume Palaestinas," CZA KKL5/46681 (n.d.): "aber lieblicher als alle ist der 'Juedische Baum,'" der Eukalyptusbaum, mit seinen vielen Blaettern und vieltausandfachen Bewegungen. Wie liebe ich ihn, das froehliche Geschoepf, den Eukalupstusbaum!" Later, the irony of the olive tree as the new "Jewish" tree is that the idea would obviously not take. The olive tree could never be successfully appropriated from the Arab. Max I. Bodenheimer, chairman from 1907 until 1914 of the JNF Board of Directors, in summing up a trip to Palestine in 1912, recommended the abandonment of the olive tree because "they are too Arab" (Cologne, August 1912; CZA KKL1/468).

22. "What a beautiful idea that of a Herzl Olive Grove in Palestine is! It will

be a fine sight which every visitor to Palestine will wish to see. It will give, as it now giving [sic], Jewish laborer an opportunity to work; and, besides this, the incomes from the olive-bearing trees is to be set aside for school purposes in Palestine. A great olive grove with its trees of eternal green and Jewish farmers working in happiness to plant these trees in the land of Israel, Jewish children having instruction in the tongue of their fathers by reason of the proceeds from the grove—what better memorial can the Jews of the world erect to Theodore Herzl!" A letter signed by Harry Friedenwald, J. L. Magnes, and E. W. Erwin-Epstein (Köln, July 7, 1908; CZA KKL1/463).

23. Ussishkin noted at the meeting of the Grosses Actions-Comite of the JNF (GAC) in April 1904, when the issue was discussed, that the olive trees would produce no fruit for some years. From Penslar's account, after this point, the justifications for the campaign became more cultural and less economic, even though the explicitly stated goals always remained economically driven to some degree. While Warburg might have still harbored the desire that these "experimental projects would result in the 'creation of the base for private initiative,'" the motivation for that endeavor was becoming less and less tied to personal economic benefit. One moment of prescience on Ussishkin's part was the criticism that, as Penslar notes, "Jewish workers would be unwilling to work as wage laborers for an administered domain, and that they would demand something for themselves." With the profit motive in place, Ussishkin and Warburg's plans remained at odds, but in a nationalist model of colonial settlement that saw collective redemption in the land—that is, replacing a bourgeois model of class conflict with the emerging ascendance of constructivism and syndicalism of national productivity and creation—a project of national domains worked by laborers would succeed, and this is precisely what happened. See Penslar, *Zionism and Technocracy*, 74–75.

24. CZA KKL1/458; CZA KKL1/452; CZA KKL1/449.

25. The protest stages, one could argue, a "subject's self-understanding" that "arises from a togetherness-in-opposition with the objectified material seemingly most alien to it," as Rosalind Krauss states generally about the modernist project in *The Picasso Papers* (New York: Farrar, Straus and Giroux, 1998), 13. Krauss is responding to Adorno, who outlined a dialectical relationship between nature and artifice, opposites that imply and engage the other's presence in aesthetics: "The concept of natural beauty rubs on a wound, and little is needed to prompt one to associate this wound with the violence that the artwork—a pure artifact—inflicts on nature. Wholly artificial, the artwork seems to be the opposite of what is not made, nature. As pure antitheses, however, each refers to the other: nature to the experience of a mediated and objectified world, the artwork to nature as the mediated plenipotentiary of immediacy." Theodor W. Adorno, *Aesthetic Theory* (Minneapolis: University of Minnesota Press, 1997), 61–62.

26. "Te'udat ha-shiloaḥ" (Ha-shiloaḥ manifesto), in *Kol kitvei Aḥad Ha'am*, 128. For an excellent discussion of this debate and its consequences for Hebrew poetry, see Gluzman, *The Politics of Canonicity*, 15–25.

27. Quoted in Yosef Ḥayim Brenner, "Micha Yosef Berdichevsky," in *Ktavim* (Writings) (Tel Aviv: Ha-kibbutz Ha-meuḥad, 1985), 3:831.

28. The first, and most important, of these travel dispatches was "Emet meeretz yisra'el" (Truth from Eretz Israel) (1891), in *Kol kitvei Aḥad Ha'am*, 23–30, and first published in *Ha-melits* on June 30, 1891. Aḥad Ha'am's second visit in 1893 also produced a provocative essay, *Kol kitvei Aḥad Ha'am*, 30–34, originally published in *Ha-melits* on August 17, 1893.

29. For an important discussion of this period for Brenner, see Hever, *Producing the Modern Hebrew Canon,* 19–45.

30. On Brenner's early days in the country, see Zohar Shavit, *He-ḥayim ha-sifrutiyim be-eretz yisra'el, 1910–1939* (The literary life in Eretz Israel, 1910–1939) (Tel Aviv: Porter Institute, 1982), 29–31.

31. In *Reshafim,* July 1909; reprinted in Yosef Ḥayim Brenner, *Ktavim* (Writings) (Tel Aviv: Ha-kibbutz Ha-meuḥad,1985), 3:303–18.

32. When Aḥad Ha'am writes of his first trip to Palestine in 1891, as part of a delegation to investigate Ḥovevei Tsiyon and Bnei Moshe land-purchasing activities and to report in general on the conditions of settlement in the First Aliyah, he titles the report "Truth from Eretz Israel" and begins by setting up the distinction between the conjured place and his encounter with the real:

> After many years of thinking about and imagining the land of our ancestors and the rebirth of our people there, I was finally able to see with my own eyes the subject of my dreams, this land of wonders that pulls toward it so many hearts from all the peoples and from all the countries. I was there about three months. I saw its deserts—the remnants of its past life; I saw the horrible condition of its present; but I took special notice of the future, and everywhere I went one question was constantly before my eyes: what are our hopes here in the end? Is the land still able to return and be rejuvenated? It wasn't difficult for me to find an answer to the land question: it was enough to travel through the land for a few days, to see the mountains and the valleys, the fields and vineyards, which give their fruit in spite of the lazy Arabs, to come to the opinion that the miracle is still there, and the strength of the past is the strength now: to give life and happiness to multitudes of her sons, who will return to her with full hearts and skillful hands, which will work her. But against this, it was not easy to find an answer to the question of Israel, to bring judgment on the strength of the workers, to learn from the deeds about the doers, about how qualified they are to bring us to our sought-after goals.

Aḥad Ha'am, "Emet me-eretz yisra'el," in *Kol kitvei Aḥad Ha'am,* 23.

33. Brenner, "Be-fa'am ha-me'ah," in *Ktavim* 3:303. All ellipses are in the original.

34. For a discussion of naming, especially as it is developed in the work of Walter Benjamin, see Susan Buck-Morss, *The Dialectics of Seeing* (Cambridge, Mass.: MIT Press, 1989), 229ff.

35. Solipsism had become the dominant narrative mode of the labor movement, according to Brenner, who saw in it the facile and unproductive projection of the self onto the land. During the first decades of the twentieth century, *Ha-po'el ha-tsa'ir* published plenty of essays such as M. Vilkansky's "My First Days of Work," which wallows in a romantic egoism of the self, completely closed to any encounter beyond the subjective drivel of impressions: "To the vastness of the field, I went out, far from any person, far from the gardens, to celebrate my triumph. I went out—and I danced and recited poetry about the world that surrounded me—both what was revealed and what lay hidden. At that time I received work for the next day; and this was very special, an important occasion in my life; in my life at that time and in the life of my world. I was not then 'green' in the country. I had already spent the summer months here, and had spun for myself already many dreams in the holiness of the land of the forefathers, land of the sons." *Ha-po'el ha-tsa'ir* (February-March 1908).

36. Brenner's dialectics of Zionist subject and the object of the land are governed by a modernist poetics that stresses the "effects linked to the message and not to its referent," Roland Barthes, "To Write: An Intransitive Verb?" in *The Rustle of Language* (Berkeley: University of California Press, 1989), 11. In this, Brenner seems to enact Barthes's notion of diathesis, which "designates the way in which the subject of the verb is affected by the action." Ibid., 18.

37. Mendele's own views on First Aliyah Zionism are discussed in Zeev Goldberg, "Mendele Mokher Sfarim veha-ra'ayon ha-tsiyoni" (Mendele Mokher Sfarim and the Zionist idea), *Ha-tsiyonut* 20 (1996): 31–54.

38. Brenner consistently criticized a nonnaturalistic writing of the nation, especially in the tendency toward interior solipsism. See his most famous article on the subject, "Ha-janer ha-eretz-yisra'eli va-avizarehu" (The genre of Eretz Israel and its devices), in *Ktavim*, vol. 3, 569–78, first published in 1911; and "Le-Shalom Aleichem" (For Sholom Aleichem), in *Ktavim*, 4: 1422–28. For a discussion of Brenner's literary criticism and influence, see Iris Parush, *Kanon sifruti ve-ideologiyah le'umit* (National ideology and literary canon) (Jerusalem: Mosad Bialik, 1992).

39. Brenner, *Ktavim*, 3:311.

40. Yosef Ḥayim Brenner, *Shkhol ve-khishalon* (Bereavement and failure), in *Ktavim*, vol. 2.

41. Gershon Shaked, *Ha-siporet ha-ivrit, 1880–1980*, vol. 3 (Tel Aviv: Hakibbutz Ha-meuḥad, 1988), 52.

42. Yosef Ḥayim Brenner, "Atsabim" (Nerves), in *Ktavim*, 2:1229–61.

43. Yosef Ḥayim Brenner, *Ktavim*, 2:1687–88.

44. Moshe Smilansky (Hawaja Musa), *Bnei arav* (Tel Aviv: Dvir, 1945).

45. "[The Administration of Palestine] shall introduce a land system appropriate to the needs of the country having regard, among other things, to the desirability of promoting the close settlement and intensive cultivation of the land." British Mandate, art. 11, in Walter Laqueur and Barry Rubin, eds., *The Israel-Arab Reader: A Documentary History of the Middle East Conflict* (New York: Penguin, 1995), 33.

46. The displacement of Arab farmers in the Yishuv will be discussed below. Also, see Kenneth Stein, *The Land Question in Palestine, 1917–1939* (Chapel Hill: University of North Carolina Press, 1984).

47. Even before the First World War, the Zionist Executive was consistently preoccupied with gathering expert assessments on Palestinian conditions of weather, soil, hygiene, and the like. The first notable effort of a comprehensive sort was initiated during the war when most JNF functions were transferred to the neutrality of the United States, thus assuring unfettered communications among the various JNF branches which, left in Europe, would have been cut off from one another. The shift to America not only echoes the major immigrant movement of the eastern European Jewish community, but also reinforces the consistent use of the trope of California as the goal of the transformation process. In a memorandum on sending experts to Palestine, dated May 6, 1919, a Mr. Robison remarks, in terms of goals for an agricultural expert they would send, "This is also needed so as to have him make a study of the productive possibilities of the various sections of Palestine and to bring to the subject his expert knowledge of results in other countries, especially California, to which Palestine has been so often compared by experts on the subject." CZA Z4/1721.

48. Kligler worked at the Rockefeller Institute in New York. His article, "Sanitary Survery of Palestine" is found among Akiva Ettinger's personal papers (CZA A111/40) under the heading, "His Public Settlement Activities in Eretz Israel."

49. John Cropper, "The Geographical Distribution of Anaphilisia and Malarial Fever in Upper Palestine," *Journal of Hygiene* 2, no. 1 (1902): 47–57. The Zionist establishment was obviously aware of Cropper's work as early as 1906; in that year, a review of Cropper's article "The Malarial Fevers of Jerusalem and Their Prevention," *Journal of Hygiene*, (1905): 460ff., appeared in *Altneuland*.

50. The cultural importance of malaria for the Zionist movement is further emphasized by the way that trachoma has been so easily ignored within political and social histories of the country. Certainly, the acute and chronic morbidity of malaria made it a more likely candidate than trachoma to become the focus of popular imagination. But trachoma's disappearance from the natural and political history of the country also implies another reading. Trachoma, unlike malaria, was a disease of human contact, of touching and interaction; it was passed along within interior spaces. Malaria, on the other hand, both before and after the discovery of the microbial pathology of the disease in 1897, was a disease of the landscape. In its morbidity it was also a disease of the mind, and this fact captured the Hebrew imagination, which then worked to develop the equation of the ridding of malaria as the ridding of a particular mentality.

51. Ever-Hadani, *Ḥaderah*, 96, makes note of competing methods.

52. Certainly by 1937, the eucalyptus was long forgotten as a scientific and utilitarian agent, and the mythology of settlement (*hityashvut*) was being popularized with ditching and oiling at center stage. In November 1937, Yosef Weitz drew up preliminary plans for a settlement museum in Palestine (CZA A111/51). The museum was to include four halls, of which the third was to deal with "soil and water." The story of Nahalal and the drying up of the marsh there takes up a good portion of the space. Ironically, the major division in this hall is between *yibush* (drying) and *hashka'ah* (irrigation), which were not originally conceived of together or in terms of how the first would affect the second. The eucalyptus only figures as a historical footnote in the museum, in a section on the history of Jewish settlement, where it is discussed for its role at Ḥadera and Petaḥ Tikvah during the First Aliyah. For late defenses of the eucalyptus on mainly economic grounds and not for health reasons, see Zeev Breen, "Ta'asiyat ha-ekaliptus" (The eucalyptus industry) and Raskin, "Die Baume Palaestinas," CZA KKL5/7312 and 46681.

53. *Eretz*, a journal of "belletristic literature and criticism," appeared in 1919 in Odessa, with Eliezer Steinman as part of the board of editors; *Gvulot* first was published in Vienna in 1918 and was the most European and cosmopolitan of these new journals; *Ha-ezraḥ* specifically tied its program to "matters of the people and the land [*eretz*]": "For the spiritual renaissance of our nation, for social awareness, and for cultural action in our country—*Ha-ezraḥ* presents itself"; and *Ma'abarot*, with Ya'akov Fichman as its editor, was specifically devoted to constructivist ideals: "We believe that hard bodily work is necessary for the work of a happy spirit, and the Hebrew workers in Eretz Israel have already demonstrated who has real need for literature and spiritual values."

54. Unsigned manifesto of *Ha-me'orer* (The Awakener), vol. 1, no. 1 (1906).

55. The manifesto for *Ha-adamah* was published in the corresponding political journal of the United Labor Movement of Palestine (Aḥdut Ha-avodah), called *Kuntres* and edited by Berl Katznelson, vol. 1, no. 6 (1919).

56. N. Wagman, "Center of Gravity," *Ha-adamah* 1 (1919): 56.

57. Alexander Ziskind Rabinovitch, "Sibah doḥah sibah mekarevet" (Opposite forces), *Ha-adamah* 1 (1919): 1–9.

58. Ibid., 2.

59. Ibid., 4. *Effendi* is a Turkish phrase for landlord.

60. Ibid., 5.

61. See Mitchell Cohen, *Zion and State: Nation, Class, and the Shaping of Modern Israel* (New York: Columbia University Press, 1992), 105–19.

62. Rabinovitch, 5.

63. Ibid., 3.

64. Ibid., 5.
65. Ibid., 9.
66. "If literature is a particular form by means of which objective reality is reflected, then it becomes of crucial importance for it to grasp that reality as it truly is, and not merely to confine itself to reproducing whatever manifests itself immediately and on the surface. . . . Lenin repeatedly insisted on the practical importance of the category of totality: 'In order to know an object thoroughly, it is essential to discover and comprehend all of its aspects, its relationships and its "mediations." We shall never achieve this fully but insistence on all-around knowledge will protect us from the errors and inflexibility.'" Georg Lukács, "Realism in the Balance," in Ernst Bloch et al., *Aesthetics and Politics* (London: NLB, 1977), 34.
67. "What if Lukács's reality–a coherent, infinitely mediated totality–is not so objective after all? What if his conception of reality has failed to liberate itself completely from Classical systems? What if authentic reality is also discontinuity? Since Lukács operates with a closed, objectivistic conception of reality, when he comes to examine Expressionism he resolutely rejects any attempt on the part of artists to shatter any image of the world, even that of capitalism. Any art which strives to exploit the *real* fissures in surface inter-relations and to discover the new in their crevices, appears in his eyes as a willful act of destruction. He thereby equates experiment in demolition with a condition of decadence," Ernst Bloch, "Discussing Expressionism," in Bloch et al., *Aesthetics and Politics*, 22.
68. Adorno, *Aesthetic Theory*, 61–62.
69. Keren Kayemeth Le Israel (Jewish National Fund), *Avodot ha-havra'ah be-emek yizra'el / Sanitation Works in the Valley of the Jesreel* (Jerusalem: JNF, 1925). While no author is given for the title, Akiva Ettinger, one of the JNF's chief agronomists, certainly worked on the pamphlet and edited extensively. An edited draft with his markings exists among his personal papers (CZA A111/45).
70. JNF propaganda also told a slightly different version that worked more in concert with a constructivist mythology of building from nothing. In the late 1920s, the JNF prepared a series of scripted slide shows ("illustrated talks") that were then translated into the languages where fund-raising efforts were strongest. No. 10, "A Trip Through the Emek Jezreel," dates from the mid to late 1920s and relates the origins of Nahalal with a more organic and nostalgic spin, completely ignoring the professionalism of the operation:

> To appreciate Nahalal it is not sufficient to look at it as it is today. One must look too into its beginnings which took place not so very long ago. In 1921 three men came out to inspect this spot which they and their followers were to settle. They knew that a Homeland could not be built up with sweat and blood, but the swamps and desolation that faced them was none the less depressing. . . . Undaunted, however, the three reconnoiters returned a few months later together with their fellows. . . . In the course of the work the dreaded malaria laid numbers of them low; hostile Bedouins attacked the encampment and robbed them of all that might be removed. But the Halutzim [pioneers] persisted. . . . To the Jews who are returning to Palestine, life in the old-new Homeland must be normal, and the backbone of a normal people is its peasantry. That is why the foundations of the new Palestine are to be laid in the "Emek," deep in the soil with plough and pick.

(CZA KKL5/3490/1): p. 14–15 of the script.
71. *Sanitation Works*, 32 (English); 21 (Hebrew). The technological victory over the swamp, however, was not couched in strictly modernist terms. In fact, the working of the soil not only restored the land to its look of ancient times, but it directly connected the Jewish worker to that ancient time: improvement itself

was figured as a tie to the land, and the Arab years intervening are marked both by the desolation the Arab caused and the technological neglect of those years. In a pamphlet published about the Jezreel by Keren Ha-yesod in 1926, these connections are made clear: "In the Emek are remains of drainage works and canals from ancient times. Nuris for instance has embankments built perhaps even before the conquest of the Romans, who doubtless improved on the existing waterworks. When the Jews began work afresh in Nuris it was found that the Arabs had neglected these earlier irrigation systems and had merely irrigated in primitive fashion in important areas. Experts then submitted plans for laying out concrete canals, iron pipes, and dikes." The Jewish reclamation of the Jezreel was certainly also figured as an ethnic occupation: "I remember quite vividly my first glimpse of Emek Yizreel thirty years ago, as I passed through it on my way from Haifa to Nazareth. The Emek was an absolute wilderness, dangerous to traverse. I had to be accompanied by two armed Turkish *zaptes*, or gendarmes, for protection against the Bedouins, the whole of the way. On both sides of the impossible road extended immense swamps. I could not then imagine that after so very many years the whole region would be cleared both of Bedouins and malaria." From Akiva Ettinger's reminiscences on settlement of the Jezreel. Both items from CZA A111/12.

72. See McClintock, *Imperial Leather*, and John Tagg, "God's Sanitary Law: Slum Clearance and Photography in Late Nineteenth-Century Leeds," in *The Burden of Representation* (Minneapolis: University of Minnesota Press, 1993), 117–52.

73. The film *Travail et Solennités en Palestine*, produced by the JNF in the 1920s tells a similar story linearly where human intervention in the land only works to make it more natural, the grid and the imposition of modernity needed to rejuvenate the place. The plot seems clear: starting with an aerial shot of Nahalal, the grid sets the entire stage for the improvement of the site, a land of "marais" that will be transformed into "en champs fertiles." The improvement is mostly underground: the digging of ditches and the laying of cement to make channels, the burying of pipes for drainage and irrigation, the planting of trees. The result is not then the settlement itself, but nature more naturalized, more itself, as water, now emerging from an electric pumping station, feeds an artificial pond next to a field where ducks are swimming: "Par des travaux d'améliorative de grande—nuergue le Keren Kajemeth Lejisrael a transformé toute—ette région, où auparavant—'étendaient des marais, en champs fertiles."

74. The grid reverses the common wisdom about itself. As Rosalind Krauss writes: "The grid states the absolute autonomy of the realm of art. Flattened, geometricized, ordered, it is anti-natural, anti-mimetic, anti-real. It is what art looks like when it turns its back to nature. . . . In the over-all regularity of its organization, it is the result not of imitation, but of aesthetic decree. . . . The grid declares the space of art to be at once autonomous and autotelic." *Grids: Format and Image in 20th Century Art* (New York: Pace Gallery, 1979), no page number. Obviously, the engineers and settlers of the Jezreel Valley in the 1920s thought otherwise.

Chapter 3

1. For an excellent discussion of constructivism in Palestine, see Mitchell Cohen, *Zion and State: Nation, Class, and the Shaping of Modern Israel* (New York: Columbia University Press, 1992).

2. "A fundamental error rests in the outlook of a majority of the 'builders of the Yishuv,' or rather in the outlook of most of those who provide employment to those who have come to work in Eretz Israel. Employers look at the employees as on 'workers' in the standard meaning, and because of this tend to exploit this relationship. The employee is to work and to do what is ordered of him, and the employer is to order and pay a salary, and sometimes to give the worker housing, and sometimes food—everything according to the conditions [of employment]. . . . Many understand in fact that our workers have come here for the sake of our ideal. . . . Idealism in action and in life is required by the worker, and only in this way does he feel he has the right to think of himself as participating in building the Yishuv and, through his creative efforts, a new life." May 31, 1912, in *Mikhtavim u-reshimot* (Letters and short articles), in *Kitvei A. D. Gordon,* 3:50–51.

3. On Brenner's standing in the Hebrew world, see Nurit Govrin, *Brenner: "Oved-etsot" u-moreh-derekh* (Brenner: "Nonplussed" and mentor) (Tel Aviv: Misrad Ha-bitaḥon and Universitat Tel Aviv, 1991).

4. The question of "engagement" and "commitment" in literature has been dominated by postwar assessments of the failures of interwar art to prevent the devastation of the Second World War. See, for instance Charles G. Whiting, "The Case for 'Engaged' Literature," *Yale French Studies* 1 (1948): 84–89; Jean Paul Sartre, *What Is Literature?* (1949; New York: Washington Square Press, 1966); Mark Carroll, "Commitment or Abrogation? Avant-Garde Music and Jean-Paul Sartre's Idea of Committed Art," *Music & Letters,* 83, no. 4 (2002): 590–606; Renato Poggiolo, *The Theory of the Avant-Garde* (Cambridge, Mass.: Harvard University Press, 1968); Peter Bürger, *Theory of the Avant-Garde* (Minneapolis: University of Minnesota Press, 1984).

5. For the European debates of the 1930s, see Bloch et al., *Aesthetics and Politics.*

6. Shlonsky later criticized the specific effects of Jewish naturalism in terms of perpetuating a diaspora mentality, easily the most persistent cultural insult in the history of Zionism; see Avraham Shlonsky, *Pirkei yoman* (Chapters of a diary) (Tel Aviv: Sifriyat Po'alim, 1981), 59.

7. Walter Benjamin, "The Author as Producer," in *Reflections* (New York: Schocken Books, 1986), 220–21. Emphasis is in the original.

8. Anita Shapira, *Berl: Biografiyah* (Tel Aviv: Am Oved, 1980), 1:259.

9. "Lamah ha-shtikah?" (Why the silence?) *Davar,* September 7, 1925.

10. Berl Katznelson [signed B. K.], "El ha-shotkim" (To those silent), *Davar,* September 7, 1925.

11. Ibid.

12. David Ben-Gurion, "Aḥdut ha-avodah veha-histadrut" (Aḥdut Ha-avodah and the Histadrut), *Kuntres,* February 6, 1925, p. 10. Mitchell Cohen quotes this statement to point out the totalistic vision of the labor movement under Ben-Gurion, and his and Katznelson's attempts to bring about that unity in the 1920s through Aḥdut Ha-avodah and the Histadrut. Cohen, *Zion and State,* 114–15. Cohen's vision of unity, however, is limited to political power and does not extend to an analysis of the discursive instruments developed to fulfill those goals. Zeev Sternhell, on the other hand, accuses Ben-Gurion of much greater desires for centralized control over all aspects of life in the Yishuv: "Ben-Gurion described th[e] absence of control in all areas of the Histadrut economy as anarchy. This was the cause of the Histadrut's great weakness, and, as he put it, 'We must now put an end to this anarchy.' Ben-Gurion judged all forms of social life by a single criterion: the extent to which they ensured control of the leadership responsible for building the country and absorbing immigration." Sternhell. *The*

Founding Myths of Israel, 124. Ben-Gurion's quotation is from "Proposals to the Aḥdut Ha-avodah Convention," *Kuntres* 4, no. 92 (1921): 3.

13. Action was, in fact, the obsession of constructivism, which allowed for little activity other than building as a mode of self-expression: "And the settler, who has come to the soil and succeeded in drying its swamps and in transforming it from a failing land into a fecund and blossoming land, looks around at the big sea of land [*karka*] surrounding the island of settlement and asks: . . . there will not be new settlements as a continuation of our efforts and needs?" Y. Ori, "Be-ein karka," *Ha-po'el ha-tsa'ir* July 11, 1924.

14. Avraham Shlonsky [signed A. Sh.], "Musaf le-shabatot ule-mo'adim—o hosafah sifrutit" (Sabbath and holiday supplement—or literary section), *Davar* October 16, 1925.

15. Ibid.

16. Hever, *Paitanim u-viryonim,* 71.

17. On Brenner's publishing in *Ha-adamah,* see Hever, *Paitanim u-viryonim,* 70ff.

18. The tie to Mayakovsky was very close. Shlonsky published a translation of Mayakovsky's "How to Make a Poem?" (Eikh la'asot shir?) in *Ktuvim* in 1927 (December 22), a futurist primer stressing complexity and the avant-garde dependence on individualism, tinged always with socialism. Shlonsky's notes to Mayakovsky stress that aspect of the paradox: "True poetry was, is, and will always be 'tendentious,' but it will never be a subservient underling serving the powers that be. There is just one dictate—the dictate of the artistic conscience. And one legislator—the divine voice that is in the heart of man [*adam*]."

19. Shlonsky, "Sabbath and Holiday Supplement."

20. Avraham Shlonsky, "Ha-melitsah" (Poesy), *Hedim* 6 (1923): 189–90. For an excellent discussion of the political legacy of these ideas about language, see Naomi Seidman, "Lawless Attachments, One-Night Stands: The Sexual Politics of the Hebrew-Yiddish Language War," in *Jews and Other Differences,* ed. Jonathan Boyarin and Daniel Boyarin (Minneapolis: University of Minnesota Press, 1997), 301–3.

21. *Ha-aretz,* October 15, 1928.

22. "Gilboa" first appeared in Avraham Shlonsky, *Ba-galgal* (Tel Aviv: Davar, 1923); and reprinted in Avraham Shlonsky, *Shirim* (Poems) (Merḥaviyah: Sifriyat Po'alim, 1965), 1:162–203. In 1947, Shlonsky returned to nature poetry with "Harei at" (You are hereby), in Shlonskly, *Shirim,* 2:254. For an insightful stylistic analysis of the poem, see Chana Kronfeld, *On the Margins of Modernism: Decentering Literary Dynamics* (Berkeley: University of California Press, 1996), 103–9.

23. Shlonsky, *Shirim,* 1:162. This particular phrase, *la'alot la-torah,* resonates with religious meaning: the act of reading the Torah. However, I have purposely rendered it ambivalent, because *la'alot* also connects to the physical domain of the represented content of the poem, that is, the Gilboa and the Jezreel Valley in general. As will become obvious in the fourth poem of the cycle, "Amal" (see discussion below), this ambivalence and ambiguity seem important. As I remark below in criticizing Leah Goldberg's reading of Shlonsky, I believe the mistake of standard Hebrew and Jewish criticism has been its reading of phrases like this outside of their immediate textual and political context.

24. Shlonsky here borrows a concept articulated in Shakespeare's *The Winter's Tale* (see Chapter 1 above) where "wildness" is already the instantiation of culture and represents the collapse of any opposition between culture and nature. See Leo Marx, *The Machine in the Garden.* Shlonsky was well familiar with Shakespeare through Russian translation and repeatedly boasted of being Shakespeare's

Hebrew translator; see, for example, William Shakespeare, *Hamlet, nesikh Denmark*, trans. Avraham Shlonsky (Tel Aviv: Hotsa'at La-am, 1946).

25. Shlonsky, *Shirim*, 1:162.

26. An analysis of Shlonsky's deployment of futurist stylistics is in Kronfeld, *On the Margins of Modernism*, 103–4.

27. Shlonsky, *Shirim*, 1:163.

28. *King Lear* was Shlonsky's other major translation of Shakespeare, in *Maḥazot*, trans. Avraham Shlonsky (Merḥaviyah: Sifriyat Po'alim, 1971).

29. Shlonsky, *Shirim*, 1:164.

30. Ibid., 165.

31. Leah Goldberg, "Al arba'a shirim shel A. Shlonsky" (On four poems by A. Shlonsky), *Moznayim* 5–6, 37 (1974). Dan Laor discusses the poems in "Gilboa" as a general reflection of the ethos and political ideology of the Third Aliyah in "Shirei 'Gilboa' veha-etos shel ha-aliyah ha-shlishit: He'arot-ptiḥah" (The poems of "Gilboa" and the ethos of the Third Aliyah: Introduction), *Moznayim* 49 (1979): 134–40.

32. There is some historical precedence beyond the reproduction in literary anthologies for reading this fourth section of "Amal" as separate from the previous three. As Laor points out, Shlonsky published the poems that would eventually be collected into "Gilboa" beginning in 1922, Laor, "Shirei 'Gilboa,'" 135. Even as part of books of poems under his authorship, Shlonsky published the poem twice in the mid-1920s, once in *Ba-galgal* (Tel Aviv: Davar, 1923) and another time in *Le-aba-ima* (Tel Aviv: Ketuvim, 1927). In *Ba-galgal*, "Amal" appears with all four sections as part of "Gilboa," which is almost intact and in the same order as it will later appear in the collected poems. However, in *Le-aba-ima*, "Halbishini ima ksherah . . ." appears as the last poem in a cycle under the volume's title. It appears alone, without any of the other parts of "Amal" and without the designation of "Amal."

33. Goldberg misses the entire notion of voice in her analysis and understands words as inherently capable of carrying independent meanings. My own understanding of voice and inflection is derived from Paul de Man, *Allegories of Reading* (New Haven, Conn.: Yale University Press, 1979).

34. If modern Hebrew really did mean to cast off the otherness of its oriental roots and reinvent itself in the reflection of European language and modern sensibilities, then the pronouncement of the strong subject position—the "I" of the poetic speaker, separate and isolated from the syntax of a grammatical morphology that would subsume that position—must certainly be read as part of that transformation. On this subject, see Harshav, *Language in the Time of Revolution.*

35. Shlonsky, *Shirim*, 1:172.

36. Ibid.

37. Edmund Wilson, *To the Finland Station* (New York: Farrar, Straus and Giroux, 1972), 511ff. Shlonsky translated Trotsky's autobiography into Hebrew in 1930: Leon Trotsky, *Ḥayai* (My life), trans. A. Shlonsky (Tel Aviv: Mitspeh, 1930).

38. If we can describe Shlonsky as taking on the subject side of a dialectic, then Fogel was certainly on the object side. Nature, for Fogel, only reinforced the objective nature of experience, the way that the individual could never achieve a true subject position. On a personal level, this division led to a mutual disregard for the other's work. For Fogel on Shlonsky, see "Lashon ve-signon be-sifrutenu ha-tse'irah" (1930), in *Siman Kriah* 3/4 (1974): 382–91; translated as "Language and Style in Our Young Literature," in *David Fogel and the Emergence of Hebrew Modernism, Prooftexts* 13, no. 1 (1993): 15–20. For Shlonsky on Fogel, see his review of Fogel's *Lifnei ha-sha'ar he-afel* (Before the dark gate) in *Hedim* 6 (1923):

66–67. See also Uzi Shavit, "Bein Shlonsky le-Fogel" (Between Shlonsky and Fogel), *Ha-sifrut* 2, no. 1: 251–57; and Michael Gluzman's analysis of the relationship in terms of maximalist and minimalist poetics, "Unmasking the Politics of Simplicity in Modernist Hebrew Poetry: Rereading David Fogel," *Prooftexts* 13, no. 1 (1993): 21–43; and in his *Politics of Canonicity*, 72–76.

39. Shlonsky, *Shirim*, 1:172.

40. The relation of stars and constellations to ideas about modernist articulations of expressive independence might best be understood through Walter Benjamin's aphorism: "Ideas are to objects as constellations are to stars," *The Origin of German Tragic Drama* (London: NLB, 1977), 34.

41. Shlonsky, *Shirim*, 1:176.

42. Ibid.

43. See Buck-Morss, *The Dialectics of Seeing*, 229ff.

44. Carolyn Abbate, *Unsung Voices: Opera and Musical Narrative in the Nineteenth Century* (Princeton, N.J.: Princeton University Press, 1991), 11.

45. Shlonsky, *Shirim*, 1:173.

46. "Schopenhauer conceives of the Will as a blind impulse that forever strives. It fails ever to achieve final satisfaction. Is our experience of music then comparably frustrating? Not according to Schopenhauer. The experience of music as the highest form of aesthetic experience is 'remote from pain' because it is without phenomenal reality. . . . In becoming completely absorbed in the music, in the Will's pure expression, we become identified with the Will itself. . . . Music offers us, then, even if for just a brief moment, a release from our perpetual suffering. In its purely metaphysical state, Schopenhauer next claims, music promises the true philosophy." Lydia Goehr, in *The Quest for Voice: On Music, Politics, and the Limits of Philosophy* (Berkeley: University of California Press, 1998), 24.

47. Shlonsky, *Shirim*, 1:182.

48. Ḥayim Arlosoroff, "Milḥemet ma'amadot ba-metsi'ut ha-eretz-yisra'elit" (Class war in the Eretz Israeli reality)," in *Kitvei Ḥayim Arlozorov* (The writings of Ḥayim Arlosoroff), 2nd ed. (Tel Aviv: Stybel, 1934), 3:126. This is also quoted in Cohen, *Zion and State*, 118.

49. As Mitchell Cohen points out, for Arlosoroff, it meant ignoring a growing urban working class because of a need to read Palestine as an intrinsically and immanently natural place. Cohen, *Zion and State*, 119.

Chapter 4

1. Shlonsky's major work from the 1930s was titled *Avnei bohu* (Stones of chaos) (Tel Aviv, 1934).

2. Yigal Zalmona, "Mizraḥah! Mizraḥah? Al ha-mizraḥ be-omanut yisra'el/ To the East? Orientalism in Israeli Art," in *Kadimah: Ha-mizraḥ be-omanut yisra'el/To the East: Orientalism in the Arts in Israel* (bilingual), ed. Yigal Zalmona and Tamar Manor-Fridman (Jerusalem: Israel Museum, 1998), 63–67, xii.

3. Of the two poets discussed here—Esther Raab, *Kimshonim* (Tel Aviv: Hedim, 1930), and Raḥel Bluwstein, *Mi-neged* (Tel Aviv: Davar, 1930) and *Nevo: Shirim aḥaronim* (Tel Aviv: Davar, 1932)—Bluwstein had previously published a volume in 1927, *Safiaḥ* (Tel Aviv: Davar, 1927).

4. In particular, in *Hedim*, which published Raab's first volume, *Kimshonim*, and where Bluwstein's poetry appeared very early alongside Shlonsky's.

5. Dan Miron argues against the marginalization of these women poets in *Imahot meyesdot, aḥayot ḥorgot: Hofa'atan ve-hitkablutan shel ha-meshorerot ha-ivriyot*

ha-rishonot (Founding mothers, stepsisters: On two beginnings in modern Eretz Israeli poetry) (Tel Aviv: Ha-kibbutz Ha-meuḥad, 1991). In this, Miron confuses a political affinity with poetic inclusion, making a fundamental error in his political assessment of culture. Even popular literature can be marginalized from the nation's canon. What any argument about gendered aesthetics must avoid is an essentialization of those poetics, where marginalization in the literary system *determines* political allegiances.

6. Berl Katznelson, "Yizkor," *Kuntres* 29 (1920). Also in Berl Katznelson, *Kitvei B. Katznelson* (The writings of B. Katznelson) (Tel Aviv: Workers' Party of Eretz Israel, 1946), 1:202. On the military use of the prayer, see Charles S. Liebman and Eliezer Don-Yeḥya, *Civil Religion in Israel: Traditional Judaism and Political Culture in the Jewish State* (Berkeley: University of California Press, 1983). Connections between the two are also discussed by Zerubavel, *Recovered Roots*, 45, who links the text to Masadah and Bar-Kokhba. It is important to note that in Katznelson's original publication of "Yizkor," the phrase *eretz yisra'el* never appears. Instead, the land is described using the more physical term, *admat yisra'el* (the soil of Israel) and action on it, *ga'al adamah* (redemption of the soil).

7. Zerubavel discusses the very early co-optation of Tel Ḥai among both Labor and the revisionists, divided between the tropes of plow and gun. Zerubavel, *Recovered Roots*, 148–57.

8. Berl Katznelson, "Meginei tel ḥai be-ḥayehem uve-motam" (Defenders of Tel Ḥai in life and in death) (1929), in *Kitvei B. Katznelson*, 4:17.

9. Katznelson's response to Tel Ḥai has striking discursive and political similarities to Aḥad Ha'am's response to Kishinev. Cf. Aḥad Ha'am, *Kol kitvei Aḥad Ha'am*, 501–3, and Chapter 1 above.

10. Katznelson, "Defenders of Tel Ḥai," 17.

11. Ibid.

12. Cf. the discussions of Aḥad Ha'am, Shimon Dubnov, and Yosef Ḥayim Brenner in Chapters 1 and 2 above.

13. Berl Katznelson, "Mi-matsor le-bitsaron" (From siege to stronghold) (1929), in *Kitvei B. Katznelson*, 4:95. Katznelson also wrote a more immediate reaction to the August riots, "Le-aḥar ha-ma'arakhah" (After the battle) (1929) in *Kitvei B. Katznelson*, 4:61–63. That article, as the title implies, responds to the collective response of the Yishuv during the disturbances, a topic that he obviously develops into a more complete political idea in "From Siege to Stronghold."

14. For an interesting firsthand account of the violence, see Maurice Samuel, *What Happened in Palestine* (Boston: Stratford Co., 1929).

15. Katznelson, "From Siege to Stronghold," 98.

16. Zalmona and Manor-Fridman, *To the East*, 63–67 xii.

17. The arbitrariness of the assignation of meaning in the landscape was not lost on the Zionist establishment, who mounted their own series of scientific inquiries into Palestine throughout the years of the British Mandate. Scientific definition of the landscape went far toward justifying political attitude; see CZA A111/40.

18. My understanding of the term obviously derives from Edward Said. But I do not mean to employ "Orientalism" in an unproblematic or static way. In this, my use of the term depends more on Said's critical definition of Orientalism in *Orientalism* (New York: Vintage, 1979) than on his unrestrained ideological use of the concept in *Culture and Imperialism* (New York: Vintage, 1994). Orientalism must certainly be viewed through the perspective of Gramsci and Foucault, but that type of cultural criticism should not flatten a critical understanding of the complexities of the mechanisms involved in its employment.

19. One of the few voices of exception was Ḥayim Arlosoroff's, who, in reaction to the Shaw Commission, began to argue for viewing Jewish settlement in Palestine as basically urban; Arlosoroff defended agricultural settlement, but saw it in conjunction with urban expansion. See Ḥayim Arlosoroff, "Din ve-ḥeshbon shel va'adat ha-ḥakirah" (Report of the Commission of Inquiry) (1931), in *Kitvei Ḥayim Arlozorov,* 1:157–219. This was a departure from viewing agriculture as absolutely primary in spite of its dependence on urban markets. See, for instance, Arthur Ruppin, *Ha-hityashvut ha-ḥakla'it shel ha-histadrut ha-tsiyonit be-eretz yisra'el (1907–1924)* (Zionist agricultural settlement in Eretz Israel [1907–1924]) (Tel Aviv: Dvir, 1925). In his chapter on the forms of intensive and extensive cultivation, Ruppin acknowledges the ties between agriculture and the urban market but explicitly points out the lack of a sufficiently large urban market in Palestine in order to argue against the expansion of intensive agriculture in the country. Of course, at that point in the mid-1920s, Arlosoroff also could see the Yishuv in strictly agricultural terms; cf. "Milḥemet ma'amadot ba-metsi'ut ha-eretz-yisra'elit" (Class war in the Eretz Israeli reality)," in *Kitvei Ḥayim Arlozorov,* 3:121–32.

20. Great Britain, Commission on the Palestine Disturbances of August 1929, and Walter Shaw, *Report of the Commission on the Palestine Disturbances of August 1929: Presented by the Secretary of State for the Colonies to Parliament by Command of His Majesty, March 1930* (London: H. M. Stationery Office, 1930), 162.

21. I am referring to the history surrounding the Balfour Declaration, which developed a maximalist understanding of Palestine based on national claims in it. See Evyatar Friesel, *Ha-mediniyut ha-tsiyonit le'aḥar hatsharat Balfour, 1917–1922* (Tel Aviv: Tel Aviv University, 1977); and Isaiah Friedman, *The Question of Palestine, 1914–1918: British-Jewish-Arab Relations* (New York: Schocken Books, 1973).

22. For detailed discussions of Zionist reactions to restrictions on land transfer and immigration in this period, see Stein, *The Land Question in Palestine.*

23. This issue became the most important of the entire period: the question of Jewish treatment of the *fellah* in land transfer transactions. The Zionist leadership had to argue, of course, that the Jews were not displacing the Arab peasantry, even though the evidence suggests that their claims were highly specious. For extended discussion of this important issue, see Stein, *The Land Question in Palestine.*

24. Anita Shapira writes about the impact the initial publication of the Shaw Commission report had on the Yishuv, in *Berl: Biografiyah,* 322. On the other hand, in *Ḥerev ha-yonah* (Land and power), 239, Shapira specifically downplays the significant effects of the riots, even though she admits to the impact they had on the Jewish public in the country.

25. The accomplishment of Arlosoroff in focusing on the issues of the British commission comes into relief against the refusal of many in the Zionist leadership to admit to a problem of Arab displacement in the country. Ruppin, while acknowledging fears of a Zionist inability to counter Arab claims of land alienation because of Jewish purchases and expulsions, simply states that the claims of tenants being driven off land have no foundation (December 20, 1929; CZA 525/4207). Yehoshua Ḥankin takes a similar position in an interview published in both *Davar* and *Ha-aretz:* "The intrigues now being carried on against us, and aiming at the foundations of a national structure are the work of professional inciters, and sowers of discord whose occupation this was in Turkish times too. . . . The Balfour Declaration not only did the Arabs no harm, but it did them, and them in particular, a lot of good" (November 11, 1929; CZA 525/4207).

26. For the wording of the Mandate Authority, see Laqueur and Rubin, eds., *The Israel-Arab Reader*, 33. See Chapter 2 above for a discussion of the implications of article 11; also, see Stein, *The Land Question in Palestine.*

27. Ruppin, *Ha-hityashvut ha-ḥakla'it*, 110–24. The argument has a long history within the Zionist movement and became a decisive factor during the 1910s in shaping Zionist policy toward land purchase and immigration settlement.

28. Arlosoroff, "Din ve-ḥeshbon," 186.

29. Ibid. To hit home, Arlosoroff then quotes from two Australian scholars of colonial settlement, citing their criticism of the labor practices of white settlers, which had led to an "indentured labor" of the indigenous people.

30. On women's exclusion from the canon, see Yael S. Feldman, *No Room of Their Own: Gender and Nation in Israeli Women's Fiction, Gender and Culture* (New York: Columbia University Press, 1999), Michael Gluzman, "The Exclusion of Women from Hebrew Literary History," *Prooftexts* 11, no. 3 (1991); Miron, *Imahot meyesdot, aḥayot ḥorgot*; Seidman, *A Marriage Made in Heaven*; Wendy Zierler, "Chariot(ess) of Fire: Yokheved Bat-Miriam's Female Personifications of Erets Israel," *Prooftexts* 20, nos. 1–2 (2000).

31. Raḥel Bluwstein, *Shirat Raḥel*, 29th ed. (Tel Aviv: Davar, 1982), 62.

32. The irony of the enduring image of Bluwstein writing poetry in the landscape she lyricized was nicely commented upon in Israel Moskovitz, "Masa shorashim," in the Tu bi-shvat edition of *Yediot Aḥaronot*, February 1, 1999.

33. On simplicity in poetry as a political-literary issue, see Gluzman's discussion in *The Politics of Canonicity.*

34. Bluwstein, *Shirat Raḥel*, 37.

35. Bluwstein published her thoughts praising Jammes in an article that appeared in *Hedim*: "Francis Jammes," in *Hedim* 1 (1922): 35.

36. Amy Lowell, *Six French Poets: Studies in Contemporary Literature* (Boston: Houghton Mifflin, 1921), 215. Amy Lowell's holding up of Jammes as "modern" represented a modernism of exteriority, of a desire to finish the romantic project through poetic description. Much of that aesthetic seems relegated to feminine expression, that is, to the counterarticulation of the maximalist poetics of Eliot or Pound himself, even though it was he who invented imagism and pushed H.D. in the direction of "exteriority." As Pound wrote of imagism, and of H.D. in particular: "Objective—no slither—no excess of adjectives. etc. No metaphors that won't permit examination.—It's straight talk—straight as the Greek!" Quoted in Hugh Kenner, *The Pound Era* (Berkeley: University of California Press, 1971), 174. Pound's staking out the ground did not prevent Amy Lowell from co-opting the name, much to Pound's consternation; see Hugh Kenner, *A Homemade World: The American Modernist Writers* (Baltimore: Johns Hopkins University Press, 1989), 9–10.

37. Ehud Ben-Ezer, *Yamim shel la'anah u-dvash: Sipur ḥayehah shel ha-meshoreret Esther Raab* (Days of gall and honey: The biography of the poet Esther Raab) (Tel Aviv: Am Oved, 1998).

38. Esther Raab, *Kol ha-shirim* (The complete poems) (Tel Aviv: Zmorah Bitan, 1988), 24.

39. The artist Ephraim Moshe Lilien, the unofficial illustrator of the early Zionist movement, created an iconology replete with Orientalist images that cast the Jew within an imagined biblical landscape. The image of the female lover entwined in nature was one he used for the design of Otto Warburg's personal bookplate.

40. Raab, *Kol ha-shirim*, 22.

41. Hannan Hever, "Ha-yam ha-tsiyoni: Simbolizm u-le'umiyut ba-shirah ha-ivrit ha-modernistit" (The Zionist sea: Symbolism and nationalism in modernist Hebrew poetry), in *Aderet le-Binyamin* (An overcoat for Benjamin), vol. 2, ed. Ziva Ben-Porat (Tel Aviv: Porter Institute and Ha-kibbutz Ha-meuḥad, 2001), 13–35.

42. See, for instance, Ben-Gurion's comments from 1937 in the midst of the Arab Revolt when the port in Tel Aviv opened: "If I should be asked what event looms most important in the history of Palestinian colonization during 1936, I should unhesitatingly answer: neither the disturbances nor the riots, but the inauguration of the Tel Aviv port." He then goes on to tie ocean access directly to a response to the violence of the previous year. David Ben-Gurion, "Going Down to the Sea," in *Jewish Frontier Anthology, 1934–1944* (New York: Jewish Frontier Association, 1945), 274.

43. Anita Shapira, *Ḥerev ha-yonah,* 195; in English, *Land and Power,* 139.

44. Hever, "Ha-yam ha-tsiyoni," 13–35.

45. Zalmona makes the connection to 1929 explicit in Zalmona and Manor-Fridman, *To the East,* "The Orientalist-romantic illusion of the local Jewish community was to be shattered in the political confrontation between Arabs and Jews. The Arab riots in August of 1929 . . . were experienced as a recurrence of the calamities of Jewish history. . . . The fact that the East, of all places, chose to reject the Jews who sought to be reintegrated into it brought on a sharp ideological reversal among the local Jewish public and intelligentsia alike" (xii). Needless to say, the fuller Hebrew version of the essay is much more circumspect and nuanced in its treatment of 1929 and the results it had for Zionist culture. However, even in Zalmona's original Hebrew, the message is clear that 1929 marks a definite break, and that the ideology of separation postdates the riots (Zalmona and Manor-Fridman, *To the East,* 63).

46. Hannan Hever has read "Albatross" in terms of Zionism's turning away from an ideology of becoming acclimatized to the political neighborhood of the Middle East and turning back to Europe for political and culture models. See Hever, "Ha-yam ha-tsiyoni," 28–31.

47. An obvious reference to Bialik's connections between forest and knowledge made in *Ha-breikhah* (The pool). See Chapter 1 above.

48. Avraham Shlonsky, "Yas'ur" (Albatross), in *Avnei bohu,* 20–21.

49. As more than one recent critic has noted, usually with the assumption that thorns and indigenous plants somehow stand outside history in a synchronic phantasmagoria of an authentic place of Palestine. See, for instance, Anne Lapidus Lerner, "'A Woman's Song': The Poetry of Esther Raab," in *Gender and Text in Modern Hebrew and Yiddish Literature* (New York: Jewish Theological Seminary, 1992); Anne Lapidus Lerner, "The Naked Land: Nature in the Poetry of Esther Raab," in *Women of the Word: Jewish Women and Jewish Writing* (Detroit: Wayne State University Press, 1994); Barbara Mann, "Framing the Native: Esther Raab's Visual Poetics," *Israel Studies* 4, no. 1 (1999).

50. Bluwstein, *Shirat Raḥel,* 138–39. Esther Raab, who figures significantly below, also turned to maternal foremothers after 1929, describing them as well within the landscape; in her untitled poem "Holy Grandmothers in Jerusalem," the speaker discovers these grandmothers precisely through the mediation of the land:

סַבְתּוֹת קְדוֹשׁוֹת בִּירוּשָׁלַיִם,
זְכוּתְכֶן תָּגֵן עָלַי:
רֵיחַ סְמָדַר וּפַרְדֵּסִים פּוֹרְחִים
עִם חֲלֵב אֵם הֻשְׁקֵיתִי

Holy grandmothers in Jerusalem,
Your virtue will protect me:
The fragrance of buds and blossoming orchards
With mother's milk I was nourished (*hushketi*)

Esther Raab, *Kol ha-shirim*, 14. The last word in the quotation, *hushketi*, is a wonderful play on settlement and naturalness in the land, deriving its primary function in the Zionist Hebrew lexicon from its meaning "to irrigate," as in a field. Raab was far too smart to use this lexical figure innocently—indeed, even without consciousness on the poet's part, the usage indicates the extent to which settlement and landscape depiction were part and parcel of a similar nature fantasy. Miron discusses the poem as a depiction of biblical mothers and the landscape, but only in terms of how that impinges on a canonical poetics of Bialik, with little relation to the internal dynamics of the poem itself. In this, Miron merely rehearses a similar dismissal to the one he ostensibly describes and critiques; see Miron, *Imahot meyesdot*, 145–48.

51. In a review of Raab's *Kimshonim*, published in 1930, Sh. Bass emphasizes the "healthy primitiveness" of the poetry as a new and significant contribution to the expression of the nation. *Ha-do'ar* 41 (1930): 690–91.

52. Esther Raab, *Gan she-ḥarav: Mivḥar sipurim ve-shiv'ah shirim* (Tel Aviv: Misrad Ha-bitaḥon, 1983), 187–91. All quotations cited here are from this edition. The story has also been reprinted in Ehud Ben-Ezer's recent anthology of Hebrew literary depictions of Arabs: Ehud Ben-Ezer, ed., *Be-moledet ha-ga'agu'im ha-menugadim* (The Arab in Israeli fiction: An anthology) (Tel Aviv: Zmorah Bitan, 1992), 120–23. That book appeared in English translation, including a version of "Rose Jam": Ehud Ben-Ezer, ed., *Sleepwalkers and Other Stories: The Arab in Hebrew Fiction* (Boulder, Colo.: Lynne Rienner, 1999), 37–40.

53. The word resonates with biblical meaning and elides between fear and awe in the face of the Divine. Even in contemporary Hebrew slang, some of that paradoxical elision is maintained in how *nora* can refer both to something "terrible" and something "terribly" good.

54. Moshe Shokeid, "Jewish Existence in a Berber Environment," in *Jewish Societies in the Middle East*, ed. Shlomo Deshen and P. Zenner (Washington, D.C.: University Press of America, 1982), 107.

55. SueEllen Campbell has made a similar critique of Edward Abbey: "Magpie," in *Writing the Environment: Ecocriticism and Literature*, ed. Richard Kerridge and Neil Sammells (London: Zed Books, 1998), 13–26. As Campbell asks, with the double entendre of knowing the overlap and interpenetration of metaphor and landscape description: "Just how solid are these rocks" upon which criticism stands? What Campbell points out is that nature—*object*-ness itself, the realm of ontological firmness and sublime truth—cannot escape the vicissitudes of personal and cultural fantasy, and so even self-reflection, which is meant to ward off the arrogance of unconscious authority, falls prey to its own critical blindness: "We have a world of words here, even when it's about rocks, and if [Abbey's] part of Utah is now in some real way 'Abbey's country,' it isn't because he possessed or loved it but because he wrote about it. Still, if Abbey were to throw a rock at my head, I'd duck." It's in that last phrase that writing about nature always falls short, for the land will never relent in exerting itself as the real. Campbell faults Abbey for what he leaves out of his considerations of the environment around Arches National Park in *Desert Solitaire*: the human element of the environment, the way that human history not only makes environmental history (mostly through destructive transformation) but is constituent of that history. But despite her

acknowledgment of the limitations of writing, nature is still allowed to constitute the real.

Chapter 5

1. Arlosoroff, "Din ve-ḥeshbon."

2. The history of electrification of Jewish Palestine is intimately involved with architecture and a modernist reinvention of labor, nature, and the city. See Eli Shaltiel, *Pinḥas Rutenberg: Aliyato u-nefilato shel "ish ḥazak" be-eretz-yisra'el, 1879–1942* (Pinhas Rutenberg: 1879–1942, life and times) (Tel Aviv: Am Oved, 1990).

3. The port at Ashdod-Tel Aviv was completed in 1936. See Ben-Gurion, "Going Down to the Sea," 274–79.

4. Joachim Schlör, *Tel Aviv: From Dream to City* (London: Reaktion, 1999).

5. Arieh Sharon, *Kibbutz + Bauhaus: An Architect's Way in a New Land* (Stuttgart: Karl Krämer Verlag, 1976), 46.

6. Sharon was one of three architects who, upon returning to Palestine from studies in Europe, actively campaigned for International Style dominance in Tel Aviv in the 1930s. In Nathan Harpaz, "Mi-'batei ḥalomot' le-'batei kufsa'ot': Ha-mahapakh ha-adrikhali shel shnot ha-shloshim be-tel-aviv" (From "dream houses" to "box houses": The architectural revolution of the thirties in Tel Aviv), in *Tel aviv be-reshitah, 1909–1934* (Tel Aviv in its beginnings, 1909–1934), ed. Mordecai Naor (Jerusalem: Yad Yitsḥak Ben-Tsvi, 1984), 91–106, Harpaz makes mention of a meeting in 1933 that Sharon had with Joseph Neufeld, who had worked before then for Erich Mendelsohn, and Ze'ev Rechter, just returned from France where he had imbibed the spirit of Le Corbusier (91).

7. For Le Corbusier's direct influence on architecture in Tel Aviv and Israel in general, see Michael Levin, "The Transformation of Villa Savoye into the National Library: Le Corbusier's Influence on Two Generations of Architects in Israel," *Journal of Jewish Art* 3–4 (1977): 103–21. Levin emphasizes Rechter as the earliest Jewish Palestinian architect to design in the style of Le Corbusier (103). He also mentions the significance of Shmuel Barkai, who shared an office with Rechter in Tel Aviv in 1926 and worked in Le Corbusier's studio in 1933–34, and Benjamin Tchlenov, each of whom later had Tel Aviv offices and designed in a modernist style heavily influenced by Le Corbusier. See also Michael Levin, *Ir levanah: Adrikhalut ha-signon ha-beinle'umi be-yisra'el* (White city: International Style architecture in Israel (Tel Aviv: Tel Aviv Museum, 1984), esp. 23–28; and Michael Levin, "The White City: International Style in Israel," *Progressive Architecture* 65 (1984): 114–21.

8. Levin certainly highlights this explanation in *Ir levanah*, 11–12. Others do as well: Ita Heinze-Greenberg, "Immigration and Culture Shock: On the Question of Architectural Identity in 'Altneuland,'" in *Tel Aviv: Modern Architecture, 1930–1939*, ed. Winfried Nerdinger (Tübingen/Berlin: Ernst Wasmuth Verlag, 1994), 36–39; and Schlör, *Tel Aviv*. Schlör's entire book expands on the idea of Tel Aviv as the bourgeois space as opposed to the rural settlement of socialist Palestine. This ignores, as Ḥayim Arlosoroff noted in the late 1920s (see Chapter 3 above), the great complexity of the city and, on a mundane analytical level, the fact that the first major International Style building projects in the city were workers' housing. For Schlör, the achievement of Tel Aviv and its architecture reflected completely the needs and actions of the new German immigrants: "These buildings were created between 1930 and 1939, at the time of the immigration from Germany and Austria. Those immigrants, mostly urban and mainly

European in their outlook, found themselves in a new country, under wholly different climatic conditions, required to adapt themselves to new work, a new language, a new way of thinking—but the architecture which they and their presence were instrumental in creating allowed the shock of initial strangeness to be softened and reduced by an element of familiarity" (236).

9. Daniel Bertrand Monk, review of *Bauhaus on the Carmel and the Crossroads of Empire* by Gilbert Herbert and Silvina Sosnovsky, *AA Files* 28 (1994): 94–99.

10. Gilbert Herbert and Ita Heinze-Greenberg, *Erich Mendelsohn in Palestine* (Haifa: Technion, 1994).

11. Ibid.

12. For an extensive discussion of the significance of "appropriateness" within the Yishuv subsequent to the 1929 riots, see Stein, *The Land Question in Palestine.*

13. Sharon, *Kibbutz + Bauhaus, 46.*

14. The original idea behind Tel Aviv was decidedly suburban; see Batya Karmiel, "Tsiyunei derekh be-hakamat tel-aviv, 1906–1918," in *Tel-aviv be-tatslumim: He-asor ha-rishon, 1909–1918* (Tel Aviv in photographs: The first decade, 1909–1918) (Tel Aviv: Eretz Israel Museum, 1990), 17–20; Gideon Biger, "Hitpatḥut ha-shetaḥ ha-banui shel tel-aviv ba-shanim 1909–1938" (The development of the built area of Tel Aviv in the years 1909–1938), in Naor, *Tel aviv be-reshitah, 1909–1934,* 42–44. Ya'akov Shavit and Gideon Biger state that, in actuality, there was a wider metropolitan vision for Tel Aviv from early on, in *Ha-historiyah shel tel-aviv* (The history of Tel Aviv), vol. 1, *Mi-shkhunot le-ir (1909–1936)* (The birth of a town [1909–1936]) (Tel Aviv: Tel Aviv University, 2001), 19–22.

15. Most standard histories leave the impression (cf. Schlör, *Tel Aviv,* as noted above) that Bauhaus modernism entered Palestine with the influx of the German immigrants of the Fifth Aliyah. However, the three principal players in this aesthetic transformation, Sharon, Rechter, and Neufeld all had formative experiences in Palestine before traveling to Europe to study. Rechter and Barkai had even practiced architecture before leaving Tel Aviv for France. And Sharon's return to Palestine did not coincide with the Nazi pressures that pushed along the mechanisms of the Fifth Aliyah after Hitler ascended to the premiership of Germany in 1933. Indeed, of the major modernist architects in Tel Aviv in the 1930s, only about half had immigrated with the Fifth Aliyah; see Nerdinger, *Tel Aviv: Modern Architecture,* 236–45. The rest were more local products who either were born in Palestine or had immigrated earlier. Of course, these facts do not nullify the idea of an imported aesthetic, as indeed International Style architecture was. On the other hand, the acknowledgment of a large number of non-Germans involved and even spearheading this aesthetic drive in Palestine goes far to undermine the assumptions of modernism as the importation of bourgeois taste and German experience into the country. Obviously, modernism spoke to a larger concern, one that resonated more fully throughout the Zionist settlement.

16. Sharon, *Kibbutz + Bauhaus,* 15.

17. Raymond Williams, *The Country and the City* (New York: Oxford University Press, 1973). For another important dialectical reading of city and country that argues nicely and convincingly for the country as supplementary to the industrial city, see Roberto Maria Dainotto, *Place in Literature: Regions, Cultures, Communities* (Ithaca, N.Y.: Cornell University Press, 2000). This is, of course, the same dialectical relationship that William Cronon works through in *Nature's Metropolis: Chicago and the Great West* (New York: W. W. Norton, 1991), although he works completely in an economic historical mode.

18. S. Ilan Troen, "Frontier Myths and Their Applications in America and

Israel: A Transnational Perspective," *Israel Studies* 5, no. 1 (2000): 312. Troen notes that Nahalal's designer, Richard Kaufmann, was "a devotee of Ebenezar Howard and his 'garden-city' concept."

19. Sharon, *Kibbutz + Bauhaus*, 46.

20. Several recent analyses of *Altneuland* have begun to question the strict bourgeois liberalism that Herzl seems to support throughout his fantasy about Palestine's future. See, in particular, Gluzman, "Ha-kmihah le-heterosexualiyut; and Press, "Same-Sex Unions in Modern Europe." Both Gluzman and Press read into Herzl's novel a homoerotic sexual fantasy and its resolution/repression through the state. See also Yigal Schwartz, "'Handasat ha-adam' ve-itsuv ha-merḥav ba-tarbut ha-ivrit ha-ḥadashah ("The engineering of man" and the design of space in modern Hebrew culture) *Mi-kan* 1 (May 2000): 9–24, who writes about the reconciliation between place as a deterritorialized concept and place in the specifics of Palestine.

21. Of particular importance for a European critique of urban civilization at the end of the nineteenth century, see Max Nordau's *Degeneration* (1982; Lincoln: University of Nebraska Press, 1993). The most famous connection between *Degeneration* and Zionism involves Nordau's call for Jews with muscles. But the various criticisms of Western urban civilization and culture in the book resonate with Zionist values, both of the political and cultural wings of the movement.

22. Georg Simmel, "The Metropolis and Mental Life," in *On Individuality and Social Forms* (Chicago: University of Chicago Press, 1971), 324.

23. Ibid., 337.

24. Erich Mendelsohn, *Palestine and the World of Tomorrow* (Jerusalem: Jerusalem Press, 1940).

25. Gil Aldema and Nathan Shahar, eds., *Sefer ha-shirim la-talmid* (The book of songs for students) (Tel Aviv: Culture and Education Enterprises, 1995), 1:200–201.

26. David Tartakover, *Hatsagah rishonah: Krazot kolno'a, tel aviv, shnot ha-shloshim* (First show: Film posters, Tel Aviv, 1930s) (Jerusalem: Jerusalem Cinemateque, 1995).

27. See, for instance, "A Trip Through the Emek Jezreel," which was part of "a series of illustrated talks on various aspects of the new life in Eretz Israel," CZA KKL5/3490/1. The document is not dated, but the narrative indicates it was prepared in late 1929.

28. Juda Leman and Keren Ha-yesod, which is currently available in a VHS version: *The Land of Promise: The First Palestine Sound Picture* (1935; Teaneck, N.J.: Ergo Media, 1992). The film also went by the Hebrew title *Le-ḥayim ḥadashim* (Toward a new life).

29. For similar images of camels in the urban environment, relating the camel as a working instrument for building projects, see Rudi Weissenstein, *Tsalmaniyah: Rudi Weissenstein—retrospektivah* (Tel Aviv: Am Oved, 2002), 49–50.

30. Karin Kirsch, *The Weissenhofsiedlung Experimental Housing Built for the Deutscher Werkbund, Stuttgart, 1927* (Stuttgart: Deutsche Verlag-Anstalt, 1992).

31. In the film, this idea of construction tied to place is given direct visual imagery by the use of camels in the scenes of Tel Aviv. There, in the context of construction sites and workers, camels, with no human hand to guide them, walk through the scene in an interesting and somewhat eerie recreation of the poster. The difference between them lies in the poster's ability to abstract and isolate these two complementary elements of the landscape, away from the contextualization of a crowded cityscape.

32. Aga Films, 1935.

33. The story of Bracha Tsfira's encounter with Einstein, as well as much of the biographical data available on her, is included in the autobiographical essay that opens her book of songs: Bracha Tsfira, *Kolot rabim* (Many voices) (Tel Aviv: Masadah, 1978), 11–31.

34. Ibid.

35. Adorno, "The Idea of Natural History," 115.

36. Ibid., 113. Of course, Adorno did not have in mind the great outdoors or even landscape when he writes about "nature": "Although the topic is natural history, it is not concerned with natural history in the traditional pre-scientific sense of the history of nature, nor with the history of nature where nature is the object of natural science" (111). Instead, nature, before it devolves into the dialectical relationship of natural history, is the immutable element of ontology that is not contingent to human thought. In that, ideas of nature as wilderness and landscape certainly do adhere, and easily fall victim, in general, to Adorno's critique.

37. Ester Levinger, *Andarta'ot la-noflim be-yisra'el* (War memorials in Israel) (Tel Aviv: Ha-kibbutz Ha-meuḥad, 1993).

38. Words in Natan Alterman, *Pizmonim ve-shirei-zemer* (Tel Aviv: Ha-kibbutz Ha-meuḥad, 1976), 310–11; words and music in Aldema and Shahar, *Sefer ha-shirim*, 1:140–41.

39. Words in Alterman, *Pizmonim*, 308–9; words and music in Aldema and Shahar, 1:142–43.

40. Words in Alterman, *Pizmonim*, 302–3; words and music in Aldema and Shahar, 1:144–45.

41. I am referring to Bialik's "Hakhnisini taḥat knafekh" (*Kol shirei Ḥayim Naḥman Bialik*, 178) and Shlonsky's fourth poem in the "Amal" cycle (Shlonsky, *Shirim*, 1:165).

42. Adorno, "The Idea of Natural History," 119–20.

43. Dan Miron, "Reshitah shel shirat tel-aviv" (The beginnings of Tel Aviv poetry), in *Ir ve-utopiyah* (City and utopia), ed. H. Lusky (Tel Aviv: Ha-ḥevrah ha-yisra'elit, 1991), 184–207. Miron's recent first volume of an in-depth biography of Alterman, *Parpar min ha-tola'at* (From a worm a butterfly emerges) (Tel Aviv: Open University, 2001), only addresses Alterman's work until 1935.

44. Miron, "Reshitah shel shirat tel-aviv," 199.

45. Ibid.

46. Natan Alterman, *Shirim she-mikvar* (Tel Aviv: Ha-kibbutz Ha-meuḥad, 1972). See especially the poems in the third and fourth sections, many of which explicitly engage urban themes.

47. Ibid., 86.

48. Ibid., 90.

49. Ibid., 87.

50. Simmel, "Metropolis and Mental Life," 336.

51. Ibid., 335.

52. For Simmel, while a money economy "interposes the perfectly objective and inherently quality-less presence of money and monetary value between the person and the particular object," it was somehow seemingly unavoidable and determined the forms of modern life: "The streams of modern culture rush in two seemingly opposing directions: on the one hand, toward leveling, equalization . . . ; on the other hand, toward the elaboration of the most individual matters, the independence of the person, the autonomy of its development. Both tendencies are supported by the money economy." "Money and Commodity Culture," in *Simmel on Culture*, ed. David Frisby and Mike Featherstone (London: Sage Publications, 1997), 244, 247.

53. Despite the architectural origin of the entire era, wall and tower history and criticism completely avoids any critical encounter with architecture itself. In *Yemei ḥomah u-migdal, 1936–1939* (The days of wall and tower, 1936–1939), ed. Mordechai Naor (Jerusalem: Yad Yitsḥak Ben-Tsvi, 1987), an excellent collection of articles on the history and culture of the period, not one addresses the specific architectural implications of the design iconography. The icon abounds within the volume, both in historical documentation and photographs of the settlements, and in later visual, poetic, and musical representations of wall-and-tower settlements and the settlement ethos of the time. But the politics of the aesthetic, beyond the politics of political confrontation and settlement expansion reflected in the icon, are never questioned. The extension of the iconographic power of the symbol of the tower is further explored in *Migdelei ha-mayim be-yisra'el, 1891–1993* (Water towers in Israel, 1891–1993), ed. Mordechai Omer (Tel Aviv: Genia Schreiber University Art Gallery, Tel Aviv University, 1993), but not its political origin or effect. Maoz Azaryahu, in a contribution to this exhibition catalogue, "Migdelei mayim be-nof ha-zikaron: Negbah ve-yad mordekhai" (Water towers in the landscape of memory: Negba and Yad Mordechai), 37–40, comes tantalizingly close to a political account of the icon's presence in the landscape, but only as a result of political circumstances happening around the tower which later changes the architectural element into a national symbol. The political implications of the aesthetic *as* a design aesthetic are never mentioned or explored even though Azaryahu admits that "during the '30s, and particularly during the '40s, the water tower became a common element in the iconography of the Zionist settlement landscape" (37).

54. Katznelson, "Mi-matsor le-bitsaron," 95–98. See discussion in Chapter 4 above.

Conclusion

1. Shaul Tcherniḥovsky, "Yeshnah od tel aviv aḥat" (There is another Tel Aviv), in *Tel aviv: Mikra'ah historit-sifrutit* (Tel Aviv: A historical-literary reader), ed. Yosef Arikha (Tel Aviv: Tel Aviv Municipality, 1942), 294. A similar sentiment was articulated earlier in 1934 by Asher Barash in his novella *Ish u-veito nimḥu* (A man and his house disappeared) (1934; Tel Aviv: Misrad Ha-bitaḥon, 1978), which also laments the growing urbanizaton of Tel Aviv as a new generation comes to populate the city and push out (and destroy) an older population and older homes. Barash pays less attention to nature as part of this originary Tel Aviv, but the description of the house and its gardens in the novella definitely echoes the aesthetic that Tcherniḥovsky describes. Visually, the best representations of the nostalgic Tel Aviv house surrounded by trees and garden are probably those by Naḥum Gutman, who painted and wrote nostalgically about this period in Tel Aviv history.

2. Shmuel Yosef Agnon, *Tmol shilshom* (Only yesterday) (1945; Jerusalem: Schocken, 1979), 7.

3. Gershon Shaked's article on settlement literature, "'Livnot u-lehibanot bah': Al roman ha-hityashvut" ("To build and be built": On the settlement novel), in *Proceedings of the Sixth World Congress for Jewish Studies* (Jerusalem: World Union of Jewish Studies, 1976), 517–27, discusses the thematic variants of the genre, concentrating mostly on texts from the 1920s, the height of the genre, according to Shaked. The best reading of these lines, and the intertextual allusions entwined within them, is certainly at the beginning of Amos Oz's essay on the novel, "Guilt

and Orphanhood and Fate," in *The Silence of Heaven: Agnon's Fear of God*, trans. Barbara Harshav (Princeton, N.J.: Princeton University Press, 2000), 63–65.

4. Barbara Harshav's recent translation into English of *Tmol shilshom* renders the title as *Only Yesterday* (Princeton N.J.: Princeton University Press, 2000). The Hebrew phrase from which the title is taken probably has no equivalence in English, and Harshav's version nicely invokes how the legacy of the Second Aliyah—in all its fumbling and tragedy—might live on within the present of the late 1940s, on the very dawn of statehood. The more traditional translation, "All Our Yesterdays" (traditional if only because it was commonly used in English-language references to the untranslated novel) emphasizes even more the sense of legacy and inheritance in Zionist culture and might just be that much more cynical.

5. Keren Kayemeth Le Israel (Jewish National Fund), *Avodot ha-havra'ah be-emek yizra'el.*

6. Gordon described the landscape as the natural environment of man, implying that this is precisely what the Jew had been cut off from for so many centuries. Gordon paints an analogy to fish and water, thereby calling upon the natural health of man within the landscape; see Gordon, *Ha-adam veha-teva.* The fish analogy, of course, does not begin with Gordon, and it seems important to note its precedence in Spinoza's *Theological-Political Treatise*, where he writes of the natural rights of man: "By the right and established order of Nature I mean simply the rules governing the nature of every individual thing, according to which we conceive it as naturally determined to exist and act in a definite way. For example, fish are determined by nature to swim, and the big ones to eat the smaller ones." Benedictus de Spinoza, *Tractatus Theologico-Politicus* (Indianapolis: Hackett Publishing, 1998), 179. The notion of "oneness" is a bit too modern for Gordon himself, but has been invoked by Gordon's later commentators; see Nathan Rotenstreich, *Jewish Philosophy in Modern Times: From Mendelssohn to Rosenzweig* (New York: Holt Rinehart and Winston, 1968), 239–52: Rotenstreich's analysis of Gordon is punctuated by section titles such as "The Yearning to Be at One with the World" and "Being One with the World and Its Expression."

7. Agnon, *Tmol shilshom*, 42.

8. This was a general theme of Gordon's work, but see, in particular, Gordon, *Ha-adam veha-teva.*

9. The scientific aspects of the impact of Zionist environmental policies have recently been analyzed by Alon Tal in *Pollution in a Promised Land: An Environmental History of Israel* (Berkeley: University of California Press, 2002). As the title makes clear, the general thrust of the book couples environmental history to the very notion of pollution, allowing little room for anything but a negative interpretation of Zionist intervention in the land.

10. As Tom Segev points out in *1949: Ha-yisra'elim ha-rishonim* (1949: The first Israelis) (Jerusalem: Domino, 1984), the call to the cultural side became explicit after 1948. In the introduction, Segev relates the tale that David Ben-Gurion called together various *anshei ruaḥ* to ask them to help support and define the nascent state (15).

11. Sternhell, *The Founding Myths of Israel*, 37.

12. Gil Aldema and Nathan Shahar, eds., *Sefer ha-shirim la-talmid* (The book of songs for students) (Tel Aviv: Culture and Education Enterprises, 1995), 1:139.

13. Ibid.

Bibliography

Archival Sources

Central Zionist Archives, Jerusalem (CZA)

Institutional Archives

KKL1: Jewish National Fund, Vienna–Cologne–The Hague
KKL2: Jewish National Fund, Cologne–The Hague
KKL3: Jewish National Fund, Jaffa–Tel Aviv–Jerusalem
KKL4: Jewish National Fund, Berlin
KKL5: Jewish National Fund, Jerusalem
Z1: Central Zionist Office, Vienna
Z2: Central Zionist Office, Cologne
Z3: Central Zionist Office, Berlin
Z4: The Zionist Organization/The Jewish Agency for Palestine/Israel–Central Office, London

Private Archives

A15: Max Bodenheimer
A24: Menachem Ussischkin
A107: Arthur Ruppin
A111: Jacob Akiva Ettinger
A120: Israel Zangwill
A148: Jacob Thon
A202: Abraham Granott (Granovsky)
A238: Yehoshua Chankin
A246: Josef Weitz

Steven Spielberg Jewish Film Archive, Jerusalem

Gnazim, Bet Ha-Sofer, Tel Aviv

Journals and Newspapers

Davar
Ha-adamah
Ha-aretz
Ha-po'el ha-tsa'ir
Ha-shiloaḥ
Hedim
Ktuvim
Kuntres

Books and Articles

Abbate, Carolyn. 1991. *Unsung Voices: Opera and Musical Narrative in the Nineteenth Century*. Princeton, N.J.: Princeton University Press.

Adorno, Theodor W. 1981. *Prisms*. Cambridge, Mass.: MIT Press.

———. 1984. The Idea of Natural History. *Telos* 60: 111–24.

———. 1997. *Aesthetic Theory*. Minneapolis: University of Minnesota Press.

———. 1998. *Critical Models*. New York: Columbia University Press.

Agnon, Shmuel Yosef. 1945 [1979]. *Tmol shilshom*. Jerusalem: Schocken.

———. 2000. *Only Yesterday*. Translated by Barbara Harshav. Princeton, N.J.: Princeton University Press.

Aḥad Ha'am. 1946. *Kol kitvei Ahad Ha'am*. Tel Aviv: Dvir.

Aḥad Ha'am, Shimon Dubnov, and Judah Leib Benjamin Katzenelson. 1906. *Ha-lashon veha-ḥinukh: Ne'umim be-ḥevrat "Mefitsei haskalah be-yisra'el."* Krakow: Hotsa'at Lishkat ha-merkaz shel "Ivriyah" Bran.

Aharon David Gordon: Bibliografiyah. 1979. Degania A: Yaḥdav and Bet Gordon.

Al admatam: Mivhar mi-yetsirot sofrim ve-omanim ba-hityashvut ha-ovedet. 1959. Tel Aviv: Mesilot.

Aldema, Gil, and Nathan Shahar, eds. 1995. *Sefer ha-shirim la-talmid*. 2 vols. The Nissimov Music Library, no. 374. Tel Aviv: Culture and Education Enterprises.

Almog, Oz. 1997. *Ha-tsabar: Deyokan*. Tel Aviv: Am Oved.

———. 2000. *The Sabra: The Creation of the New Jew*. Berkeley: University of California Press.

———. 2003. From *Blorit* to Ponytail: Israeli Culture Reflected in Popular Hairstyles. *Israel Studies* 8 (2): 82–117.

Almog, Shmuel. 1990. Ha-ge'ula ba-retorikah ha-tsiyonit. In *Ge'ulat ha-karka be-eretz yisra'el*, edited by Ruth Kark, 13–32. Jerusalem: Yad Yitsḥak Ben Tsvi.

Alterman, Nathan. 1972. *Shirim she-mikvar*. Tel Aviv: Ha-kibbutz Ha-meuḥad.

———. 1976. *Pizmonim ve-shirei-zemer*. Tel Aviv: Ha-kibbutz Ha-meuḥad.

Anderson, Benedict. 1983. *Imagined Communities*. London: Verso.

Arad, Gulie Ne'eman, ed. 1995. *Israeli Historiography Revisted*. Special Issue, *History and Memory* 7, no. 1.

Arikha, Y. A. 1937. *The Redeeming of Names*. Jerusalem: Jewish National Fund.

Arikha, Yosef, ed. n.d. *Tel aviv: Mikra'ah historit-sifrutit*. Tel Aviv: Iriyat Tel Aviv.

Arlosoroff, Ḥayim. 1934–35. *Kitvei Ḥayim Arlozorov*. 7 vols. Tel Aviv: Stybel.

Arpaly, Boaz. 1992. *Ha-ikar ha-shlili: Ideologiyah u-foetikah be-"mi-kan umi-kan" uve-"atsabim" le-Y. Ḥ. Brenner*. Tel Aviv: Ha-kibbutz Ha-meuḥad.

Ashbel, A., ed. 1969. *Shishim shnot hakhsharat ha-yishuv*. Jerusalem: Ḥevrat Hakhsharat Ha-yishuv.

Avitsur, Shmuel. 1965. *Avodot ha-ya'ar.* Tel Aviv: Ha-makhon Le-yediyat Ha-aretz Veha-am.

Bacon, Yitzhak. 1972. *Yosef Ḥayim Brenner: Mivḥar ma'amarei bikoret al yetsirato ha-sipurim.* Tel Aviv: Am Oved.

———. 1975. *Brenner ha-tsa'ir: Ḥayav ve-yetsirotav shel Brenner ad le-hofa'at "Ha-meorer" be-London.* Tel Aviv: Ha-kibbutz Ha-meuḥad.

———. 1981. *Bein ha-shurot.* Tel Aviv: Papirus.

———. 1982. *Mi-tokh ha-ḥavurah.* Tel Aviv: Papirus.

Baer, Gabriel. 1971. *Mavo le-toldot ha-yaḥasim ha-agrariyim ba-mizraḥ ha-tikhon, 1800–1970.* Tel Aviv: Ha-kibbutz Ha-meuḥad.

Bahat, Yaacov. *Avraham Shlonsky: Ḥeker ve-iyun be-shirato uve-haguto.* Tel Aviv: Yaḥdav.

Barash, Asher. 1934 [1978]. *Ish u-veto nimḥu.* Tel Aviv: Misrad Ha-bitaḥon.

Bardenstein, Carol. 1997. Territorialism and Desire in Palestinian and Israeli Discourses of Exile and Return. *European Journal for Semiotic Studies* 9, no. 1: 87–114.

———. 1998. Threads of Memory and Discourses of Rootedness: Of Trees, Oranges and the Prickly-Pear Cactus in Israel/Palestine. *Edebiyat* 8: 1–36.

———. 1999. Trees, Forests, and the Shaping of Palestinian and Israeli Collective Memory. In *Acts of Memory: Cultural Recall in the Present,* edited by Mieke Bal, Jonathan Crewe, and Leo Spitzer, 148–68. Hanover, N.H.: Dartmouth College, University Press of New England.

Barthes, Roland. 1989. *The Rustle of Language.* Berkeley: University of California Press.

Barzel, Hillel, ed. 1975. *Measef 10: Mukdash le-yetsirat Ḥayim Naḥman Bialik.* Ramat Gan: Masadah.

———. 2001. *Shirat eretz-yisra'el: Avraham Shlonsky, Natan Alterman, Leah Goldberg.* Tel Aviv: Sifriyat Po'alim.

Bateson, M. C. 1966. "A Riddle of Two Worlds": An Interpretation of the Poetry of H. N. Bialik. *Daedalus* 95: 740–62.

Be'er, Haim. 1992. *Gam ahavatam, gam sinatam: Bialik, Brenner, Agnon: Ma'arkhot-yaḥasim.* Tel Aviv: Am Oved.

Bein, Alex. 1976. *Toldot ha-hityashvut ha-tsiyonit mi-tkufat Herzl ve-ad yameinu.* 4th ed. Ramat Gan: Masadah.

Ben-Ari, Eyal, and Yoram Bilu. 1997. *Grasping Land: Space and Place in Contemporary Israeli Discourse and Experience.* Albany: State University of New York Press.

Ben-Artzi, Yosi, Ruth Kark, and Ron Aaronson. 1988. Ḥanim o mivne aḥuza? Le-she'alat tafkidam ha-mekori shel atarei ha-hityashvut ha-yehudit be-nof eretz-yisra'el (1882–1914). *Tsiyonut* 13: 263–84.

Ben-Ezer, Ehud. 1998. *Yamim shel la'anah u-dvash: Sipur ḥayehah shel ha-meshoreret Esther Raab.* Tel Aviv: Am Oved.

Ben-Ezer, Ehud, ed. 1992. *Be-moledet ha-ga'agu'im ha-menugadim.* Tel Aviv: Zmorah Bitan.

———. 1999. *Sleepwalkers and Other Stories: The Arab in Hebrew Fiction.* Boulder, Colo.: Lynne Rienner.

Ben-Gurion, David. 1945. Going Down to the Sea. In *Jewish Frontier Anthology, 1934–1944,* 274–79. New York: Jewish Frontier Association.

Ben-Porat, Ziva. 1995. The "Kibbutz" as Reality and Utopia: Mimesis and Representation of a Cultural Concept. In *Ideal Places in History—East and West,* 121–36. Kyoto: International Research Center for Japanese Studies.

———. 1996. Zionist Reads Palestinian: Interpretation and Dialogue in the

Light of Cultural Differences and Political Conflicts. In *Arcadia: Festschrift für Allgemeine und Vergleichende Literaturwissenschaft*, edited by H. Rüdiger. Berlin: Walter de Gruyter.

Benjamin, Walter. 1977. *The Origin of German Tragic Drama*. London: NLB.

———. 1986. *Reflections: Essays, Aphorisms, Autobiographical Writings*. New York: Schocken Books.

Berdichevsky, Micha Yosef (Ben-Gurion). 1948. *Kitvei Micha Yosef Ben-Gurion (Berdichevsky): Ma'amarim*. Tel Aviv: Dvir.

Berger, Tamar. 1998. *Dionysus ba-senter*. Tel Aviv: Ha-kibbutz Ha-meuḥad and Siman Kriah.

Berkowitz, Michael. 1997. *Western Jewry and the Zionist Project, 1914–1933*. Cambridge: Cambridge University Press.

Berlinger, Se'ev, Zwi Silberstein, Paula Arnold, Michael Berlinger, and Brakha Levy Avigad. 1963. *Trees and Shrubs in Israel / Arbres et arbustes d'Israël*. Haifa: Department of Education.

Berlovitz, Yafa. 1991. Sifrut ve-tḥiyah le'umit: *Bnei arav* le-Moshe Smilansky—ha-sipur ha-patroni. *Iyunim bi-tkumat yisra'el* 4: 400–421.

Bhabha, Homi. 1990. *Nation and Narration*. London: Routledge.

Biale, David. 1986. *Power & Powerlessness in Jewish History*. New York: Schocken Books.

Bialik, Ḥayim Naḥman.1938. *Igrot Ḥayim Naḥman Bialik*. Edited by P. Lachover. 5 vols. Tel Aviv: Dvir.

———. 1940. He-ḥaluts. In *Sefer he-ḥaluts*, edited by M. Basok. Jerusalem: Ha-sokhnut Ha-yehudit.

———. 1965. *Divrei sifrut*. Tel Aviv: Dvir.

———. 1970. *Kol shirei Ḥayim Naḥman Bialik*. Tel Aviv: Dvir.

Bialik, Ḥayim Naḥman, and Yaakov Goren. 1991. *Eduyot nifge'ei Kishinev, 1903: Kfi she-nigbu al-yedei Ḥ. N. Bialik va-ḥaverav*. Ramat Efal: Yad Tabenkin; Tel Aviv: Ha-kibbutz Ha-meuḥad.

Biger, Gideon. 1984. Hitpatḥut ha-shetaḥ ha-banui shel tel aviv ba-shanim 1909–1938. In *tel aviv be-reshitah, 1909–1934*, edited by Mordechai Naor. Tel Aviv: Yad Yitsḥak Ben-Tsvi.

Bloch, Ernst, et al. 1977. *Aesthetics and Politics*. London: NLB.

Bloch, Jean-Richard. 1928. Der Jude zwischen Orient und Okzident. In *Der Jude: Sonderheft zu Martin Bubers fünfzigstem Geburtstag*: 52–58.

Bluwstein, Raḥel. 1922. Francis Jammes. *Hedim* 1: 35.

———. 1926. *Safiaḥ*. Tel Aviv: Davar.

———. 1930. *Mi-neged*. Tel Aviv: Davar.

———. 1932. *Nevo: Shirim aḥaronim*. Tel Aviv: Davar.

———. 1982. *Shirat Raḥel*. 29th ed. Tel Aviv: Davar.

Bohlman, Philip Vilas. 1989. *"The Land Where Two Streams Flow": Music in the German-Jewish Community of Israel*. Urbana: University of Illinois Press.

———. 1992. *The World Centre for Jewish Music in Palestine, 1936–1940: Jewish Musical Life on the Eve of World War II*. Oxford: Clarendon Press.

Bordo, Jonathan. 2000. Picture and Witness at the Site of Wilderness. *Critical Inquiry* 26 (Winter): 224–47.

Borochov, Ber. 1984. *Class Struggle and the Jewish Nation: Selected Essays in Marxist Zionism*. Edited by M. Cohen. New Brunswick, N.J.: Transaction Books.

Bradbury, Malcolm and J. W. McFarlane. 1978. *Modernism: 1890–1930*. New York: Penguin.

Braslavsky, M. 1966. *Tnuat ha-po'alim ha-eretz-yisra'elit: Korot u-mekorot*. 2nd ed. Vol. 1. Tel Aviv: Ha-kibbutz Ha-meuḥad.

Brecht, Bertolt. 1966. *Die Hauspostille—Manual of Piety*. New York: Grove.
Brener, Uri, and Yitsḥak Kafkafi. 1991. *Al Y. Ḥ. Brenner: Od zikhronot*. Tel Aviv: Ha-kibbutz Ha-meuḥad; Ha-Merkaz le-tarbut ule-hinukh shel ha-histadrut ha-klalit.
Brenner, Benjamin. 1978. *Gdolah haitah ha-bedidut*. Tel Aviv: Am Oved.
Brenner, Yosef Ḥayim. 1940. *Igrot Y. Ḥ. Brenner*. Tel Aviv: Davar.
———. 1977 and 1985. *Ktavim*. 4 vols. Tel Aviv: Ha-kibbutz Ha-meuḥad.
Brinker, Menachem. 1988. Brenner's Jewishness. *Studies in Contemporary Jewry* 4: 232–49.
———. 1990. *Ad ha-simtah ha-teveryanit: Ma'amar al sipur u-maḥashavah bi-yetsirat Brenner*. Tel Aviv: Am Oved.
Buck-Morss, Susan. 1989. *The Dialectics of Seeing: Walter Benjamin and the Arcades Project*. Cambridge, Mass.: MIT Press.
Buell, Lawrence. 1995. *The Environmental Imagination*. Cambridge, Mass.: Harvard University Press.
Bürger, Peter. 1984. *Theory of the Avant-Garde*. Minneapolis: University of Minnesota Press.
Burke, Edmund. 1990. *A Philosophical Enquiry into the Origin of the Ideas of the Sublime and Beautiful*. Oxford: Oxford University Press.
Campbell, SueEllen. 1998. Magpie. In *Writing the Environment: Ecocriticism and Literature*, edited by Richard Kerridge and Neil Sammells, 13–26. London: Zed Books.
Carmi, Shlomo. 1996. Le-she'alat ha-"mukdam" veha-"meuḥar" ve-she'alat ha-"sibah" veha-"mesuvav" be-tḥiyat ha-lashon ha-ivrit uve-ḥeker gormehah ve-toldotehah. *Ha-tsiyonut* 20:55–76.
Carmi, S., and H. Rosenfeld. 1971. Immigration, Urbanization, and Crisis: The Process of Jewish Settlement in Palestine in the Twenties [in Hebrew]. *Mi-bifnim* 33, no. 1: 49–62.
Carmi, Shulamit, and Henry Rosenfeld. 1989. The Emergence of Militaristic Nationalism in Israel. *International Journal of Politics, Culture, and Society* 3, no. 1: 5–49.
Carroll, Mark. 2002. Commitment or Abrogation? Avant-garde Music and Jean-Paul Sartre's Idea of Committed Art. *Music & Letters* 83, no. 4: 590–606.
Cohen, Shaul Ephraim. 1993. *The Politics of Planting: Israeli-Palestinian Competition for Control of Land in the Jerusalem Periphery*. Chicago: Chicago University Press.
Cohen, Adir. 1971. *Yetsirato ha-sifrutit shel Yosef Ḥayim Brenner*. Tel Aviv: Goma.
Cohen, Erik. 1970. *The City in the Zionist Ideology*. Jerusalem Urban Studies, no. 1. Jerusalem: Hebrew University Institute of Urban and Regional Studies.
Cohen, E. 1976. Environmental Organization: A Multidimensional Approach to Social Ecology. *Current Anthropology* 17, no. 1: 49–70.
Cohen, Mitchell. 1992. *Zion and State: Nation, Class, and the Shaping of Modern Israel*. New York: Columbia University Press.
Cohen, Yaakov, and P. Lachover, eds. 1936. *Knesset: Divrei sofrim le-zekher Ḥ. N. Bialik*. Tel Aviv: Dvir.
Cordova, Abraham, and Hanna Herzog. 1978. The Cultural Endeavor of the Labor Movement in Palestine: A Study of the Relationship Between Intelligentsia and Intellectuals. *YIVO Annual of Jewish Social Science* 17: 238–59.
Cronon, William. 1991. *Nature's Metropolis: Chicago and the Great West*. New York: W. W. Norton.
———. 1995. *Uncommon Ground: Toward Reinventing Nature*. New York: W. W. Norton.
Cropper, John. 1902. The Geographical Distribution of Anaphilisia and Malarial Fever in Upper Palestine. *Journal of Hygiene* 2, no. 1: 47–57.
———. 1905. The Malarial Fevers of Jerusalem and Their Prevention. *Journal of Hygiene* (October): 460ff.

Dagon, Gadi. 2003. *Keren kayemit u-matzlemat: Tmunot meha-kuftsah ha-kḥolah 1903–2003.* Jerusalem: Jewish National Fund.

Dainotto, Roberto Maria. 2000. *Place in Literature: Regions, Cultures, Communities.* Ithaca, N.Y.: Cornell University Press.

Dan, Hillel. 1963. *Be-derekh lo slulah: Hagadat solel boneh.* Jerusalem and Tel Aviv: Schocken.

Dayan, Shmuel. 1937. *Ḥatsi yovel shanim shel Degania.* Tel Aviv: Stybel.

Deleuze, Gilles, and Félix Guattari. 1986. *Kafka: Toward a Minor Literature.* Minneapolis: University of Minnesota Press.

De-Lima, N. 1942. *On Labor in Palestine: The Jewish National Fund from the Beginnings of Its Activities in Palestine until the Purchase of the Valley* [in Hebrew]. Jerusalem: Jewish National Fund.

DellaPergola, Sergio. 1999. Arthur Ruppin Revisted: The Jews of Today, 1904–1994. In *National Variations in Jewish Identity,* edited by S. M. Cohen and G. Horencyzk, 53–84. Albany: State University of New York Press.

De Man, Paul. 1984. *The Rhetoric of Romanticism.* New York: Columbia University Press.

Doleve-Gandelman, Tsili. 1987. The Symbolic Inscription of Zionist Ideology in the Space of Eretz Yisrael: Why the Native Israeli Is Called *Tsabar.* In *Judaism Viewed from Within and from Without: Anthropological Studies,* edited by Harvey E. Goldberg. Albany: State University of New York Press.

Dorman, Menakhem, and Uzi Shavit. 1984. *Maḥbarot Brenner.* Vol. 3/4. Tel Aviv: Ha-kibbutz Ha-meuḥad and Tel Aviv University.

Doukhan-Landau, Leah. 1979. *Ha-ḥevrot ha-tsiyoniyot li-rekhishat karka'ot be-eretz yisra'el, 1897–1914.* Jerusalem: Yad Yitsḥak Ben-Tsvi.

Dowty, Alan. 2000. Much Ado About Little: Aḥad Ha'am's "Truth from Eretz Yisrael," Zionism, and the Arabs. *Israel Studies* 5, no. 2: 154–81.

Druyanov, A. 1919. *Ktavim le-toldot ḥibat tsiyon ve-yishuv eretz yisra'el.* Odessa: Ha-va'ad le-yishuv eretz yisra'el.

Dubnov, Shimon. 1937. *Mikhtavim al ha-yahadut ha-yeshanah veha-ḥadashah.* Tel Aviv: Dvir.

———. 1972. *Jewish History: An Essay in the Philosophy of History.* Freeport, N.Y.: Books for Libraries Press.

Dubnov-Erlich, Sophie. 1991. *The Life and Work of S. M. Dubnov: Diaspora Nationalism and Jewish History.* Trans. Judith Bowles. Bloomington: Indiana University Press.

Dubnow, Simon. 1937. *Mein Leben.* Berlin: Jüdische Buchvereinigung.

Efrati, Nathan. 1991. *Mi-mashber le-tikvah: Ha-yishuv ha-yehudi be-eretz-yisra'el be-milḥemet ha-olam ha-rishonah.* Jerusalem: Yad Yitsḥak Ben-Tsvi.

Efros, Israel, ed. 1965. *Selected Poems of Hayyim Nahman Bialik.* New York: Bloch.

Eliav, Mordechai, ed. 1991. *Be-matsor uve-matsok: Eretz-yisra'el be-milḥemet ha-olam ha-rishonah.* Jerusalem: Yad Yitsḥak Ben-Tsvi.

El-yesh, Ephraim. 1977. *Mi-sipurav shel roeh tson.* Tel Aviv: Am Oved.

English Zionist Federation, ed. 1907. *The Physical and Political Conditions of Palestine.* London: London Zionist League.

Even-Shoshan, Ts. 1946. *Ha-histadrut: Me'asef.* Tel Aviv: Ha-va'ad ha-po'el shel ha-histadrut ha-klalit shel ha-ovdim ha-ivriyim be-eretz yisra'el, maḥleket "he-ḥaluts."

Ever-Hadani, Aharon. 1951. *Ḥaderah (1951–1891): Shishim shnot koroteha.* Tel Aviv: Hotsa'at masadah ve-"ḥevrat meyesdei ḥaderah."

Feldman, Yael S. 1979. From Dostoyevsky to Brenner. *Hebrew Annual Review* 3: 91–104.

———. 1999. *No Room of Their Own: Gender and Nation in Israeli Women's Fiction, Gender and Culture.* New York: Columbia University Press.

Fogel, David. 1923. *Lifnei ha-sha'ar he-afel.* Vienna: Ma'ar.

———. 1930 [1974]. Lashon ve-signon be-sifrutenu ha-tse'irah. *Siman Kriah* 3/4: 382–91.

———. 1993. Language and Style in Our Young Literature. In *Prooftexts,* special issue, *David Fogel and the Emergence of Hebrew Modernism* 13, no. 1: 15–20.

Fraenkel, Josef. 1963. *Dubnow, Herzl, and Ahad Ha-am: Political and Cultural Zionism.* London: Ararat Publishing Society.

French, L. 1932. *Reports on Agricultural Development and Land Settlement in Palestine.* Jerusalem: Palestine Government.

Friedman, Isaiah. 1973. *The Question of Palestine, 1914–1918: British-Jewish-Arab Relations.* New York: Schocken.

Friesel, Evyatar. 1977. *Ha-mediniyut ha-tsiyonit le'aḥar hatsharat Balfour, 1917–1922.* Tel Aviv: Tel Aviv University.

Gavrieli, Ḥayim, ed. 1935. *Avodah ivrit.* Tel Aviv: Ha-histadrut.

Gertz, Nurit. 1988. *Sifrut ve-ideologiyah be-eretz-yisra'el bi-shnot ha-shloshim: Mikra'ah.* Tel Aviv: Ha-universitah Ha-ptuḥah.

———, ed. 1988. *Nekudot tatspit: Tarbut ve-ḥevrah be-eretz-yisra'el.* Tel Aviv: Ha-universitah Ha-ptuḥah.

Ginosar, Pinḥas. 1993. Hariyono, ledato, ḥayav u-moto shel ha-yarḥon "ha-adamah." *Iyunim bi-tkumat yisra'el* 3: 224–69.

Gluzman, Michael. 1991. The Exclusion of Women from Hebrew Literary History. *Prooftexts* 11, no. 3: 259–78.

———. 1997. Ha-kmihah le-heterosexualiyut: Tsiyonut u-miniyut be-*Altneuland. Teoriyah u-vikoret* 11 (Winter): 145–62.

———. 2003. *The Politics of Canonicity: Lines of Resistance in Modernist Hebrew Poetry.* Stanford, Calif.: Stanford University Press.

Goehr, Lydia. 1998. *The Quest for Voice: On Music, Politics, and the Limits of Philosophy.* Berkeley: University of California Press.

Goldberg, Harvey E., ed. 1987. *Judaism Viewed from Within and from Without: Anthropological Studies.* Albany: State University of New York Press.

Goldberg, Leah. 1974. "Al arba'a shirim shel A. Shlonsky." *Moznayim* 5–6, no. 37.

Goldberg, Zeev. 1996. Mendele Mokher Sfarim veha-ra'ayon ha-tsiyoni. *Ha-tsiyonut* 20: 31–54.

Goodblatt, Chanita. 1993. Natan Alterman: The "Other" as "Wanderer" in His Early Poetry. In *Israeli Writers Consider the "Outsider,"* edited by Leon I. Yudkin. Rutherford, N.J.: Fairleigh Dickinson University Press.

Gordon, Aharon David. 1938. *Selected Essays.* Translated by Frances Burnce. New York: League for Labor Palestine.

———. 1955. *Kitvei A. D. Gordon.* 3 vols. Tel Aviv: Ha-sifriyah Ha-tsiyonit.

Gorny, Yosef. 1968. Ha-ideologiyah shel "kibush ha-avodah." *Keshet* 10, no. 2: 66–79.

———. 1982. Yosef Haim Brenner's Attitude Toward Socialism and the Workers' Movement. *Studies in Zionism* 6: 185–209.

———. 1983. Hope Born out of Despair. *Jerusalem Quarterly* 26: 84–95.

———. 1984. Utopian Elements in Zionist Thought. *Studies in Zionism* 5, no. 1: 19–27.

Gouldner, Alvin. 1976. *The Dialectic of Ideology and Technology: The Origins, Grammar, and Future of Ideology.* New York: Seabury Press.

Govrin, Nurith. 1985. *Tlishut ve-hitḥadshut: Ha-siporet ha-ivrit be-reshit ha-meah ha-20 ba-golah uve-eretz-yisra'el.* Tel Aviv: Misrad Ha-bitaḥon.

———. 1991. *Brenner: "Oved-etsot" u-moreh-derekh.* Tel Aviv: Misrad Ha-bitaḥon and Tel Aviv University.
———. 1994. Brenner and the Palestinian Peace Agreement. *Ariel* 95: 5–12.
———. 1998. *Ktivat ha-aretz: Artsot ve-arim al mapat ha-sifrut ha-ivrit.* Jerusalem: Carmel.
Govrin, Nurith, and Yoram Gal. 1995. *Tserivah: Shirat-ha-tamid le-Brenner.* Tel Aviv: Misrad Ha-bitaḥon.
Graicer, Iris. 1990. The Valley of Jezreel: Social Ideologies and Settlement Landscape, 1920–1929. *Studies in Zionism* 11, no. 1: 1–23.
Granovsky (Granott), Abraham. 1936. *The Land Issue in Palestine.* Jerusalem: Jewish National Fund.
———. 1940. *Land Policy in Palestine.* New York: Bloch.
———. 1944. *She'alat ha-karka likrat ha-atid.* Jerusalem: Jewish National Fund.
Great Britain. Commission on the Palestine Disturbances of August 1929, and Walter Shaw. 1930. *Report of the Commission on the Palestine Disturbances of August 1929: Presented by the Secretary of State for the Colonies to Parliament by Command of His Majesty, March 1930.* London: H. M. Stationery Office.
Haefrati, Yosef. 1974. Tmurot be-shirat ha-teva ke-degem shel ma'avar mi-tkufah le-tkufah shel ha-sifrut. *Ha-sifrut* 17 (September): 50–54.
———. 1976. *Ha-mar'ot veha-lashon: Le-toldot ha-te'ur ba-shirah ha-ivrit ha-ḥadashah.* Tel Aviv: Porter Institute.
Hakak, Lev. 2001. *Modern Hebrew Literature Made into Films.* Lanham, Md.: University Press of America.
Halmish, Aviva. 1993. Aliyah ve-hityashvut. *Iyunim bi-tkumat yisra'el* 3: 98–113.
Halperin, Hagit, and Galia Sagiv. 1997. *Me-agvaniyah ad simfoniyah: Ha-shirah ha-kalah shel Avraham Shlonsky u-paraodiyot al shirato, Sefer Shlonsky 3.* Tel Aviv: Makhon Kats and Sifriyat Po'alim.
Harpaz, Nathan. 1984. Mi-'batei ḥalomot' le-'batei kufsa'ot': Ha-mahapakh ha-adrikhali shel shnot ha-shloshim be-tel aviv. In *Tel aviv be-reshitah, 1909–1934,* edited by Mordechai Naor. Jerusalem: Yad Yitsḥak Ben-Tsvi.
Harshav, Benjamin. 1993. *Language in the Time of Revolution.* Berkeley: University of California Press.
Hashulami, Ya'ir, and Adin Shulami. 1995. *Olam holekh ve-ne'elam: Ha-ḥakla'ut ba-moshavah ha-ivrit bi-shnot ha-esrim shel ha-meah ha-esrim: Pirkei zikhronot.* Tel Aviv: Milo.
Hazony, Yoram. 2000. *The Jewish State: The Struggle for Israel's Soul.* New York: Basic Books.
Headrick, Daniel. 1988. *The Tentacles of Progress: Technology Transfer in the Age of Imperialism, 1850–1940.* New York: Oxford University Press.
Heinze-Greenberg, Ita. 1994. Immigration and Culture Shock: On the Question of Architectural Identity in "Altneuland." In *Tel Aviv: Modern Architecture, 1930–1939,* edited by Winfried Nerdinger. Tübingen/Berlin: Ernst Wasmuth Verlag.
Herbert, Gilbert, and Ita Heinze-Greenberg. 1994. *Erich Mendelsohn in Palestine.* Haifa, Israel: Technion.
Herbert, Gilbert, and Silvina Sosnovsky. 1993. *Bauhaus on the Carmel and the Crossroads of Empire: Architecture and Planning in Haifa During the British Mandate.* Jerusalem: Yad Yitsḥak Ben-Tsvi.
Herlihy, Patricia. 1986. *Odessa: A History, 1794–1914.* Cambridge, Mass.: Distributed by Harvard University Press for the Harvard Ukrainian Research Institute.
Hertzberg, Arthur, ed. 1959. *The Zionist Idea: A Historical Analysis and Reader.* Garden City, N.Y.: Doubleday.
Herzl, Theodor. 1960. *Old New Land.* New York: Bloch.

Hever, Hannan. 1990. Hebrew in an Israeli Arab Hand: Six Miniatures on Anton Shammas's *Arabesques*. In *The Nature and Context of Minority Discourse*, edited by Abdul R. JanMohamed and David Lloyd. New York: Oxford University Press.

———. 1994. *Paitanim u-viryonim: Tsmiḥat ha-shir ha-politi ha-ivri be-eretz-yisra'el.* Jerusalem: Mosad Bialik.

———. 1995. *Bi-shvi ha-utopiyah: Masah al meshiḥiyut ve-politikah ba-shirah ha-ivrit be-eretz-yisra'el bein shtei milḥamot ha-olam.* Beersheva: Ben-Gurion University Press.

———. 2001. Ha-yam ha-tsiyoni: Simbolizm u-le'umiyut ba-shirah ha-ivrit ha-modernistit. In *Aderet le-Binyamin*, vol. 2, edited by Ziva Ben-Porat. Tel Aviv: Porter Institute and Ha-kibbutz Ha-meuḥad.

———. 2002. *Producing the Modern Hebrew Canon: Nation Building and Minority Discourse.* New York: New York University Press.

———. 2004. *Moledet ha-mavet yafah: Estetikah ve-politikah be-shirat Uri Zvi Greenberg.* Tel Aviv: Am Oved.

———. 2006. "The Origins of Eretz Israeli Poetry." In *Jewish Literature and History*, edited by Sheila Jelen and Eliyana Adler. College Park, Md.: University of Maryland Press.

Heymann, Michael, editor. 1977. *The Minutes of the Zionist General Council: The Uganda Controversy*, vol. 2. Jerusalem: Ha-sifriyah Ha-tsiyonit.

Hirschfeld, Ariel. 1994. "My Peace unto You, My Friend": On Reading a Text by Yosef Haim Brenner Concerning His Contacts with the Arabs. *Palestine-Israel Journal* 2: 112–18.

Holtzman, Avner. 1998. Poetics, Ideology, Biography, Myth: The Scholarship on J. H. Brenner, 1971–96. *Prooftexts* 18: 82–94.

Ḥug le-sifrut ivrit, Tel Aviv University. 1975. *Maḥbarot le-ḥeker yetsirato u-fo'olo shel Y. Ḥ. Brenner.* Vol. 1. Tel Aviv: Tel Aviv University.

Hullot-Kentor, Bob. 1984. Introduction to Adorno's "Idea of Natural History." *Telos* 60: 97–110.

Jackson, John Brinckerhoff. 1994. *A Sense of Place, a Sense of Time.* New Haven, Conn.: Yale University Press.

Jammes, Francis. 1920. *Romance of the Rabbit.* New York: N. L. Brown.

———. 1967. *Jammes.* Translated by Teo Savory. Unicorn French Series. Santa Barbara, Calif.: Unicorn Press.

Jewish Frontier Association. 1945. *Jewish Frontier Anthology, 1934–1944.* New York: Jewish Frontier Association.

Jusdanis, Gregory. 1991. *Belated Modernity and Aesthetic Culture: Inventing National Literature.* Minneapolis: University of Minnesota Press.

Kark, Ruth. 1990. *Ge'ulat ha-karka be-eretz-yisra'el.* Jerusalem: Yad Yitsḥak Ben-Tsvi.

Karmiel, Batya. 1990. Tsiyunei derekh be-hakamat tel aviv, 1906–1918. In *Tel aviv be-tatslumim: He-asor ha-rishon, 1909–1918.* Tel Aviv: Eretz Israel Museum.

Katz, Shmuel. 1982. "Ha-telem ha-rishon": Ideologiyah, hityashvut ve-ḥakla'ut be-petaḥ-tikvah, be-asor ha-shanim ha-rishonim le-kiyumah. *Cathedra* 23: 57–124.

Katz, Yosef. 1986. Ideology and Urban Development: Zionism and the Origins of Tel Aviv, 1906–1914. *Journal of Historical Geography* 12, no. 4: 402–24.

Katznelson, Berl. 1946. *Kitvei B. Katznelson.* 11 vols. Tel Aviv: Workers' Party of Eretz Israel.

Katznelson-Shazar, Rachel. 1975. *The Plough Woman: Memoirs of the Pioneer Women of Palestine.* New York: Herzl Press.

Keith, Michael, and Steve Pile, eds. 1993. *Place and the Politics of Identity.* London and New York: Routledge.

Kenner, Hugh. 1989. *A Homemade World: The American Modernist Writers.* Baltimore: Johns Hopkins University Press.

Keren Kayemeth Le Israel (Jewish National Fund). 1925. *Avodot ha-havra'ah be-emek yizra'el / Sanitation Works in the Valley of the Jesreel.* Jerusalem: Jewish National Fund.

Kerridge, Richard, and Neil Sammells. 1998. *Writing the Environment: Ecocriticism and Literature.* London: Zed Books.

Kimmerling, Baruch. 1983. *Zionism and Territory.* Berkeley: Institute of International Studies, University of California.

Kirsch, Karin. 1992. *The Weissenhofsiedlung Experimental Housing Built for the Deutscher Werkbund, Stuttgart 1927.* Stuttgart: Deutsche Verlag-Anstalt.

Klauzner-Bar, Aliza. 1975. Al hashpa'ato shel Aḥad Ha'am al Ḥayim Naḥman Bialik. In *Mukdash li-ytsirat Ḥayim Naḥman Bialik,* edited by Hillel Barzel. Ramat Gan: Agudat Ha-sofrim and Masadah.

Klein, Shmuel. 1937. *Ha-karka: Skirah historit al she'elat ha-karka be-eretz yisra'el.* Jerusalem: Jewish National Fund.

Krauss, Rosalind E. 1980. *Grids: Format and Image in 20th Century Art.* New York: Pace Gallery.

———. 1998. *The Picasso Papers.* New York: Farrar, Straus and Giroux.

Kronfeld, Chana. 1996. *On the Margins of Modernism: Decentering Literary Dynamics.* Berkeley: University of California Press.

Kurzweil, Baruch. 1968. *Bialik ve-Tschernihovsky: Meḥkarim be-shiratam.* Tel Aviv: Schocken.

Kushner, M. 1947. *A. D. Gordon: Zikhronot ve-divrei-ha'arakha.* Tel Aviv: Ha-histadrut–Ha-merkaz Le-tarbut.

Lachover, Fischel. 1953. *Shirat Bialik.* Jerusalem: Mosad Bialik.

Laor, Dan. 1979. Shirei "Gilboa" veha-etos shel ha-aliyah ha-shlishit: He'arot-ptiḥah. *Moznayim* 49:134–40.

———. 1983. *Ha-shofar veha-ḥerev: Masot al Natan Alterman.* Tel Aviv: Tel Aviv University and Ha-kibbutz Ha-meuḥad.

Laqueur, Walter, and Barry Rubin, eds. 1995. *The Israel-Arab Reader: A Documentary History of the Middle East Conflict.* New York: Penguin.

Larson, Neil. 1990. *Modernism and Hegemony.* Minneapolis: University of Minnesota Press.

Laskov, Shlomit. 1981. *Ha-biluyim.* Tel Aviv: Ha-sifriyah Ha-tsiyonit.

Lehmann, Siegfried. 1928. Über die erzieherischen Krafte von Erde und Volk. In *Der Jude: Sonderheft zu Martin Bubers fünfzigstem Geburtstag,* 58–69.

Leman, Juda, and Keren Ha-yesod. 1935 [1992]. *The Land of Promise: The First Palestine Sound Picture.* Teaneck, N.J.: Ergo Media.

Lerner, Anne Lapidus. 1992. "A Woman's Song": The Poetry of Esther Raab. In *Gender and Text in Modern Hebrew and Yiddish Literature,* edited by Naomi B. Sokoloff, Anne Lapidus Lerner, and Anita Norich, 17–38. New York: Jewish Theological Seminary of America; distributed by Harvard University Press.

———. 1994. The Naked Land: Nature in the Poetry of Esther Raab. In *Women of the Word: Jewish Women and Jewish Writing,* edited by Judith R. Raskin, 236–57. Detroit: Wayne State University Press.

Levin, Michael. 1977. The Transformation of Villa Savoye into the National Library: Le Corbusier's Influence on Two Generations of Architects in Israel. *Journal of Jewish Art* 3–4: 103–21.

———. 1981. Ha-adrikhalim she-heviu et ha-bauhaus le-yisra'el. *Kav* 2 (January): 65–79.

———. 1984. *Ir levanah: Adrikhalut ha-signon ha-beinle'umi be-yisra'el.* Tel Aviv: Tel Aviv Museum.

———. 1984. The White City: International Style in Israel. *Progressive Architecture* 65: 114–21.
Levin, Yisra'el, ed. 1981. *Sefer Shlonsky I: Meḥkarim al Avraham Shlonsky ve-yetsirato.* Tel Aviv: Sifriyat Po'alim.
Levinger, Ester. 1993. *Andarta'ot la-noflim be-yisra'el.* Tel Aviv: Ha-kibbutz Ha-meuḥad.
Lichtenbaum, Joseph. 1967. *Yosef Ḥayim Brenner: Ḥayav vi-ytsirato.* Tel Aviv: Niv.
Liebman, Charles S., and Eliezer Don-Yeḥya. 1983. *Civil Religion in Israel: Traditional Judaism and Political Culture in the Jewish State.* Berkeley: University of California Press.
Lifschitz, Nili, and Gideon Bieger. 1994. Mediniyut ha-yi'ur shel ha-memshal ha-briti be-eretz yisra'el. *Ofekim be-geografiyah* 40–41: 5–16.
Lowell, Amy. 1921. *Six French Poets: Studies in Contemporary Literature.* Boston: Houghton Mifflin.
Lukács, Georg. 1971. *The Theory of the Novel: A Historico-Philosophical Essay on the Forms of Great Epic Literature.* Cambridge, Mass.: MIT Press.
Lusky, H., ed. 1991. *Ir ve-utopiyah.* Tel Aviv: Ha-ḥevrah ha-yisra'elit.
Malachi, Zvi. 1977. *Al shirah ve-siporet: Meḥkarim ba-sifrut ha-ivrit.* Tel Aviv: Tel Aviv University and Makhon Kats.
Mann, Barbara. 1999. Framing the Native: Esther Raab's Visual Poetics. *Israel Studies* 4, no. 1: 234–57.
———. 2001. The Vicarious Landscape of Memory in Tel Aviv Poetry. *Prooftexts* 21, no. 3: 350–78.
Marx, Leo. 1964. *The Machine in the Garden: Technology and the Pastoral Idea in America.* New York: Oxford University Press.
McClintock, Anne. 1995. *Imperial Leather: Race, Gender, and Sexuality in the Colonial Conquest.* New York: Routledge.
Megged, Aharon. 1998. One-Way Trip on the Highway to Self-Destruction. In *Zionism: The Sequel,* edited by Carol Diament. New York: Hadassah Books.
Megged, Matti. 1978. A Vision Alive: The Thought of Yosef Haim Brenner. *Response* 35: 49–60.
Melamed, David. 1984. Requiem for a Landscape. *Modern Hebrew Literature* 9, nos. 3–4: 69–72.
Mendelsohn, Erich. 1940. *Palestine and the World of Tomorrow.* Jerusalem: Jerusalem Press.
Mikhaeli, Yitsḥak. 1983. *Be-shadmot Yosef Ḥayim Brenner: Bibliografiyah.* Tel Aviv: Ha-kibbutz Ha-meuḥad.
Mintz, Alan L. 1984. *Hurban: Responses to Catastrophe in Hebrew Literature.* New York: Columbia University Press.
Miron, Dan. 1991. *Imahot meyesdot, aḥayot ḥorgot: Hofa'atan ve-hitkablutan shel ha-meshorerot ha-ivriyot ha-rishonot.* Tel Aviv: Ha-kibbutz Ha-meuḥad.
———. 1991. Reshitah shel shirat tel aviv. In *Ir ve-utopiyah,* edited by H. Lusky, 184–207. Tel Aviv: Ha-ḥevrah ha-yisra'elit.
———. 1993. *Ḥadashot me-ezor ha-kotev: Iyunim ba-shirah ha-ivrit ha-ḥadashah.* Tel Aviv: Zmorah Bitan.
———. 1999. Ahavah ha-tluyah be-davar: Toldot hitkablutah shel shirat David Fogel. In *Aderet le-Binyamin,* vol. 1, edited by Ziva Ben-Porat. Tel Aviv: Porter Institute and Ha-kibbutz Ha-meuḥad.
———. 2000. *H. N. Bialik and the Prophetic Mode in Modern Hebrew Poetry.* Syracuse, N.Y.: Syracuse University Press.
———. 2001. *Parpar min ha-tola'at.* Tel Aviv: Open University.

Mitchell, W. J. T. 2000. Holy Landscape: Israel, Palestine, and the American Wilderness. *Critical Inquiry* 26 (Winter): 193–223.

Monk, Daniel Bertrand. 1994. Review of *Bauhaus on the Carmel and the Crossroads of Empire,* by Gilbert Herbert and Silvina Sosnovsky. *AA Files* 28: 94–99.

———. 2002. *An Aesthetic Occupation: The Immediacy of Architecture and the Palestine Conflict.* Durham, N.C.: Duke University Press.

Morahg, Gilead. 1986. New Images of Arabs in Israeli Fiction. *Prooftexts* 6, no. 2: 147–62.

Morris, Benny. 1988. The New Historiography: Israel Confronts Its Past. *Tikkun* 3, no. 6: 19–23, 99–102.

———. 1990. *1948 and After: Israel and the Palestinians.* Oxford: Clarendon Press.

———. 1993. *Israel's Border War, 1949–1956.* Oxford: Clarendon Press.

———. 2000. *Tikun ta'ut: Yehudim ve-aravim be-eretz-yisra'el, 1936–1956.* Tel Aviv: Am Oved.

Murphy, Patrick D. 2000. *Farther Afield in the Study of Nature-Oriented Literature.* Charlottesville: University Press of Virginia.

Nakhimovsky, Alice S. 1992. *Russian-Jewish Literature and Identity: Jabotinsky, Babel, Grossman, Galich, Roziner, Markish.* Baltimore: Johns Hopkins University Press.

Naor, Mordechai, ed. 1986. *Yemei ḥomah u-migdal, 1936–1939.* Jerusalem: Yad Yitsḥak Ben-Tsvi.

Navon, Ofira, curator. *Landscapes in Israel Art.* 1984. Jerusalem: D. K. Graubart.

Nerdinger, Winfried, ed. 1994. *Tel Aviv: Modern Architecture, 1930–1939.* Tübingen/ Berlin: Ernst Wasmuth Verlag.

Nordau, Max. 1892 [1993]. Degeneration. Lincoln: University of Nebraska Press.

Ofaz, Gad. 1990. Yetsirat "am adam": Ha-utopiyah ha-le'umit shel Aharon David Gordon. *Ha-tsiyonut* 15: 55–76.

Ofrat, Gideon. 1980. *Adamah, adam, dam: Mitos he-ḥaluts u-fulḥan ha-adamah be-maḥazot ha-hityashvut.* Tel Aviv: Tscherikover.

Omer, Mordechai, ed. 1993. *Migdelei ha-mayim be-yisra'el, 1891–1993.* Tel Aviv: Genia Schreiber University Art Gallery, Tel Aviv University.

Oppenheimer, Yochai. 1999. The Arab in the Mirror: The Image of the Arab in Israeli Fiction. *Prooftexts* 19: 205–34.

Oz, Amos. 1985. *Israeli Literature: A Case of Reality Reflecting Fiction.* Colorado Springs: Colorado College.

———. 2000. *The Silence of Heaven: Agnon's Fear of God.* Trans. Barbara Harshav. Princeton, N.J.: Princeton University Press.

Pappé, Ilan. 1988. *Britain and the Arab-Israeli Conflict, 1948–51.* New York: St. Martin's Press.

Parush, Iris. 1992. *Kanon sifruti ve-ideologiyah le'umit: Bikoret ha-sifrut shel Frishman be-hashva'ah le-vikoret ha-sifrut shel Klozner ve-Brenner.* Jerusalem: Mosad Bialik.

Patterson, David. 1980. Yosef Hayyim Brenner. *Jewish Book Annual* 38: 117–26.

Penslar, Derek J. 1991. *Zionism and Technocracy: The Engineering of Jewish Settlement in Palestine, 1870–1918.* Bloomington: Indiana University Press.

Penueli, Shemuel Yeshayahu. 1964. *Brenner u-Gnesin ba-sipur ha-ivri shel reshit ha-meah ha-esrim.* Tel Aviv: Tel Aviv University.

Perry, Menakhem. 1986. The Israeli-Palestinian Conflict as a Metaphor in Recent Israeli Fiction. *Poetics Today* 7, no. 4: 603–19.

Piterberg, Gabriel. 2002. Postcards from Palestine. *New Left Review* 17 (September/ October): 150–57.

Poggiolo, Renato. 1968. *The Theory of the Avant-Garde.* Cambridge, Mass.: Harvard University Press.

Poran, Zevulun. 1984. *Yohshua Henkin: Go'el ha-adamah.* Jerusalem: Jewish National Fund.

Press, Jacob. 1997. Same-Sex Unions in Modern Europe: *Daniel Deronda, Altneuland,* and the Homoerotics of Jewish Nationalism. In *Novel Gazing: Queer Readings in Fiction,* edited by Eve Kosofsky Sedgwick. Durham, N.C.: Duke University Press.

Raab, Esther. 1930. *Kimshonim.* Tel Aviv: Hedim.

———. 1983. *Gan she-ḥarav: Mivḥar sipurim ve-shiv'ah shirim.* Tel Aviv: Misrad Ha-bitaḥon.

———. 1988. *Kol ha-shirim.* Tel Aviv: Zmorah Bitan.

———. 2001. *Kol ha-proza.* Tel Aviv: Astrolog.

Ram, Uri, ed. 1993. *Ha-ḥevrah ha-yisra'elit: Hibatim bikortiyim.* Tel Aviv: Breirot Publishers.

Ramraz-Rausch, Gila. 1979. *Y. Ḥ. Brenner veha-sifrut ha-modernit.* Tel Aviv: Eked.

Reisner, Marc. 1993. *Cadillac Desert: The American West and Its Disappearing Water.* New York: Penguin Books.

Ross, Ronald, and Liverpool School of Tropical Medicine. 1900. *Instructions for the Prevention of Malarial Fever: For the Use of Residents in Malarious Places.* Liverpool: University Press of Liverpool.

Rotenstreich, Nathan. 1968. *Jewish Philosophy in Modern Times: From Mendelssohn to Rosenzweig.* New York: Holt Rinehart and Winston.

———. N.d. *Ha-umah be-torato shel A. D. Gordon.* Jerusalem: Ha-histadrut; Keren Ha-yesod; Reuven Mas.

Ruppin, Arthur. 1925. *Ha-hityashvut ha-ḥakla'it shel ha-histadrut ha-tsiyonit be-eretz yisra'el (1907–1924).* Tel Aviv: Dvir.

———. 1936. *Three Decades of Palestine: Speeches and Papers on the Upbuilding of the Jewish National Home.* Jerusalem: Schocken.

———. 1936 [1975]. *The Agricultural Colonization of the Zionist Organization in Palestine.* Westport, Conn.: Hyperion Press.

Sadan-Loebenstein, Nilli, and Avidov Lipsker. 1991. *Siporet shnot ha-esrim be-eretz yisra'el.* Jerusalem: Sifriyat Po'alim.

Said, Edward. 1979. *Orientalism.* New York: Vintage.

———. 1994. *Culture and Imperialism.* New York: Vintage.

———. 2000. Invention, Memory, and Place. *Critical Inquiry* 26 (Winter): 175–92.

Samuel, Maurice. 1929. *What Happened in Palestine: The Events of August 1929, Their Background and Their Significance.* Boston: Stratford Co.

Sandbank, Shimon. 1976. *Shtei brekhot ba-ya'ar.* Tel Aviv: Tel Aviv University.

Sartre, Jean Paul. 1949 [1966]. *What Is Literature?* New York: Washington Square Press.

Schama, Simon. 1995. *Landscape and Memory.* New York: A. A. Knopf; distributed by Random House.

Schechter, Yosef. 1957. *Mishnato shel Aharon David Gordon.* Tel Aviv: Dvir.

Schlör, Joachim. 1999. *Tel Aviv: From Dream to City.* London: Reaktion.

Schneider, Samuel. 1994. *Olam ha-masoret ha-yehudit be-kitvei Yosef Ḥayim Brenner.* Tel Aviv: Reshafim.

Schor, Naomi. 1987. *Reading in Detail: Aesthetics and the Feminine.* New York: Methuen.

Schorske, Carl. 1981. *Fin-de-Siècle Vienna.* New York: Vintage.

Schwartz, Yigal. 2000. "Handasat ha-adam" ve-itsuv ha-merḥav ba-tarbut ha-ivrit ha-ḥadashah. *Mi-kan* 1 (May): 9–24.

Schweid, Eliezer. 1970. *Ha-yaḥid: Olamo shel A. D. Gordon.* Tel Aviv: Am Oved.

Segev, Tom. 1984. *1949: Ha-yisra'elim ha-rishonim.* Jerusalem: Domino.

Seidman, Naomi. 1997. Lawless Attachments, One-Night Stands: The Sexual Politics of the Hebrew-Yiddish Language War. In *Jews and Other Differences: The New Jewish Cultural Studies,* edited by Jonathan Boyarin and Daniel Boyarin, 279–305. Minneapolis: University of Minnesota Press.

———. 1997. *A Marriage Made in Heaven: The Sexual Politics of Hebrew and Yiddish.* Berkeley: University of California Press.

Sela, Rona. 2000. *Tsilum be-palestin: Eretz-yisra'el bi-shnot ha-shloshim veha-arba'im.* Herzliyah: Muze'on Herzliyah Le-omanut; and Tel Aviv: Ha-kibbutz Ha-meuḥad.

Selwyn, Tom. 1995. Landscapes of Liberation and Imprisonment: Towards an Anthropology of the Israeli Landscape. In *The Anthropology of Landscape: Perspectives on Place and Space,* edited by E. Hirsch and M. O'Hanlon. Oxford: Clarendon Press.

Shafir, Gershon. 1996. *Land, Labor, and the Origins of the Israeli-Palestinian Conflict, 1882–1914.* Berkeley: University of California Press.

Shaked, Gershon. 1973. *Le-lo motsa.* Tel Aviv: Ha-kibbutz Ha-meuḥad.

———. 1976. "Livnot u-lehibanot bah": Al roman ha-hityashvut. In *Proceedings of the Sixth World Congress for Jewish Studies.* Jerusalem: World Union of Jewish Studies, 517–27.

———. 1978. The Man Who Was Not Job: An Analysis of the Composition of *Breakdown and Bereavement* by J. H. Brenner. *Scripta Hierosolymitana* 27: 155–73.

———. 1988. *Ha-siporet ha-ivrit, 1880–1980.* Vol. 3. Tel Aviv: Ha-kibbutz Ha-meuḥad.

Shakespeare, William. 1938. *The Works of William Shakespeare.* New York: Oxford University Press.

———. 1946. *Hamlet, nesikh Denmark.* Translated by A. Shlonsky. Tel Aviv: Hotsa'at La-am.

Shaltiel, E. 1990. *Pinḥas Rutenberg: Aliyato u-nefilato shel "ish ḥazak" be-eretz-yisra'el, 1879–1942.* Tel Aviv: Am Oved.

Shapira, Anita. 1980. *Berl: Biografiyah.* 2 vols.Tel Aviv: Am Oved.

———. 1992. *Ḥerev ha-yonah: Ha-tsiyonut veha-koaḥ, 1881–1948.* Tel Aviv: Am Oved.

———. 1992. *Land and Power: The Zionist Resort to Force, 1881–1948.* New York: Oxford University Press.

Shapira, Anita, and Derek Jonathan Penslar, eds. 2003. *Israeli Historical Revisionism: From Left to Right.* Portland, Ore.: Frank Cass.

Shapira, Avraham. 1996. *Or ha-ḥayim be-"yom ktanot": Mishnat A. D. Gordon u-mekoroteha ba-kabalah uva-ḥasidut.* Tel Aviv: Am Oved.

———. 1997. Revival and Legacy: Martin Buber's Attitude to A. D. Gordon. *Journal of Israeli History* 18, no. 1: 29–45.

Sharon, Arieh. 1976. *Kibbutz + Bauhaus: An Architect's Way in a New Land.* Stuttgart: Karl Krämer Verlag.

Sharoni, Edna. 1983. Edenic Energy: Esther Raab's Unmediated Vision of Nature. *Modern Hebrew Literature* 8, nos. 3–4: 62–69.

Shavit, Jacob, and Gideon Biger. 2001. *Ha-historiyah shel tel aviv.* Tel Aviv: Tel Aviv University.

Shavit, Uzi. Bein Shlonsky le-Fogel. *Hasifrut* 2/4: 251–57.

———. ed. 1988. *Sefer Shlonsky II: Meḥkarim al Avraham Shlonsky ve-yetsirato.* Tel Aviv: Sifriyat Po'alim.

Shavit, Uzi, and Ziva Shamir. 1995. *Al sfat ha-brekhah: Ha-poemah shel Bialik bi-re'i ha-bikoret.* Tel Aviv: Ha-kibbutz Ha-meuḥad.

Shavit, Zohar. 1982. *He-ḥayim ha-sifrutiyim be-eretz yisra'el, 1910–1939.* Tel Aviv: Porter Institute.

———. 1994. Aliyatam ve-nefilatam shel ha-merkazim ha-sifrutiyim be-eropah uve-amerikah ve-hakamat ha-merkaz be-eretz-yisra'el. *Iyunim bi-tkumat yisra'el* 4: 422–77.

Shilony, Zvi. 1990. *Ha-keren ha-kayemet le-yisra'el veha-hityashvut ha-tsiyonit, 1903–1914.* Jerusalem: Yad Yitsḥak Ben-Tsvi.

———. 1998. *Ideology and Settlement: The Jewish National Fund, 1897–1914.* Jerusalem: Magnes Press.

Shlonsky, Avraham. 1923. *Ba-galgal.* Tel Aviv: Davar.

———. 1923. Ha-melitsah. *Hedim* 6: 189–90.

———. 1927. *Le-aba-ima.* Tel Aviv: Ketuvim.

———. 1934. *Avnei bohu.* Tel Aviv.

———. 1960. *Yalkut eshel.* Tel Aviv: Sifriyat Po'alim.

———. 1965. *Shirim.* 2 vols. Merhaviyah: Sifriyat Po'alim.

———. 1981. *Pirkei yoman.* Tel Aviv: Sifriyat Po'alim.

———, trans. 1971. *Maḥazot.* Merhaviyah: Sifriyat Po'alim.

Shoham, Reuven. 1975. Bat ha-aretz. *Shdemot* 15: 74–93.

———. 1998. The Role of the Mythic Birth Narrative in Modern Hebrew Poetry: Bialik, Shlonsky, Greenberg. *Hebrew Studies* 39: 75–97.

Shokeid, Moshe. 1982. Jewish Existence in a Berber Environment. In *Jewish Societies in the Middle East,* edited by Shlomo Deshen and P. Zenner. Washington, D.C.: University Press of America.

Silberstein, Laurence J. 1999. *The Postzionism Debates: Knowledge and Power in Israeli Culture.* New York: Routledge.

Simmel, Georg. 1971. The Metropolis and Mental Life. In *On Individuality and Social Forms.* Chicago: University of Chicago Press.

———. 1997. Money and Commodity Culture. In *Simmel on Culture,* edited by David Frisby and Mike Featherstone. London: Sage Publications.

Slutzky, Yehuda. 1973. *Mavo le-toldot tenu'at ha-avodah ha-yisra'elit.* Tel Aviv: Am Oved.

———, ed. 1975. *Tnu'at ha-avodah ha-eretz-yisra'elit.* Tel Aviv: Agudat Ha-studentim.

———, ed. 1978. *"Po'alei tsiyon" be-eretz-yisra'el 1905–1919 (te'udot).* Tel Aviv: Tel Aviv University.

Smilansky, Moshe. 1930. *Jewish Colonisation and the Fellah: The Effect of Jewish Land Settlement in Palestine on the Native Rural Population and on Agricultural Development in General.* Tel Aviv: "Misḥar ve-Ta'asiyah" Publishing Co.

———. 1945. *Bnei arav.* 2 vols. Tel Aviv: Dvir.

Smolly, Eliezer. 1931 [1982]. *Anshei be-reshit.* Tel Aviv: Am Oved.

———. 1942. *Ḥayei rishonim.* Tel Aviv: Am Oved.

Snir, Mordecai. 1971. *Yosef Ḥayim Brenner: Mivḥar divrei-zikhronot.* Tel Aviv: Tarbut ve-ḥinukh.

Spinoza, Benedictus de. 1988. *Tractatus Theologico-Politicus.* Indianapolis: Hackett Publishing.

Stanislawski, Michael. 2001. *Zionism and the Fin-de-Siècle: Cosmopolitanism and Nationalism from Nordau to Jabotinsky.* Berkeley: University of California Press.

Stein, Kenneth W. 1984. *The Land Question in Palestine, 1917–1939.* Chapel Hill: University of North Carolina Press.

Sternhell, Zeev. 1998. *The Founding Myths of Israel: Nationalism, Socialism, and the Making of the Jewish State.* Princeton, N.J.: Princeton University Press.

Strauss, Arieh. 1959. *Be-darkei ha-sifrut.* Jerusalem: Mosad Bialik.

Tabenkin, Yitzḥak. 1969. *Be-darkei ha-shliḥut: Mivḥar dvarim bi-she'elot ha-histadrut u-tnu'at ha-po'alim.* Tel Aviv: Tarbut ve-ḥinukh.

Tagg, John. 1993. God's Sanitary Law: Slum Clearance and Photography in Late Nineteenth-Century Leeds. In *The Burden of Representation,* 117–52. Minneapolis: University of Minnesota Press.

Taharlev, Yoram, and Mordechai Naor. 1992. *Shiru habitu u-re'u: Ha-sipurim sheme-aḥorei ha-shirim.* Tel Aviv: Misrad Ha-bitaḥon.

Tal, Alon. 2002. *Pollution in a Promised Land: An Environmental History of Israel.* Berkeley: University of California Press.

Tal, Alon, N. Ben-Aharon, and Amir Idelman. 2002. *Sevivah u-mediniyut: Kovets meḥkarim.* Jerusalem: Mekhon Yerushalayim; Ha-merkaz li-mediniyut svivatit.

Tartakover, David. 1995. *Hatsagah rishonah: Krazot kolno'a, tel aviv, shnot ha-shloshim.* Jerusalem: Jerusalem Cinemateque.

Tcherniḥovsky, Shaul. 1942. Yeshnah od tel aviv aḥat. In *Tel aviv: Mikra'ah historit-sifrutit,* edited by Yosef Arikha. Tel Aviv: Tel Aviv Municipality.

Thon, Ya'akov, ed. 1948. *Sefer Warburg.* Herzliyah: Masadah.

Troen, S. Ilan. 2000. Frontier Myths and Their Applications in America and Israel: A Transnational Perspective. *Israel Studies* 5, no. 1: 301–29.

———. 2003. *Imagining Zion: Dreams, Designs, and Realities in a Century of Jewish Settlement.* New Haven, Conn.: Yale University Press.

Trotsky, Leon. 1930. *Ḥayai* (My Life). Translated by A. Shlonsky. Tel Aviv: Mitspeh.

Tsemaḥ, Adah. 1984. *Tnuah be-nekudah: Brenner ve-sipurav.* Tel Aviv: Ha-kibbutz Ha-meuḥad.

Tsfira, Bracha. 1978. *Kolot rabim.* Tel Aviv: Masadah.

Tsur, Muki. 1998. *At enekh bodedah ba-marom: Mikhtavim me-A. D. Gordon ve-elav.* Tel Aviv: Ha-kibbutz Ha-meuḥad.

Tsur, Muki, Gavriel Barkai, and Eli Shiller, eds. 1999. *Ha-kineret ve-svivatah.* Jerusalem: Sifriyat Ariel.

Tsur, Reuven. 1985. *Yesodot romantiyim ve-anti-romantiyim be-shirei Bialik, Tcherniḥovsky, Shlonsky, ve-Amichai.* Tel Aviv: Papyrus.

Turner, Yehudit. 1984. *Ir levana: Tatslumim.* Tel Aviv: Tel Aviv Museum.

Ussishkin, Menahem. 1905. *Our Program.* Translated by D. S. Blondheim. New York: Federation of American Zionists.

———. 1929. *Kol ha-adamah.* Jerusalem: Jewish National Fund.

———. 1935. *Ha-ishah ha-ivrit ve-ge'ulat ha-karka.* Jerusalem: Jewish National Fund.

———. 1942. *The Call of the Land.* London: Jewish National Fund.

Vigouroux, F. 1909. *Emet me-eretz.* Odessa.

Warburg, Otto. 1948. *Sefer Warburg.* Edited by Ya'akov Thon. Herzliyah: Masadah.

Warnke, Martin. 1995. *Political Landscape: The Art History of Nature.* Cambridge, Mass.: Harvard University Press.

Weinberg, David H. 1996. *Between Tradition and Modernity: Haim Zhitlowski, Simon Dubnow, Ahad Ha-Am, and the Shaping of Modern Jewish Identity.* New York: Holmes and Meier.

Weinberg, Robert. 1993. *The Revolution of 1905 in Odessa: Blood on the Steps.* Bloomington: Indiana University Press.

Weisbord, Robert G. 1968. *African Zion: The Attempt to Establish a Jewish Colony in the East Africa Protectorate, 1903–1905.* Philadelphia: Jewish Publication Society of America.

Weiss, Aviezer, ed. 1975. *Avraham Shlonsky: Mivḥhar ma'amarim al yetsirato.* Tel Aviv: Am Oved and Keren Tel Aviv le-sifrut ule-omanut.

Weiss, Meira. 2002. *The Chosen Body: The Politics of the Body in Israeli Society.* Stanford, Calif.: Stanford University Press.

Weissenstein, Rudi. 2002. *Tsalmaniyah: Rudi Weissenstein—retrospektivah.* Tel Aviv: Am Oved.

Weitz, Yosef. 1929. *Ha-ya'ar be-eretz yisra'el.* Tel Aviv: Omanut.

———. 1939. *Dibat ha-aretz: Le-verur ba'ayat ha-karka be-eretz yisra'el.* Jerusalem: Jewish National Fund.
———. 1947. *Hitnaḥalutenu bi-tkufat ha-sa'ar.* Merḥaviyah: Sifriyat Po'alim.
———. 1949. *Mediniyut ha-yi'ur be-yisra'el.* Jerusalem: Jewish National Fund.
———. 1950. *The Struggle for the Land: Selected Papers.* Tel Aviv: Lion the Printer.
———. 1955. *Nof ve-adam.* Tel Aviv: Masadah.
———. 1970. *Ha-ya'ar veha-yi'ur be-yisra'el.* Ramat Gan: Masadah.
Whiting, Charles G. 1948. The Case for "Engaged" Literature. *Yale French Studies* 1: 84–89.
Williams, Raymond. 1973. *The Country and the City.* New York: Oxford University Press.
Wilson, Edmund. 1972. *To the Finland Station.* New York: Farrar, Straus and Giroux.
Ya'ari-Poleskin, Jacob. 1922. *Me-ḥayei Yosef Ḥayim Brenner.* Tel Aviv: D. Sharek.
Yalkut aḥdut ha-avodah. 1932. 2 vols. Tel Aviv: Aḥdut Ha-avodah.
Yoffe, A. B. 1979. *Esrim ha-shanim ha-rishonot: Sifrut ve-omanut be-tel aviv ha-ktanah, 1909–1929.* Tel Aviv: Ha-Kibbutz Ha-meuḥad.
Yoffe, Abraham B. 1966. *A. Shlonsky: Ha-meshorer u-zmano.* Merḥaviyah: Sifriyat Po'alim.
Yudkin, Leon I. 1974. *Escape into Siege: A Survey of Israeli Literature Today.* New York: Routledge and Kegan Paul.
Zait, Shibolet. 1997. The Life and Poetry of Esther Raab. Ph.D. dissertation, Columbia University.
Zalmona, Yigal, and Tamar Manor-Fridman, eds. 1998. *Kadimah: Ha-mizraḥ be-omanut yisra'el / To the East: Orientalism in the Arts in Israel.* Jerusalem: Israel Museum.
Zerubavel, Yael. 1995. *Recovered Roots: Collective Memory and the Making of Israeli National Tradition.* Chicago: University of Chicago Press.
———. 1996. The Forest as National Icon: Literature, Politics, and the Archaeology of Memory. *Israel Studies* 1, no. 1: 60–99.
Zierler, Wendy. 2000. Chariot(ess) of Fire: Yokheved Bat-Miriam's Female Personifications of Erets Israel. *Prooftexts* 20, nos. 1–2: 111–38.
Zikhronot eretz-yisra'el. 1947. 2 vols. Jerusalem: Ha-histadrut.
Zipperstein, Steven J. 1993. *Elusive Prophet: Ahad Ha'am and the Origins of Zionism.* Berkeley: University of California Press.

Index

Abbate, Carolyn, 116
Abraham, 36. *See also* Genesis
absorptive capacity, 10, 20, 126–28, 130–31, 138
"Adamah" (Soil). *See* Shlonsky, Avraham
Adorno, Theodor: on "immanent criticism," 17–18; on "natural history," 162–63, 169, 173; on nature, 85; on "second nature," 21, 47
Agadati, Baruch, 165, 166; *Das ist das Land*, 165–67; poster illustration, 166
Agnon, Shmuel Yosef, 182–84; *Tmol shilshom* (Only Yesterday), 182–84, 185
agriculture, 5, 6, 75; in Natan Alterman's poetry, 172; and British colonialism, 10, 20, 124–25, 129, 130, 141–42; extensive agriculture and Zionist ideology, 8, 10, 125, 127–28, 129–31, 184–85; in Hebrew fiction, 81–83, 148–49; intensive agriculture and colonialism, 5, 74–75, 77, 129; intensive versus extensive within Zionist debates, 74–75, 77; as Jewish labor, 54, 57–58, 78, 81, 115; and Jewish National Fund, 59–60, 86–90; in *The Land of Promise*, 169–70, 172; and urbanism, 162, 172. *See also* Orientalism; Rothschild colonies
Aḥad Ha'am (Asher Ginzberg), 7, 23, 24–25, 33, 59, 123; attacks on political Zionism, 29; "Binyan" (Building), 30–31; and Yosef Ḥayim Brenner, 64–65, 67, 68, 69; Shimon Dubnov and concepts of deterritorial nationalism, 5–6, 24, 79; influence on Ḥayim Naḥman Bialik, 33–34, 36, 37, 40, 42, 52; on language, 42; "Letter to the Brethren," 28–29; on Palestine's physical poverty, 25, 64–65; Pinsker's tenth *jahrzeit*, 29; poesy debate, 33–34, 37, 63–64, 93, 96, 98; reaction to Kishinev, 19, 28–32
Aḥdut Ha-avodah (the United Labor Movement of Palestine), 9, 78, 79, 91, 94, 95, 97
akedah: inversion in Ḥayim Naḥman Bialik's "Be-ir ha-hareigah," 36
allegory: in Natan Alterman's "Shir boker" (Morning Song), 170, 171, 172, 175; in Ḥayim Naḥman Bialik's "Ha-breikhah," 43–46; "constitutive" allegory, 44; land as, 66; rejection of personal allegory in Ḥayim Naḥman Bialik's poetry, 44–45, 48, 51; in Avraham Shlonsky's poetics, 115, 117, 141; and solipsism in Zionist writing, 113; in Zionist discourse, 2
Alterman, Natan, 109; "Be-harim kvar hashemesh melahetet" (In the Mountains the Sun Is Already Ablaze), 170; in contrast to Georg Simmel, 177–78; as inheritor of Shlonsky's legacy, 119; *Kokhavim ba-ḥutz* (Stars Outside), 175; as lyricist for *Land of Promise* soundtrack, 170; Dan Miron's analysis of, 173–75; nature and city in poetry, 173–74; in relation to Bialik and Shlonsky, 172, 173, 175; "Shir boker" (Morning Song), 170–75; "Shir ha-emek" (Song of the Valley), 170; "Shir ha-kvish" (Song of the Road), 170; as Tel Aviv poet, 152, 173–74; "Yom ha-shuk" (Market Day), 175–79
Altneuland (agronomy journal), 60

Acknowledgments

The idea to write about nature and the development of Hebrew aesthetics emerged from conversations with my brother Tom Zakim, whose own work on the cultural history of Los Angeles served as both a model and an inspiration. I am grateful for his indefatigable energy in discussing research and for his boundless generosity, especially when it comes to sharing ideas.

Eric Goldberg, Lee Perlman, Raviv Schwartz, Danny Shapiro, and Ron Skolnik—along with the rest of Garin Sasa-Barkai on Kibbutz Harel—introduced me to the land of Israel (both *adamah* and *eretz*) and throughout the years have supported and challenged me on this intellectual journey. They will always have my gratitude.

Many other friends and colleagues contributed generously to this project by reading, commenting on, and discussing various drafts and ideas as I have been able to offer them. In this process, I am particularly grateful to Kalman Bland, Roberto Dainotto, Michael Gluzman, Hannan Hever, Mark Jacobs, and Daniel Bertrand Monk. Nancy Berg, Eugene Carr, Leo Ching, miriam cooke, Ellyn Kusmin, Bruce Lawrence, Sarah Lipton, Walter Mignolo, Lucas Van Rompay, Irene Tucker, Jing Wang, Annabel Wharton, and Michael Zakim have all helped at different stages in this project. My current colleagues at the University of Maryland, in particular Bernard Cooperman, Einat Gonen, Sheila Jelen, Hayim Lapin, Elizabeth Papazian, and Marsha Rozenblit, have consistently offered their support and provided a collegial environment where I could pursue my interests. To all of them, my sincerest thanks.

In the course of conducting research for this book, I benefited greatly from help provided by Reuven Koffler at the Central Zionist Archives in Jerusalem; Yfaat Rothenberg at the Steven Spielberg Jewish Film Archive in Jerusalem; and the staff of the African and Middle Eastern Reading Room at the Library of Congress in Washington, D.C.

Avraham Shlonsky's "Adamah," "Hineh," "Yas'ur," and "Amal" are reprinted in this book by permission, copyright by Avraham Shlonsky and Acum. Esther Raab's "Le-eineikha ha-orot, ha-mele'ot" and "Nof ha-tmarim" are reprinted by permission, copyright by Esther Raab and Acum. Natan Alterman's "Shir boker" and "Yom ha-shuk" are reprinted by permission, copyright by Natan Alterman and Acum. The lyrics for "Mi yivneh" are reprinted by permission, copyright by Levin Kipnis and Acum. The lyrics for "Horah mamterah" are reprinted by permission, copyright by Yeḥiel Mohar and Acum.

At the University of Pennsylvania Press, Jerome Singerman has been a wonderful editor; Ted Mann has assiduously attended to the details leading to publication; and Erica Ginsburg has followed the book through production with a very precise eye. I have been fortunate to work with such professionals.

The publication of this book has been generously supported by grants from the Joseph and Rebecca Meyerhoff Center for Jewish Studies at the University of Maryland and the University of Maryland General Research Board. I am truly grateful for their support and hope that this book lives up to the high intellectual standards they are working to promote.

Finally, not a word would have found its way to the page without the support, love, and infinite patience of my family, Yael and Jonah.